READING SEMINARS I AND II

SUNY Series in Psychoanalysis and Culture

Henry Sussman, Editor

READING SEMINARS I AND II

LACAN'S RETURN TO FREUD

Seminar I: Freud's Papers on Technique
Seminar II: The Ego in Freud's Theory and in
the Technique of Psychoanalysis

EDITED BY

| Richard | Bruce | Maire |
| Feldstein | Fink | Jaanus |

The Paris Seminars in English

STATE UNIVERSITY OF NEW YORK PRESS

Published by
State University of New York Press, Albany

©1996 State University of New York

Jacket photograph courtesy of Jacques Six.

For information, address State University of New York Press,
194 Washington Avenue, Suite 305, Albany, NY 12210-2384

Production by Laura Starrett
Marketing by Terry Abad Swierzowski

Library of Congress Cataloging-in-Publication Data

Reading seminars I and II : Lacan's return to Freud / edited by
    Richard Feldstein, Bruce Fink, and Maire Jaanus.
          p.   cm. – (SUNY series in psychoanalysis and culture)
     Includes bibliographical references and index.
     ISBN 0-7914-2779-X. – ISBN 0-7914-2780-3 (pbk.)
     1. Lacan, Jacques, 1901-1981 .2. Psychoanalysis. I. Feldstein,
Richard. II. Fink, Bruce, 1956-   .   III. Jaanus, Maire.
IV. Series.
BF109.L28R43   1996
150.19'52–dc20   94-12517
                                                      CIP

10 9 8 7 6 5 4 3

CONTENTS

PREFACE

∾

Bruce Fink

Seminars I and II are far and away the most accessible of Jacques Lacan's works, and yet little attention has been devoted to date to exploring them in print. That should not be taken to imply that they are self-explanatory. Indeed, a great deal of background is required to grasp what Lacan is up to in these early seminars in which his "return to Freud" is first announced. His early influences run the gamut from psychiatry to surrealism, existentialism to linguistics, phenomenology to structuralism, and Greek philosophy to the Church fathers. Successively a Jaspersian psychiatrist, a Hegelian dialectician, and a Kleinian psychoanalyst, Lacan begins to weave the strands of his own interests together in the early 1950s, achieving a return with a twist: the "Lacanian twist," as it were.

Each of the speakers whose papers are collected in this volume presents this stage of Lacan's work in his or her own way, emphasizing theoretical and/or clinical notions, relating Lacan's work to his earlier influences and later developments, and so on. Many of the speakers were asked to cover specific chapters of Seminars I and II, and thus a great deal of the material found in those seminars is systematically presented here, above all in Parts I, II, and III. The reader interested in getting a handle on the most basic of Lacan's concepts, such as the imaginary, the symbolic, and the real, will be pleased with the *clarity* of the exposés. More advanced readers will relish the way the speakers here use these early Lacanian texts as a springboard for sophisticated discussions of transference, interpretation, hysteria, and other concepts, which are based on many of Lacan's later developments as well. Indeed, many of the texts included here operate at several levels simultaneously, presenting seemingly simple notions, while surreptitiously introducing far more complex issues in analytic theory, epistemology, and ethics.

Jacques-Alain Miller devotes his first three talks to outlining Lacan's development prior to Seminar I, presenting the philosophical backdrop of Lacan's early explorations, and allowing us to understand the questions foremost in Lacan's mind in the first few seminars. Françoise Koehler explains Lacan's early (1930s) interest in and critique of Melanie Klein's work. Anne Dunand highlights Lacan's borrowings and later divergences from Lévi-Strauss' structural approach. My paper, "Logical Time and the Precipitation of Subjectivity," explores the presuppositions at work in Lacan's 1946 article "Logical Time and the Assertion of Anticipated Certainty." And Slavoj Žižek explains Hegel's early and enduring influence on Lacan.

Turning to Seminars I and II themselves, Colette Soler, Marie-Hélène Brousse, and Éric Laurent present many of the most basic notions constitutive of Lacan's theoretical perspective in the mid-1950s and thereafter, including the symbolic, the imaginary, and the real; full speech and empty speech; transference, countertransference, identification, and interpretation; the other, the Other, and the subject; Lacan's reconceptualization of the Oedipus complex; and so on.

Robert Samuels shows how Lacan's categories—real, imaginary, and symbolic—can help us better understand the historical development of Freud's technique. My paper on "The Nature of Unconscious Thought" explains Lacan's models of the functioning of the symbolic order in the unconscious, first developed in Seminar II and then in "The Seminar on 'The Purloined Letter.'" Jacques-Alain Miller provides an exceptionally clear introduction to Lacanian diagnostic criteria, which are already visible in Lacan's early seminars. Françoise Gorog, Claude Léger, and Dominique Miller present specific cases which fall into the different diagnostic categories, giving us a sense of the wide variety of clinical phenomena Lacan helps us understand.

The reader will note that we have included at the end of this volume the first English translation to appear in print of Lacan's article from the *Écrits*, "On Freud's '*Trieb*' and the Analyst's Desire." It is a fine companion piece to Seminars I and II as it emphasizes the central role of the analyst's desire in psychoanalytic practice, a notion which, while not explicitly stated in those seminars, makes sense of much of what Lacan says in them. This 1964 text is also alluded to in a number of the papers presented in this volume.

Jacques-Alain Miller and Seuil have been kind enough to allow us to include this text here; the royalties associated with it and with the cover photo were generously covered by Barnard College, which financed the index of this book as well. Miller has also provided us with a short commentary he made on this article by Lacan in the course of his 1993–94 seminar, *Donc.* In addition, we have included two talks given by Miller in the United States, "On Perversion" and "A Discussion of Lacan's 'Kant with Sade,'" and the text of a seminar given by Colette Soler in Israel, "Hysteria and Obsession."

Rather than summarize all of these contributions, and the other papers on related aspects of Lacanian theory and practice, let me simply provide a little background on this collection.

Richard Feldstein, Professor of English at Rhode Island College, editor of the journal *Literature and Psychology*, and author of numerous books on psychoanalysis and cultural theory, came up with the idea of holding in Paris a several week long seminar in English, with the members of the *École de la Cause freudienne* (ECF, the school of psychoanalysis Lacan founded shortly before his death) giving the lion's share of the lectures. He approached Jacques-Alain Miller—head of the ECF, Chairman of the Department of Psychoanalysis at the University of Paris VIII, and general editor of all of Lacan's seminars—who put him into contact with me (I was finishing my analytic training at the ECF at the time). With the assistance of Ellie Ragland, author of two books on Lacan, Roger Williams University instructor Kate Mele, whose organizational energy and enthusiasm were indispensable, and the organizational and moral support of many members of the ECF, we organized two "Lacan Seminars in English," the first in June 1989 on Lacan's Seminars I and II, and the second in July 1990 on Seminar XI (see the companion volume to this one published by State University of New York Press in 1995).

The members of the ECF who generously gave of their time by lecturing to the participants, and whose contributions are collected here, include Jacques-Alain Miller, Colette Soler, Éric Laurent, Marie-Hélène Brousse, Anne Dunand, Vincent Palomera, Dominique Miller, Claude Léger, Françoise Koehler, and Françoise Gorog; the first four contributors are also professors in the Department of Psychoanalysis at the University of Paris VIII, Saint-Denis. Lectures by a number of other members of the ECF and other Lacan Seminar faculty could not be included in the present volume due to inadequate tape recordings: our sincere apologies to Dominique Laurent, Michael Turnheim, Henry Sullivan, Darian Leader, Stuart Schneiderman, Mark Bracher, Robert Groom, and Russell Grigg.

Maire Jaanus is a Professor of English at Barnard College, author of *Literature and Negation*, and one of the editors of this volume. Robert Samuels is the author of *Between Philosophy and Psychoanalysis: Lacan's Reconstruction of Freud*. Slavoj Žižek is a researcher at the Institute for Sociology in Ljubljana, Slovenia, and author of numerous books on Lacan, politics, and film.

On behalf of the three editors of the present volume, I would like to thank all of the speakers here for their gracious generosity in speaking to us in what was for many of them a foreign tongue, and for so clearly and elegantly formulating Lacan's views for us. Special thanks go to Dr. Françoise Gorog, who organized two very stimulating day-long series of talks and case presentations at Sainte-Anne Hospital, and to the whole of her staff who gave us a very warm welcome two years in a row. Judith Miller helped provide us with classroom space at the *Collège freudien* and the ECF, and welcomed us into her home, as did Françoise Gorog, Colette Soler, and Jean-Jacques Gorog. Jacques-Alain Miller, apart from lecturing and inviting us into his home, made the whole of the seminar possible by supporting the idea and its realization every step of the way.

Special thanks go to Josefina Ayerza and Mark Bracher who each transcribed one of Miller's talks in the United States and made those transcriptions available to us. Jacques Peraldi transcribed and Catherine Bonningue edited the French version of Miller's commentary on Lacan's article from the *Écrits*. Yotvat Elberbaum and Susy Pietchotka transcribed and completed the initial editing of Soler's "Hysteria and Obsession." Many other people assisted in many ways in the preparation of the manuscript: Héloïse Fink, Ashley Hoffman, Tom Ratekin, Yan Shen, Suzette Thibeault, Sara Williams, Paula Delfiore, Ling Xiao Hong, Susan Beller, Ann Murphy, and Rituja Mehta. On behalf of all of the editors, I would like to express heartfelt thanks for what was often an extremely fastidious task.

This volume represents no ordinary collection of papers. Unlike most conferences and conventions, where at least a majority of the contributors are native speakers of the language in which the conference is held, or where interpreters render a talk in the speaker's native tongue into that of the people in the audience, we decided to invite primarily French-speaking lecturers to address an English-speaking (primarily non-French-speaking) audience in English. This allowed for greater contact between speakers and participants, but vastly complicated the work of the editors of this volume.

The transcription of the tapes of the lectures was, in and of itself, a formidable undertaking. Each lecture was then extensively edited, our goal being less to preserve the "letter" of the talks than to ensure their comprehensibility. In no case have we tried to make the text say something other than what it seemed the speaker meant to say; we have, however, sought to eliminate Gallicisms, grammatical formulations based on French structure, repetitions, and inaccuracies. A modicum of informality is lost thereby, but we feel that the gains in understanding far outweigh the losses. While the essence of communication remains miscommunication, we have nevertheless managed to remove some of the more obvious obstacles.

Questions and answers during and after lectures were particularly difficult to transcribe from the tapes, and have for the most part been left out despite their important contribution to the conference as a whole. Wherever possible, references to the English editions of Lacan's work have been provided, but we have taken numerous liberties with the existing translations of Lacan's work—

their inadequacies are becoming ever more glaring as our understanding of Lacan's work grows. Page references to the Seminars always correspond to the Norton editions: Seminar I, translated by John Forrester, published in 1988; Seminar II, translated by Sylvana Tomaselli, published in 1988; and Seminar XI, translated by Alan Sheridan, published in 1978. "*Écrits* 1966" refers to the French edition published by Seuil in Paris, while "*Écrits*" alone refers to Alan Sheridan's 1977 English translation published by Norton.

PART I

INTRODUCTION

AN INTRODUCTION TO SEMINARS I AND II

Lacan's Orientation Prior to 1953 (I)

∞

Jacques-Alain Miller

The lecturers for the "Lacan Seminar in English" have decided to focus on Lacan's first two seminars: Books I and II. I feel that we shall have attained our objective if you go home having read at least one of them, or being able to do so with interest. While Lacan doesn't always have a reputation for readability, I believe these two texts are readable. He himself said that his writings only became clear to people ten years after their publication; ten years is perhaps too short a timespan. But these seminars were held with French participants in 1953 and 1954, and I believe that in 1989 they are fairly accessible to many people. Only a few very recent books by American and English writers can, conceptually speaking, be considered contemporary with these thirty-five-year-old seminars.

Having reread these books, what I'd like to do tonight is introduce Lacan—Lacan in 1953—to get you acquainted with the context of his first seminars: who he was when he gave them, and how he came to offer this new reading of Freud. Who was Jacques Lacan in 1953? I can't describe him at that time from personal experience as I only met him ten years later, in January of 1964, when he began his eleventh seminar, *The Four Fundamental Concepts of Psychoanalysis*. He was fifty-two in 1953, having been born in April 1901, not too far from here, I believe. As far as I know, his family lived near the Boulevard Raspail, and he attended the nearby Stanislas school. It was a Catholic school where students were taught by Jesuits, and it catered to the Parisian bourgeoisie. It was there that Lacan learned Latin and Greek and was instructed in religious matters. As you may know, Lacan was quite knowledgeable about religion. I've met Islamic scholars who've said they were sure Lacan had studied the Koran as they had found many echoes of it in the *Écrits*. And there are Marxists who believe that Lacan's work is primarily Marxist. Others think the Other is another name for God. Lacan is many things to many people, but I'll try to limit my attention to psychoanalysis tonight.

I won't provide a biographical account of Lacan's life, firstly because I do not have the material—sometimes I was curious and would ask him things about himself, but he wasn't interested in discussing biographical matters—and secondly, because he was very scornful of biographers. In the *Écrits* you'll find references to Jones that are so scornful that, for a Lacanian to become Lacan's biographer, he'd have to overcome that scorn—and I never did. As a matter of fact, in the 1970s, people offered to interview him concerning his life; the publishing house, Seuil, asked him to speak with a journalist who they wanted to do a book on his life, and he unhesitatingly refused.

In the *Écrits*, Lacan provides a clue as to his intellectual trajectory in saying that he considers that his work, the work associated with his name, began in 1952: what came before counted in his mind as his "antecedents." He doesn't thereby cancel out what came before, but stresses a cut in his own intellectual development that occurred around 1952–1953. The starting point of his teaching was "Function and Field of Speech and Language in Psychoanalysis," a paper written for a 1953 conference in Rome. Why was this text so significant to him—a landmark, in his opinion? The seminar you have before you, *Freud's Papers on Technique*, is the immediate sequel to "Function and Field." The paper was published in September, Lacan came back to Paris, and two months later this seminar began. The seminar and the paper must thus be thought together. The seminar could be said to be an application of "Function and Field" to psychoanalytic technique or practice. In some sense it answers the question, 'what psychoanalytic technique can be deduced from the thesis: the unconscious is structured like a language?' If we admit that the unconscious is so structured, how can we practice psychoanalysis?

The ethical point of view always takes precedence over technique. Therefore, the technique discussed here must be supplemented by the ethics of psychoanalysis, found in Seminar VII. You'll see that Seminar I is not a "How to Do Psychoanalysis According to Lacan"—it's not the *Complete Angler* of psychoanalysis. The book has to be read in conjunction with Freud's texts, and you'll see that Lacan's approach here is quite general. Two of Lacan's published articles are clearly related to this seminar for, as you know, it was simply an oral seminar that Lacan gave from notes; it was never written up, nor was it tape-recorded at the time, as the Japanese perhaps had not yet discovered the tape recorder. There was a stenographer who took shorthand and typed it up. Lacan kept that version for many years until I began working on it in 1975. The stenographer's version circulated among a small number of students for years by photocopy, and then spread more and more. People at that time did not so often refer to the seminar as to his published articles based on certain ideas developed in the seminar. In the *Écrits*, you find *"Variantes de la cure-type."* It was part of an encyclopedia article, the first part of which, called "The Standard Treatment," was given to another analyst to write, Lacan—already considered to be some sort of deviant—being assigned "Variations on the Standard Treatment." He makes fun of the title right at the beginning of the article, and I believe this seminar was unfolding while he was researching the material for it. The part on Balint, for instance, was certainly inspired by the article, and there are many other interconnections.

In chapter 5 of Seminar I, one finds a presentation by Jean Hyppolite of Freud's *Die Verneinung.* Hyppolite was a philosopher and the first person to translate Hegel's *Phenomenology of Mind* into French; he was a student at the *École normale supérieure* at the same time as Sartre and a friend of Sartre's; he was interested in Lacan's work, and regularly attended his seminar then. Hyppolite was quite open-minded at a time when other French philosophers found Lacan too difficult to understand. In chapter 5 of Seminar I we find Hyppolite's talk on Freud's text, and Lacan's introduction and commentary. Lacan rewrote the introduction and reply as a separate text that appears in the *Écrits*, and there will no doubt be scholars who will compare the oral version that appears in the seminar with the careful rewriting thereof that appears in the *Écrits*. Thus "Variations on the Standard Treatment" and the "Introduction and Reply to Hyppolite" are two texts which are intimately related to Seminar I.

But there are others as well, and I will mention at least two of them. The second part of this seminar concerns the imaginary, centering around chapter 11 where we find the distinction between "ideal ego" and "ego ideal" and a complicated mirror structure. Lacan didn't write anything based on this part of the seminar until 1960; in other words, he waited seven years before giving a definitive formulation of what he tried to pinpoint therein. In the *Écrits*, that formulation appears in the "Remarks on Daniel Lagache," complete with a definitive mirror schema. The stenographer did not copy Lacan's schemas at the time of the seminar, and thus it was very difficult to check them—Lacan didn't remember exactly how he'd drawn them in 1953, that is, exactly what stage they were at. I went through the notes of some of his students, and then he and I eventually compromised on something.

Yet another instance can be found in chapter 21, where truth is said to emerge from mistakes, for Lacan refers directly to the same notion in 1968 in a short and rather difficult article: *"La méprise du sujet supposé savoir"* ("The Mistaking of the Subject Supposed to Know"). In a word, we find echoes of Seminar I in all the rest of Lacan's teaching.

In the overture itself (page 2, paragraph 4), Lacan stresses the importance of symbols for scientific reflection: when he mentions that Lavoisier introduced an appropriate concept of the symbol at the same time as his phlogistics, we can already see an anticipation of Lacan's emphasis on mathemes, that is, the symbolism he invented for thinking psychoanalytic experience. While stressing the importance of symbols for science, we see that Lacan himself is beginning to forge a special symbolism for psychoanalytic experience, though he has not yet invented object *a* or the rest of the symbolism that grows out of his work.

Another historical note: while *Freud's Papers on Technique* is considered Book I of the seminar, Lacan had in fact already begun his seminar two years prior to that. In 1951–1952, he gave a seminar on the Dora case, echoes of which can be found in "Intervention on Transference" in the *Écrits*; in 1952–1953, he gave another on the Wolf Man, some of which is reflected in "Function and Field." For the first two years, the seminar was given in his living room at home; there were perhaps fewer people attending then than are here tonight, I don't know. No stenographer was there to take shorthand, and there are but a few, not altogether reliable, notes. Only in 1953 did he start giving his seminar at Sainte-Anne Hospital with a stenographer present. But as you can see, the first lesson of the seminar is nevertheless missing, and further on there's another gap as well.

From 1953 to 1963, Lacan was reading Freud in his seminars, at the rate of one or two texts per year. For twelve years he presented himself as but a careful reader of Freud; Seminar I concerned Freud's technical writings, just as the year before had been devoted to a case history, and Seminar II was devoted to *Beyond the Pleasure Principle* and *The Ego and the Id*. Lacan advocated a return to Freud's texts at a time when Freud's texts were less often read in the United States and England than those of other analytic writers. I suspect Freud's texts are now more widely read, largely as a result of Lacan's advocacy. Future historians will confirm or refute that point, but that is my sense.

Four years ago, at Columbia Institute, just prior to the "elimination" of certain members, I spoke with the president of the United Psychoanalytic Association, Dr. Cooper. He told me that "we've made progress since Freud"; when you hear such views, you understand why in 1953 already, people in America were saying that Freud was old-fashioned. They figured they knew better than Freud what it was all about, and clearly considered his early work to be naive and archaic. In 1963, for example, a book by Arlow and Brenner sought to demonstrate that Freud's second topography—the id, ego, and superego—completely supersedes the first topography, that is, the distinction between conscious, preconscious, and unconscious; in so doing, they discarded more than half of Freud's work as utterly antiquated. Thus, while I haven't checked with historians, I suspect that we can take Lacan at his word when he says that people were neglecting to read Freud.

Now what led Lacan in 1953 to believe he was really beginning to grasp the functioning and essence of psychoanalysis? That's not a biographical question—it's a theoretical one. What did 1953 represent in that sense? He was of course already at odds with the International Psychoanalytical Association (IPA), and was obliged to teach in order to maintain some sort of professional existence among peers and friends; but I won't go into that. The theoretical moment is best characterized by the fact that Lacan managed to locate a point of convergence between phenomenology and structuralism. From the very beginning of his work in psychiatry—for Lacan was a psychiatrist, not a philosopher or an academic—he was phenomenologically oriented. By phenomenology, I mean Husserlian phenomenology, for it was Husserl's version thereof which was incorporated into psychiatry by Karl Jaspers.

I believe Lacan may be deemed an existentialist up until 1953. Which is going a bit too far, as he was certainly not Sartrian, but I would nevertheless accept his being qualified thusly. Nineteen fifty-three was not the year he abandoned existentialism/phenomenology for structuralism, but rather the year he blended the two: "Function and Field" is a blending of the two. Lacan's theory of speech at that time is, in a sense, existentialist and phenomenological, while his theory of language is structuralist.

He refers to Husserl (and in the background Heidegger, Sartre, and Merleau-Ponty) and Hegel, on the one hand, and Saussure, Jakobson, and Lévi-Strauss on the other. As a philosophy student in 1963, I remember how entranced I was the first time I read "Function and Field." I was fascinated to see how everything being hotly debated in the early 1960s, and above all the widespread movement to discard existentialism and flock to a popular form of structuralism, had been discussed by Lacan ten years earlier when he was blending the two.

I'm trying to give you a compendium of Lacan's theoretical itinerary, a sort of "Pilgrim's Progress" starring Lacan. It would be fun to present it as a kind of "Pilgrim's Progress." Though a very serious psychiatrist by the 1930s, I have the sense that Lacan may have had some other vocation before that. The dates don't work out quite right, between the end of his secondary schooling, college, and medical school, and I suspect he spent some two years doing something else—but it's just a conjecture. Whatever the case may be, let us keep in mind that Lacan was a psychiatrist, and the colleague of someone who was, for nearly half a century, the dominant force in French psychiatry: Henri Ey. In the *Écrits*, you will find an article written in 1945 that discusses Henri Ey's main ideas.

As a reference point, let us take Lacan's thesis: *On Paranoid Psychosis in Relationship to Personality*. Published in 1932, and republished in 1975,[1] it was by no means his first publication. But it helps us understand what Lacan was looking for between 1932 and 1953. The thesis is on paranoia, a very specific psychiatric category that was classically described by Kraepelin and generally accepted by French psychiatry. It contains three chapters, the second of which is entirely devoted to a single case history—rather original at a time when most theses compared a great many cases, covering each of them in very little detail. Lacan states that he has drawers full of case studies but prefers to develop just one at length to get to the heart of the matter. His first chapter provides a review of all psychiatric work on paranoia. The third chapter offers some perspectives arising from the lengthy case study, and refers to Freud. Thus, it is in this psychiatric study of psychosis that Freud is first mentioned in Lacan's work, and we know that Lacan entered analysis just after completing it. I would say he was driven to psychoanalysis chiefly because of his work on psychosis—not on hysteria.

Now what does Lacan do in his thesis? He invents a new category—"psychosis of self-punishment"—which is symmetrical to Freud's "neurosis of self-punishment." While Freud was elaborating the concept of the superego and demonstrating the importance of guilt in neurosis, Lacan was attempting to transfer the Freudian superego into the field of psychosis and demonstrate its similar functioning therein. He takes the case of a young woman who, in a delirious paranoid state, attacked a well-known actress with a knife. The event was mentioned in all the newspapers at the time, and the young woman was brought to Sainte-Anne Hospital where Lacan was practicing. Lacan notes that shortly after her incarceration, that is, shortly after the onset of punishment, her delusions abated dramatically. Caught by the police and imprisoned on the high-security ward of Sainte-Anne, her delirious state subsided. Lacan concludes that, to some extent, she seems to have wanted to be punished, and construes it as a case of "psychosis of self-punishment."

Still more important is the fact that Lacan's interest in psychoanalysis stems from Freud's concept of the superego. Which already tells us something about the Lacanian "self": it is intimately related to self-punishment. In other words, it has nothing to do with unity, harmony, equilibrium, or enjoyment. Rather, it is already a divided self. There's a problem with the term "superego": you get the sense of there being something above and something else below. But "superego" simply means that the supposed self doesn't want that which is conducive to its own good. When Freud says that it is the superego that organizes symptoms, he thereby qualifies the internal division of a self that doesn't want what is conducive to its own good. It wants, on the contrary, punishment, suffering, and displeasure. The supposed Lacanian self thus works against itself, not for its own good—as if in pursuit of unhappiness, if I may be permitted to reverse the famous phrase in the American constitution. "Superego" means that the self pursues unhappiness.

There is a connection between the division of the self and the fundamentally masochistic status of the self: the fact of finding satisfaction in displeasure. The concept of unconscious self-punishment found in Freud's work means that the supposed self finds satisfaction in displeasure, pleasure in pain. That spells masochism. Up until the end of his teaching, and ever more clearly, to Lacan's mind the subject was fundamentally masochistic. This already gives us a clue as to why Lacan was interested in the mirror stage, for—as a description and analysis of the relation between a subject's own body (the self's own body) and its image—the mirror stage is based upon a divided self: it is a commentary on the divided self, a way of approximating the division of the self in another way. That is the most predominant topic in Lacan, even more predominant than language.

It is important to grasp Lacan's perspective in his work on the case study included in his thesis. It is that of phenomenological psychiatry. It won't be easy to give you a compendium of Husserl's phenomenology in the space of a few short minutes, but I'll give it a try nonetheless.

Let us compare it with Descartes' views. What is the truth of what we see and feel? What we see and feel as the outside world is not matter but rather extension, according to Descartes. It is through extension that he pinpoints the difference between cogito and thought. He distinguishes two realities: that of thought and that of extension. By extension he means that the truth of perception is given by scientific geometry. If we see our finger as bigger than the moon, it's simply corporeal illusion. Perceptual truth is given by science: astronomy and geometry provide truth about the outside world. Descartes takes an objective point of view of the world, the truth being God's viewpoint, that is, science. Science dictates the form for everyone from above, in other words, from a vantage point that no one can attain.

Now what does Husserl say? He takes it quite seriously that when I look from one specific point in space, I see one person seated just before me, and behind that person another whom I can see only in part, etc. We may adopt God's point of view and state where each person present is seated, or we can map it out, and *that* would be the truth. But I, nevertheless, am here, and have a perspective of my own: perspective is a fundamental concept of phenomenology. You cannot nullify your own perspective and you may thus philosophize about your own perspective. An axiom of true everyday life is that you cannot but perceive things one beside the other or with one thing blocking your perception of another. There is no *actual* perception without perspective. We can formulate that as a law.

We can now precisely simulate perspective: we are developing a science of perspective (in fact we are redeveloping it, as there was in the past a science of perspective). As a matter of fact, we might say that phenomenology opened up a field of philosophy concerning one's own body. As there is no such thing as a mind without a body, so we cannot think of the various objects in the world as being mere parts of God's extension: there is something objective that is always present—my own body—and I have a relationship with it that is different from the relationship I have with any and every other object. Let us philosophize about that.

This view had a seminal influence on the twentieth century. The popular worship of what is lived and felt, related to the idea of the importance of one's own body, stems from Husserl. It is so widespread now that no one any longer knows where it is grounded. Running counter to science's objective point of view, phenomenology strove to develop a rigorous philosophy of subjectivity. It agreed that there were natural sciences wherein objective causal explanations could be found, but stipulated that when it comes to man as a being of perspective and a speaking subject, something else has to be taken into account: meaning.

Dilthey stated that even before Husserl, but it wasn't until Jaspers that meaning was brought into psychiatry. Jaspers opposed the psychiatrists who said, 'You have a mental illness? Let us find the objective, biological causes and constitutional makeup that explain it, just as we would explain any physical illness.' Jaspers brought to psychiatry an interest in the meaning of madness, taking into account the language spoken by the subject, and so on. Lacan explicitly refers to Jaspers in his thesis.

Heidegger's work stemmed from Husserl's. Heidegger defined what he called—not man—but rather *man's being-in-the-world*. It is not pure consciousness: it is always in a worldly context with a certain perspective, that is, there are always things he does not see but which are nevertheless around him. As a being-in-the-world, man has a project, that is, a sense of the future, something he wants to do. Thus, he projects his life from the point he is at into the future. Heidegger originated the very important existentialist concept of the "project." I am *here* physically, but I *project* myself into the future, and I conceive of what I want to do. It is on the basis of what I want to do that I can experience difficulties and obstacles. Sartre developed this point at length: things are not obstacles in and of themselves, they are only obstacles if you want something. It is because you want something to happen further along that retroactively things are experienced as obstacles. You find the same idea in another guise in Lacan's work.

Even in Heidegger's writings one comes upon the idea that man—being connected to the environment and to the future—is always projecting himself outside himself. What Heidegger called *Dasein* is not an interiority. He defines the existence of man not as interiority, an inner something like ideas or feelings, but rather as a constant projecting outside. Heidegger himself invented the notion of ex-sistence—*stare* outside—that Lacan took up; Heidegger himself invented the distinction between ex-sistence and insistence. Having no interiority, one projects outside, and this repeats itself; Lacan's wordplay on "*L'instance de la lettre*" ("The *Instance* [meaning "agency" or "insistence"] of the Letter") stems in reality from Heidegger.

Sartre radicalized Heidegger's point of view by saying that, fundamentally speaking, consciousness is nothing. If we take Heidegger seriously when he says that man is always outside himself, we can simplify it by saying that consciousness is nothing–nothing more than a movement of intentionality towards the outside. That's *Being and Nothingness* in a nutshell. Sartre goes so far as to define consciousness as nothing, yet connected to intentionality. In defining consciousness, Sartre himself used the expression "lack of being" (*le manque d'être*) that Lacan recast as the *manque-à-être*. It's difficult to translate into English, but Lacan translated it as "want-to-be," rendering thereby the impact of desire.

The problematic from Husserl to Sartre can be stated as follows: if meaning is given to the world by man's project, we may still ask what gives meaning to a person's individual world. The project is one's perspective, not at the level of pure perception, but rather at that of history: an individual's perspective at the historical level. We may therefore ask someone, 'Why did you rebel?', and he may reply, 'I rebelled because something was intolerable.' Let's suppose your project is to defend democracy; you feel the resistance of bureaucracy, and thus experience some sort of obstacle in your path; you try to overthrow it, but at times the obstacle gets the better of you, as happened very recently in China. The obstacle is defined by a project which is a perspective; a subject takes on history, and gives it a meaning. If any of you happen to be members of the American Communist Party, you might, for example, view the recent events in China as indicative that class warfare will prevail, attributing thereby a certain meaning to the events. Consequently, you see the connection between projects, meaning as based on projects, and lack of being. I apologize for going so quickly–it's half a century of philosophy.

Phenomenology was of capital importance to Lacan as it introduced anti-objectivism. Lacan, in a sense, transferred many phenomenological considerations to the unconscious. It was essential to him that the unconscious not be taken as an interiority or container in which some drives are found over on one side and a few identifications over on the other–associated with the belief that a little analysis helps clean up the container. He took the unconscious not as a container, but rather as something ex-sistent–outside itself–that is connected to a subject who is a lack of being.

Just after the war an essayist/sociologist, Jules Monroe, wrote a book entitled *Social Facts Are Not Things*, which criticized Durkheim. Monroe used a phenomenological point of view to explain that social facts have meaning to people, and if you want to understand sociology you have to return to the meanings people give things. Things are not things in and of themselves. In Seminar I and "Function and Field," Lacan develops the idea that while psychical facts are not things, they can be reconstructed. Lacan forces us to ask ourselves how meaning is given to certain things by neurotics, psychotics, and perverts. He recounts the story of a child who, when slapped, asked whether it was meant kindly or as punishment. If the slapper said it was intended as punishment, the child cried, whereas if he said it was meant kindly, the child did not cry. The child realized that a great deal hinged on the meaning attributed to the slap. Lacan asserts that the same is true of so-called instinctual developments that biology tries to pass off as objective. According to Freud, all events involving "instinctual development" are *meaningful* events; with a patient, one must reconstruct the meaningful events of his life, analyzing why he chose certain meanings and not others, and how certain meanings came to be attributed to certain events.

What distinguished Lacan from phenomenologists right from the outset in his thesis—I don't have the time here to comment upon it in detail—was that whereas he took meaning to be fundamental in psychiatry and psychoanalysis, he also stressed the importance of seeking the laws of meaning. He didn't consider meaning to be some kind of dainty thing floating in the air here and there which alights on something, gives it meaning, and then disappears. The fact that meaning is grounded in the subject—the fact that meaning is not a thing—does not imply that there are no laws of meaning. In 1932, Lacan was already studying linguistics to discover the laws of meaning. And, true to himself, in the overture of Seminar I, he stressed it anew: "Our task, here, is to reintroduce the register of meaning, a register that must itself be reintegrated on its own level" (p. 1)—in other words, his standpoint was still an existentialist/phenomenological one. In 1932, he was explicitly Jaspersian. In *"Propos sur la causalité psychique" (Écrits* 1966), within the context of his debate with Henri Ey, he was an existentialist; but at the same time he was preoccupied with logical time. Why so? There is objective time, as measured by clocks, and subjective time: time of maintained interest, time to end—which we are rapidly nearing—and so on. From a phenomenological point of view, you may distinguish between objective and subjective time. But Lacan doesn't approach subjective time through a description of feelings which cannot be narrated, attempting to grasp the inner feeling of temporality (as found in poetry, for example); he tries to find the logic of subjective time. His work on the mirror stage lies in the interim between his thesis and his debate with Henri Ey, but we'll skip that here to proceed to the moment where structuralism connects with existentialism.

Lacan probably read Lévi-Strauss, Jakobson, and Saussure in 1949 (and thus cannot be considered a founder of post-structuralism, a movement which began in the late sixties). He found what he was looking for therein: the laws of meaning. Certain aspects of existentialism and phenomenology were completely at odds with structuralism, but he managed to reconcile others. Structuralism taught him that the Husserlian attempt to describe one's immediate intuition of the world—feeling one's own body or being in a perspective—is illusory because language is always already there. Lacan thus rejected the phenomenological illusion of immediacy, and realized that the question of the origin of language was not a scientific one, the notion of structure undercutting the search for origins. In some sense there is no origin of structure: we cannot think unless language is already there. Language is an order (a reference to Saussure's idea of the symbolic order), that is, a whole composed of interrelated elements. A differential order must be conceived of as a whole, the different component elements being interrelated; none of the elements is absolute. What is the minimum number of elements in such an order? The minimal order consists of two related elements. After a great deal of thought, Lacan adopts S_1 and S_2 as the constituent elements of the minimum structural order.

Hence, we see that Lacan is not concerned with consciousness, but rather with the subject of meaning. He adopts Hegel's notion that the subject of meaning is always related to an other; in order to be myself, I must recognize another person who recognizes me. This clues us in as to how Lacan understands the relationship of the subject to the Other. The points embodied in Schema L crop up throughout Seminar I, as Lacan distinguishes the relationship between the subject (as subject of meaning) and the Other from the mirror stage relations between the subject and his own image (*Écrits*, p. 193). Lacan's primary emphasis in this seminar, though unfortunately I have no time to go into it now, is to distinguish, when tackling any psychoanalytic question, the level of language and symbols from the level of the imaginary. The imaginary/symbolic distinction is the main thrust of this seminar.

Question: You talked briefly about Heidegger as a sort of subtext at certain points in Lacan's work. How did Heidegger influence Lacan? Seminar VII, for example, pretty much ends with being-unto-death.

Miller: You think Heidegger is very present in Seminar VII?

Question: Towards the end, at any rate, Lacan uses the term "being-unto-death."

Miller: I think Lacan very much admired Heidegger, but I don't think his influence was as great as one might imagine. It was certainly far more pronounced at the beginning of Lacan's teaching than later on. An American Heideggerian came to see me some ten years ago, convinced that Lacan was a follower of Heidegger's. I disappointed him a great deal in saying that in some sense Lacan agreed with Heidegger—which was perhaps an excessive way of putting it—but nevertheless was not Heideggerian. I tried, on the contrary, to point out his phenomenological streak, situating him on the fringes of French psychiatry, objectivism, and biologically oriented psychoanalysis. Lacan had already adopted the perspective of meaning before taking up psychoanalysis. In 1932, he stressed the need to seek meaning in madness itself, that is, the inner logic of the patient's discourse. In that sense he considered himself to be Jaspersian. His path was diametrically opposed to that of researchers trying to detect the part of the brain affected in madness. Lacan, like Freud, was truly listening to what his patients said. There were French psychiatrists who, while believing madness to be biologically determined, were nevertheless good listeners. Lacan claimed to have learned more from his biologically oriented professor of psychiatry than from any of the others. From the outset, he adopted a concern for meaning derived from phenomenology: he was looking for the laws of meaning and seeking to account for the emergence of meaning.

Structuralism led him to believe that he had to start building on the basis of Saussure's distinction between the signifier and the signified. Saussure stressed the existence of structure at the level of the materiality of language, asserting the existence of a symmetrical structure for the signifier which he himself never developed. Lacan modified that in stating that a certain signified, that is, a certain signification or meaning, is produced by a specific combination of signifiers. He sought out a law such that meaning would appear as a function of signifiers. In the end he isolated two fundamental combinations of signifiers: metaphor and metonymy. In the latter you have a combination of two signifiers which produces a certain effect of meaning, a certain signified (let's call it elision); in metaphor, you have another type of combination, which produces a positive effect of meaning.

Notes

1. [*De la psychose paranoïaque dans ses rapports avec la personnalité, suivi de premiers écrits sur la paranoïa*, Paris: Seuil, 1975.]

AN INTRODUCTION TO SEMINARS I AND II

Lacan's Orientation Prior to 1953 (II)

∞

Jacques-Alain Miller

Continuing in my attempt to present Lacan's orientation prior to Seminar I, I might mention that it has given me an opportunity to work out the theoretical chronology of Lacan's early work. Lacan left behind his psychiatric perspective for a psychoanalytic one, a moment we see at the end of his 1932 thesis on psychiatry; as I mentioned last week, he tried therein to establish a new category, "paranoia of self-punishment," built on the model of the "neurosis of self-punishment," that is, incorporating Freud's second topography, and in particular, the function of the superego, into the investigation of psychosis. Lacan entered analysis in 1932 when he finished his thesis, and we can trace his careful, systematic, and highly personal approach to psychoanalytic theory from that moment on.

In Seminar I, Lacan's main objective is clear, and it is perhaps the same objective at work in Lacan's teaching for thirty years thereafter: to change the way psychoanalysis is transmitted. In repeating over and over that he was addressing his fellow analysts, which sometimes seemed a bit exaggerated as there were many other people attending his classes as well, he thereby stressed the fact that the core of the Other he was addressing consisted of fellow analysts, and that his goal was to change the way psychoanalysis was practiced at the time. We no longer know very much about how it was practiced at that time—we have to reconstruct it from Lacan's critique. Ego psychology, for instance, is no longer in its prime, and we do not know exactly what ego psychology practice was like when it was in full bloom. By the way, I read in the newspaper yesterday a quote by someone claiming that there were never any French ego psychologists, an astounding pronouncement to say the least. In any case, Lacan was not interested in changing psychoanalysis for the sake of changing it, but to know how it works. Lacan again and again returned to the question 'how does analysis work?'

It may come as some surprise to you that Lacan's goal at that time was simplicity. On page after page of the seminar you find very simple conceptualizations of how analysis works, and you can trace the development of his views. His ideal of simplicity was similar to Freud's. In *Civilization and Its Discontents*, Freud states that science aims at simplification, that is, at finding concepts that may seem abstract, but which enable you to grasp what is going on in what Lacan at one point spoke of as "analytic experience." That expression is perhaps more widely employed nowadays, but Lacan seems to have been the first to use it in 1938.

Returning to the question of chronology, we know that Lacan entered analysis in 1932 after finishing his thesis. He gave his first public psychoanalytic presentation on the "Mirror Stage"in 1936 at the Marienbad Convention. Just after that convention, he wrote his first article on psychoanalysis, which is not very well known as we only have the first half of it; he never completed the second half. I want to focus first on this very early perspective that Lacan adopted regarding analytic experience while still in analysis, after having undergone four years of it. From August to October 1936, he wrote an article called "Beyond the 'Reality Principle'" which you can find in the French version of the *Écrits*. It is a very surprising article which is not often read because it contains a number of somewhat vague ideas about reality and Einstein, and about reality and science—all of which seems a bit irrelevant to most readers. Lacan was clearly trying to emulate Freud: Freud had written *Beyond the Pleasure Principle*, and thus Lacan, at age thirty-five, wrote "Beyond the 'Reality Principle.'" It is not very clear in the article, which is unfinished, exactly what he wanted to say, except that reality is much more complicated than we think and that Einstein's notion of relativity has something to do with it.

I will focus here on what Lacan offered as a first theoretical take on what he called analytic experience. The subtitle of his article, "Beyond the 'Reality Principle'," was "A Phenomenological Description of Analytic Experience." He was thus a phenomenologist when he was a psychiatrist, and he remained a phenomenologist when he was an analysand trying to present what he referred to as analytic experience. A phenomenological description entails trying to present what is going on without any preconceptions. Some of you might want to state that in a more complex fashion, but in any case it involves the suspension of all preconceived notions and theoretical constructs: you are simply to describe the phenomena. In adopting this perspective, what Lacan found to be the fundamental datum of analytic experience was language. It is striking to see that in 1936, when Lacan was just leaving psychiatry behind and starting to work on psychoanalysis. He only really began to develop this idea in 1953, when he wrote "Function and Field of Speech and Language in Psychoanalysis" (*Écrits*), and continued to develop it in Seminar I. But it was already there in 1936. We can see how he built on that idea from 1936 onward.

This notion was not in the forefront at the outset. Lacan simply stated that what seems specific to Freudian practice, when compared to psychiatric practice, is that in psychoanalysis you work on the basis of what the patient says. In other words, you do not try to replace what he says with some objective description of his symptom as you do in psychiatry; rather, you listen to the patient's own testimony about his symptom. As simple as this point may seem, it is constitutive of a whole new approach. It is the Archimedean point of Lacan's teaching. It cannot be explicitly found in Freud's writings, but it stems from Freud's description of analytic experience. It implies that in psychoanalysis proper, you do not refer anything that is said to what is. You do not verify what the patient says. Freud began by doing that and was still doing it even in the case of the Wolf Man; but after that he stopped. Asking the patient or his or her family for proof in order to ascertain the veracity of what he or she says is not analysis. Lacan's standpoint here is that references to reality are replaced by the notion of the internal coherence of the patient's discourse, that is, of what he or she says. You do not compare what he or she says to something that can be found in reality; you simply check whether his or her discourse is consistent. You look for discrepancies within the discourse itself, not for cross checks in reality.

Thus, Lacan's point of departure is that language is the main datum of analytic experience. Now if that's true, and phenomenologically speaking it is true, then psychoanalysis functions through language and a problem arises: What is language? From 1936 to 1953 and afterward, you see a progressive enrichment of the concept of language in Lacan's work. He finds his way, in some sense, when he encounters structural linguistics. But he had been awaiting that encounter since 1936, and even since his thesis in 1932. In 1936, Lacan considered language to amount to signs. Even this simplistic view of language allowed him to present some kind of alternative. A sign signifies something when you take the sign to refer to something in reality or in your mind: you connect the sign with that something that is referred to. Lacan says that in psychoanalysis what is important is rather that the sign signifies *to someone*. In this very simple analysis of the sign, something essential is being presented. Prior to signifying something, a sign signifies to someone. Lacan thereby emphasized the fact that a patient speaks *to* someone. He shifted from language to communication: what appeared to be most important in the structure of language was communication, or "interlocution" as he called it. He stressed the social function of language—language as a social link. In the 1970s, Lacan presented his notion of discourse as fundamentally a social link, but it was already there in embryonic form much earlier. It is not so much the thing referred to that is important but the other to whom one speaks. The discussion, granted but one page in the 1930s, nonetheless presents what Lacan spent years developing.

Even if you do not understand what a patient is saying, even if in analysis you do not question the credibility of what he is saying, the fact remains that he wants to speak—he wants to say something, and thus the "want to say"[1] can already be isolated. Lacan later talks about it in terms of desire, but it is already clear here that the analysand wants an answer. What kind of answer does the analyst provide? And what kind of other is the analyst in this very unusual kind of interlocution constitutive of psychoanalytic experience? What kind of other is an analyst?

Lacan's answer at that time was very simple: an other who tries to be as anonymous as possible: an other without qualities (to paraphrase the title of Robert Musil's book) who makes himself invisible, rarely answers, and consequently enables the patient to project images onto him which are of fundamental importance to the patient. We already have here a conceptualization: The analyst is to be seen as the Other of language;[2] he is "imaginarized" by the speaking subject because he is an unusual kind of other.

On the basis of this point of departure you can already provide a new foundation for the dependency that arises in analytic experience, which has always been difficult to account for. Why does a person who enters analysis generally, in a very short space of time, begin to feel so emotionally dependent on the analyst, thereby initiating regression and transference? Lacan's first answer is that *dependency arises out of the "dissymmetrization" of the structure of psychoanalytic communication.* In normal communication situations between speaking subjects, we are speakers and listeners in turn. A type of equalization or egalitarianism is produced thereby. In this lecturing situation, the more I talk, the more dependent upon you I become. In psychoanalysis, we deliberately "dissymmetrize" communication. One person is chiefly the speaker, and the other the listener. Dependency can be directly deduced therefrom, for if you admit that a speaker is dependent upon a listener, regression, repetition, and transference follow, assuming that the listener remains anonymous. The speaker invents this listener on the model of the people who have listened to him call out and cry out his whole life long.

Lacan continually worked on the structure of communication, trying to be more and more precise—and twenty years later, his account was more sophisticated—but he always held to the thesis that psychoanalytic experience makes an unusual use of the general structure of communication. For instance, in "Variations on the Standard Treatment" you find the same emphasis on uncommon communication. It is always the listener as such who is master of the truce, that is, it is he who says yes or no, accepts or rejects, decides to take at face value or literally what I say, or decides to understand what I'm alluding to. Everything depends on the listener's reaction, and while that may shift in the course of a conversation, it is still always the listener who is in the position of master: the master of meaning. Whatever I say, the other may take it as a cry for help or as a rejection of some kind. It is always interpreted at the place of the listener. This property of communication is greatly multiplied in the analytic situation. Lacan says as much in that paper published in 1956, but he was working from the very same foundation he laid down in 1936; the later version was far more developed and lively, but was nevertheless fundamentally the same. At the end of that article he says that, in his discussion of the structure of communication, he has tried to formulate something that is already clear in Freud's doctrine.

Now we are going to tackle his libido theory. Lacan very early on divided Freud's work and the psychoanalytic field as a whole into that which is based on communication and language, on the one hand, and the libido theory, that is, metapsychology, on the other. If you approach psychoanalysis from the vantage point of language and meaning alone, you can't account for everything. The theory of sexual development, with its various stages, drives, etc., escapes your grasp. By 1936, Lacan was already separating Freud's theory of language from his theory of libido. A fundamental problem in teaching Lacan is to always try to reformulate the theory of the drives and the libido in terms of the theory of language. In speaking of the relationship between signifiers and jouissance, as we now do, we continue to grapple with this division. In 1953, in "Function and Field of Speech and Language in Psychoanalysis," you can see that the very terms "speech" and "language" indicate a disentangling of techniques for deciphering the unconscious from the theory of instincts or drives. Meaning, deciphering, and interpretation are set apart from instincts and drives.

Lacan seemed to be asking himself whether there are in fact two different directions implicit in Freud's work and thus in psychoanalysis as a whole, or whether they are reducible to a common core; and, if so, at what cost? In what sense can drives be reduced to or inscribed within the structure of language? Lacan essentially answered with object (a). He invented it to try to integrate drives into the structure of language. In so doing, he paid a price; for in the structure of language, you have signifiers and meanings, but he was obliged to invent something which is neither, but rather something else altogether. That may seem a bit abstract, but it will serve as a compass in finding our way in Lacan's opus.

Now to add a little flesh to this bare-bones framework. If we accept the notion that speaking *to* someone is more important than speaking *about* something, that is, if we stress the social character of language, its character of constituting a connection with others, then we have a problem with the things which appear in Freud to be biological functions. If you view analytic experience as a communication experience of an unusual kind, you stress the social character of the experience and of language. But what do you do with Freud's seemingly biological functions?

Lacan sets out to prove that the drives are completely embedded in language, and that they are structured like a language, which is easy enough to prove in Freud's work. Drives are part of the mythology of psychoanalysis. They are not as natural as all that. The theory of drives is metapsychological. Drives are presented by Freud through grammatical transformations: seeing—being seen; he uses all the verb tenses in analyzing drives. If you refer to his article on "Instincts and Their Vicissitudes," you'll see this. There is necessarily a problem between the social and the biological, between language and libido.

I won't go into it here, but his 1938 text on *Family Complexes*,[3] a general clinical presentation centered on the family, contains nothing on analysis as such; but it is clear that when he talks about Freud, he never simply repeats Freud—he tries to find his own path within Freud's work, seeking his own perspective. In *Family Complexes* he invents his own concept of complexes, or generalizes Freud's concept. He considers that the main defect in Freud's theory is its neglect of structure, privileging instead a dynamic approach. It neglects fixed form. In 1938, Lacan was, extraordinarily enough, already using the word structure, and already looking to reformulate Freud's work in terms of structure. When he began reading Lévi-Strauss and Jakobson in the late 1940s, it was something he had been looking for for a long time.

What he stresses in *Family Complexes* is the autonomy of forms. Freud was too much of an atomistic thinker for Lacan, and even the term "free association" stems from the atomist tradition. Lacan tries to formulate what he calls "complexes" as fixed forms in which a behavior or emotion is typified. He rewrites Freud's developmental stages as structures, which he calls complexes. Thus, he takes the word "complex" from the Oedipus and castration complexes, and makes it equivalent to the word "structure." It's as if he said to himself 'Freud thought he could ground his concept of complexes in instinct, and I'm going to do just the opposite. I'm going to take the concept of complex as primary, and clarify the concept of instinct on its basis.' Now if you do that, instinct in humans appears to be dependent on structure as social; already in *Family Complexes* Lacan tries to show that instincts in human beings have nothing to do with instincts in animals. What we call instincts in human beings are open to manipulation and differentiation. There is clearly an unsatisfied appetite in man which cannot be reduced to simple instinct. It hardly seems to require any proof, it's so obvious. Consider advertising: Imagine dogs watching TV, desiring and identifying with a man or a dog in a commercial. That can happen with domestic animals. As Lacan said, animals living in a sea of language are always a bit neurotic and always develop some kind of disorder.

Complexes are always cultural. Lacan opposed instincts and nature to complexes and culture, and showed that, in man, social structure—language—goes to the farthest reaches of the organism. It may seem that drives are purely organic, but they are not.

Let us skip what Lacan wrote during World War II because he didn't publish anything; he didn't want to publish while France was occupied by Germany. There was a wonderful intellectual life in Paris during the German occupation; many leftist intellectuals obtained authorization from the Nazis to publish and put on plays. Lacan was not a leftist intellectual, but it is worth mentioning that he had the decency not to publish anything during the occupation. It was only in 1945, upon France's liberation, that he gave an article to a small unknown artistic journal, a short logical piece called "Logical Time and the Assertion of Anticipated Certainty."[4] That was written in 1944 and published in 1945. Then came his article "Remarks on Psychical Causality" (*Écrits* 1966) written in 1946, which I will also leave aside, in order to proceed directly to an article that is really the sequel to "Beyond the 'Reality Principle'": "Aggressivity in Psychoanalysis" (*Écrits*), written in 1948. Here, Lacan refines his conception of language, the sign, the other, etc. You can understand why he took up the subject of aggression in 1948, because at that time it was a popular topic in psychoanalysis; it was what the ego psychology psychoanalysts considered acceptable in Freud's notion of the death instinct, that is, in his notion that there is not only libido, but also the death drive. After World War II, which seemed to have demonstrated the existence of some kind of death drive, after five years of world war, concentration camps, the atom bomb, etc., the idea that there might be such a thing as a death drive in humanity didn't seem so far-fetched. So, it was a timely topic.

As you perhaps already know, Lacan's view of aggressivity grows out of what he says about the mirror stage: the imaginary relationship is a perpetual war against the other due to the fact that the other usurps my place. That enables Lacan to account for aggression at the imaginary level at that time: aggression is always grounded in narcissism. But correlatively, how does that relate to the phenomena of analytic experience? In analytic experience, on the contrary, we have dialogue—Lacan adopted that term at the time though it's a bit too symmetrical—and dialogue as such is a renunciation of aggression. Thus, you see how he built upon this already developed position. The imaginary level is fundamentally characterized by aggression, so we have to distinguish the level of language, where understanding and dialogue are possible, from the level of the imaginary. Hence the distinction between the imaginary and the symbolic. The imaginary is war; the symbolic level of speech is language, and its fundamental phenomenon appears to be peace.

In this article from 1948, Lacan expands upon his mirror stage article using phenomenological vocabulary, conceptualizing analytic experience as intersubjectivity. He provides a still more precise definition when he says that what is essential in verbal communication is meaning, not reference. His two axioms, which define the intersubjectivity of meaning, are that only a subject can understand a meaning (which is the first definition of the subject in Lacan's work: the subject is the agency that understands meaning, the agency correlated with meaning) and every meaningful phenomenon implies a subject. If you find meaning somewhere, you have a subject. It is here that Lacan first begins to introduce the notion of a subject in psychoanalysis: the subject of meaning. You can take it as a formal definition, like that of a triangle as such and such. We call "subject" that instance or agency which understands meanings or is correlated thereto, such that there is no meaning without a subject.

We could perhaps establish a more complex relationship between the subject and meaning, but if we say correlation it is sufficiently general. It allows us to distinguish between the individual and the subject, the former, according to Aristotle's definition, implying a body, a soul, etc. When it comes to the subject, we are not concerned with the individual—that is true in psychoanalysis as well. I was surprised to hear today that my son—who is trying to get into the main engineering and math school in France, the *École Polytechnique*—is obliged, in addition to the usual examinations in math, physics, English, Spanish, and French, to pass a swimming test as well. And tomorrow he has to run. He is not taken, in such a case, as the subject of knowledge or as a subject of meaning who has to explain something. He must be accepted as a body as well. It changed my view of the school: my literary/philosophical sense was that one should be able to get into the school as a pure self, a pure subject of meaning and knowledge, without having to run. Next thing you know, one will have to be able to repair cars!

What Lacan says about psychoanalysis is that you enter as a subject of meaning. 'Let no one enter here who is not a subject of meaning.' Even after having seen a patient for a very long time, you may not know whether or not he can swim. You may very well not know his capacities at the individual level. As Lacan said, you will not know the intensity of his tastes; there is a great deal of data you will not know, even after years of analysis of the subject—the subject of meaning—and that is a very radical definition of what may enter into the artificial setting of analysis.

We must also differentiate between the subject and the ego. That is a fundamental distinction in Lacan's work from 1948 on. He gives a definition of the ego, similar to the definition Sartre provided in a seminal text, prior to *Being and Nothingness*, entitled *Transcendence of the Ego*,[5] in which Sartre radicalized certain of Husserl's notions, defining consciousness as nothingness and the ego as an object in the world—in your supposedly inner world, but an object nevertheless. Self-consciousness is by definition transparent, and thus the ego seems to be opaque as an object; you do not know what is inside: it is like an object in the world. That inspired Lacan to define the ego as the core of given consciousness, but as opaque to reflection; fundamentally, he defines the ego at the level of the imaginary. The subject, on the other hand, is defined at the level of the symbolic. When defined as the subject of meaning, it is on the side of the signified, not of the signifier. If you understand the notion of the subject of meaning, you see that the concept of the subject in Lacan is situated at the symbolic level, while the ego is at the imaginary level. At this early stage, he situates the subject on the side of the signified; later, however, he situates the subject on the side of the signifier. Thus, he shifts from the signified to the signifier.

If we speak of the subject of meaning, and we consider that meaning changes as you speak, understanding also changes. The concept of the subject takes on new meaning for you as I continue to talk about it. The meaning of what I say changes constantly as I add to it. On the one hand, we have the problematic of continuously changing meaning and the subject that goes with it, and on the other we have an imaginary relationship characterized by inertia. Hence, we have two relationships: the imaginary relationship which is fixed and involves aggressivity, and the relationship between the subject and the Other at the symbolic level (see Schema L, *Écrits*, p. 193; p. 127 below) where meaning is constantly shifting—inertia on the one hand, and change on the other. This is found at the end of Seminar II and in Seminar III, but you can find it in Seminar I as well. The symbolic is the axis of the subject as such.

A fundamental opposition between subject and ego is as follows: If you take the subject as a subject of meaning, it is constantly emerging, as meaning is constantly emerging; the subject is not a fixed point: it is mobile. The ego, on the other hand, has a certain inertia and fixity. That is why Lacan characterizes analytic experience as a "realization of the subject." The subject, which upon entry into analysis is nothing—that's Sartre's nothingness—realizes him or herself through changing meanings and becomes something. Thus, there is an opposition between the value of inertia on the side of the ego, and the value of mobility and self-realization on the side of the subject. There is a constant movement back and forth between the two, which brings up the question of transference.

As long as Lacan defined transference as imaginary, it remained a moment of inertia in psychoanalytic experience. For example, in his 1951 article, "Intervention on Transference" (*Écrits* 1966), he says that transference becomes obvious in analytic experience at the moment of stagnation. When the patient stops talking, the analyst can always interpret: the patient is thinking about me. That can also be found in Seminar I. Transference appears when the subject reverts to silence, thereby establishing an imaginary relationship with the analyst.

His theory of transference changes when he tries to offer a *symbolic* definition of transference. He provides such a definition when he proposes the expression "the subject supposed to know." The subject supposed to know is the pivotal point of transference; and this definition has nothing to do with emotion, projection, or inertia.

Consider what happens in analytic work with obsessive neurotics. An obsessive patient seems to speak more to himself than to another person, so much so that when you interpret something for him, he is disturbed by your intrusion and wants to continue his own train of thought. It seems that the subject wants to talk to himself: he asks questions but wants to provide his own answers. That is why Lacan speaks of the "intrasubjectivity" of obsessive patients.

On the contrary, you might say that it is really the hysterical patient who solicits an answer from the other. Hysterical patients cannot bear the analyst's silence and anonymity. They want the analyst to be someone with a face, someone they can touch and feel as a living body, whereas the analyst's body appears dead to the hysterical patient. That is why, for instance, if you insist on strict respect for the rules of the analytic setting, many hysterical patients feel rejected, and you wind up rejecting schizophrenics as well, because you do not understand that part and parcel of the hysteric's question is "is this other dead or alive?"

In psychosis, the Other clearly speaks to the subject in his or her own head. In some sense, the concept of the Other stems from Lacan's work as a psychiatrist and from the notion of mental automatism (Clérambault isolated the phenomenon of someone speaking inside the patient's own head). The Other as agency or instance is present in the very structure of communication. In some sense, psychotics are simply more lucid than we are: they know better than we do that we are spoken. The paranoid subject who complains of being talked about behind his back, people saying bad things about him, is far more lucid about his situation than we are, because we are fundamentally talked about, even before we are born. There is a discourse which precedes and conditions our appearance in the world.

Lacan differentiated clinical categories according to the different fundamental questions posed by different subjects. The subject of meaning is, in and of itself, a question. The subject is a question mark. He or she doesn't know, nor do we know, what he or she will in the future reveal about the past, because of the retroaction I spoke of last time.

Question: I have a question about Darwin. I think it's at the very beginning of the second seminar that Lacan talks about a Copernican revolution, and he occasionally compares the behavior of human beings to that of animals. One of the interesting things about Darwin and about Freud is that they both demote human beings. Darwin showed the continuity between human beings and non-human animals; Freud continued that same sort of debasement. What is interesting here is that, once you dispense with the need for the centrality of instincts in Freud's theory, psychoanalysis no longer appears to continue the series of Copernican revolutions brought about by Copernicus, Darwin, and Freud.

Miller: Yes, that could give one the impression that Lacan was on the side of sublimation, rejuvenating the narcissism of human beings. In the 1950s, you sometimes sense some sort of exaltation, but even then pure instinct is minimized by Lacan. But man's homogeneity with animals is conserved and extended by Lacan on the imaginary level. He shows, at that level, that we find the same things in human psychology as in ethology. He constantly refers in his early work to the animal kingdom. In his early seminars, he constantly takes examples from ethology to demonstrate the material importance of images. In 1946, for example, he explains that some pigeons cannot mature if they cannot see other pigeons like themselves. He uses that to show that images have a material efficiency. They are not mere illusions, but have materiality. It is a given in Lacan's work for years that human psychology is animal psychology, but that there is another level that intersects the animal level: that of the realization of the subject. At times, Lacan seems very enthusiastic about the power of the symbolic; in 1953, he's really changing things—he is free of all the fretting of the IPA. But soon thereafter he adopts a more Freudian pessimism. To many, it was horrifying to see how sarcastic he was about the existence of human beings. If you are looking for a debasement of humanity, read Lacan.

Notes

1. [Cf. the French expression *vouloir dire*: to mean (literally, to want to say).]

2. [*l'Autre du langage*: linguistic Other, Other as language, the Other that language is.]

3. [*Les complexes familiaux*, Paris: Seuil, 1984.]

4. [The English translation by Bruce Fink and Marc Silver can be found in *Newsletter of the Freudian Field*, 2, 1988, pp. 4–22.]

5. [Written in 1936 and published in *Recherches philosophiques*, VI, 1936–1937, pp. 85–123; for the English translation see *Transcendence of the Ego: An Existentialist Theory of Consciousness*, trans. Forrest Williams and Robert Kirkpatrick. New York: Noonday Press, 1957.]

AN INTRODUCTION TO SEMINARS I AND II

Lacan's Orientation Prior to 1953 (III)

∞

Jacques-Alain Miller

I've been presenting Lacan's work prior to Seminars I and II to see how Lacan arrived at that point in his "Pilgrim's Progress," from being a psychiatrist and a phenomenologist to being an analyst. Let me remind you that Lacan already conceived of himself as a phenomenologist when he was a psychiatrist and viewed his dissertation in psychiatry as following in the footsteps of Karl Jaspers. When we follow this path for twenty years, from 1932, the date of his thesis, up until 1952–1953, the beginning of Seminar I and the era of "Function and Field of Speech and Language," we see a progressive transformation or embedding of phenomenology into structuralism. In some way, Lacan's own personal past is a compendium of the intellectual history of the French intelligentsia, and what appeared to the public to be a sudden revolution in the 1960s—a sudden move away from existential Sartrism, a sudden public shift away from Sartre and Merleau-Ponty to structuralism—was, in Lacan's case, based on a great deal of intellectual work which I have tried to reconstruct in my previous talks here.

What I have carefully reconstructed so far is the central role played by Lacan's concept of the subject even before he asserts that the unconscious is structured like a language. That thesis is subordinate to the concept of the subject. The concept of the subject encapsulates much of phenomenology's view of consciousness. But what had developed in phenomenology since Husserl was the concept of unconsciousness.

The Lacanian twist is to transfer the phenomenological view of conscious-ness to the concept of the subject, that is, the subject of the unconscious. What phenomenologists like Husserl and his French pupils, Sartre and Merleau-Ponty, developed through their concept of consciousness was the fundamental anti-objectivist or non-objectivist status of consciousness. They stressed the fact that consciousness is not an object in the world and that you must not describe or analyze self-consciousness with the same categories you use to describe objects in the world.

In trying to describe—and description is essentially different from analysis—the inner life of consciousness, none of the categories you use to describe the world is useful or adequate. You may have a category with which to describe an object in the world—"substance" or some such term—but if you accept the idea of consciousness, there is no objectivist or positive category with which to describe it.

Last time I provided a careful description of the *Lebenswelt*, the "life world" as understood by Husserl and adopted by Merleau-Ponty, the perspec-tive that the relationship of consciousness to the body proper is that the body is always localized, and that means that the subjective world or world of con-sciousness is always localized: you only reach it through a perspective, accord-ing to the notion of the "project" taken from Heidegger. What we are talking about when we speak of consciousness is not something which exists once and for all. Rather, consciousness is something which forms and becomes; it is not something which is, but something which evolves and becomes from a localized point. In Heidegger's work we can already see the theme of the project which takes on such importance in Sartre's *Being and Nothingness*. In Sartre's work, being, which is what it is, is opposed to self-consciousness, which is nothing-ness: a working nothingness. It is Sartre's nothingness—which transforms being, and makes holes in the totality of being—which paves the way for the Lacanian subject defined as a lack of being (*manque-à-être*).

Thus, there are many connections between phenomenology and Lacan's work. Consciousness is not a thing. In some ways it is no thing, and yet it becomes. In *Being and Time*, Heidegger resisted speaking about consciousness because he already felt that the kind of object consciousness is ought to be qual-ified not as consciousness but as *Dasein*, because it is always a localized con-sciousness. In some sense, Lacan transfers the whole of phenomenological anal-ysis to the subject of the unconscious, and much of Lacan's teaching is a reformulation of this phenomenological theme in psychoanalysis.

The subject as something that becomes is very difficult to understand because it is what all classical Anglo-Saxon philosophy has always rejected: the idea of a defective nothingness, a nothingness that is not a pure and simple nothing, but rather an active nothing. That is Hegel's central tenet: there is a nothing which is not simply nothing at all, but which is a dialectical and active nothing. That has always been rejected by empiricists, and especially by Hume. It was rejected by positivism, and it was rejected by Butler who said: "A thing is what it is and nothing more."

Americans have recently become fascinated with the idea that, indeed, nothingness could be something, with the idea that what Butler said perhaps is not true. Maybe Hegel was not a madman. Hegel has always been considered a madman by mainstream Anglo-Saxon philosophy; the whole dialectical tradition was considered sheer madness conducive to Nazism. Americans could understand its appeal at the end of World War II but could not fathom how it could remain an active ideological position.

You have to understand that this conception of the subject as nothing implied, for instance, the term "realization": how is this subject, who is fundamentally nothing, realized or actualized through his or her project and what s/he becomes? That is why the first part of "Function and Field of Speech and Language," Lacan's long article on which the first two seminars are grounded, is called "The Realization of the Subject." The concepts of full speech and empty speech are elaborated in relation to the realization of the subject.

Moreover, the subject as a nothing which becomes and evolves implies the importance of the *history* of the subject. You can grasp the subject in his or her development as history, and so you have a promotion of the concept of history grounded on nothingness. Lacan considered an analytic session to be a construction of history, of spoken history, history constructed with its meaning by the subject. Only now are American analysts beginning to rediscover psychoanalysis as narration, a notion which was clearly already central in "Function and Field." The history which is spoken in analysis is a reconstruction of the subject's project.

Furthermore, it implies that you distinguish between the subject and the ego. That can already be found in Sartre's short text which preceded *Being and Nothingness*, called *Transcendence of the Ego*, where Sartre explained the difference between self-consciousness and the ego, self-consciousness being nothing and the ego being an object for the subject, an object in the world, something he does not know, something which is a concretion. Thus this concept of the subject required that it be distinguished from the ego as an object in the world, and this is clearly what Lacan says in his article on the mirror stage. The mirror stage provides a definition of the ego as an image, a worldly image, a hodgepodge of images: the ego constitutes an opaque object for the subject. The subject is fundamentally at the receiving end. The subject is weighed down by his ego and narcissism which he may even experience as an obstacle to his subjective realization.

Therefore, the distinction between the subject and the ego is really a fundamental orientation of Lacan's in Seminars I and II, and repeatedly he tries to make sense of and illustrate it. The ego is conceptualized on the basis of the mirror stage, that is, on the basis of the relationship between two similar objects: one's self and the image of oneself. This distinction is of the utmost importance. The relationship between the ego and the alter ego is a worldly relationship.

Lacan constructs a relationship for the subject in Seminars I and II that corresponds to that for the ego in the mirror stage. I won't go back into how Lacan defines this subject as a subject of meaning, every meaning being correlated with a subject, there being no meaning without a subject. On the side of the subject, Lacan constructs an S (which is distinct from the ego), and S's correlate, which at the end of Seminar II he calls the Other (Subject-Other [S-A]). It corresponds to the two terms of the imaginary relationship laid out in the mirror stage (a-a'). He constructs a corresponding relationship between the subject and the Other at the level of meaning, where the problem is how the subject is going to become realized.

The difference between subject and ego is similar to that between the "Other" and the "other." They are corresponding distinctions: you go from the distinction of the ego—this is still a central point for American psychoanalysts, the most advanced of whom have finally begun to think of psychoanalysis as narration, but if they go a bit further to think of narration as operative for the individual, they will not be able to escape the notion of the subject. By reformulating meaning, what do you change? You don't change the individual. It is not because you go into analysis that you get three arms or four eyes. What changes? You have to define what is supposed to change through a change in meaning and that is what Lacan did with the subject. The subject is exactly what changes due to changes in meaning. You are all aware of the two axes: the imaginary axis and the symbolic axis. They are not presented as parallel. He could have said, on the one hand, there is the imaginary and, on the other hand, the symbolic, and the relationship is parallel. I'm both the subject of meaning and, at the same time, an image: I'm a body or image and I'm a substance; you could represent that as parallel.

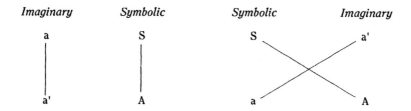

The twist you see at the end of these seminars is that, as the two axes are constructed, they are situated in such a way as to intersect and constitute a cross. The imaginary relationship—in other words, the relationship that derives from the mirror stage–is an obstacle to the establishment of a truly symbolic relationship. You have to trespass upon or cross over the imaginary in order to pave the way to the symbolic.

This immediately connects with Freud's work on resistance in the psychoanalytic session. On this basis, Lacan can define imaginary resistance as, for example, when a patient and his or her analyst get involved in a dual relationship like that described in the mirror stage, characterized by the phrase "You're in my space" or "You're usurping my role." This accounts for many phenomena in the analytic session where we find imaginary resistance which must be overcome.

Lacan affirms that the fundamental resistance in analysis is the analyst's, due to the fact that the analyst places himself in a dual relationship with his patient. Thus Lacan's famous adage that the *only* resistance in analysis is the analyst's.

But there is yet another resistance: the resistance of the symbolic axis when the subject has to elaborate a new meaning. There are paradoxes at the symbolic level which Lacan points out: there is resistance within the analysand's discourse and it is logically deducible.

What I have said thus far should supply you with a grid by which to read these two seminars: whenever you encounter some difficulty trying to understand what he is saying, try to apply this grid. When I published Lacan's *Television*, which reads like a highly contrived text with a great deal of difficult rhetoric, I included a number of schemas in the margins to indicate that Lacan's rhetoric constitutes a commentary of a very precise nature.

In the case of the first two seminars, you would have to indicate in the margin that, while Lacan constructed these two axes, there is in fact a third which I will come to later. Lacan's objective here is to apply this grid in order to understand the imaginary relationship between egos. What he is trying to do in Seminars I and II is to elaborate something specific to this relationship that was not provided by the mirror stage.

How did Lacan conceptualize the imaginary relationship? His conceptualization was not solely experimental or based on observation alone. He conceptualized the imaginary relationship using the grid provided by Hegel: he constructed it as a relationship between master and slave, as a dialectical relationship of alienation, and in some sense he didn't look any further. For instance, he wrote an article in 1951 called "Intervention on Transference" which is a rereading of the Dora case. At that point he clearly applied the Hegelian grid to the relationship of the subject to the other. He applied what he had already developed in the mirror stage, presenting the relationship between Freud the analyst and Dora as subject as a dialectical relationship along the lines of a Hegelian model. When he wrote a short preface to that article in 1966 for the *Écrits,* he said that at that time he was merely accustoming his students to the concept of the subject. He used the concept of the subject in a very interesting way. He opposed a relationship of one subject to another—and by that time, the other subject was the Other—to objectivization. He combatted the objectivization of the subject.

At that point in time, he defined transference as essentially imaginary. Transference, narcissism, and love were all considered imaginary phenomena, situated on the imaginary axis a-a'; a reference to the mirror stage is very appropriate in the case of narcissism. Lacan then considered transference as an imaginary phenomenon which interrupts the subject's creative realization. Thus, his notion of transference was, at that time, solely negative.

That allows you to understand how far Lacan took this reference to the Hegelian grid; even later, when he reformulated it through structuralism, he continued to refer to this dialectical relationship between subject and Other. Let me indicate the central matrix of his graph of desire, which he provided only ten years later in 1960 (see "Subversion of the Subject and Dialectic of Desire" in *Écrits*). The central matrix of the graph is given by the correlation between the subject and the Other. How can we understand this on the symbolic level? The subject has to accept or recognize the other as another subject in order for the other to recognize him in an adequate or valid way. And you first have to acknowledge the existence and value of the other in order for the other to recognize you. In Hegel's work, the impasse of the master's position is that he doesn't recognize the slave as a subject. Thus the master loses out because he cannot be recognized by anyone. The master does not recognize the slave as a subject and so the slave's submission does not constitute recognition of the master. The slave's submission merely acknowledges the master's strength; it in no way recognizes him as a subject.

The slave, on the other hand, triumphs in history because he is the one who works, and, through his work, makes nothingness effective. Marx took up this dialectical process and used it as the basis for the promise that, in the end, the true master of history will be the slave.

On that basis, Lacan constructed the highly democratic necessity for the subject to acknowledge the existence of an other so that the other may recognize him. He gives as an example the phrase "You are my wife," uttered by a husband, indicating that the subject (the husband) recognizes the other (his wife) as occupying a certain position; only on that basis can he be recognized by the other he has recognized. In Lacan's terms, this means that the subject cannot recognize himself because he does not know what he is; he cannot say "I am your husband." He is obliged to say "you are such and such" in order to receive feedback from the other. This justifies the analytic situation: you need an other. It explains why in the session, the analyst incarnates this other subject from whom you can receive your identity. It implies that to recognize the other is to be recognized by him. It implies that the fundamental desire of a human subject is to be recognized. For many years Lacan expanded on that, conceiving Freud's *"Wunsch"* as the desire to be recognized by the other. He took it so far in fact that he eventually concluded that it didn't fit in with psychoanalysis.

What I find so appealing about this is not simply the fact that Lacan finally rejected notions such as reciprocity, the other, creative speech, etc. It was not an offhanded dismissal of everything, the kind post-structuralists are inclined to engage in. Lacan carefully deconstructed all of those elements, pitting them against each other until the very structure of phenomenology began to crumble.

The desire of a human being is to be recognized by the Other, and as the graph of desire shows that the subject's desire is fundamentally the Other's desire, what the subject hears from the Other is the inversion of his own message. At the very moment at which you believe that you yourself are speaking, it is the Other who is speaking. That is why Lacan transformed this Other, who was initially another subject, into the unconscious itself. That is why he said in 1953 that "The unconscious is the Other's discourse." He transformed the Hegelian model from within and, by the end of Seminar II, he defined the Other no longer as simply another subject, but also as a locus. In the end, the Other was no longer another subject at all, but rather the locus of the unconscious.

Therefore, Lacan progressively "structuralized" a model which was fundamentally Hegelian at the outset. He connected dialectic and structure. He conceptualized speech and language as two fundamental connections and, moreover, as two antinomial concepts. He emphasized this in "Function and Field of Speech and Language" and, at the very end of Seminar II, he was still demonstrating this connection and antinomy of speech and language. In chapter 22, "Where Is Speech, Where Is Language?," his fundamental point is to draw a distinction between speech and language. It is a Saussurian distinction, expounded in Saussure's *Course in General Linguistics* and taken up by Jakobson; Saussure distinguishes between language as a fixed, universal, global structure and speech as a particular function, a creative function. Lacan presented language as an order, a structured order that includes the dictionary and grammar of language, in other words, everything that is fixed or ordered. Speech stems from that fixed order. Speech is a particular ordering that may eventually find its way into the dictionary.

What is the meaning of a word? A word's meaning is constituted by the different uses of the word and the created uses of the word that give rise to a shift in meaning. A new meaning stems from some particular use which appears at one moment and is repeated so often that it winds up in the dictionary. "Psychoanalysis," for example, is a word that was created at one time and is now found in most dictionaries. The French Academy is very slowly preparing its dictionary--after twenty years of work I think they are finally up to the letter "C" or "D," since they are very careful: they meet on Thursdays, not everyone shows up, and so they proceed very slowly. Last year they expressed their view that they should not include much psychoanalytic vocabulary as it is too new and they are not sure it will last. Language resists the admittance of new words and shifts in meaning. The "life of a language" involves constant shifts in meaning thanks to speech that is engaged in a dialectic with reality.

Lacan opposed language as a fixed structure to speech as a creative function. He deduced therefrom his own position regarding the history of psychoanalysis. Since Freud, to whom speech and language were of paramount importance, there had been an ever greater forgetting of the role of speech and language in psychoanalysis right up until 1953. Lacan showed that psychoanalysts had objectivized the unconscious. They had forgotten all about the creative function of speech. Lacan viewed his historical mission, his return to Freud, as a return to the foundations of speech. All psychoanalytic concepts are grounded in speech and it is in speech that psychoanalysis is active.

Hence, we have a number of distinctions: between the subject and the ego, the Other and the other, speech and language (the creative function of speech and the fixed order of language), and the symbolic and the imaginary, which leaves the real as a third and rather unknown quantity. At that time, Lacan was only operating with the symbolic and the imaginary, the real being something which did not enter into the imaginary relationship. You don't know what is real: it is neither symbolic nor imaginary. With that opposition Lacan began a systematic reformulation of Freud's work. He was aware that Freud had not formulated an unequivocal shift based on speech and Lacan found this Archimedean point from which to reformulate all of Freud's work. On the basis of his understanding of speech, Lacan began to reformulate clinical experience, theorizing that various clinical phenomena result from dysfunctions of one or another of the axes.

The first step towards structuralizing this is—and I am skipping some intermediate steps here—to try to focus on speech and language. Where is speech? Where is language? He makes a connection which is very strange from a Hegelian point of view, by attempting to situate language in this schema—a schema which would normally include only two subjects: one subject and another subject. When I speak to another subject, I have to speak his language in order to be understood; for instance, in speaking to you I am speaking your language. Lacan demonstrates that language is necessary to speech: a fixed order is necessary if the creative function of speech is to be exercised. The structural order of language is always situated in the locus of the Other. Lacan therefore begins to change the meaning of the other from another subject to the Other as a fixed order and structure.

What is fundamental in a structuralist point of view is that language is a fixed order of differential elements which is always already there (see Saussure, Jakobson, and Lévi-Strauss, in particular the latter's introduction to Marcel Mauss). The very idea of language, from a structuralist point of view, precludes any idea of its genesis as a global order, that is, it implies that language always precedes the speaking subject. That is why Lacan always criticized experiments on language acquisition, his fundamental view being that, prior to any learning by the subject, language is already there in the world. Everyone is born into a world where language is already operative. Consequently, the question is how the subject gets inside language and not the other way around.

Chomsky views language as a kind of organ that develops inside, but Lacan's point of view is strictly opposed to that: language is there and the question is how an individual subject gets inside it. According to structuralism, language is an order that precedes the subject. At that time, Lacan tried to deduce the subject from language and to show that the subject is an effect of certain linguistic relationships. In "Function and Field of Speech and Language," the symbol makes the man: man is what he is because of symbols. There Lacan introduces all the anthropological references from Levi-Strauss showing that even in the case of the most "primitive" peoples, their lives are organized by a highly structured order of references and their inscription in an order of symbols is very precise. The discontent in our civilization may come from the fact that our symbolic order is far more contradictory than that of primitive peoples: it is overly complicated.

Considering the Other to be the locus of the structure of language, Lacan goes on to identify the primordial law, the law of Oedipus, with the structure of language. In all of this, the fundamental term is acknowledgement by the Other, acknowledgement of one's existence by the Other, compared to what occurs in the mirror stage. The imaginary is war; the symbolic order is fundamentally peace and dialogue. Hence, Lacan could define desire at that time as a search for this symbol of peace, which seems difficult when you consider the very existence of psychoanalysis. That is why he then shifted away from that position.

To understand the difference between speech and language, for instance, in "Function and Field" Lacan isolated three central paradoxes, situations, or subjective positions wherein speech and language seem distinct. The first paradox he called the paradox of madness, defining madness as stereotypical: in madness we see an absence of speech instead of the creative function of speech. We find language only as a fixed form without creativity or dialectic. He defines the madman as someone who doesn't recognize the Other, who exercises an unthinkable, negative freedom not to recognize any Other. The madman knows no dialectic and Lacan goes even further by saying that, in mental automatism, the Other speaks directly to the subject instead of being symbolic. It borders on the dimension of the real; instead of receiving the symbolic order from the linguistic Other, you receive something in the real and so you hear what the Other is saying in your head. That is a rough sketch, but you can see that even his analysis of the Schreber case is based on the antinomy of speech and language.

Second, Lacan considers symptoms, inhibitions, and anxiety (borrowing the three terms of Freud's 1925 title) as illustrations of the relationship between speech and language; he considers the analytic symptom as a kind of speech or message which has not been able to be realized in discourse, and which is expressed in the body or in images instead. It is a symbolic message that has not been expressed through articulated discourse, and which is expressed in the real of the body or the imaginary as displaced speech. One must recognize therein the structure of language.

Third, Lacan analyzes what he calls the objectivization of discourse, characteristic of our situation in civilization, where everything has already been said, where the creative function of speech is reduced. Only objective discourse remains, a wall of language, as he says, a fixed form, a wall of structure opposed to speech. Thus the role of psychoanalysis in civilization is to vindicate the rights of creative speech over and against this fixed order, a view which clearly has certain romantic and anarchistic overtones. From this he deduces a new psychoanalytic technique which restores Freud's technique. In other words, he deduces therefrom what interpretation must be and what the role of time in the session must be. In the second half of the third part of "Function and Field," Lacan explains at length why this implies the variable-length session. I don't believe I have any time to explain it to you today.

PART II

SYMBOLIC

THE SYMBOLIC ORDER (I)

∞

Colette Soler

I'd like to welcome you to Paris and to the Freudian Field. You are an unknown to me, an X, but I already have a strong link with you, because it was for you that I learned English. I didn't know that it would be you, exactly those of you who are here today, but it was for you that I learned English, that's a fact. But you are still an X, and I suppose something about you—it's only a supposition. I suppose that, even if you have read a lot about Lacan, Lacan is still an X for you. So I will try, if I can, to make the two Xs meet to some extent.

My goal today is to say something about Seminar I. I have noticed that, to French people, Lacan's first seminar often seems easier than his later seminars. But to me now, in rereading the seminar, it seems a bit difficult. And that is because by 1953 Lacan hadn't precisely and definitively constructed the structure he went on to construct afterward: he hadn't yet constructed the graph of speech, elaborated the structure of language, or developed mathemes. Nor had he yet laid out the distinction between signifier and signified or the structure of metaphor and metonymy which these mathemes considerably simplified, providing important conceptual tools. What exactly was he up to in the first seminar? What exactly was he doing?

When he began the seminar, he had just written "Function and Field of Speech and Language in Psychoanalysis" (*Écrits*) the summer before. Thus, he had already made the fundamental distinction between the imaginary and symbolic orders, and had already introduced that between the ego and the subject (S). There is something perhaps which seems a bit confused in the first seminar, and I believe it is because at that time, Lacan was *forging* a distinction; he was trying to make people understand something which did not exist at that time. Before 1953, the distinction between imaginary and symbolic, which for us in 1989 is a very common distinction, did not exist. It was a Lacanian accentuation or creation. And we can see in this case that to create something new in the field of language is very difficult. It is not enough to introduce new words and set them in opposition to each other: "imaginary" versus "symbolic." That is the first step, of course. But afterward it is necessary to give meaning to the opposition, to demonstrate that the opposition is more operational, stronger, and more appropriate to experience than other conceptual distinctions. It seems to me that at that time Lacan was struggling with the spirit of the times, and there is something twisted or skewed, because while Lacan was explaining what the symbolic is and what symbolization is, at the same time he was demonstrating, in the act of giving his own seminar, how it is possible to introduce a new symbolization. That is a great achievement and yet difficult to grasp. The way he works is an example of a symbolic invention. So we see the appearance in the world of something new, something that did not previously exist.

Now let me say something about the context. What was Lacan's problem to begin with? It was to make psychoanalytic experience understandable. And from about 1950 on, he took a very simple point of view concerning psychoanalytic experience. He explored the psychoanalytic method as a method which uses speech alone. Now that's an obvious fact, but it is surprising that we had to wait until 1950 for this fact to be highlighted. The psychoanalytic method uses speech alone, and Lacan insisted upon the fact that psychoanalysis cannot be defined by the means it must forego. It can only be defined by the means at its disposal: they alone suffice to constitute a domain (he sustains this in 1953), a domain whose limits define the relativity of its operation.

We can therefore state the problem very simply: in psychoanalysis one speaks and symptoms change (sometimes, but sometimes is good enough). We can logically conclude then that symptoms have something to do with speech, that is, that symptoms and speech are in some respect homogeneous, and that the same holds true for the unconscious and speech. Starting with this main point, Lacan sets out to explain what speech is, what language is, and how, with speech and language, we can change something which apparently is not speech. Hysterical conversion apparently is not speech, but rather something involving the body. Bungled actions and the forgetting of words apparently concern action, not speech. Obsessions do not seem to concern speech either. But if speech can change all of these symptoms, we are forced to conclude that they have something in common.

Here I should remind you of Lacan's preliminary elaborations. Before stressing speech, Lacan constructed a theory of the ego. In his article "On My Antecedents" (*"De nos antécédents,"* *Écrits* 1966), Lacan himself declares that the real Lacan starts with "Function and Field of Speech and Language," referring to his earlier texts as "antecedents." These latter elaborated a consistent theory of the ego, and perhaps it is worth recalling this theory; for our problem today concerning the seminar is to understand what the subject, the symbolic, and speech are—too many questions for one lecture, but I will examine primarily the structure of speech here today. I noticed that "Remarks on Psychical Causality" ("*Propos sur la causalité psychique,*" *Écrits* 1966) has not yet been translated into English: what a pity, for the text is the most precise one concerning the ego. The main idea therein is that the ego is a system of identifications, and so we can write what the ego is for Lacan in the same way that we write the subject: one signifier over or which represents a subject: $S_1/\$$.

We can write the ego in this way, interpreting it as one imago that represents an ego. Retrospectively, that provides an accurate account of what Lacan says about psychical causality. The idea is that there is something called an "imago"—it's not an image or a signifier, but rather something between the two—an image erected as something fixed which has the role of a signifier. The ego is a totality of the imagos assimilated by the subject. So we have to stress—and Lacan did so at that time—the fact that there is a disjunction between being and identification, that is, an alienation: Through identification, the subject is alienated and loses his own being; this latter is constituted like something repressed or put aside.

I was wondering how to give another simple definition of the ego, based on the idea that the ego is a system of identifications. Here is a translation: the ego is what one looks like; it is the totality of the appearances of someone who is called a subject. But if you say it that way, you immediately perceive that we have to ask: "What is a subject?" If the ego is the system of identifications which command the different appearances of the subject, then we have to ask who the subject is. Thus, the idea is that the ego alienates the subject; psychoanalysis, consequently, is an attempt to go beyond the ego-alienation of the subject and to make something of the subject, something of being itself, appear.

How is it possible to make what is beyond the ego appear? The only way to make the subject beyond the ego appear is through speech. Perhaps you are wondering, "then what about behavior?" Behavior is not useful to know what a subject is. I don't want to speak about behavior, but it is a manifestation or appearance of a subject. If we are to situate behavior, Lacan would have us align it with the ego, rather than with the subject. Speech is what will perhaps make the subject appear. The problem is that speech is also used for ego purposes. A great deal of the first seminar tries to draw a distinction between two uses of speech: ego-related uses and subject-related uses. For it is a fact that the ego speaks. Let us examine the distinction, on pages 48–50, 108, and 126 in the first seminar, concerning the function of speech.

Speech in the field of the ego has a function of what Lacan calls "mediation"; and speech in the field of the subject has a completely different function that he calls "revelation." We have to try to understand what revelation is. Clearly it is a word that has religious, not scientific, overtones. And perhaps today it seems old-fashioned to introduce a term like "revelation" into a practice that claims to maintain ties with science—it seems a bit odd. A bit of work is required to see why Lacan introduces this word.

Speech's mediating function designates the use of speech with an intention to establish a link with the other, that is, the alter ego. The ego's partner is the alter ego, that is, the other as someone who can understand you, who might possibly love you, and who can know something about you. Lacan sets out to define the extension and limits of speech's mediating function.

> Speech is no doubt mediation, mediation between subject and other, and it implies the coming into being of the other in this very mediation. An essential element of the coming into being of the other is the capacity of speech to unite us to him. This is above all what I have taught you up to now, because this is the dimension within which we are always moving.

> But there is another side to speech—revelation (p. 48).

I want to emphasize the idea that the function of mediation *unites* one with the other. That is, in this uniting, we can extract a link, but not a mere link: a link that is essentially unifying, the idea of something that is possible with the other. Speech's mediating function is at work, for example, when one addresses the other as a witness, and when one addresses the other with seductive intentions or with the intent of making oneself lovable. It is also at work when one intends to transmit one's feelings, knowledge, or experience: one intends to share something. What is the function of the other in mediation? The other fundamentally fulfills a function of comprehension, comprehension by way of identification. Here I am summarizing what Lacan says about speech as mediation in the seminar. Now what does the other intend to understand? And what does s/he do when s/he cannot understand what you are saying? Lacan answers the question precisely: s/he projects. Projection and understanding are thus the tasks of the other in the field of speech as mediation.

Now as concerns the subject: how is the true subject revealed in speech, and in particular in psychoanalysis? (In general, as well, but here we can take the problem to the extreme in psychoanalytic experience.) How can revelation come about in speech? We must realize that speech is not a solitary activity; it implies an other who responds. This is the thesis introduced by Lacan in his text, "Function and Field of Speech and Language": "There is no speech without a response, even if speech only encounters silence, because silence too is a response." So the first point to stress is that revelation is not expression; it is produced *between two subjects*. Revelation in speech is produced between the subject who speaks and the subject who listens. More precisely, what produces revelation—and revelation in speech is revelation for the subject him or herself—is interpretation. What corresponds to projection and understanding (in the field of the ego) is interpretation in the field of true speech. Quite simply we can say that the ego wants to make itself understood. And when the ego is a listener it has to understand. As for subjects, we must say that subjects want to make something appear, and the Other has to make something appear through interpretation.

Perhaps an example would be useful here to illustrate the structure we are speaking about, that is, to illustrate the between-two of the truth. But first, I'm not sure you appreciate the full weight of the word "revelation": it implies that truth is not known by the subject who speaks, nor by the subject who listens. Truth is produced, it emerges as something new between the two subjects. And what proves that truth emerges as something new? The subject's own surprise. When s/he speaks truly in an analysis, the surprise when s/he hears what s/he has said constitutes the proof we are seeking. And what has been said depends on what the analyst has interpreted. It is a complicated structure implicitly present in the seminar that Lacan develops at greater length later.

Here is an example Lacan uses in the seminar. It is an example he uses in different ways, but it can be used to provide an example of revelation. Freud first describes it as the forgetting of a word: "Signorelli." Speaking with someone, Freud forgets the name Signorelli, the name of the famous painter responsible for the fresco of the Last Judgement. How does Lacan exemplify the difference between the ego's empty speech and the subject's full speech in this example? Freud is speaking with an alter ego in a train; he is travelling and speaking with a doctor about people, but his thoughts turn to death and the power of doctors—or more precisely their lack thereof; those are his intimate thoughts, and he rejects them. Why? Because he is not there to reveal his innermost feelings. He is speaking normally with an alter ego, and so rejects something from his thoughts, continuing his speech as mediation with the other; he talks about the people, the country, and so on. What happens is that Freud at that point forgets the name Signorelli. If you look at Freud's account, the problem with the example is that the speaker and the listener are one and the same therein, that is, it is Freud who forgets and Freud who interprets the forgetting. Thus it is not a classical example, but we can take the forgetting of "Signorelli" as a small, momentary symptom. It reveals Freud's deeper thoughts, assuming someone interprets it. We associate the forgetting with the subject who speaks; we associate Freud, of course, with the Other who interprets, but the interpretation makes Freud's deeper thoughts—those concerning death and powerlessness—appear behind the forgetting of "Signorelli." We see in this example that before the interpretation, the truth—that is, the meaning of the forgetting—was inexistent, literally non-existent. *Its meaning or truth appears only through the mediation of interpretation.* We must conclude that the forgetting had no meaning prior to interpretation: it was simply a failure of the action of speech.

Therefore, what Freud designates as unconscious, the forgotten name "Signorelli," while but a very minor example, is clearly not something that intends to express itself. The Freudian unconscious is not expression, and is only present in some failure of activity: speech, memory, or bodily action. Before Freud's time—before their invention by a person who interpreted all such failures—these failures had no meaning. For centuries, people have bungled actions, had dreams, and experienced symptoms, but they had no meaning; for meaning exists only in speech, through the mediation of the ego, I might add.

Let me raise one last problem before opening up the discussion: how do we know that the interpreter is not inventing? How do we know that the meaning that appears between the subject who speaks (in general, or through his or her symptom or the failure of his or her action) and the interpreter is not invented by the latter? There can only be one form of proof, but it's decisive: the fact that symptoms are transformed when they are interpreted. The only proof of the unconscious as speech is the effectiveness of interpretation on symptoms. Here we are led to ponder over the nature of truth—not truth as exactitude. Subjective truth is only a form of truth; there are others. But the truth of a subject is not exactness concerning facts; it is something which is produced in speech. When you manage to put something into words, you transform it. That is where what we call a subject comes in. A subject is not a person or the whole reality of a man or woman. Psychoanalysis operates a cut in reality: what we refer to as a subject—what Lacan referred to as a subject at that time—is something implied by what happens in speech.

Question: I'm trying to understand the relationship between speech and relationship. The truth emerges in a relationship between two people: why is it "failed speech" that you talk about it, rather than a "failed relationship" that did not allow for the truth earlier, whereas now you have a new relationship that allows for it?

Soler: When we use the expression "relationship between two people," we see that such a relationship implies four terms. When you have two people, you have two couples, two egos and two subjects. Thus, the notion of "relationship" is insufficient, because we have to know if we are speaking about the axis between the two egos or between the two subjects.

When you attempt to make yourself understood by the other, your alter ego, you use your own identifications, and the other understands you by way of his or her own identifications. If, for example, we have some problem communicating or dialoguing, it is because we don't belong to the same culture, the same country, etc.: we don't have the same references, at least in part. Hence our problems identifying with one another. But when you speak with someone who lives in the same town as you, goes to the same school, reads the same books, does the same work, and so on, you speak very fluently together, and everyone believes that you understand each other immediately. Successful communication always depends upon a certain level of identification. What is lost when communication is successful? The particularity or singularity of each person. Though you may understand an alter ego very well, there is always a fundamental difference between two subjects. Successful communication eliminates the possibility of making your own particularity appear. Successful communication means that singularity fails to appear. In everyday life, such communication is obviously necessary to sociality. If everyone was solely concerned with making his or her own singularity appear, life would be impossible; but in psychoanalysis our intent is to make what is most singular and most intimate appear. The analysand starts by speaking just as s/he does in everyday life. Truth as singularity is thus lost. Where can we find the remains of this singularity? In the failures of one's actions. Singularity is obliged to manifest itself through the failure of common action.

Question: You mentioned that truth only arises from the relationship between the subject and the Other? Is that on the symbolic axis of Schema L? Lastly, what is the relationship between truth and the subject's desire?

Schema L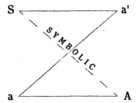

Soler: Yes, of course, the truth must be situated on that axis alone. Let me say first how I understand the question: When Lacan explains that subjective truth exists only in speech, and that truth's appearance necessitates the intervention of the Other—the Other being the master of truth, a radical thesis—we have a problem. As concerns the subject, we have something that seems not to be at the mercy of interpretation, namely what Freud discovered as unconscious desire: something that insists and is always present. The symptom is not simply a failure of speech. It is something constant, something that makes life impossible. It is clear that we have to put these two theses together: the insistence of the symptom in the field of the subject, and Lacan's statement, demonstrated in the structure of speech, that truth depends on the Other. We can resolve the problem: in the field of the subject we have the constancy of the symptom, and the suffering that accompanies it.

Subject	*Other*
symptom	interpretation
suffering	
unconscious desire	

Can we say that the symptom has a meaning before interpretation? No. The symptom is something that impedes life: it has no meaning; it is no more than an insistence. The interpretation by the Other gives meaning, that is, changes suffering into meaning, into something that has to do with truth. We could almost say that interpretation converts suffering into truth and has an effect on the subject, in the best of cases. So regarding unconscious desire, I situate it in the field of the subject as something that insists. Lacan perhaps at first translates the Freudian expression "unconscious desire" as truth of the symptom (*vérité de symptôme*).

Question: Does interpretation produce meaning or non-meaning?

Soler: Lacan of course insists on the presence of non-meaning, but that's a complementary point. Meaning has a lot to do with non-meaning, as truth has a lot to do with lies and error. Lacan often stresses the function of non-meaning, that is, the structural limit of meaning. And it is clear that the symptom shows itself to be divided into two parts, one that is translatable into meaning through interpretation, another that resists meaning, in other words, a part of non-meaning.

Question: In *The Ego and the Id*, Freud speaks of the ego as subject and object, as actor and process of binding. In Lacan's work, it seems the ego is more an imago, mask, or misrecognition. I understand that, but I don't understand what happens to the identificatory and binding processes: what happens to the functions that were prominent in ego psychology, notably the ego's synthesizing function? How do they work here?

Soler: There is an extensive psychoanalytic debate about the ego in Freud's work. Our thesis is that "ego" does not always mean the same thing in Freud's work: in his early work, he does not yet have the distinction between superego, id, and ego, and the latter is a sort of dynamic subject. Later, the ego is not the same; if the ego is a system of identifications, you cannot think of it as having a synthesizing function. *Lacan worked very hard to explain that there is no such thing as ego synthesis.* He thus has a problem explaining how shared, collective reality is constructed. The fact is that there is no function of synthesis in the ego or the subject. Hence there is no answer to that question—which does not point to a lack in Lacan's teaching, but rather to a problem in the way in which the question is posed.

THE SYMBOLIC ORDER (II)

∞

Colette Soler

I would like to begin today with the idea that the unconscious is linked to symptoms through speech. Lacan set out to think psychoanalysis on the basis of this notion, and to understand it we must immediately specify what speech is. I will not be able to discuss every aspect of speech as it is a vast topic. But I must remind you that, according to Lacan, speech—that is, full or true speech—is an act. An act is something that has a creative function; it brings something new into the world. The creative function of speech is the main thing you have to understand if you want to enter into Lacan's teaching, but it is not very easy to understand.

Second, I would like to remind you that speech implies the Other. We have to specify who the Other is. The Other, in the simplest sense, that is, the Other in the case of speech, is the listener: the person who can respond. The listener is the person who can introduce the symbolic order. In my talk last week I stressed the ambiguity of speech—the fact that speech has two different functions: one of mediation between two others or egos, and another of revelation. Today I will speak only of the level of full speech, that is, revelation. For that is the level encountered in psychoanalysis, that is, when psychoanalysis is really psychoanalysis!

Let us recall the structure of speech. When someone speaks, we symbolize the movement of speech by an arrow from the subject to the other who listens.

subject – — - — ➤ other

Now if you are the listener, you hear the statements made by a subject—simple enough. And you ask yourself, "what does s/he mean?" The problem is that there are many answers to that question. In trying to answer the question, "what does s/he mean?" or "what does s/he want to say?", you can first seek out the meaning or signification of his or her statements, that is, their grammatical signification. But beyond that meaning, a meaning you can obviously explain to other people, another question arises: What is the subject's intention when s/he transmits these significations? What does s/he want with these significations?

The very question of what s/he wants to say has a double meaning, the first possible meaning relating to the subject's conscious intention. For example, I am speaking, and I have a conscious intention to explain certain notions in Lacan's work. But beyond that conscious intention, there is always what we call an-other intention: an unconscious intention, that is, something I don't know about. Why is that? Speech has many strata. Is there a point at which the ambiguity of speech stops? Yes there is. But it is not situated on the side of the subject, but rather on that of the Other. For ambiguity stops when the listener decides or chooses what he has heard. When he decides, the subject's message becomes precise. The subject himself usually doesn't like the message the Other hears in the subject's statements (in fact he is quite certain not to like it), and at times protests. He may try to explain what he has said, but try as he might, the same process recurs.

The general structure of speech is such that, at the end of the subject's statement, the Other's after-the-fact decision determines the subject's message. That is why Lacan writes the subject's message as s(A), that is, as signified by the Other (A), not by the subject.[1] The statement is made by the subject, but the message is chosen by the Other. Later, if we have time, we can play a little game. I'll bet that you cannot come up with an unambiguous statement, and I'll go on to demonstrate to you that it's impossible—well, we probably won't have time, so . . .

Now, this general structure of speech works in psychoanalysis, but with a few differences. In psychoanalysis, the speaking subject is asked to obey the rule of free association. He or she is supposed to speak without what one might call se f-control. The second difference is that in psychoanalysis the Other appears as an interpreter, someone whose job it is to interpret unconscious messages. There is a third difference as well that is perhaps less obvious: the subject submits to the rule of free association, but what is at stake for him or her in his or her analysis is not just any old thing—it's who s/he is, and the why and wherefore of his or her symptoms and problems. S/he is out to discover the cause of his or her problems. That aim changes something in the field of speech.

In psychoanalysis, the interpreter is situated on the side of the Other.

subject - ⋯ — ⋯ ▶ Other
interpreter

But there is a problem: if the listener chooses what s/he hears, what constitutes a guarantee for the subject that s/he will be heard [*entendu*]?[2]

How is the all-powerfulness of the listener to be regulated? What can discipline his or her interpretative activity? How can we be sure the listener is not simply inventing what s/he hears? This is a fundamental question in psychoanalysis, because the subject wants to be heard, and does not want to undergo suggestion due to inventions on the listener's part. The revelation of subjective truth implies a good listener, and the listener has to reveal a truth which is not his or her own truth; if the listener interprets on the basis of his or her own truth, s/he cannot make a real interpretation; such interpretation amounts to what Kleinians call projection. It seems to me that the projection that goes on in psychoanalysis is above all projection by the analyst. That is what Lacan means when he tells us not to understand: 'Don't project your own truth or your own point of view onto the patient.' So how are we to interpret properly?

Let's look at the example, given by Lacan in Seminar I (pp. 196–97), of the patient who had a peculiar symptom related to the use of his arm. I will comment upon this example to try to illustrate what interpretation is all about.

In the example, we have a subject, an interpreter, and something else in the middle.

subject - ⋯ — — - Other
symptom   interpreter

The subject presents a symptom involving his arms. His first analyst offers an interpretation which has no effect: the symptom persists. His interpretation is, according to Lacan, a simple, classical one: it interprets the symptom by the drive (p. 196). In effect, the first analyst interprets the paralysis of the subject's hand—his inability to use his hand—as related to a primary prohibition of infantile masturbation. Such an interpretation is quite obvious, as little boys often use their hands to masturbate. And surely the first analyst was able to detect in the analysand's childhood a prohibition of masturbation. Thus he interpreted the symptom as a displacement of the prohibition of masturbation onto the instrument of masturbatory jouissance. It is a well-made interpretation, applicable to a great many people.

As the prohibition of masturbation is very widespread, it is not a very individual interpretation; it is general, not particular. I could invent another interpretation, if I wanted to, on the basis of Freud's idea that people often have a need for punishment: the analysand can't use his arm, because unconsciously he doesn't want to succeed in his intellectual activity, needing instead to punish himself. It is always possible to invent such an interpretation. If I were this patient's analyst I could try it, and if I were lucky it might have some effect.

Now Lacan is first struck by the fact that the analysand, though raised in an Islamic context and region, is, as he says, estranged from the Koranic law, and even has an aversion to it. We immediately see how Lacan hears: he devotes special attention to the subject's symbolic context. That is to say that his attention introduces, between subject and interpreter, the Other—not as listener, but rather as symbolic context, that is, as the locus of a discourse, the Other as a discourse already constituted before the subject's birth.

subject	Other	other
symptom		interpreter

Lacan stresses the fact that, as listeners, we always have to ask ourselves what position the subject occupies with respect to the symbolic order that envelopes him. In this example, it is very precise: his position is one of refusal, aversion, and estrangement. What Lacan discovers in giving such attention to the symbolic level is that as a child, the patient had "been caught up in a whirlwind, both private and public, which amounted to the following, that he had heard it said—and it was quite a scene, his father being a civil servant and having lost his position—that his father was a thief and must therefore have his hand cut off" (p. 197). Lacan thus discovers a legal proposition that is part and parcel of the patient's symbolic context: "A thief must have his hand cut off." This proposition comes to the subject from the Other, the Other of discourse: as a proposition, it is present in the subject's tradition. An event occurred. Something happened by chance, a contingent event in his life: his father was denounced as a thief. Therefore, we have three elements: a proposition present in the Other, a father denounced as a thief, and a son. One is a proposition, another is a contingent fact—and we see that the symptom realizes or applies the Koranic law: the son's hand is cut off. Not really, but its functioning is cut off through his symptom.

This point should be emphasized. The interposition of the Other's discourse between the subject who speaks to an analyst and the analyst's interpretation introduces something objective, an objective level. The analyst does not conjure up the proposition, "a thief must have his hand cut off," and inject it into the Other's discourse. That proposition is objective; it is objectively present in the subject's social context or discourse. And we have an objective event: the childhood incident. Lacan's interpretation emerges from the link between these two objective facts.

Now we don't know the exact interpretation Lacan made as he doesn't come right out and say it; he only gives us the objective signifiers (the proposition and the thieving father) on the basis of which he interpreted. There are perhaps many interpretations possible on the basis of the three terms: thieving father, law, and son. One could, for example, say that the paralysis of his hand means that he considers himself to be a thief, or that he feels he has to pay for his father's crime. We have a set of signifiers, and our interpretation has be grounded in that set of signifiers; but beyond that there is a certain amount of play: there are a number of degrees of freedom at the level of the precise interpretation, if one calls interpretation the act of giving the subject his message.

This example helps us address another theme. What is the relationship between a symptom and the unconscious? We see in this example that a symptom is a memory (it is perhaps other things as well), that is, it fulfills a memory function here. Consciously, the subject doesn't want to know anything about the Koranic law into which he was born, but his unconscious and his symptom remember the law he himself has rejected. Thus we see his symptom as the memory of a trauma, for we can naturally deduce that the unveiling of his father as a thief was traumatic for him. And we see that the unconscious is the conservation of a piece of discourse, namely the legal proposition that "a thief must have his hand cut off." The unconscious here is the symptomatic operativity of its implicit presence in the subject; the conscious subject is unaware of the presence and efficiency within himself of this proposition deriving from the Other.

This example allows us to see that the unconscious is a split or schism in the subject's symbolic world: there are things the subject can synthesize about himself and his own history, and others that he cannot. Hence Lacan's description, at that time, of psychoanalysis as a process of symbolic integration of one's history, that is, of the parts put aside in the unconscious. When Lacan speaks of history, you must remember that history for Lacan is not a set of pure facts: there is no such thing as a pure fact. History, of course, consists of objective facts, but those facts are linked together and organized by the meaning the subject gives them. Thus history in itself is always a symbolic construction. Hence Freud's notion of ex post facto traumatism—see the Wolf Man, a case in which a trauma is only constituted after the fact. A fact without meaning is not a fact; a fact without subjective meaning is not a subjective fact; a trauma is a fact that has received meaning from a subject. When I say that speech is creative, the first way to understand that is by saying that speech creates meaning.

What I would like to stress with this example is that meaning is always present in Lacan's theoretical understanding of psychoanalytic experience. What allows for the objectivity of psychoanalysis—what allows psychoanalytic practice to have some degree of objectivity, and to maintain a link with science— is *the interposition of the symbolic order between the subject and listener.* In the first phase of Lacan's teaching, he broached the symbolic order as an order linked to speech; in later phases, he stressed the Other as the locus of language's mechanisms—and language does not have the same structure as speech. Toward the end of his life, the objective symbolic order was reduced to logic alone: the logic of signifiers, the logic of discourse. But his main goal remained the same throughout: to reconstruct the symbolic laws which envelope and determine—not completely, only partially—the subject. Obviously they do not completely determine him or her, for otherwise there would be no subject (no subject who could lie, for example); we would have a machine if symbolic determination were complete.

There are always two aspects in Lacan's work: on the one hand, one must construct the symbolic determination that allows for a kind of psychoanalytic action which is not pure suggestion, respecting as it does the set of signifiers determining the subject; but, on the other hand, we constantly encounter the idea of the subject's freedom. Symbolic determination does not contradict subjective responsibility, and when one speaks of responsibility, one implies a level of choice; for without choice it is impossible to conceive of responsibility.

Let me make one last observation: this clinical example can also be used to shed light on the difference between repression and foreclosure. For our example shows that when there is repression, a signifier is nevertheless present, having been admitted into the subject's unconscious. Repression supposes what Freud called *Bejahung*—not "affirmation," as it has often been translated, but rather "admission"—admission into the symbolic. Signifiers are first present in the Other; they have to be admitted by the subject into the symbolic order, and *Bejahung* is Freud's term for this admission. In this case, we have an admission of the law into the unconscious: a pathological admission; this admission is attested to by the symptom. In his unconscious, this subject is a rebel: he revolts against the law, but that law is not foreclosed, being present in his symptom. It is not present in his conscious discourse, only in his symptom.

Repression	*Foreclosure*
Bejahung of the signifier into the unconscious; negation of it in consciousness (secondary): refusal	no admission of the signifier; what is not admitted into the symbolic is seen in hallucination: that is, in perception

In the case of foreclosure, we have a sort of imaginary—or more precisely real—presence of the signifier.

Question: In the example you gave, the Koranic law stood out for Lacan because it was not part of *his* symbolic order; isn't there a much larger problem when the patient and the analyst are both immersed in the same symbolic order? It seems that the capacity for making the symbolic order objective becomes problematic when they both share it.

Soler: Perhaps. As an analyst from the Catholic tradition, I know the main signifiers of that tradition; and when I have a Catholic patient who dreams of someone named Mary, it's impossible for me not to think of the religious connotations, even if Mary is merely the patient's girlfriend. Perhaps it is better when the analyst belongs to another symbolic context, that is, when the analyst is quite foreign or different. But his or her job is the same, regardless: to grasp the main signifiers belonging to the patient's symbolic order and operate on the subject. In the example I gave, it just so happened that Lacan knew a lot about the Koranic law. He had such a wide-ranging culture. You just can't imagine the extent of his culture: such people no longer exist in France. But even when the analyst knows nothing of the analysand's culture, as long as s/he is not stupid, s/he should immediately think that, when someone from such a background says s/he doesn't want to talk about the Koranic law, it's probably of the utmost importance.

Question: I was struck by what you said about the ways in which symbolic laws affect the subject, and about what symbolic law is. In this case history, there is a crossing between two registers of law: psychoanalytic and juridical, and in the question of theft, there is a crossing of the registers of property law and the law of the phallus; I was wondering if this kind of crossing of registers is important when looking at what a symbolic law means, how it is constituted, and how it constitutes a subject.

Soler: What are you calling psychoanalytic law?

Question: The involvement of castration, castration not coming under juridical law, "you will lose your hand if you steal" being juridical.

Soler: Castration is not a psychoanalytic law. Castration is an effect of language on living beings. It is something Freud discovered, but it is not introduced by psychoanalysis; it is something that is concomitant with the appearance of subjectivity.

I will try to provide a general answer to your question concerning the relationship between juridical law and symbolic law. In Lacan, one finds that the symbolic order—and by that I mean the level of language—well, it's not so easy to give a short answer. My main hypothesis would be that language has effects on living beings; it transforms living beings into subjects. Perhaps we don't have to call this effect "law"; it is a real effect of language as encountered in discourse. Therein we encounter an order; relationships between human beings are ordered by a system of laws, with different levels. What we find is that every law, regardless of its level, always has the same goal: it sets out to limit what Freud called drives, and what we Lacanians call jouissance: it regulates the links between people. The possibility of a social link implies limitations on individual jouissance, limitations and transformations, because the jouissance of living beings is closed in upon itself, solipsistic, in a sense. Jouissance doesn't establish any link in and of itself; you need the whole order of the symbolic and speech to have a bond with others, and for your own jouissance to become compatible with that of those around you. The effect of language on the real, that is, on jouissance, is therefore an effect that limits and regulates every satisfaction. Hence, it has something to do with law.

A subject's position with respect to juridical law is not necessarily an indication of his or her unconscious insertion into the law; this example shows us that you can have a subject who seems to refuse juridical law, but who in reality unconsciously accepts the limitations imposed by it. Thus it is incorrect to assert that a subject's insertion into the law inevitably results in his or her conforming to society. That is a very important point; people sometimes speak of psychoanalysis as something that tries to make people conform to the requirements of the social order. That is not the case in Lacanian theory. Conformity to the social order is sometimes compatible with psychosis—not always, but sometimes. There are a lot of comments I could make here. Let me just say that, in a certain sense, considerable insertion in the symbolic law allows a subject more freedom in regard to regulations.

Question: I would like you to say something more on the topic of individual responsibility.

Soler: I never said "individual responsibility." Words are things, and when Lacan speaks of a "subject's responsibility," it's not the same as "individual responsibility." We have to carefully distinguish between what depends on the subject and what doesn't. Subjective responsibility is an important topic in Lacan's work, and when he gave Seminar VII, *The Ethics of Psychoanalysis*, he showed that ethics makes no sense without the dimension of subjective responsibility; the ethics of psychoanalysis was a subject of considerable concern to Lacan, but to go into it would involve a whole other lecture. Simply stated, *I take subjective responsibility to be one's responsibility for meaning, regardless of the events to which one has been subjected.* Occasionally you meet a subject who has been confronted with very difficult experiences: mourning, war, abandonment, and the like; whatever those events may be, s/he alone gives them meaning. That meaning determines the way s/he experiences the events. You come across subjects who have lived in apparently very easy circumstances, for example, but who are always unhappy and always complaining; they seem to complain for no reason, but that is not true. They complain because they give the meaning of suffering to their life events. On the other hand, there are people all around Paris with objective difficulties who bear them well because the meaning they give them is different. The subject is thus always responsible.

Question: When you say it like that, it sounds like the subject is describing something rather than taking responsibility by acting.

Soler: In psychoanalysis, a subject speaks of his or her history, of his or her father, mother, brothers, and sisters, of what has happened, and of his or her wants; there is of course something related to description in psychoanalysis. The patient criticizes those who were around him or her while the psychoanalyst thinks the patient needs to realize his or her own responsibility for what happened. That is why, when the Rat Man told Freud he felt guilty, Freud immediately said to him that he was right to feel guilty. If you feel guilty, it is because you are guilty.

Just one more word: as an example of subjective responsibility, I said that the subject is responsible for meaning; but the meaning given by the subject to what happens is linked to a form of satisfaction. When I speak of meaning, you should not therefore assume that the register of jouissance is absent.

Notes

1. [On this point, cf. pp. 306 and 313 of "Subversion of the Subject and Dialectic of Desire" in *Écrits*].

2. Let me make a brief remark here on terminology: there are two aspects of speech, that of mediation between one ego and another—and in this context in French we use the term "*compréhension*," meaning comprehension or understanding—and a second involving the subject and the Other (no symmetry intended here), and in this case Lacan uses the term "*entendre*" [to hear or understand]. The latter means to understand *without* comprehension, identification, or similitude.

TRANSFERENCE

∞

Colette Soler

My intention this week is to speak about transference. My goal is to say something about the nature of time in psychoanalysis, and though I may not be able to say much about it today, hopefully I will next week. There is a huge debate in psychoanalysis about time: the length of treatment, the duration of sessions, and so on. I want to take up the problem directly, but I will begin today with a statement from Seminar II. It is a short statement, and one can easily read it without realizing its importance. It says that transference, with its link with time, is the concept of psychoanalysis itself. What does that mean? It implies that psychoanalytic practice and transference are identical. It is indicative of Lacan's intention to come up with a definition of transference which includes all aspects of psychoanalytic practice. That is not so easy because there are different elements in psychoanalysis. There is speech and there is love as well. What is the link between speech and transference love?

One can read all of Lacan's work with transference as one's guiding light and, if one does so, one can see that he defines and redefines transference as he develops the structure of analytic discourse. At the beginning, for example, he adopts a political position with respect to the rest of the psychoanalytic movement by saying that true transference is not situated at the level of object relations. It may seem a bit paradoxical to say that transference is not an object relation because between an analysand and a psychoanalyst there is apparently a relationship which produces feelings, feelings which concern the analysand's love object. But Lacan seems to me to give us the key to his position when he says that people who believe that transference is an object relation can't explain why, in psychoanalysis, we speak. At that time, he is looking for a definition which allows us to understand the function of speech in psychoanalysis, and in the 1970s his definition of transference is analytic discourse. The matheme of transference at the end of Lacan's teaching is the analyst's discourse. This position implies the distinction between what Lacan, after Seminar II, calls the constituting aspects and the constituted aspects of transference. It is a fundamental distinction, and we can translate the distinction into other words such as "cause" and "effect."

With this distinction, Lacan manages to situate all the most obvious transference phenomena—all levels of transference feelings. There are plenty of feelings in transference: love, anger, hope, and so on. Lacan doesn't set out to erase them, but rather considers them to be effects, effects of something else which has a causal function. Obviously you can't operate with effects. If you want to achieve something in psychoanalysis, you have to discover the level of causality. First he constructs the level of signifying causality, which is itself twofold: there is the causality of speech and the causality of signifying structure. And there is a further distinction which comes afterward. But in the end he completes this causality with the idea of an object-like causality. He reintroduces the function of an object in transference, but it is not the same object he criticized at the beginning in his critique of object relations theory. This distinction can be illustrated very simply using Schema L. All the object relations that psychoanalytic theory speaks about are localized by Lacan along the imaginary axis or arrow, and they constitute an enormous set of phenomena.

Schema L

Question: Does that include love?

Soler: It includes all transference feelings, with one exception I will perhaps speak about later. It includes love, hate, anger. . . .

Question: Does it include anxiety?

Soler: It did at the time of Seminar II, for he had not yet elaborated his theory of anxiety or angst as the only feeling which indicates a relationship to the real. I think that in Seminar II he would have situated anxiety in the imaginary.

It may be a bit surprising to you that in Seminar II Lacan situates the drives at the imaginary level; it is a bit surprising, but he had not yet distinguished between the imaginary and the real. The real had not yet been elaborated. For example, if you look at pages 269 and 272 where Lacan speaks about obsessive neurotics, you see that he denounces the kind of analysis which aims at getting the subject to recognize his or her drives. That is precisely what he considers to be the wrong orientation of psychoanalysis, especially with obsessives. One must not stress the drives which are situated between the ego and the other. In Seminar II he localizes the play of the drives between two egos, and one must realize the full extent of the imaginary: what Lacan calls the imaginary is not merely images—it also includes the body and the drives. Later he makes a distinction—whereas he begins with a certain confusion between the imaginary level and the level of drives, including drives in the imaginary dialectic, he later changes totally on this point. In Seminar XI, for example, he says that transference enacts the reality of the unconscious, and that the reality of the unconscious is the drives. Thus, in 1964, Lacan links the drives and the unconscious, but in 1955 there seems to be a certain amount of confusion in his mind about the localization of the drives.

A moment ago, I was stressing the vast array of phenomena localized along the imaginary axis. Now, if you situate all transferential feelings and drives in the relationship between the ego and the other, what remains on the symbolic axis? The subject. But what is the subject? What is the subject if you subtract all the phenomena which fill up one's life? What remains? That is exactly what is at stake in transference. Lacan changes his definition of transference, but there is something which never changes in his teaching: the idea that transference has to do with being. Being and time. You might mistake him for Heidegger. But he is just a reader of Heidegger's work.

Being and time are always present in the problem of transference. In Lacan's early work, he asserts that psychoanalysis is a process of revelation. I stressed the word "revelation" last week in what Lacan calls the "revelation of being." On the symbolic axis, we are thus looking for a revelation of being. Then, around 1973, Lacan asserts that by the end of psychoanalysis, the analysand has to *se faire à être:* get used to being, become able to bear being. Something becomes bearable for the analysand: he becomes able to bear something that is difficult to bear. Between the two expressions, there is a change in Lacan's definition of being. It is not a philosophical question. Of course, philosophy has always been interested in being, but if it is a philosophical question we have to say that the psychoanalyst has philosophical interests. For the question of being is a question raised by the analysand. Before explaining that I will give some indication of the definition of being.

The word is not very easy to grasp. Is being the real? No. In Lacan's work, being is not the real if we define the real as that which remains unsymbolized. That is the simplest definition of the real. The real is that which subsists without us, that is to say outside of symbolization. Being has no meaning outside of the symbolic, and if we want to situate being with our three categories—imaginary, symbolic, and real—being is mainly linked to the symbolic. There is a relationship between the imaginary and being which Lacan terms alienation: every imaginary identification alienates being. Every identification alienates being, fixes it, and at the same time represses it. Thus, the link between being and the imaginary is a first alienation (there is a second alienation via the symbolic). What is the relationship between being and the real? It is possible to say that being is the real as symbolized—that would be a simple definition—the real as spoken. The matheme of the relationship between being and the real would be written:

$$\frac{\text{Symbolic}}{\text{Real}}$$

There the symbolic substitutes for the real. That is Lacan's first idea of being: revelation of being when, through something symbolic like speech, you manage to make something new appear in the real. I am not saying that you manage to "express" it. That is a taboo word in Lacanian theory. You don't express with the symbolic. In a truly symbolic elaboration, you create, you make something appear which is produced by the symbolic. Thus being is, in a certain way, the real, but a real transformed by symbolization.

It is a first definition and is not far from identifying subject and being: if the subject is a subject created by speech, subject and being are virtually identical. Lacan later changes on this point. When he says that the analysand has to become able to tolerate being, what he then calls being is not the real, for the analysand has managed to say it. Rather, being is the real as impossible to say. In the end, he sometimes calls being the part that is impossible to symbolize, that remains impossible to symbolize, and that is what he calls object *a*. If analysis is always situated as a relation to being, it is not always in the same sense. There is an evolution which is, in fact, a complete reversal.

Now, I will come back to the question of being. The question of being is very simple. Who am I? or what is "I"? if you prefer. It is clearly a clinical question, especially for the hysterical subject. The hysterical subject ($) has strong feelings about the impossibility of making her or his being appear, a deep feeling of alienation in images and signifiers. The question "who am I?" is a clinical question: it implies the very notion of the unconscious. When we deal with symptoms and unconscious formations, that is, something impossible to control or grasp, you have to ask who is the subject of these manifestations? Who is the subject? What allows us to say that there is a subject is that symptoms and unconscious formations are possible to decipher; and when you decipher you make speech or signifiers appear beyond the symptoms and unconscious formations. So it is simple: it is nothing more than a series of implications. There is the fact that deciphering is operative: symptoms change through deciphering. That is the main fact of psychoanalysis. Deciphering implies the presence of the signifier, because only the signifier can be deciphered. And when you have a signifier, by definition you have a subject: there is no signifier without a subject in the world. In the pure world of the real, there is no signifier and no subject. Hence, the signifier implies a subject, but as an unknown, enigmatic being.

The matheme of transference Lacan provides before he develops the formula for the analyst's discourse is what he calls the "signifier of transference." When you emphasize the signifier of transference in a clinical case, you have to find the signifier of transference at the beginning of the cure, before the beginning of the cure. I don't have time to explain it in detail now or justify it, but we can, for example, identify the signifier of transference with the signifier of the symptom, the first signifier of the symptom. For when someone goes to see an analyst, it is because something is not working. The signifier of transference is the first emergence of what isn't working which the person presents to the analyst. Thus Lacan draws an arrow in the direction of the analyst; he writes the signifier of the analyst as a *"signifiant quelconque"*—any old signifier representing any analyst whatsoever. The idea is that if there is a first signifier, a subject is implied—Saussure's matheme says as much. But something else is implied: unconscious knowledge. Lacan writes unconscious knowledge as a second supposition: $S_1, S_2, \ldots S_n$. We can abbreviate that as S_2. Why does he write transference like that in 1967? Why does he introduce the idea that the signifier of the symptom implies the signifier of the unconscious?

I'll begin with the more apparent, not the logical, level. When someone seeks out a psychoanalyst, what does s/he expect? S/he expects a lot of things: to get better, to be happy, to be cured, and perhaps to become a psychoanalyst him or herself. But more essentially s/he expects interpretation. When a subject goes to see a doctor, s/he expects a lot of things, but not interpretation. When s/he goes to see a psychoanalyst or agrees to establish a relationship with a psychoanalyst, s/he expects interpretation. Interpretation consists, at the first level, in giving meaning to the symptom, and to give meaning is to complete the first signifier, the signifier of the symptom (S_1), with a second signifier which produces the meaning of the first signifier. At the beginning, the first signifier had no meaning. When you speak with an analyst qua interpreter, the presence of the signifier which allows meaning to be produced is implied.

Perhaps we should stop there today. Next time I will speak more directly about time, which I have introduced only indirectly with the notion of the patient's expectations (*attente* in French means both waiting and expecting). The patient waits for an interpretation, but beyond interpretation, he also waits for the revelation of who s/he is.

TIME AND INTERPRETATION

∞

Colette Soler

Today is the last day of the seminar and I will make only a couple of points.

First: What is a psychoanalyst's duty? You can take the word "duty" in two different ways: either in an ethical sense or an economic sense. You can ask what the psychoanalyst offers his or her patient, in other words, what you pay for in psychoanalysis. It is a fact that you pay and that you even pay a lot, but why and for what? You can see that such questions are not strictly intellectual—they are common questions from people who ask about psychoanalysis, and you must realize that this kind of question is determined by something which dominates everyone: not the law of the father, but rather the law of profit. We are in a society in which everyone everyday asks how much everything costs and what benefit will I reap if I buy, and if I pay such and such a price; this law dominates everyone. It works without your agreement; it is a product, an indirect product, of science. It is a secondary effect of the development of science and of the production of objects science needs to produce. Whether or not psychoanalysis will survive is not clear, but if psychoanalysis survives this attack, perhaps psychoanalysis is not very compatible with the great law of profit.

Lacan stresses the fact that psychoanalysis is linked with science and that psychoanalysis too—psychoanalysis as a practice and as a theory—is dependent on the existence of science; that is, psychoanalysis would not have been possible in antiquity, for example. Psychoanalysis is made possible by science, but from an ethical point of view psychoanalysis is not compatible with science. There is something not exactly opposed, but you immediately see the divergence in that science blindly produces knowledge, ever more knowledge. Psychoanalysis has something to do with knowledge, but the aim of psychoanalysis is to interrogate truth, which is not the same, and even to interrogate truth as knowledge, but in any case to interrogate truth. Truth does not mean universal knowledge, but rather the singular truth of one subject.

A psychoanalyst need not be impressed by the question "what is profit?" S/he has to be a psychoanalyst and work as one. S/he is not a nurse; if the subject needs nursing s/he has to call upon a real nurse. The analyst is not a doctor even if s/he is an M.D. In his or her work as a psychoanalyst, s/he is not a doctor. S/he is not a priest who offers confession nor is s/he an adviser, giving advice to guide the subject in life, in love problems, work problems, and so on. S/he is someone who holds out the promise of interpretation.

A psychoanalyst obviously must not take just anyone into analysis because, before taking someone into analysis, s/he first has to obtain a change in that person's subject position. If someone comes to a psychoanalyst looking for something very precise, for example, to solve a precise family problem, s/he cannot be taken into analysis immediately because the aim of psychoanalysis is not directly to solve the person's family problem. The aim of psychoanalysis is to bring out what Freud called the unconscious desire which is causing the family problem; thus, before taking someone into analysis you have to obtain a change in his or her subjective position. There is a problem in that the psychoanalytic subject does not ask to know what s/he doesn't know about his or her truth. S/he knows what happens to him or her, what is done by the Other. Sometimes s/he asks for help or relief, but not to know what s/he already knows.

The analyst's only duty is to provide interpretations, but if you want to provide interpretations you need something to interpret. To interpret you need a subject who lets you interpret, and that is not always the case. You need a subject who agrees to speak in the way you are asking him or her to speak, by freely associating. Before s/he can be an interpreter, the analyst has to do something else: s/he has to manage to become the cause of the patient's speech. This problem is clearly visible in Freud's work—though not in the same terms I am using here. Freud stressed that what a psychoanalyst has to do is interpret, but in time he discovered that interpretation sometimes meets with obstacles—transferential obstacles. In 1915, in "Remembering, Repeating and Working Through," Freud says that he discovered the need to work on transference to make interpretation possible. It is true that in psychoanalysis there is a therapeutic effect. That effect is fundamental because it proves that the unconscious exists—it proves the effectiveness and operativity of speech, the signifier, and the symptom. But what we have to see is that that is not the goal. We try to obtain a change in psychoanalysis, not merely relief, and the subject may or may not have the feeling that psychoanalysis is helping him or her, that s/he is better off after psychoanalysis. In the case of a negative therapeutic reaction, the subject and analyst discover that the subject was happier before s/he entered analysis. That is not the most frequent case, but it happens. In general, the subject feels that s/he is happier afterwards, but this positive change is seen from the vantage point of common discourse which demands that everyone be happy and successful. We are subject to the law of current discourse. I was speaking of the law of profit earlier—perhaps there is a superego of happiness now. It is a pure effect of current discourse.

All the changes you obtain in psychoanalysis are dependent on the fact of speaking. Change occurs because the patient has said something: the therapeutic effect of psychoanalysis is due to saying, but saying what the rule of psychoanalysis commands you to say: everything. Which especially means the unsayable, because to say everything is a technique. But Freud's aim, when he asked his patients to say everything that comes to mind, was not to understand everything, but to be aware, to hear something very precise: that which is the most intimate, evil, and shameful to the subject. We ask the patient to say everything to make the unsayable appear. The rule of free association does not ask you to say whatever you feel like saying. The rule requires you to say exactly what you don't feel like saying and it is a kind of forcing. It is not the forcing of the master signifier. There is also a forcing of the master signifier which consists in its indicating to you what you have to desire, what you have to do, what you have to want—for example, success, money, and so on. In psychoanalysis, there is also a forcing, but it is not a forcing which says to you what you have to desire; it is a forcing that gets you to say what you mean, what you want without knowing it—what Freud called the indestructible unconscious desire which is ever present, always the same, and always hidden.

Let me also say something here about time in psychoanalysis. If the patient pays for psychoanalysis to obtain some kind of revelation about him or herself, s/he pays for interpretation, not for time. The psychoanalyst doesn't owe the patient time, s/he owes him or her interpretation, and interpretation supposes other things: interpretation supposes presence. The psychoanalyst owes presence—it is a serious responsibility for him or her to be in his or her office at the appropriate time every day, all year long. Time is something else; it is not possible to completely deal with the problem of time in psychoanalysis today, but I will make a couple of points. Time in psychoanalysis is not only the time of the session, but also the time of psychoanalysis itself, the duration of the treatment. The problem of time in psychoanalysis has to be conceived of as subjective time, the time of the subject. If you have to reveal the subject, the question of time has to be approached with only one reference: what is the time of the subject? On this point, Lacan didn't always say the same thing and I am giving you the impression that it is very simple, but the first question concerns the time of the speaking subject—the temporality of the subject who is defined only by his or her subordination to speech. The first point is that there is a specific temporality of the subject and that temporality is not, for example, the temporality of living beings: animal temporality. There is such a thing as animal temporality: it is what we might call the temporality of instinctual tension. If you observe the animal world, you see a temporality which is regulated by instinctual tension, that is to say by the rhythm of instincts, elemental and sexual instincts; the temporality of the subject is not instinctual tension, nor is it clock time.

I'd like to say something about clock time; Lacan speaks in the second seminar about the invention of the clock and the measurement of time. The psychotic subject, Jean-Jacques Rousseau for example—Lacan called him a paranoid genius—has trouble with clock time. It is an important moment in Rousseau's life when he decides to abandon his watch, because all discourse imposes the measurement of time. Without the measurement of time you can't have appointments or social meaning. But the psychotic can decide to no longer have a watch and no longer see what time it is except day and night.

The temporality of the subject is neither clock time, nor the temporality of living beings; it is the temporality of the signifier. What is the temporality of the signifying chain? It is a twofold temporality between anticipation and retroaction; it is what Lacan called reversible time. In other words, the temporality of speech is a time shared between the anticipation, while you are speaking, of the moment of conclusion (the moment at which you can grasp what you meant), and retroaction, for when you arrive at the anticipated end point, all previous speech takes on new meaning, that is to say, new meaning emerges retroactively. It is a time split between "I don't know yet" and "Oh yes, I already knew that." The time of the subject is the time linked in the first definition with the problem of the temporality of signification, engendered by the signifier. The time of the session is the time of the scansion of speech, and the analyst, as listener, determines what the subject said.

I won't develop this point any further here, but a very consistent theory links the structure of speech with the time of the subject, and the time of the subject with the intervention of the listener. But that is not all Lacan says about time. Next year we will speak about Seminar XI where Lacan says that there is a time of the signifying chain, but it is mixed with other things, with what might be called the time of the object. What is that? Freud says that the unconscious is not in time and that unconscious desire is indestructible. That means that there is something constant, something which doesn't change; there is something which changes, but also something which doesn't change, and we can make a distinction between two elements in psychoanalytic experience: the signifier with its reversible time and something which is a constant: object *a*. These two times are mixed up in psychoanalysis, and Lacan tries to show in Seminar XI how the insistence or inertia of something interferes with the dialectical time of the signifier. Jacques-Alain Miller spoke Wednesday about dialectics, and dialectical time is the time of signifiers, not the inertia of constancy. That is more or less the idea. The reversible time of psychoanalysis is mixed up with another temporal element which is opening and closing, that is to say a *battement* or beat between the moment in which the subject articulates something of the unconscious with signifiers, and the moment in which the signifier is silent.

The subject of the signifier is a subject who has a lot of peculiarities, but the main peculiarity of the subject in the signifying chain is lack, lack of being, lack of knowledge, lack of jouissance, lack of the object desired. The subject asks the analyst for what s/he lacks—something which could put a stop to his or her lack, to his or her want to be, to his or her want of knowledge or being. What is the role of the psychoanalyst? In a word, it is to incarnate what the subject lacks. The subject lacks knowledge and an object. The psychoanalyst is supposed, in the transference, to be able to restore the knowledge the subject lacks and at the same time to be the locus of the object. The psychoanalyst is called upon to serve as the locus of lack, which means that s/he is called upon to serve as a complement, something which obturates the lack of the object. What is love if not to encounter an object which permits one to forget lack? The psychoanalyst is called upon to serve as just such an object.

It is not easy to handle transference in this respect because there is a contradiction, opposition, or tension between the necessary elaboration by the analysand and his or her complementation by the analyst. Because when you are obturated, you are not incited to speak; the motor force is always lack. When you achieve completion through transference, you do not engage in the work required to say what you would like to be. That is why it is one of the main preoccupations of a psychoanalyst, before interpretation, to decomplete the subject, to make the complementation of the subject's lack impossible. This task sometimes implies preventing presence and speech—everything the patient is asking for—and the short session, even reduced to one second, follows the main rule of separation. Separation sometimes implies suffering, frustration, and indignation.

To put it in an extreme fashion, in psychoanalysis you pay for loss. In some sense, in psychoanalysis we lose an inadequate loss. Some kinds of losses are in reality profits, but not the profits or benefits you expect at the beginning. I want to stress that this perspective can be found in Freud's work. When Freud, in chapter 7 of "Analysis Terminable and Interminable," speaks about what he calls the main transferential resistance, it is what he describes as the patient's claim that the other owes him or her something. What Freud describes is a case in which the subject never stops complaining that s/he is not getting what s/he is paying for. Freud called this something the phallus. The subject pays for the signifier of something which has value, jouissance value. Freud's philosophical position was that the psychoanalyst does not give this something because s/he can't; it is not because s/he doesn't, but because s/he can't. Something is lost that is related to the fact of being a speaking subject. That loss is thus inevitable. The consent of the subject is a way for him or her to accept the loss, and is related to the therapeutic effect.

What have I said today? I have said that the problem of time is to be considered a function of the subject as lack and his or her complement. Second, I have linked the problem of time with the ethical aim of psychoanalysis and it is impossible not to do so. The question of time has to be reflected in the aim or finality of psychoanalysis.

THE OEDIPUS COMPLEX

∞

Éric Laurent

I have chosen to address the status of the Oedipus complex in Lacan through the end of Seminar II. In a sense, you cannot isolate particular seminars as being indicative of the Oedipus complex. Yet at the same time, it is discussed throughout Seminar II. In Lacan's analysis of "The Purloined Letter," for example, the king, the queen, and the letter are read as an allegory or a new presentation of the structure of the Oedipus complex.

The cover of the French edition of Seminar II is a detail of Mantania's painting, on exhibit at the Louvre, where you see two Roman soldiers throwing dice at the foot of a cross. That painting presents the whole theme of the seminar. The status of the father is related to the fact that it is the son's cross. What exactly is the status of the father, not only once those soldiers throw the dice, but once cognitive sciences appear on the intellectual scene? What is the situation of the father once science appears in a new form, which is now known as cognitive science, but which in 1954 was known as cybernetics?

The lecture included in the seminar as chapter 23, "Psychoanalysis and Cybernetics or On the Nature of Language," would today be entitled "Psychoanalysis and Cognitive Sciences or On the Nature of Language." In the first part of this lecture Lacan makes a distinction he maintains throughout his teaching: that between "conjectural sciences" and "exact sciences." He introduces his notion of conjectural sciences in straightforward opposition to *sciences humaines* as they were called in French at that time. Lacan wanted to emphasize the fact, not that the "human sciences" are somehow more human than the exact ones or just as human, but rather that they address something

67

which is not exactly human, but which is subjective: the calculus of conjecture. And when he discusses the conjectural sciences, he refers to the origins of probability in the seventeenth century, probability as an economic calculus, and he says that probabilities were first introduced in thinking about throwing dice and all manners of gambling.

The problematic Lacan introduces in that lecture is still quite interesting to us today. I read in the *Times Literary Supplement* last week a critique of a book by Lorraine Daston entitled *Classical Probability in the Enlightenment* (Princeton: Princeton University Press, 1988). During the past decade or so, one of the most exciting controversies in the history of ideas has concerned the origin of contemporary ways of thinking about probability. For instance, we can now interpret probability either subjectively or objectively. I don't see why the critic who discusses Daston's book says that it is only today that we can interpret probability either subjectively or objectively, when three decades ago Lacan stated that we have to address probability and the calculation of probabilities as the problem of what appears on the subjective side or the objective side. The critic goes on to make a very interesting point about Daston's book; Daston criticizes a book by Ian Hacking entitled *The Emergence of Probability* (Cambridge: Cambridge University Press, 1984). It is a very good book, I might add, in the French tradition of Pascal, Condorcet, Poisson, and Laplace, as opposed to the English tradition which flourishes with Keynes and Ramsey. It poses the problem of whether these probabilities have an effect as such on the status of the subject. Condorcet's position was that they do, in speaking about social mathematics just before the French Revolution, probabilities on the subjective side having been repressed. Probability used only as a statistical calculus was the main interpretation or the main sense in which probabilities as such were or are considered. And if we stick to the statistical approach, as opposed, let's say, to the social mathematical approach, probabilities have no consequence at all on the status of the subject. The status of the subject is beyond the reach of that type of calculus.

In his lecture, Lacan begins with the fact that, for psychoanalysis, cybernetics continues the tradition of what started in the seventeenth century with probability; psychoanalysis has a great deal to do with a new status of the subject that was introduced at that time. Cybernetics has developed through a variety of approaches that can be labelled "cognitive science" or "artificial intelligence." The status of the subject with which psychoanalysis is confronted has to be considered through this introduction of the subject of science into our work. Lacan stresses the fact that in the seventeenth century—between 1659, which marks the invention of Huygens' pendulum, and the calculus introduced by Pascal in the second half of the seventeenth century—science changes status in a crucial way: what had been the science or calculus of what was in one place (essentially the planets that always return to the same place) was replaced by the calculus or science of the combination of places.

Lacan introduces the crucial term: "The science of what is found at the same place is replaced by the science of the combination of places as such. It arises in an ordered register which assuredly assumes the notion of the throw, that is, the notion of scansion" (p. 299).

I think that some of you have already encountered the term "scansion" in Lacan's other texts on interpretation in the practice of psychoanalysis. It is interesting that it was introduced along with the notion of probability at the end of the seventeenth century. Scansion goes with the idea of chance, chance not randomness, which introduces the idea of *la rencontre scandée* (translated as "scanned encounter" on p. 300)—the "scanded encounter" or the fact that, after that date, any encounter can only be determined by the fact that the places as such are already numbered. If we read Lacan in a Champollionesque way, reading only the terms themselves and not what they mean or what we suppose them to mean, we see nothing but that kind of approach. The "scanded encounter" is a term used by Lacan not only in an epistemological way but as applicable to interpretation as such. This Champollionesque approach is confirmed in Lacan's text on Gide in the *Écrits* where he speaks about nightmares and the presence of death in nightmares—Gide had a nightmare that he was in a house and that death was already there; Lacan says that Gide wandered in the labyrinth of life knowing that death had already numbered the places. That was a reference to this type of problematic.

The encounter always has to do with the subject as Lacan tries to isolate him or her in the practice of analysis: the subject always encounters what s/he is looking for through a previous scansion or numbering of the places s/he cannot define. We can refer to Gide or to the analysis of "The Purloined Letter"— there too, in one sense, the places are perfectly numbered, and the letter the subject explores can only occupy a certain number of places.

This is merely a logification of what Freud said when he claimed that *Objekt-findung*, the finding of the object, is always a refinding of the object. The place where the object is found has already been numbered. The scanded encounter to which Lacan refers is a presentation, from a logical point of view, of the fact that the object one is seeking—pleasure—has already been numbered.

That leads us to the questions Lacan raises in this lecture on cybernetics: what exactly is the status of chance in the unconscious? That question implies a reformulation of the status of free association. What exactly is the status of the "freedom" in free association? The problem does not disappear simply because we think there is no freedom at all since there is repetition. Of course there is repetition. That does not eliminate the problem.

That leads us to the critique Lacan provides here of the object relations approach in psychoanalysis which was new at that time. As he says, there are

two schools in psychoanalysis. Is it a matter in analysis of co-optation of fundamental images for the subject, that is rectification or normalization in terms of
the imaginary, or of a liberation of meaning in discourse, the continuation of
the universal discourse in which the subject is engaged?–that is where the
schools diverge.

To update the problem a bit more, you would have to replace the fundamental images with fantasies. Is psychoanalysis merely an exploration of the
repetition of the subject's fantasies? At the end of an analysis do we have to
attain the point where one knows one's crucial fantasies and can thus stick to
them? In the 1960s, Lacan calls that the fixation of the subject on his fantasies
(*Discours à l'EFP*). When he speaks of "fixating the subject on his shit," a technique, especially in the analysis of the obsessive neurotic, fixating him on his
anal fantasies, he is criticizing a technique which was employed by Bouvet. And
Bouvet was not the only one to use that technique. By fixating the obsessive
neurotic on his shit, Bouvet stressed that at the end of his analysis, the patient
can be completely devoted to an ideal: that of giving to others–that is, he
becomes the object to be given.

With the introduction of the "scanded encounter," Lacan proposes an
objective for psychoanalysis: not to fixate the subject on his fantasies, but to lib-
erate meaning in discourse. But what exactly does that mean, the liberation of
meaning in discourse? First, who can be against something like that? Everybody
is for liberation in everything. But what does that mean, especially in the context of the lecture? It's certainly odd to come across an expression like the "liberation of meaning" in a lecture in which Lacan explains that what is especially
useful for us in cybernetics is the fact that these scanded encounters can transmit a message, and that using some very simple cybernetics—0 and 1—you can
create a message which has no meaning at all, and which is reduced through
the very steps used to generate it.

This is presented in that lecture in a very simple way, but Lacan analyzes
"The Purloined Letter" as different steps that can transmit a message which, in
the end, is nothing but the steps the message took. The message in "The Purloined Letter" doesn't have the same meaning at the different stages. When
the queen has the letter, it's a love letter; when the minister has the letter, it's
his only power over the queen; when Dupin has the letter, it means that he can
take revenge; and at the end when the queen has it again, it's a useless power,
or more precisely the letter at the end has no exact meaning. It persists as a
pure message, incorporating the different steps it has been through: it has no
precise meaning. Rather, it is a dejection of the different steps it has gone
through.

Now, when Lacan says that what is useful in cybernetics is the fact that the
message has no meaning at all and can be reduced to the logical steps it has
gone through, what does that have to do with the liberation of meaning? What

does that nothingness—appearing as the construction or pure logical step of that message which confronts us with pure nothingness at the end, the nothingness in meaning—have to do with the liberation of meaning?

That is a crucial point in Lacan's theory, and it's precisely at that point that Oedipus can help us. The nothingness with which we are confronted at the end had already struck some of Lacan's students. In the seventeenth chapter, entitled "Questions to the Teacher," there's a question by Clémence Ramnoux who was a most distinguished analyst and wrote a number of books on Greek tragedy which I can only recommend—one of which was called *Enfants de la nuit* (*Children of the Night*). She questions the Greek tradition in, let's say for those of you who know the English edition, more or less the same way as Dodds, stressing the irrational aspects of the rational presentation of the self in Greek myth. Her question to Lacan runs as follows: "I managed to figure out why Freud called the source of repetitive symptoms a death instinct, because repetition manifests a kind of inertia, and inertia is a return to an inorganic state, hence to the most remote past. I thus understood how Freud could associate that with the death instinct. But, after having thought about your last lecture, I realized that these compulsions stem from a kind of indefinite, multiform desire, without any object, a desire for nothing. I understand it very well, but now I no longer understand death" (pp. 207–208).

It is in answering Ramnoux's question that Lacan introduces Oedipus. And not only Oedipus in Thebes but also at Colonus, Lacan emphasizing a part of the tragedy that had generally been ignored in psychoanalysis hitherto. In *Oedipus at Colonus*, Oedipus, who has endured his whole destiny and has castrated himself, lies in the temple at Colonus, and the citizens of Thebes try to get him to come back to the city. They are willing to have him back in the city, regardless of his status. Regardless of his doings, he is still part of the history of the city. He doesn't have to stay at Colonus, and they beg him to come back to Thebes. They send his son to beg him to come back and, of course, Oedipus refuses. At that precise moment, Oedipus mentions his father's name to his son. After Oedipus refuses to come back to the city, his son looks back and sees the transformation, the impossible instantaneous disappearance of Oedipus in something that cannot be named as such. It seems to me that that's the moment at which Oedipus is transformed from the name he was up until then into an object that has no name at all. That object has no name—it has only a place which Lacan designates as object *a*. The theory of that object had not yet been adumbrated when Lacan gave Seminar II. But I think we can use it here to explain why Lacan stressed *Oedipus at Colonus* and Oedipus in Thebes rather than *Oedipus Rex*.

In the drama, Oedipus is constituted as the Name-of-the-Father or as the son related to his father, Laius. And what is he, after he has taken all the different steps and traversed all the possibilities introduced by his name? What is the meaning of the existence of Oedipus? What does all that mean? It is only at Colonus that there is meaning in it all. The meaning is the fact that, in his fundamental being, he is transformed into an object.

The second example Lacan takes is from "The Facts in the Case of M. Valdemar" by Poe. The story is always of interest when people try to reduce transference in psychoanalysis to hypnotic suggestion. Most interestingly, Poe saw that the point of abdication of the problem of suggestion or hypnotic suggestion is the moment when the subject dies. It's the whole point of that tale, and that is exactly the same theme found in *Oedipus at Colonus*.

We can see why Lacan is not so interested in the fullness of meaning. Consider the distinction he makes between conjectural sciences and exact sciences through a distinction between semantics and syntax. "In other words, within this perspective, syntax exists before semantics. Cybernetics is the science of syntax and it is in a good position to help us perceive that the exact sciences do nothing other than tie the real to a syntax." It's not so much a distinction between exact sciences as syntax of the real, and semantics, something which can be related, for instance, to life as such or to conjectural or human sciences. It's not that point that interests Lacan. Consider the works of philosophers of cognitive science like John Searl who, in the lectures he gave in 1984, stressed the difference between the machine, the computer, and the mind (published as *Minds, Brains and Science*). According to Searl, the reason why a computer program will never be the same as a mind is because the program is purely syntactical, whereas mind is semantic, in the sense that beyond its formal structure it has a content. Searl thus tries to differentiate between machine and mind through the difference between syntax and semantics.

That is precisely what Lacan tries to avoid throughout this seminar. He claims that the fact that the subject we deal with has some semantic notion about his or her feelings or emotions beyond the syntactic structure within which s/he is embedded is not sufficient for psychoanalysis. That's the same type of problem dealt with via the catchword "intentionality." "Intentionality" should be considered a catchword, because it's a real problem. It's the problem that Lacan tried to address by referring to *Oedipus at Colonus* and Poe's "Valdemar." What does it mean in psychoanalytic terms that, when we use syntactic structure, we direct ourselves toward an object? Is that intentionality? The only intentionality we know of is the fact that the subject looks for a pleasurable object, and that s/he seeks it beyond the pleasure principle. That intentionality can be recognized; but what is the answer, what does s/he find? S/he doesn't find the object. S/he finds the place or places where the object was—the place already numbered and, in that place, the response is something that cannot be named. It is something which is structured along the same lines as the encounter between the name "Valdemar" and what is in the place of Valdemar once he's dead, or what is in the place of Oedipus and responds to it once he is dead, really dead, and refuses to rejoin the living.

That introduces us to a problematic found in "Function and Field of Speech and Language in Psychoanalysis" (*Écrits*). From that article, right up to the end of Lacan's teaching, what is the relationship between the name and what responds in the real? What we can name in the real, in the final analysis, what we are looking for beyond the pleasure principle, is jouissance. There are, in Lacan's work, as Jacques-Alain Miller has stressed in one of his classes, two paternal metaphors.

The one developed in "A Question Preliminary to Any Possible Treatment of Psychosis" (*Écrits*) runs as follows: the Name-of-the-Father occupies or has to occupy the place where the desire of the mother was, and the desire of the mother is what the subject looks for; "What does she want from me?," the child asks himself. When the Oedipus complex functions, the mother is prohibited, as Freud pointed out. Lacan put it as follows: The mother has to be substituted for; there is no direct answer. Nobody can really enjoy his or her mother who is only *real* pleasure, and she is prohibited at that place—thus the father is a name. We see that in the way Lacan writes the paternal metaphor: he clearly distinguishes between a signifier and a name. He doesn't write the name within the parentheses of the set of all possible signifiers, A. There's more in a name than in a description. The point Lacan wants to make in writing the metaphor as he does is that there is a distinction between a name and the set of signifiers.

One of the possible readings of that would be that, after the functioning of the paternal metaphor, the subject knows that the only thing he can name of that forbidden jouissance of the mother is the phallic signification of everything he says, of every one of his demands throughout his life. Everything we say has phallic signification. That's the only naming we can attain. Thus, that is the first paternal metaphor in Lacan.

In that same article, he presents the way in which somebody who didn't have any access at all to the paternal metaphor (a strict definition of a psychotic for Lacan), Schreber, tried to elaborate another meaning of his fundamental language—he had no fundamental fantasy, but a fundamental language. In the end, he could name his jouissance through the new language, and Lacan describes the way in which Schreber organized his jouissance throughout the feminization he underwent. There is then a new metaphor, that Lacan at that time called the "delusional metaphor"—the second paternal metaphor in Lacan's work. The new metaphor was introduced by Lacan via the graph of desire in "Subversion of the Subject and Dialectic of Desire" (*Écrits*) in which the Other was no longer written A, but $\cancel{A}$. Which means there is a fundamental inconsistency in the Other that cannot be reduced by the functioning of the father.

The father's name, the only name that introduces law in the Other, is a consistency that gives meaning to what exists beyond the pleasure principle—the phallus—and produces an answer: a stopping point that can captivate the subject, make him or her believe that that was the pleasure or satisfaction s/he was looking for, and make him or her stop at that point. There is a fundamental inconsistency in the Other, and there is no guarantee that the subject can stop and achieve satisfaction. Hence, Lacan who had previously written the subject as S, began to write it with the same inconsistency as that characteristic of the Other, $ and Á.

In the 1960s, Lacan elaborates the status of what is left for the subject, and what appears at the end of the *Écrits* is the status of that object which only has a place and cannot be named. In Seminar XIV, *The Logic of Fantasy* (it is not the logic of fantasies, but rather the logic of the object of fantasy as such), he elaborates the logic of what can be named, what can be placed, and of the place to which anyone can travel.

By way of conclusion, let me make two points.

1) The main consequence of the second paternal metaphor was that Lacan tried to inoculate the analyst against the delusion of occupying either the place of the father or that of the mother, paternal transference and maternal transference being a vicious circle. He stressed the fact that transference is directed toward the place of the analyst; transference is fundamentally a direction, a direction introduced at the beginning of analysis through the power of language as such: the fact that any one signifier can only be interpreted through another signifier. That journey can be initiated at the beginning of analysis through the power of language, but at the end of analysis, when analysands have gone through the steps, what are the words of the gods concerning them? What was the discourse that existed before them?

When they recognize the different steps they have gone through, the liberation they can attain is the fact that their true journey consists in having tried to occupy a room in that labyrinth before it was enumerated. Yet that is impossible and, in the end, they find themselves on a new journey. Here their itinerary is only justified by the fact that that room is already occupied by someone, the analyst, who serves to embody the consistency of an object, of everything patients say during analysis. Everything they say, after five, seven, ten, or fifteen years, obtains a certain logical consistency, but not a name. As Lacan said, it's like Orpheus and Eurydice. Should analysands try to name all the truths about their love life they encounter in analysis, these truths just disappear, fade away. But at least they know what they are. They are behind them and will always follow them as a consistency. Thus, we are all, at the end of analysis, Orpheus with our Eurydice, but we cannot look back. That's one of the possible readings of the fact that the object at the end is behind and pushes.

2) Lacan called the analyst a *saint homme*, a holy man. That may seem odd for somebody who was an atheist like Lacan. Lacan says transference with the analyst is like that with a holy man. I'd like to recommend that you read

Peter Brown, an historian of late antiquity and early Catholicism. His latest book is on sexuality in early Christiandom. In *Society and the Holy in Late Antiquity,* a collection of papers, he explains what the function of the holy man was in the world of early Christiandom. He was somebody who could not be named. There is a dialogue, from the synod in 1850, a conversation between the functionary of the emperor and he who carried the sword for the emperor, about whether the functionary of the emperor had really been absolved by a priest. An enquiry is made by the envoy from the Roman legate from the pope in Rome. He asks the functionary: "What was your confessor's name ?" "I don't know him, I know only that he once belonged to the Imperial Court, but he became a monk and spent forty years on the pillar. Was he a priest? That I don't know. He was a holy man and I put my trust in his hands." Peter Brown says that, in the Western world, the localization of the holy provided the power to absolve men of their sins. We are always perfectly located and everything is strictly named by the hierarchy; but a holy man had no name. Holy men were only authorized by the fact that they had become monks at one time in their lives and stayed forty years on the pillar like Saint Simeon Stylites. The analyst, according to Lacan, is like Simeon. It's not the fact that the analyst is authorized by a hierarchy to absolve man's sins, but rather that at one time in his or her life, s/he became not a monk, but an analysand, and spent instead maybe fifteen years on a couch and then a number of years in an armchair. In a sense, the analyst's armchair has to be elevated to the dignity of the *kaidan.*[1] It's the only authorization the analyst has, and beyond the paternal and maternal position, the fact is that, on his or her seat or *kaidan,* s/he can incarnate the dejection monks incarnated in the Western world; s/he can present what the subject was looking for and then what is beyond him or her at the end of his or her analysis.

Notes

1. [Nichiren, a Japanese Buddhist, taught that there should be a sacred place of ordination (*kaidan*).]

THE SUBJECT AND THE OTHER'S DESIRE

∞

Bruce Fink

You have already heard many lecturers here speak in very general terms about our alienation in and by language, language preceding our birth, flowing into us via the discourse that surrounds us as infants and children, and shaping our wants and fantasies. Without language there would be no desire as we know it—exhilarating, and yet contorted, contradictory, and loath to be satisfied—nor would there be any subject as such.

In this talk, I will outline Lacan's view of the advent of the subject in more theoretical terms. I will begin with a general discussion of the two processes Lacan refers to as "alienation" and "separation."[1] I will then present alienation and separation, operations which can be characterized and formalized in logico-mathematical terms, more discursively in terms of the Other's desire. After that, I will turn to the operation Lacan conceives as a further separation, or a going beyond of separation: the traversing of the fundamental fantasy. At the end, I will illustrate the workings of these three operations in the analytic setting.

Alienation and Separation

Hegel's concept of alienation, according to Lacan, evokes a struggle to the death between two parties, master and slave, that leaves only one party alive—but it could be either of them. In Lacan's version, the two parties, the child[2] and the Other, are very unevenly matched and the child almost inevitably loses. By losing and submitting to the Other, the child nevertheless gains something: he or she becomes one of language's subjects, in a sense, a subject "of language" or "in language." Schematically represented, the child, submitting to the Other, allows the signifier to stand in for him or her.

$$\frac{\text{Other}}{\text{child}}$$

The child, coming to be as a divided subject, disappears beneath or behind the signifier, S.

$$\frac{\text{S}}{\$}$$

The child need not absolutely be vanquished in his or her "struggle" with the Other, and psychosis can be understood as a form of victory by the child over the Other, the child *foregoing* his or her advent as a divided subject so as not to submit to the Other as language. Freud speaks of the *choice* or *election* of neurosis,[3] and Lacan suggests that a choice of some kind is involved in the child's accepting to submit to this Other—a "forced choice," as he calls it (which is something of an oxymoron), the decision not to allow oneself to be subdued by the Other entailing the loss of oneself. That decision forecloses the possibility of one's advent as a subject. The choice of submission is necessary *if* one is to come to be as a subject, but it maintains its status as a choice since it is nevertheless possible to refuse subjectivity.

Thus, in Lacan's version of alienation, the child can be understood to in some sense choose to submit to language, to agree to express his or her needs through the distorting medium or straightjacket of language, and to allow him or herself to be represented by words.

Lacan's second operation, *separation, involves the alienated subject's confrontation with the Other, not as language this time, but as desire.*

The cause of the subject's physical presence in the world was a desire for something (pleasure, revenge, fulfillment, power, eternal life, etc.) on the part of the child's parents. One or both of them wanted something, and the child results from that wanting. People's motivations for having children are often very complex and multilayered, and a child's parents may be very much at odds concerning their motives. One or both parents may have not even wanted to have a child, or only a child of one particular gender.

Whatever their complex motives, they function in a very straightforward way as a cause of the child's physical presence in the world, and their motives continue to act upon the child after his or her birth, being responsible, to a great extent, for his or her advent as a subject within language. In this sense, *the subject is caused by the Other's desire*. This can be understood as a description of alienation in terms of desire, not simply in terms of language, though they are clearly but warp and woof of the same fabric, language being ridden with desire, and desire being inconceivable without language, being made of the very stuff of language.

If, then, alienation consists in the subject's causation by the Other's desire which preceded his or her birth, by some desire not of the subject's own making, separation consists in the attempt by the alienated subject to come to grips with that Other's desire as it manifests itself in the subject's world. As a child tries to fathom its mOther's desire—which is ever in motion, desire being essentially desire for something else—the child is forced to come to terms with the fact that it is not her sole interest (in most cases, at least), not her be-all and end-all. There is rarely, if ever, a total mother-child unity, whereby the child can fulfill all of the mother's wants in life, and vice versa. Indeed, the mother is often led to momentarily neglect her child's wants precisely because her attention is drawn to other centers of interest; a child is often obliged to await its mother's return, not only because of the demands of reality (she must procure food and other necessities for her child, not to mention the money with which to buy them), but also because of her own priorities and desires which do not involve her child. The child's unsuccessful attempt to perfectly complement its mother leads to an expulsion of the subject from the position of wanting-to-be and yet failing-to-be the Other's sole object of desire. The why and wherefore of this expulsion—this separation—will be described at some length further on.

The Vel of Alienation

Alienation is not a permanent state of affairs, though it may have seemed that way in my earlier discussion; rather it is a process, an operation which takes place at certain times. This particular operation lends itself to formalization, and Lacan begins to formalize it in 1964. Rather than trace the historical development of his concept of alienation throughout his writings—it is already there in his 1936/1949 article on the mirror stage—I will present it here in terms of what Lacan calls the "vel of alienation."

Lacan's classic example of his vel of alienation is the mugger's threat: "Your money or your life!" (Seminar XI, p. 212). As soon as you hear those words pronounced, it is clear that your money is as good as gone. Should you be so foolhardy as to try to hold onto your money, your trustworthy mugger will unburden you of your life, proceeding, no doubt, to unburden you of your money as well shortly thereafter. (And even if he doesn't, you won't be around to spend it.) You'll thus, no doubt, be more prudent and hand over your wallet or purse; but you'll nonetheless suffer a restriction of your enjoyment, as a life in this world without money is not much of a life. Uncertainty only really remains around the question of whether you'll struggle with him and perhaps get yourself killed in the bargain.

The parties to the vel of alienation that concern us here are not, however, your money and your life, but the subject and the Other, the subject being assigned the losing position (that of money in the previous example, which you had no choice but to lose). In Lacan's reading of Hegel's version of alienation, the subject and the other are on more of an equal logical footing in that they both have a chance of surviving. In Lacan's version of alienation, the sides are by no means even: in his or her confrontation with the Other, the subject imme-diately *drops out* of the picture. If alienation is the necessary "first step" in acceding to subjectivity, we must take into account the fact that this step involves choosing one's own disappearance.

Lacan's concept of the subject as *"manque-à-être"* is useful here: the sub-ject fails to come forth as a someone, as a particular being; in the most radical sense, he or she is not: he or she has no being. The subject *exists*—insofar as the word has wrought him or her from nothingness, and he or she can be spo-ken of, talked about, and discoursed upon—yet remains beingless. Prior to the onset of alienation there was not the slightest question of being: "It's the sub-ject himself who is not there to begin with" (Seminar XIV, *The Logic of Fan-tasy*, November 16, 1966); afterward, his or her being is strictly potential. *Alien-ation gives rise to a pure possibility of being*, a place where one expects to find a subject, but which nevertheless remains empty. Alienation engenders, in a sense, a place in which it is clear that there is, as of yet, no subject: a place where something is conspicuously lacking. *The subject's first guise is this very lack itself.*

Lack in Lacan has, to a certain extent, an ontological status[4]—it is the first step beyond nothingness. To qualify something as empty is to use a spatial met-aphor implying that it could alternatively be full, that it has some sort of exist-ence above and beyond its being full or empty. A metaphor often used by Lacan is that of something *"qui manque à sa place,"* which is out of place, not where it should be or usually is, that is, of something which is missing. Now for some-thing to be missing, it must first have been present and localized; it must first have had a place. And something only has a place within an ordered system—space-time coordinates or a Dewey decimal book classification, for example—that is, within some sort of symbolic structure.

Alienation represents the instituting of the symbolic order—which must be realized anew for each new subject—*and the subject's assignation of a place therein.* A place he or she does not "hold" as of yet, but a place designated for him or her, and for him or her alone. When Lacan says (in Seminar XI) that the subject's being is eclipsed by language, that the subject here slips under or behind the signifier, it is in part because the subject is completely submerged by language, his or her only trace being a place-marker or place-holder in the symbolic order.

J.-A. Miller suggests that the process of alienation may be viewed as yielding the subject as empty set, {∅}, that is, a *set* which has no elements, a symbol which transforms nothingness into something by *marking* or *representing* it. Set theory generates its whole domain on the basis of this one symbol and a certain number of axioms. Lacan's subject, analogously, is grounded in the naming of the void. The signifier is what founds the subject—the signifier is what wields ontic clout, wresting existence from the real that it marks and annuls. What it forges is, however, in no sense substantial or material.

The empty set as the subject's place-holder within the symbolic order is not unrelated to the subject's proper name. That name, for example, is a signifier which has often been selected long before the child's birth, and which inscribes the child in the symbolic. A priori, this name has absolutely nothing to do with the subject—it is as foreign to him or her as any other signifier. But in time this signifier—more, perhaps, than any other—will go to the root of his or her being and become inextricably tied to his or her subjectivity. It will become the signifier of his or her very absence as subject, standing in for him or her.[5]

Alienation thus marks the institution of the subject through the primal repression of a first signifier, founding the unconscious and creating the precondition of the possibility of subjectivity as such.

Alienation is essentially characterized by a "forced" choice which rules out *being* for the subject, instituting instead the symbolic order and relegating the subject to mere *existence* as a place-holder therein. Separation, on the other hand, gives rise to being, but that being is of an eminently evanescent and elusive ilk. While alienation is based on a very specific sort of *either/or*, separation is based on a *neither/nor*.

Desire and Lack in Separation

One of the essential ideas involved in separation seems clear enough: that of *a juxtaposition, overlapping, or coincidence of two lacks*. This is not to be confused with a lack of lack: a situation in which lack is lacking. Consider the following passage from Seminar X, *Angst*:

> What provokes anxiety? Contrary to what people say, it is neither the rhythm nor the alternation of the mother's presence-absence. What proves this is that the child indulges in repeating presence-absence games: security of presence is found in the possibility of absence. What is most anxiety-producing for the child is when the relationship through which he comes to be—on the basis of

lack which makes him desire—is most perturbed: when there is no possibility of lack, when his mother is constantly on his back (December 5, 1962).

This example fails to conform to Lacan's notion of separation, for the negatives here (the lacks) both apply to the same term—the mother, that is, the Other. The mOther must show some sign of incompleteness, fallibility, or deficiency for separation to obtain and for the subject to come to be as $; in other words, the mOther must demonstrate that she is a desiring (and thus also a lacking and alienated) subject, that she too has submitted to the splitting/barring action of language, in order for us to witness the subject's advent. The mother, in the above example from Seminar X, monopolizes the field: it is not clear whether she is alienated, whether her field or domain has been encroached upon and decompleted through an encounter with the Other.

In separation we start from a barred Other, a parent who is him or herself divided—not always aware (conscious) of what he or she wants (unconscious) and whose desire is ambiguous, contradictory, and in flux. The subject has—to change metaphors somewhat—gained, via alienation, a foothold within that divided parent: *the subject has lodged his or her lack of being (manque-à-être) in that "place" where the Other was lacking.* In separation, the subject attempts to fill the mOther's lack—demonstrated by the various manifestations of her desire for something else—with his or her own lack of being, his or her not yet extant self or being. The subject tries to excavate, explore, align, and conjoin these two lacks, seeking out the precise boundaries of the Other's lack in order to fill it with him or herself.

The child latches onto what is indecipherable in what his or her parent says. He or she is interested in that certain something which lies in the interval between the parent's words—the child tries to read between the lines to decipher *why*: she *says* X, but why is she telling me that? what does she want from me? what does she want in general? Children's endless *why's* are not, to Lacan's mind, the sign of an insatiable curiosity as to *how* things work but rather of a concern with where they fit in, what importance they have to their parents. They are concerned to secure (themselves) a place, to try to be the object of their parents' desire—to occupy that between-the-lines "space" where desire shows its face, words being used in the attempt to express desire, and yet ever failing to do so adequately.

Lack and desire are coextensive for Lacan. The child devotes considerable effort to filling up the whole of the mother's lack, her whole space of desire—the child wants to be everything to her, her be-all and end-all. Children set themselves the task of excavating the site of their mother's desire, aligning themselves with her every whim and fancy. Her wish is their command, her desire their demand.[6] Their desire is born in complete subordination to hers: *"le désir de l'homme, c'est le désir de l'Autre"* Lacan reiterates again and again. Taking the "*de*" as a subjective genitive[7] for the moment, the following translations are possible here: "man's desire is the Other's desire," "man's desire is the same as the Other's desire," and "man desires what the Other desires," all of which convey part of the meaning. For man not only desires *what* the Other desires, but he desires it *in the same way*, that is, his desire is structured exactly like the Other's. Man learns to desire *as an other*, as if he were some other person.[8]

What is posited here is a tendency to totally superimpose the mother's lack and the child's, which is to say that an attempt is made to make their desires completely coincide.

This must, however, be recognized as a chimerical, unrealizable moment. For the fact is, try as he or she might, a child can rarely and is rarely allowed (or forced) to completely monopolize the space of his or her mother's desire. The child is rarely her only interest and the two lacks can thus never entirely overlap—the subject is prevented or barred from holding at least part of that space.

The Introduction of a Third Term

Separation may be seen here as involving an attempt by the subject to make these two lacks thoroughly coincide, that attempt being abruptly thwarted. We can begin to understand how and why that occurs by examining Lacan's reconceptualization of psychosis in Seminar III, *The Psychoses*, and "On a Question Preliminary to Any Possible Treatment of Psychosis" in *Écrits*, for it seems to me that separation, as formulated in 1964, is in some respects equivalent to what Lacan in 1956 referred to as the operation of the "paternal metaphor" or "paternal function."

Psychosis, according to Lacan, results from a child's failure to assimilate a "primordial" signifier which would otherwise structure the child's symbolic universe, that failure leaving the child unanchored in language, without a compass reading on the basis of which to adopt an orientation. A psychotic child may very well *assimilate* language, but cannot come to be in language in the same way as a neurotic child. Lacking that fundamental anchoring point, the remainder of the signifiers assimilated are condemned to drift.

This "primordial" signifier is instated through the operation of what Lacan calls the paternal metaphor or paternal function. If we hypothesize an initial child-mother unity (as a logical, that is, structural, moment if not a temporal one), the father, in a Western nuclear family, typically acts in such a way as to disrupt that unity, intervening therein as a third term—often perceived as foreign and even undesirable. The child, as yet a sort of undifferentiated bundle of sensations, lacking in sensory-motor coordination and all sense of self, is not yet distinguishable from its mother, taking the mother's body as a simple extension of its own, being in "direct, unmediated contact" with it. And the mother may, if unopposed by some other member of the household or some other desire of her own, devote virtually all of her attention to the chid, anticipate its every need, and make herself one hundred percent accessible to the child. In such a situation, the father or some other member of the household, or that other desire of the mother's, can serve a very specific function: that of annulling the mother-child unity, creating an essential space or gap between mother and child. Should the mother pay no attention to the father or other member of the household, granting him or her no importance, the mother-child relationship may never become triangulated. Or should the father or other member of the household be unconcerned, tacitly allowing the unity to go undisrupted, a third term may never be introduced.

Lacan called this third term the Name-of-the-Father or the Father's Name, but by formalizing its action in the form of the paternal metaphor or function, he made it clear that it was not inescapably tied to either biological or de facto fathers, or, for that matter, to their proper names. In Seminar IV, Lacan goes so far as to suggest that the only signifier that is able to serve a paternal function in the case of Freud's "little Hans" is the signifier "horse." "Horse" is, clearly in little Hans' case, *a* name for the father, but certainly not his "proper" name. It stands in for Hans' father who is unable to serve a paternal function, because he is incapable of separating his son from his wife.[9]

The symbolic order serves to cancel out the real, to transform it into a social, if not socially acceptable, reality, and here the name that serves the paternal function bars and transforms the real, undifferentiated, mother-child unity. It bars the child's direct access to pleasurable contact with its mother, requiring it to pursue pleasure through avenues more acceptable to the father figure and/or mOther (insofar as it is only by her granting of importance to the father that the father can serve that paternal function). In Freudian terms, it is correlated with the reality principle, which does not so much negate the aims of the pleasure principle as channel them into socially designated pathways.

The paternal function leads to the assimilation or instating of a name (which, as we shall see, is not yet a "full-fledged signifier," as it is not displaceable) which neutralizes the Other's desire, viewed by Lacan as potentially very dangerous to the child, threatening to engulf it or swallow it up. In a striking passage in Seminar XVII, Lacan sums up in very schematic terms what he had been saying for years:

> The mother's role is her desire. That is of capital importance. Her desire is not something you can bear easily, as if it were a matter of indifference to you. It always leads to problems. The mother is a big crocodile and you find yourself in her mouth. You never know what may set her off suddenly, making those jaws clamp down. That is the mother's desire.

> So I tried to explain that there was something reassuring. I am telling you simple things—indeed, I am improvising. There is a roller, made of stone, of course, which is potentially there at the level of the trap, and that holds and jams it open. That is what we call the phallus. It is a roller which protects you, should the jaws suddenly close (p. 129).

It should be kept in mind that the French words I am translating by mother's desire (*désir de la mère*) are inescapably ambiguous, suggesting both the child's desire for the mother and the mother's desire per se. Whichever of the two we choose to dwell on, or whether we prefer to view the situation as a whole, the point is the same: language protects the child from a potentially dangerous dyadic situation, and the way this comes about is through the substitution of a name for the mother's desire.

Name-of-the-Father

Mother's Desire

Read quite literally, this kind of formulation (*Écrits*, p. 200) suggests that the mother's desire is for the father (or whatever may be standing in for him in the family), and that it is thus his name which serves this protective paternal function by naming the Other's desire.

Now a name is, according to Saul Kripke,[10] a rigid designator, that is, it always and inflexibly designates the same thing. We might refer to a name as a signifier, but only with the caveat that it is an unusual kind of signifier, a "primordial" signifier. A further step is required for that which replaces or stands in for the mother's desire to function as a "full-fledged" signifier: it must become part and parcel of the dialectical movement of signifiers, that is, become displaceable, occupying a signifying position that can be filled with a series of different signifiers over time. This requires a "further separation" of the kind discussed below, and it is only that further separation that allows Lacan to variously refer to the symbolic element operative in the paternal function as the Father's Name (*le nom du père*), the father's no-saying (*le non du père*), the phallus (the signifier of desire), and the *signifier* of the Other's desire, S(Ⱥ).

Signifier

Mother's Desire

The substitution implied by the paternal metaphor is only made possible by language, and thus it is only insofar as a "second" signifier, S_2, is instated (the Father's Name, at the outset, and then more generally the signifier of the Other's desire) that the mother's desire is retroactively symbolized or transformed into a "first" signifier (S_1):

$$S_2$$

$$S_1$$

S_2 here is thus a signifier which plays a very precise role: it symbolizes the mOther's desire, transforming it into signifiers. By doing so, it creates a rift in the mOther-child unity, and allows the child a space in which to breathe easy, a space of its own. It is through language that a child can attempt to mediate the Other's desire, keeping it at bay, and symbolizing it ever more completely. While in the 1950s, Lacan spoke of the S_2 involved here as the Name-of-the-Father, and in the 1960s as the phallus, we can understand it most generally as the signifier that comes to signify (to wit, replace, symbolize, neutralize) the Other's desire. The symbol Lacan provides us for it (see Seminars VI and XX) is S(Ⱥ), which is usually read "the signifier of the lack in the Other," but, as lack and desire are coextensive, can also be read "the signifier of the Other's desire."

The result of this substitution or metaphor is the advent of the subject as such, the subject as no longer just a potentiality, a mere place-holder in the symbolic waiting to be filled out, but a desiring subject.[11] Graphically speaking, separation leads to the subject's expulsion from the Other, in which he or she was still nothing. Simplistically described, this can be associated with the outcome of the Oedipal complex (at least for boys) whereby the father's castration threats—"Stay away from Mom or else!"—eventually bring about a breaking away of the child from the mOther. In such a scenario, the child is, in a sense, kicked out of the mOther.

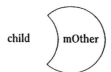

child   mOther

This logically discernable moment (which is generally quite difficult to isolate at any particular chronological moment of an individual's history, and is likely to require many such moments to come about, each building on the ones before) is a momentous one in Lacan's metapsychology, all of the crucial elements of his algebra—S_1, S_2, $\$$, and a—arising simultaneously here. As S_2 is instated, S_1 is retroactively determined, $\$$ is precipitated, and the Other's desire takes on a new role: that of object a.

Object a: The Other's Desire

In the child's attempt to grasp what remains essentially indecipherable in the Other's desire—what Lacan calls the X, the variable, or better, the unknown—the child's own desire is founded; the Other's desire begins to function as the cause of the child's desire. That cause is, on the one hand, the Other's desire (based on lack) for the subject—and here we encounter the other meaning of Lacan's dictum "*le désir de l'homme, c'est le désir de l'Autre*," which we can translate here as, for example, "man's desire is for the Other to desire him" and "man desires the Other's desire for him." His desire's cause can take the form of someone's voice, or of a look someone gives him. But its cause also originates in that part of the mOther's desire which seems to have nothing to do with him, which takes her away from him (physically or otherwise), leading her to give her precious attention to others.

In a sense, we can say that it is the mother's very desirousness that the child finds desirable. In Seminar VIII, *Transference*, Lacan points to Alcibiades' fascination with "a certain something" in Socrates which Plato (in the *Symposium*) terms "agalma": a precious, shiny, gleaming something which is interpreted by Lacan to be Socrates' desire itself, Socrates' desiring or desirousness. This highly valued "agalma"—inspiring desire in its detectors—can serve us here as an approach to what Lacan calls object *a*, the cause of desire.

This second formulation of Lacan's dictum, involving man's desire to be desired by the Other, exposes the Other's desire *as* object *a*. The child would like to be the sole object of the mother's affections, but her desire almost always goes beyond the child: there is something about her desire which escapes the child, which is beyond his or her control. A strict identity between the child's desire and hers cannot be maintained—her desire's independence from the child's creates a rift between them, a gap in which her desire, unfathomable to the child, functions in a unique way.

This approximative gloss on separation thus suggests that a rift is induced in the hypothetical mother-child unity due to the very nature of desire, leading to the advent of object *a*.[12] Object *a* can be understood here as the *remainder* produced when that hypothetical unity breaks down, as a last trace of that unity, a last *reminder* thereof. By cleaving to that rem(a)inder, the split subject, though expulsed from the Other, can sustain the illusion of wholeness; by clinging to object *a*, the subject is able to ignore his or her division. That is precisely what Lacan means by fantasy, which he formalizes with the matheme $ \$ \lozenge a $, to be read: the divided subject in relation to object *a*. It is in the subject's complex relation to object *a* (Lacan describes this relation as one of "envelopment-development-conjunction-disjunction," *Écrits*, p. 280) that he or she achieves a phantasmatic sense of wholeness, completeness, fulfillment, and well-being.

When analysands recount fantasies to their analyst, they are informing the analyst about the way in which they want to be related to object *a*, that is, the way they would like to be positioned with respect to the Other's desire. Object *a*, as it enters into their fantasies, is an instrument or plaything with which subjects do as they like, manipulating it as it pleases them, orchestrating things in the fantasy scenario in such a way as to derive a maximum of pleasure therefrom.

Given, however, that the subject casts the Other's desire in the role most exciting to the subject, that pleasure may turn to disgust and even to horror, there being no guarantee that what is most exciting to the subject is also most pleasurable. That excitement, whether correlated with a conscious feeling of pleasure or pain, is what the French call "jouissance." Freud detected it on the face of his Rat Man, interpreting it as *"horror at pleasure of his own of which he himself was unaware."*[13] And Freud states in no uncertain terms that "patients derive a certain satisfaction from their sufferings."[14] This pleasure—this excitation due to sex, vision, and/or violence, whether positively or negatively connoted by conscience, whether considered innocently pleasurable or disgustingly repulsive—is termed jouissance, and that is what the subject orchestrates for him or herself in fantasy.

Jouissance is thus what comes to substitute for the lost "mother-child unity," a unity which was perhaps never as united as all that since it was a unity owing only to the child's sacrifice or foregoing of subjectivity. We can imagine a kind of jouissance before the letter, before the institution of the symbolic order (J_1)—corresponding to an unmediated relation between mother and child, a *real* connection between them—which gives way before the signifier, being canceled out by the operation of the paternal function. Some modicum or portion of that real connection (a jouissance after the letter, J_2) is refound in fantasy, in the subject's relation to the byproduct of symbolization: object *a*, that which is produced as S_2 retroactively determines S_1 and precipitates out a subject.

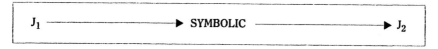

$$J_1 \longrightarrow \text{SYMBOLIC} \longrightarrow J_2$$

This second order jouissance takes the place of the former "wholeness" or "completeness," and fantasy—which stages this second order jouissance—takes the subject beyond his or her nothingness, his or her mere existence as a marker at the level of alienation, supplying a sense of being. It is thus only through fantasy, made possible by separation, that the subject can procure him or herself some modicum of what Lacan calls "being." While existence is granted only through the symbolic order (the alienated subject being assigned a place therein), being is supplied only by cleaving to the real.

Thus we see how it is that separation, a neither/nor operator applied to the subject and the Other, brings forth being: creating a rift in the subject-Other whole, the Other's desire escapes the subject—ever seeking, as it does, something else—yet the subject is able to recover a rem(a)inder thereof by which to sustain him or herself in being, as a *being of desire*, a *desiring being*. Object *a* is the subject's complement, a phantasmatic partner that ever arouses the subject's desire. Separation results in the splitting of the subject into ego and unconscious, and in a corresponding splitting of the Other into lacking Other (Ⱥ) and object *a*. None of these "parties" were there at the outset, and yet separation results in a kind of intersection whereby something of the Other (the Other's desire in this account) that the subject considers his or her own, essential to his or her existence, is ripped away from the Other and retained by the now divided subject in fantasy.

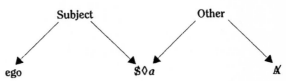

A Further Separation: The Traversing of Fantasy

Lacan's notion of separation largely disappears from his work after 1964, giving way in the later 1960s to a more elaborate theory of the effect of analysis. By Seminars XIV and XV, the term "alienation" comes to signify both alienation and separation as elaborated in 1960–1964, and a new dynamic notion is added: "*la traversée du fantasme.*"

This reformulation begins, in a sense, with Lacan's elaboration of the notion that the analyst must play the role of object *a*, the Other as desire, not as language. The analyst must steer clear of the role in which analysands often cast him or her—that of an all-knowing and all-seeing Other who is the ultimate judge of the analysand's value as a human being, and the final authority on all questions of truth. The analyst must maneuver away from serving the analysand as an Other to imitate, to try to be like, to desire like (desire's tendency being to model itself on the Other's desire), in short, an Other with whom to identify, whose ideals one can adopt, whose views one can make one's own. Instead, the analyst must endeavor to embody desirousness, revealing as few personal likes and dislikes, ideals and opinions as possible, providing the analysand as little concrete information about his or her character, aspirations, and tastes as possible, as they all furnish such fertile ground in which identification can take root.

Identification with the analyst's ideals and desires is a solution to neurosis advanced by certain analysts of the Anglo-American tradition: the analysand is to take the analyst's strong ego as a model by which to shore up his or her own weak ego, an analysis coming to a successful end if the analysand is able to sufficiently identity with the analyst. In Lacanian psychoanalysis, identification with the analyst is considered a trap, leading the analysand, as it does, to still more alienation within the Other as language and as desire. Maintaining his or her constant enigmatic desire for something else, the Lacanian analyst aims, not at modeling the analysand's desire on his or her own, but rather at shaking up the configuration of the analysand's fantasy, changing the subject's relation to the cause of desire: object *a*.

This reconfiguration of fantasy is known as the "traversing" or "crossing over" of fantasy, and implies a number of different things: the construction in the course of analysis of a new "fundamental fantasy" (the latter being that which underlies an analysand's various individual fantasies, constituting the subject's most profound relation to the Other's desire); the traversing of the square, in the graph of the split subject provided in Seminar XIV, to the lower left-hand corner; and a "crossing over" or switching of positions within the fundamental fantasy whereby the divided subject assumes the place of the cause, subjectifies the traumatic cause of his or her own advent as subject, coming to be in the place where the Other's desire had been.

$$(\$ \lozenge \overset{\blacktriangle}{a})$$

The traversing of fantasy involves the subject's assumption of a new position with respect to the Other as language and the Other as desire. A move is made to invest or inhabit that which brought him or her into existence as split subject, to become that which *caused* him or her. There where it—the Other's discourse, ridden with the Other's desire—was, the subject is able to say "I." Not "it happened to me," or "they did this to me," or "fate had it in store for me," but "I was," "I did," "I saw," "I cried out."

This "further" separation consists in the temporally paradoxical move by the alienated subject to become his or her own cause, to come to be as subject in the place of the cause. The foreign cause—that Other desire that brought him or her into the world—is internalized, in a sense, taken responsibility for, assumed (in the sense of the French word *"assomption"*), subjectified, made "one's own."

If we think of trauma as the child's encounter with the Other's desire—and so many of Freud's cases support this view (consider, to suggest but one example, little Hans' traumatic encounter with his mother's desire)—trauma functions as the child's cause: the cause of his or her advent as subject and of the position the child adopts as subject in relation to the Other's desire (the encounter with the Other's desire constituting a traumatic experience of pleasure/pain or jouissance).

The traversing of fantasy is the process by which the subject subjectifies trauma, takes the traumatic event upon him or herself, and assumes responsibility for that jouissance.

Subjectifying the Cause: A Temporal Conundrum

Temporally speaking, this operation of *putting the I back in the traumatic cause* is paradoxical. Was there subjective involvement at the outset which the subject must come to recognize and take responsibility for? Yes, in some sense. And yet subjective involvement is also brought about after the fact. Such a view necessarily contradicts the timeline of classical logic, whereby effect follows cause in a nice, orderly fashion. Separation nevertheless obeys the workings of the signifier whereby the effect of the first word in a sentence can be brought out only after the last word in the sentence has been heard or read, and whereby its meaning is only constituted retroactively by a semantic context provided after its utterance, its "full" meaning being an historical product. Just as Plato's dialogues take on a first meaning for students new to philosophy, acquiring multiple meanings as they deepen their study of them, Plato's *Symposium* has been shown to mean something else since Lacan's reading of it in Seminar VIII, and will continue to take on new meanings as it is interpreted and reinterpreted in the centuries and millennia to come. Meaning is not created instantaneously, but only ex post facto: after the event in question. Such is the temporal logic—anathema to classical logic—at work in psychoanalytic processes and theory.

Lacan never pinpoints the subject's chronological appearance on the scene: he or she is always either *about to arrive*—is on the verge of arriving—or *will have already arrived* by some later moment in time. Lacan uses the ambiguous French imperfect tense to illustrate the subject's temporal status. He gives as an example the sentence, *"deux secondes plus tard, la bombe éclatait"* which can either mean "two seconds later, the bomb exploded," or "the bomb would have gone off two seconds later," there being a possibly implicit "if, and, or but": it would have gone off two seconds later if the fuse had not been cut. A similar ambiguity is suggested by the following English wording: "The bomb was to go off two seconds later."

Applied to the subject, the imperfect tense leaves us uncertain as to whether the subject has emerged or not. His or her ever so fleeting existence remains in suspense or in abeyance. Here there seems to be no way of really determining whether the subject has been or not.

Lacan more commonly uses the future anterior (also known as the future perfect) in discussing the subject's temporal status. "By the time you get back, I will have already left": such a statement tells us that at a certain future moment, something will have already taken place, without specifying exactly when. This grammatical tense is related to Freud's *Nachträglichkeit*, deferred action, retroaction, or ex post facto action: a first event (E_1) occurs, but does not bear fruit until a second event (E_2) occurs. Retroactively, E_1 is constituted, for example, as a trauma, that is, it takes on the significance of a trauma (T)—it comes to signify something that it in no way signified before. Its meaning has changed.

$$E_1 \longrightarrow E_2 \qquad\qquad \underline{E_1} \longrightarrow E_2$$

(signification) T

In the statement, "By the time you get back, I'll have already left," my departure is retroactively determined as prior. Without your return, it would have no such status. It takes two moments to create a before and after. The signification of the first moment changes in accordance with what comes afterward.

Similarly, a first signifier does not, as we shall see below, suffice to create an effect of subjectification until a second signifier has appeared on the scene. A relation between two signifiers proves to us that a subject has passed that way, and yet we can in no sense pinpoint the subject in either time or space.

$$S_1 \longrightarrow S_2 \qquad\qquad \underline{S_1} \longrightarrow S_2$$

$$\$$$

Lacan's article on "Logical Time"[15] sets out to pinpoint the emergence of the subject in a very precise situation with a series of explicit constraints. The moments elaborated in that paper—the instant of the glance, the time for comprehending, and the moment of concluding—were later referred by Lacan to the moments of the analytic process itself.

Just as the time for comprehending is indeterminate for an outsider in the three-prisoner problem expounded in that article, the time necessary for comprehending in analysis is indeterminate—that is, it is not calculable a priori. Yet in associating the end of analysis with the prisoners' moment of concluding (Seminar XX, *Encore*), Lacan suggests a final moment of subjectification which can be forced to occur through a propitious combination of logical and/or analytic conditions.

Thus, while seemingly forever suspended in a future anterior, Lacan nevertheless holds out for us the prospect of a subjectification of the cause at a logically specific, but chronometrically incalculable, moment. We may, in a sense, think of alienation as opening up that possibility, and of this "further separation" as marking the end of the process. Separation can, nevertheless, be fostered, as we shall see, in certain situations, for example, at the moment of the cut or scansion of an analytic session, a moment which is both logical and chronological.

The traversing of fantasy can, not surprisingly, also be formulated in terms of increasing "signifierization"—a turning into signifiers—of the Other's desire.

Insofar as the subject finds, in this further separation, a new position in relation to object *a* (the Other's desire), the Other's desire is no longer simply named, as it was through the action of the paternal metaphor. As the cause is subjectified, the Other's desire is simultaneously fully brought into the movement of signifiers; as Lacan can be seen to be saying in his discussion of Hamlet in Seminar VI, it is at that point that the subject finally gains access to the *signifier* of the Other's desire, S(Ⱥ). In other words, whereas the Other's desire had simply been named through separation, that name was fixed, static, and thing-like in its unchanging effect, rigid in its limited power of designation.

In neurosis, the name generally remains to be adequately separated from the Other's desire. The name is not the death of the thing—the signifier is. As long as a rigid connection subsists between the Other's desire and *a* name of the father, the subject is unable to act: Hamlet, according to Lacan, has no access to the phallic *signifier* prior to his duel with Laertes at the end of Shakespeare's play, and that is why he is incapable of taking any action. It is only during the duel that he is able to discern "the phallus behind the king," to realize that the king is but a stand-in for the phallus (the phallus being the signifier of desire,[16] that is, of the Other's desire), and can be struck without throwing the phallus into question. Until Hamlet could finally dissociate the king and the phallus ("the king is a thing of nothing"), action was impossible, for to take revenge on the king would have threatened to make Hamlet's whole world collapse. It is only when the king (the object of the Queen's desire) is signifierized that a power can be discerned beyond the king, a legitimacy or authority which is not embodied in the king alone, but which subsists in the symbolic order above and beyond the king.

The name of the Other's desire must be set into motion—from the mother's partner, to teacher, to school, to police officer, to civil law, to religion, to moral law, etc.—and give way before the *signifier* of the Other's desire if subjectification is to take place, that is, if the subject is to become the Other's desire, leaving the signifier to its own devices. In that sense, traversing fantasy entails a separation from language itself, a separation of the subject—who will have become the cause—from his or her own discourse about his or her problem with the Other's desire, inability to deal with the lack detected in the Other, lack of success in maintaining the right distance from and relation to the Other, etc.

Neurosis is maintained in discourse, and we see in Lacan's notion of traversing fantasy the suggestion of a kind of beyond of neurosis[17] in which the subject is able to act (as cause, as desirousness), and is at least momentarily out of discourse, split off from discourse: free from the weight of the Other. This is not the freedom of the psychotic Lacan mentions in his early paper, "Aggressivity in Psychoanalysis" (*Écrits*, pp. 8–29); it is not a freedom "before" the letter but "after" it.

Alienation, Separation, and the Traversing of Fantasy
in the Analytic Setting

Imagine, for a moment, an analysand—ensconced upon the analyst's couch, talking about his or her dream from the night before, filling the room with his or her discourse, hoping that it will be interesting and satisfying to the analyst, thus in a fantasy mode ($ \diamond a$)—being suddenly interrupted with a word uttered by the analyst (not by the Other of knowledge to whom that discourse was in some sense addressed), a word which the analysand may have hurriedly glossed over or thought of no importance or interest either to him or herself or the analyst. Analysands often tailor their discourse, due to transference love, hoping to say what their analysts want them to say, what they think their analysts want to hear, and until such an interruption comes—whether with a cough, a grunt, a word, or the termination of the session—they can go on believing that they are achieving their purpose. Such interruptions often serve to jolt analysands, suddenly bringing them back to the realization that they know not what their analysts want or mean, that the latter are looking for *something else* in their discourse than what the analysands intended, that they want something else from it, something more.

It is in that sense that the Lacanian practice of "punctuating" and "scanding"[18] the analysand's discourse serves to disconnect the analysand from his or her discourse, confronting the analysand with the enigma of the analyst's desire. It is insofar as that desire remains enigmatic, never being precisely where the analysand believes it to be—and analysands devote considerable effort to divining and second-guessing that desire—that the analysand's fantasy is repeatedly shaken up in the analytic situation.[19] The Other's desire, in the guise of object *a*, is never precisely where the analysand thinks it is, or wants it to be in his or her fantasy. The analyst—serving as a "make-believe" object *a*, as a stand-in for or semblance of object *a*—introduces a further gap between $ and *a*, disrupting the fantasized relationship, $\diamond$. The analyst makes *that* relationship untenable, inducing a change therein.

Alienation and separation are involved at all times in the analytic situation, the analysand alienating him or herself as he or she tries to speak coherently, that is, in a way which will "make sense" to the analyst, the analyst taken here to be the locus of all meaning: the Other that knows the meaning of all utterances. In the attempt to make sense, the analysand slips away or fades behind the words he or she utters. Those words—due to the very nature of language—always and inescapably say more or less than the analysand consciously intends to say in selecting them. Meaning is always ambiguous, polyvalent, betraying something one wanted to remain hidden, hiding something one intended to express.

This attempt to make sense situates the analysand in the register of the Other as meaning: the analysand fades behind a discourse whose "true meaning" can only be determined and judged by the Other (whether parent, analyst, or god). That kind of alienation is unavoidable and is not (unlike alienation as understood by Marxists and critical theorists) connoted negatively in Lacanian analysis.

Nevertheless, the analyst is enjoined not to indefinitely foster this kind of alienation. Though the analyst, in his or her work with neurotics, attempts to bring into focus the analysand's relation to the Other, clearing away in the process the "interference" stemming from the analysand's imaginary relations with others like him or herself, that is by no means the end of the process, and could lead, if left at that, to a kind of solution *à la* American ego psychology, the analysand identifying with the analyst as Other.

The Lacanian analyst adopts a discourse radically different from that of the analysand—a discourse of separation. If the analyst offers something along the lines of meaning to the analysand, he or she nevertheless aims at something capable of exploding the "analyst-provides-the-meaning-of-the-analysand's-discourse" matrix by speaking ambiguously, at several levels at once, using terms which lead in a number of different directions. By intimating several, if not a never ending panorama of successive meanings, the register of meaning is itself problematized. As the analysand attempts to fathom the import of the analyst's polyvalent words or the reason why he or she terminated the session at that precise moment, the analysand is separated from meaning and confronted with the enigma of the analyst's desire. That enigma has an effect on the analysand's deep-rooted fantasy relation to the Other's desire. While the fundamental rule of free association requires the analysand to try to ever further articulate, put into words, symbolize, signifierize that relation to the Other's desire, the analyst's action serves to separate the subject to an ever greater extent from the very discourse he or she is required to forge about it.

One is the subject of a particular fate, a fate one has not chosen, but which—however random or accidental it may seem at the outset—one *must* nevertheless subjectify; one must, in Freud's view, become its subject. Primal repression is, in a sense, the roll of the dice at the beginning of one's universe which creates a split and sets the structure in motion. An individual has to come to grips with that random toss—that particular configuration of his or her parents' desire—and somehow become its subject. "*Wo Es war, soll Ich werden.*" I must come to be where foreign forces—the Other as language and the Other as desire—once dominated. I must subjectify that otherness.

It is for that reason that we can say that the Lacanian subject is ethically motivated, based as it is on this Freudian injunction so often repeated in Lacan's work. Freud's injunction is inherently paradoxical, enjoining us as it does to put the I (back) in the cause, to become our own cause; but instead of dismissing this paradox, Lacan attempted to theorize the movement implied therein and find techniques by which to induce it. The I is not already in the unconscious. It may be everywhere presupposed there, but it has to be made to appear. It may always already be there in a sense, in that its advent always comes about through a retroactive motion, but it must still be made to appear there "before."

Notes

1. Jacques-Alain Miller has extensively developed Lacan's notions of alienation and separation in his ongoing seminar, *Orientation lacanienne*, given under the auspices of the University of Paris VIII, Saint-Denis. I rely here, above all, on his classes given on March 9, 16, and 23, 1983, and on November 21 and 28, 1984, but his seminar forms the backdrop of much of what I present here.

2. I am using the term "child" here instead of subject since it does not presuppose subjectivity on the child's part, subjectivity being a result of alienation and separation. "Child" has the disadvantage of suggesting a strictly developmental stage here, which I qualify below.

3. In "Formulations on the Two Principles of Mental Functioning" (1911), Standard Edition (hereafter SE) XII, p. 224. The same expression is found in the case of the Rat Man, SE X.

4. Akin to that assigned {Ø} in set theory.

5. The subject is called upon to assume or subjectify that name, make it his or her own; the frequency with which people fail to do so is witnessed by the large number of people who change their names (when this is not done for strictly political or commercial purposes).

6. Lacan exemplifies the intrication of demand and desire with two intertwined toruses in Seminar IX, *Identification*, where a circle drawn around the tube-like surface of one torus (the circle of demand) coincides with the smallest circle around the central void in the other (the circle of desire).

Toruses:

7. See "Subversion of the Subject and Dialectic of Desire," *Écrits*, p. 814.

8. This implies alienation—in the more usual sense of the term—at the very heart of separation.

9. In the case of single parents, a lover (past or present) or even a friend or relative can, at times, fill the father's "shoes," signifying that part of the parent's desire that goes beyond the child. It is certainly *conceivable* that one of the partners in a homosexual couple might fill this role as well, one of the partners adopting the more nurturing role, the other intervening in the parent-child relationship as third term. In "heterosexual" couples, one occasionally finds biological males playing the maternal role and biological females representing the law, but it is clear that social norms do not currently foster the effectiveness of such reversals in replacing the Name-of-the-Father or paternal function.

10. See his book *Naming and Necessity* (Cambridge: Harvard University Press, 1972), which Lacan discusses in Seminar XXI.

11. As I have indicated in my discussion of substitutional metaphors in "The Subject As Metaphor" (*Newsletter of the Freudian Field*, 5, 1991), every metaphor has a similar effect of subjectification.

12. One cannot help but be reminded here of the father's role in the breakup of the mother-child dyad. I have mentioned the introduction of a *third* element, but that element is in fact always already there, structuring the apparent privacy of the initial relationship. The infant experiences an *intrusion* from the outside, an intrusion—effectuated by what one can variously characterize as the father, the Father's Name, the phallus, and object *a*—ousting him from the space of his intersection with his mother, impeding a total overlap.

The intrusion may take the form of a prohibition of his monopoly rights to his mother, which forces his interest to seek beyond her the source of the prohibition, the source of his mother's fascination—her boyfriend, lover, husband, family, neighbors, state, law, religion, God: something which may be totally undefinable and yet quintessentially fascinating.

13. SE VII, p. 167.

14. SE VII, p. 183. Today I would articulate the relations between desire, fantasy, and jouissance rather differently. Fantasy is a veil that allows the subject to overlook the fact that he or she is caused by object *a*, the latter being the cause of the subject's being and jouissance; "fantasy provides the pleasure peculiar to desire" (*Écrits* 1966, p. 773) while serving as a defense against jouissance—that satisfaction beyond pleasure, beyond the pleasure principle. Whereas desire is sustained in or by fantasy, both desire and fantasy serve, in certain respects, as barriers against jouissance.

Pleasurable conscious or preconscious fantasies, in which the subject stages or orchestrates the desired relationship to an object, may veer towards horror or displeasure as the object shows its true colors as that which satisfies the drives in total disregard for the social veneer provided by desire (associated here with the Other). A dream becomes a nightmare when the drives assert their priority over the unconscious desire (the Other's desire) that seemed to have served as the mainspring of the dream. On these and related points, see Jacques-Alain Miller's "Commentary on Lacan's Text" further on in this collection.

15. *Écrits* 1966; English translation by Bruce Fink and Marc Silver in *Newsletter of the Freudian Field*, 2, 1988.

16. *Écrits*, p. 289.

17. We can, of course, situate what I am referring to here as separation and a "further separation" in terms of Lacan's 1964 articulation of alienation and separation. Rather than saying that the neurotic is in need of a further separation—that is, needs to traverse fantasy—in the late 1950s and early 1960s Lacan says that the neurotic "identifies the Other's lack [i.e., desire] with the Other's demand. . . . [T]he Other's demand takes on the function of the object in the neurotic's fantasy" (*Écrits*, p. 321). The idea here is that the subject, in the neurotic's fantasy, ($ ◊ D), adopts as his or her "partner" the Other's demand—that is, something that is static, unchanging, ever revolving around the same thing (love)—instead of the Other's desire, which is fundamentally in motion, ever seeking something else. That essentially means that the subject does not have full access to a third term, to a point outside of the mother-child dyadic relation. Separation would then be understood as the process whereby the Other's demand (D) is replaced in the neurotic's fantasy by the Other's desire (object *a*). The neurotic subject would have already come into being, in some sense, in his or her truncated fantasy ($ ◊ D), but would achieve a greater degree of subjectivity through separation.

18. I prefer to use the neologistic "scanding" as the verb form of scansion since "scanning," the accepted verb form, has rather different connotations which could lead to considerable confusion here. On "scansion," "punctuation," and Lacanian clinical practice in general, see my *A Clinical Introduction to Lacanian Psychoanalysis* (Cambridge: Harvard University Press, 1996).

19. See chapters 17 and 18 of Seminar XI on this point.

LACAN AND LÉVI-STRAUSS

∞

Anne Dunand

I am going to talk about anthropology, and, more precisely, about Lévi-Strauss' brand of anthropology. Why, you may ask—although you have probably noticed Lacan's numerous allusions to and quotations of Lévi-Strauss' work—why give a talk on anthropology in a series of lectures focusing on Lacan's first two seminars? Well, that is just what I hope to explain. Don't worry. I do not intend to give a full account of the theories of structural anthropology or of structuralism, nor will I proceed to give a historical description of the relations between Lévi-Strauss and Lacan's writings.

What will occupy us here is more specifically the symbolic function, the point of emergence of the symbolic function, in both those fields—what we may call the initial discovery that generated for a time parallel lines of research in psychoanalysis and anthropology, as they were transformed and re-elaborated by Lacan and Lévi-Strauss.

First, let us recall that anthropology is a field of inquiry that became a branch of learning long before psychoanalysis was invented. Since its origins, it was bent on trying to understand the meaning of certain phenomena; it did not limit itself to description, even if it did nurture at the outset the ambition of describing human data in the manner of zoologists or botanists, with the same concern to remain objective and unbiased. But anthropology was obliged to borrow some elements from psychology to explain behaviors that were so different and so alien to the civilization that was its point of reference, namely that of the anthropologist.

On the other hand, psychoanalysis is an investigation into the individual's social behavior. Freud wondered why, in hysteria, one observes seemingly senseless behavior. He gave it meaning, sexual meaning. It can be understood only in relation to a satisfaction in which the Other, as language, but also as partner, is involved. What is unconscious is the primary relationship to the Other. This could not but lead him to try and understand what links the individual to the group, that is, the genesis and signification of group formations. He wrote *Totem and Taboo* to demonstrate how belonging to a group is built upon one's first relationship to an object and how societies are constituted through the mechanisms of identification, phobia, and obsessional neurosis, and the universality of the Oedipus complex. But he drew a correlation between the prohibition of incest as a universal phenomenon, and the totem, the symbol representing the father figure. Freud often returned to the problem of group consistency, clarifying it with the findings he gathered from his experience of analysis; for instance, he made use of what was revealed by infantile neurosis to buttress some of these themes in the essays in *Totem and Taboo*; and it was in that vein that he wrote his major essays on social structures: *Group Psychology and the Analysis of the Ego* (1921), *The Future of an Illusion* (1927), *Civilization and Its Discontents* (1930), and *Moses and Monotheism* (1939). Many of his other works that touch on this subject bear the mark of his study of and interest in anthropology.

After Freud, many of his followers carried on the task, such as Rank, Ferenczi, Reik, and Roheim, to mention only the most prominent. Their intent was twofold:

1. On the one hand, to criticize Western society by studying other societies, highlighting phenomena found elsewhere to bring new approaches to Western culture.

2. On the other hand, to verify the postulates of psychoanalysis, such as they emerged from the observation of Western society, and measure their applicability (or lack thereof) to other social groups.

In a certain sense, the goal was to find, above or through individual or particular ethnic features, "a universal foundation of the human mind." This last phrase is a quote from Lévi-Strauss. What he sought was a structure that could serve as a compass and give its bearings to the mass of facts encountered in anthropological studies.

We can say, therefore, that there is a similarity in the research of psychoanalysis and anthropology, and that both fields overlap, even if the main axes their research follows are fundamentally different. Anthropology, if we leave aside the times when it was put to use by religion and colonialism, does not wish to transform the society it observes and does not focus on the individual as much as it does on the institution. On the contrary, psychoanalysis really came into existence as a means of alleviating suffering that seemed as if it were pursuing only the generation of more suffering; psychoanalysis' aim was at first primarily therapeutic; it wanted to change something from the very start, either the patient's environment or the patient him or herself. Now it is not so much directed towards the relief of a symptom, but it still aims at a change of places in discourse, the discovery by the subject of another relationship to his or her desire or jouissance. This subversive design makes psychoanalysis a threat to certain societies in which the subject and his desire must remain under the control of the master's discourse. It is this factor, not the sexual signification given symptoms by Freud, that draws the line and limits between psychoanalysis and anthropology, and that stimulates a certain distrust of psychoanalysis by anthropologists; anthropologists do not aim at transforming the societies they study, their object of study. This mistrust, this rejection of psychoanalysis, was also characteristic of Lévi-Strauss.

Lévi-Strauss

Lévi-Strauss gave birth to and fostered a new stage in anthropology by putting to use the new paths opened up by linguistics. Troubetskoi, Benveniste, and Jakobson especially were the Archimedes lever with which he managed to move the mass of facts and hypotheses that were, so to speak, lying around in anthropology, often simply laid side by side.

Linguistics allowed Lévi-Strauss a new approach to anthropology by introducing the primacy of the symbolic. I will briefly introduce this connection. Lévi-Strauss noticed that there are two factors that characterize human beings: language and the prohibition of incest. As heterogeneous as these two notions may seem at first, Lévi-Strauss demonstrated that they have the same foundation and the same function.

1. *Foundation.* Let us remember that for Lévi-Strauss, nature is the opposite of culture; culture is what makes man different from animals; his actions cannot be considered wholly natural. Concerning the origins and foundation of culture, Lévi-Strauss was a disciple of Rousseau. He stated that culture started on the day man ceased to be able to survive alone.

There is, of course, in this point of view, something that leaves us in the lurch; we cannot grasp how culture can possibly arise from a state of nature, how nature can afford a passage into culture, just as it is difficult, indeed impossible, to conceive desire as a product of need alone. But to Lévi-Strauss, it is essential to maintain this passage from nature to culture, and we do not find any actual discontinuity in his theory between the symbolic and the real. In short, he gives us the same origin for culture and language in time and cause.

2. *Function.* Language and social rules serve the same function. Language has a function, that of establishing and maintaining relations between men and between groups. Social structures are like a syntax—they lay down the rules of exchange and gift giving. These rules are not the same everywhere, nor do we find the same languages spoken everywhere.

3. Now there is another element that brings anthropology close to linguistics: the similarity between phonemes and atoms of kinship. The phoneme has no signification of its own but can form meanings by groupings; in the same way, with the relations of kinship, the terms do not have any meaning in and of themselves—mother, father, son, and uncle have meaning only when articulated as a relation to the group. The prohibition of incest is an empty form that can be used to link biological groups[1] through a network of exchanges; it is a rule that operates like a syntax, akin to a grammatical syntax, between the different terms.

The reality of the phoneme is not to be found in its phonic individuality, but in the oppositional and negative relations phonemes have amongst themselves. This goes on at an unconscious level; language and social functions work at an unconscious level.

If we admit that oppositions and negations constitute language, and while we speak we do not pay any conscious attention to them, we concentrate on what we have to say rather than on the mechanism of speech—we make a choice of how to say it. From the point of view of social rules, I cannot completely ignore the laws of the group I belong to if, say, I want to marry. I am mentioning this argument in order to distinguish the unconscious, as Lévi-Strauss conceptualized it, from the Freudian unconscious. In Seminar XI, Lacan points out that it has nothing to do with the Freudian unconscious.

How does the rule of the prohibition of incest translate in Lévi-Strauss' system? We must recall that Lévi-Strauss, in *The Elementary Structures of Kinship*, reproaches Freud for not having explained why incest is forbidden and only having shown why it is desired. This is rather unfair, because Freud gives many reasons and explanations for this fact, the most outstanding of which is probably love for the father. But this demonstration is not convincing to Lévi-Strauss. He proposes another: the prohibition of incest is really the negative statement of a positive rule that makes exogamy obligatory.

Man, every man, must give up a woman in order to obtain another in exchange; women are like words: they must be exchanged, otherwise there is no communication. According to Lévi-Strauss, woman is a strange object situated midway between nature and culture. She is an object to be bartered, and what is of value is the transaction itself. Man has to give something in order to obtain something he doesn't have. It is the law of substitution that finds its cause in the obligation of substitution itself.

What does the submission to the rule depend on? Envy. I want what another man has—that is the mainspring of Lévi-Strauss' psychology. What gives value to what I don't have is already social in its very ground. Its value derives from the fact that everyone else recognizes it as having value. The law of reciprocity (that is to structural anthropology what the law of gravity is to Newton's physics) is established on the psychological basis that one must give in order to receive. The child psychology that Lévi-Strauss uses to buttress these hypotheses is borrowed from Isaacs and Piaget. What is desired is desired only because someone has it; the desire to possess is a social response and rests on the primordial need for security.[2] Hostility remains the fundamental primitive attitude.

If Lévi-Strauss makes a foray into child psychology, it is only to prove that language and society have the same foundations. Not that, as one might have expected, language allows me to know what I don't have and what the other has (what Lacan emphasized by saying that the phallus is a signifier) but because Lévi-Strauss, utilizing Jakobson's research on the language of children,[3] declares that the child, at the outset, presents in its utterances all the structures that are possible in all languages, just as the child presents all forms of sexuality—Lévi-Strauss' way of interpreting Freud's expression that the child is a polymorphous pervert. The child is polymorphously social as an infant. Society imposes upon the child to renounce all structures that are not adequate, that is, that are not those of its culture. In the same fashion, Lévi-Strauss thinks that the child will renounce all the social structures discarded by its society in order to keep only those that are admitted. This also explains the peculiarity of one society with respect to another.

But as far as universal structures are concerned, Lévi-Strauss defines the universal structure of the mind as determined by three basic, fundamental rules: the demand for rules; the notion of reciprocity, considered the most immediate form through which the opposition between ego and another may be integrated; and the synthetic character of the gift,[4] meaning that the fact of an accepted transfer of value from one individual to another individual changes them both into partners and adds a new quality to the transferred value.

That is how Lévi-Strauss transforms the data of the incest prohibition into three fundamental rules.

If we wanted to summarize his thought, we could make the following analogies:

$$\frac{\text{culture}}{\text{nature}} = \frac{\text{meaning}}{\text{sound}} = \frac{\text{rules of kinship}}{\text{incest}} = \frac{\text{reciprocity}}{\text{envy}}$$

In these oppositions there is a symbolic principle at work, organizing, regulating, fragmenting, and ordering a primitive given datum. But if we compare this approach to Lacan's, we find a fundamental difference that I will try to briefly sketch out.

Lévi-Strauss believes man wants to be equal to other men, and that social organizations have that as their aim. Once an exchange has been made, or merely foreseen, even if it must be repeated to reestablish a kind of homeostasis, there are no leftovers.

The individual is satisfied; he has obtained or will obtain what is rightly his. But for Lacan, there is something left over after the operation of language on the living being—there are consequences of the prohibition of incest; something is lost and the lost satisfaction will always break through: desire is never fulfilled, there is no reciprocal appeasement. This forever wanting something is what he calls object *a*, forever causing desire beyond satisfaction; what he refers to as the Other is what causes something to be always beyond human reach. Language and social structures are not adequate to bring about peaceful enjoyment, because there is no passage from one level of experience to the other, but rather a gap—heterogeneity between the real, symbolic, and imaginary. There is no gradual transformation of nature leading to the laws of culture. The subject is born into language, and the necessity for substitution is there even before s/he comes to life.

For Freud, the necessity of substitution is there already in the certainty that the very desire to have a child is a substitute for the desire to have a penis, so that the child, even before it is conceived, is a substitute object that takes the place of another more pleasurable one.

How Lacan Put Lévi-Strauss' Propositions to Use

Lacan refers quite often to Lévi-Strauss' writings. Apart from his friendship with Lévi-Strauss, he was quite interested in anthropology; it is difficult to imagine how psychoanalysis could ignore social structures and not want to situate itself with respect to them. Already in his first articles and in his thesis, Lacan demonstrates this: he tries to understand how crime is related to social structure, how schizographic writings depend on that structure, and how family complexes are inscribed in a wider structure. Even before Lévi-Strauss published his first major work, *The Elementary Structures of Kinship*, Lacan had started to try and grasp what language social structure speaks, and what links human beings to the symbolic function, law, ties of kinship, and the practice of writing.[5]

Today it does not seem so odd to give the symbolic function such an important place in psychoanalysis and anthropology. But we should keep in mind that before Lacan, and before Lévi-Strauss, psychoanalysis floated and literally swam in streams of ethos, pathos, and affect. The symbolic function was considered the vehicle of emotions that were thought to be causal. Lévi-Strauss, by formalizing the structures of kinship and those of myths, and Lacan, by demonstrating that analytic experience is first and foremost a practice based on language and speech, granted importance to the subject's determination by the symbolic structure. Then, in the further development of their research, and because of this first step, they were able to modify their first approach without giving up this revolutionary conception: Lévi-Strauss, through the elimination of the dimension of the subject, and Lacan, through the transformations and mathemes establishing the subject's relation to its object.

Note in passing that Lévi-Strauss cites Lacan only once, and what he cites is Lacan's 1948 article, "Aggressivity in Psychoanalysis" (*Écrits*). In his *Introduction to the Writings of Marcel Mauss*,[6] Lévi-Strauss supplies his own reading of a passage in that article: "It is only the man we call mentally sane who is able to alienate himself, since he accepts to exist in a world definable only by the relationship between the ego and an other." This quote appears in the following context: Lévi-Strauss believes that no biochemical discovery will ever be able to invalidate a purely sociological theory of mental illness because each culture is a whole consisting of symbolic systems. The alienation of the mentally sane is defined as normal thought's capacity to construct symbolic structures, and that can be brought about only at the level of social life. We have here a theory that is not psychological, strictly speaking, that explains sublimation as a participation or giving and taking of one's share in the building of the symbolic structure. Lévi-Strauss also notes that the neurotic individual plays a part in the integration of the system as a whole. If change takes place in the structures, it is for two reasons: a society is never completely symbolic, and societies are transformed by contact with other societies.

That is, as far as I know, the only time Lévi-Strauss quotes Lacan. All he seems to have gathered of Lacan's thought is the relationship of the ego to the other in its fundamentally alienating effects, and that the world, the *Umwelt*, is definable only through that relationship. Lacan, on the contrary, refers very often to Lévi-Strauss. I will point out only a few of his references, starting with those to symbolic efficiency in his article "The Mirror Stage" (*Écrits*).

In "The Effectiveness of Symbols,"[7] Lévi-Strauss describes and explains a magical operation, the cure of a sick woman obtained through an incantation. He narrates how this woman, during a difficult childbirth, gets well thanks to ritualized ministering by a sorcerer or shaman, and everything then proceeds normally. Lévi-Strauss explains this result by the fact that the structure of the myth summoned in the incantation acts on the structure of the individual, imposes itself somehow, not through its meaningful contents but through its structural pattern. Lacan's comments on this in "The Mirror Stage" do not reveal all his thoughts at once. We are confronted with a magical operation, clouded in ritual and mystery, executed by a sorcerer; in Lévi-Strauss' article there is something that attacks psychoanalysis, aiming at its efficiency; he says the psychoanalyst should proceed like the shaman, help the patient reintegrate the social structure of his own culture, and not make him produce an individual myth.

Lacan answers all of this in many ways and at several different moments; first in "The Mirror Stage," then in "The Individual Myth of the Neurotic,"[8] and later in "Science and Truth" (*Écrits* 1966). What is at stake is how psychoanalysis can work. Lacan answers this question the first time by saying that, in his daily experience, the psychoanalyst encounters the twilight of the efficiency of the symbolic when the veiled imago's outline is dimly perceived. This term, imago, that he does not use later on, is at the junction of the symbolic and the imaginary. It is the image of the individual's own body perceived in such a way that it permits him to establish a relationship of the organism to its reality. I think we see here Lacan's first formula for fantasy, keeping in mind that the object thus far is imaginary. But Lacan emphasizes the anthropologist's fascination with the junction between nature and culture, where he uncovers a knot of imaginary servitude. He lets us infer that there is, in the shaman's cure, an operation on an imaginary object using signifiers. Psychoanalysis must undo or cut this knot in a way that holds the subject in its custody, love performing this act. As short as this commentary is, we can already see that it is through the transference particular to the analytic situation that any psychoanalytic act is to be carried out, and that signifiers are used not to convey the subject back to the group's beliefs, but to produce a gap.

Lacan goes back to this theme in "Science and Truth"[9] where he brings up the problem of the efficiency of magic and *magical thinking*, which we attribute to primitives, and by that we mean anyone not like us. But there he distinguishes the place of causation in the magical operation. Lacan refers to the efficient cause for magic, the causality that Aristotle described as having its origin out of its effect but not foreign to it, and as the beginning of such an effect, with the intention of producing such an effect. As such, Lacan sees in the magical act the linking up of one signifier with another. The subject interested in the magical act is none other than the shaman, who is put in the position of receiving his message from the Other in an inverted form. What is causal here is the signifier, that carries in itself a load of signification, an implicit commandment. What Lévi-Strauss leaves aside in this reduction, notes Lacan, is the subject.

The efficiency of the symbolic is mentioned again by Lacan in Seminar II where the subject's relationship to the symbolic is discussed (p. 223). The efficiency of the symbolic is contrasted with the inertia of the symbolic that is peculiar to the subject, and characteristic of the subject of the unconscious. When the subject free associates, s/he manifests his or her symbolic inertia.

May we then say s/he submits to a law s/he ignores? Is it enough to think that, if s/he discovers this law, s/he will not be subjected to it anymore? I will leave that for you to answer, but we must note what is at stake here. We cannot consider the unconscious simply as something unknown. In "Function and

Field of Speech and Language in Psychoanalysis" (*Écrits*), Lacan makes a distinction between two symbolic forms: language and speech. This Saussurian distinction was used by Lévi-Strauss to determine the structure of myths: language pertains to the realm of time as reversible, speech to that of irreversible time. A myth can be defined by a temporal system that combines both qualities. To Lacan, speech is distinct from language essentially because it has meaning to a subject; it is a revelation of meaning, and beyond that, a revelation of being.

The dimension of the unconscious for Lacan is not of the order of what is known or knowledge, but of what is. When Lacan writes, in "Function and Field," that Lévi-Strauss, by developing the implications of the structure of language and of the social laws that regulate alliance and kinship, conquers the very ground on which Freud establishes the unconscious, we can perceive an analogy as to the place given the symbolic function by anthropology; but what are missing are its subjective sources that Freud brought out with his observation of the "*fort/da*" game in *Beyond the Pleasure Principle*. It is clear that at this point in his teaching, Lacan was bent on emptying the unconscious and the subject of their contents and attributes, the subject being reduced to the manifestation of desire (want-to-be). In this respect, the analogy between the functioning of language and the structure of kinship, or even the structure of myth, is very apropos. Language has meaning or existence only because of the absence it signifies. Myths too have meaning only inasmuch as they render manifest and veil at the same time, a contradiction that is their truth. But to say the unconscious is empty is not to say anything until it has been specified what it is empty of. Lévi-Strauss treats the prohibition of incest as an empty form; can we accept that definition when we hear at the same time that it is a reckoning: to give in order to receive in exchange?

I will conclude briefly with a question that is at the heart of Seminar II, and that concerns this prohibition (see chapter 3, "The Symbolic Universe"). The symbolic order constitutes a dialectical structure that is complete; symbolic agencies function in society from the start, and Lacan stresses the analogy with the unconscious, when it starts to *ex-sist* in relation to a subject in analysis. Lacan emphasizes the fact that the Oedipus complex is purely symbolic, and is as such both contingent and universal. This definition echoes the definition Lévi-Strauss gives of culture in *The Elementary Structures of Kinship*: culture can be defined by the fact that it is entirely ruled by laws, whereas the realm of nature is defined by an absence of rules.

Now you can understand why Lacan says that Lévi-Strauss was overcome by a kind of dizziness regarding the connection between the symbolic and the unconscious. For if there are what we call laws *in* nature, such as gravitation for instance, shall we say that they are laws *of* nature or is it only that man uses them as such to explain natural phenomena? What does Lévi-Strauss say about this?

Wherever rules are found, we know with certainty that we are at the level of culture, as when we are dealing with the relative and the particular. The order of nature is the realm of the universal and the spontaneous. The prohibition of incest belongs to both orders: it is a social rule that has the character of universality. We may understand, I think, that whenever we have a rule and not just a phenomenon that has been observed everywhere (such as gravitation), that seems to conform to a rule, the question of intentionality is raised. As soon as you take intentionality away from the subject, you find it in nature in the form of a god that makes the whole thing work. If you have a subject who desires, s/he is the one who forges the rails along which his or her desire moves. In Lacan's discussions with Lévi-Strauss, the question of the cause of desire is already present. According to Lacan, at that point, the subject seeks his or her being through the structures of language and speech. Later in his teaching, the subject discovers it in a relationship to the object.

But according to Lévi-Strauss, here and later too, it is the group that wants to outlive the individuals that constitute it; therefore, the Other is the subject; the Other wants it to last. This implies some kind of obscure will, impossible to decipher, that harks back to a very antiquated conception of nature. Culture is identified with the blind energy of nature—the two systems are fused; because Lévi-Strauss leaves open a passage from nature to culture, they are never really heterogeneous.

But the whole point is that a line cannot be drawn between nature and culture, as they are two imaginary agencies; they cannot be equated with the different levels of the real and the symbolic. It is the dynamic opposition between the real and the symbolic that Lacan designates, at the end of Seminar I, as the structuralism proper to Freud. The symbolic is the network of language thrown over the real.

It does not give the subject any sure signifying prey or bond, except for the truth of castration that is the absence of all significations. The being of the subject that Lacan situates in speech at that time, as revealed by the fullness of full speech, is the encounter with the gap in the Other, where the only reciprocity the subject can count on is that it will ensure such being with the perennial nature of his or her desire. That is the only truth that can be delivered by speech through analysis, but it happens as revelation, for it stands under no signifier.

Notes

1. Introduction by Lévi-Strauss to Jakobson's *Six Lectures on Sound and Meaning,* Cambridge: MIT Press, 1978.

2. C. Lévi-Strauss, *Les structures élémentaires de la parenté,* Paris: Mouton, 1973, p. 100.

3. R. Jakobson, *Langage enfantin, aphasie et lois générales de la structure phonique* (first published in German in 1939), Paris: Éditions de Minuit, 1969.

4. C. Lévi-Strauss, *op. cit.*, p. 98.

5. J. Lacan. *Les complexes familiaux*, Paris: Navarin 1984.

6. C. Lévi-Strauss, *Introduction à l'oeuvre de Marcel Mauss*, Paris: PUF, 1985, pp. xix–xx.

7. C. Lévi-Strauss, *Structural Anthropology*, New York: Basic Books, 1963.

8. J. Lacan, *"Le mythe individuel du névrosé"* (1953), *Ornicar?*, 17–18, 1979.

9. Translated by Bruce Fink in *Newsletter of the Freudian Field*, 3, 1989.

PART III

IMAGINARY

MELANIE KLEIN AND JACQUES LACAN

Françoise Koehler

The topic I have chosen to focus on today is fantasy in the work of Melanie Klein and Jacques Lacan. I'd like to discuss one of the questions that Lacan raised several times during his teaching, "What do we do when we analyze?" Of course it's a simple question, but the answer is always quite difficult to provide. It's all the more crucial because analysts are not very inclined to tell people how they operate. Their resistance to doing so could be considered structural, since an analyst, Lacan says, operates by *not* thinking. It nevertheless seems to me that the future of the transmission of analysis demands an effort or, as it were, a desire to put things into words.

This paradox strikes me as one of the reasons why Lacan instituted the "pass" as a way to develop a taste for transmission in the new generation of analysts. The *École de la Cause freudienne* has taken the challenge very seriously and is now engaged in the process of evaluating its first results.

Melanie Klein was someone who did not hesitate to share her analytic moments. She left us four very large volumes of her writing, and was definitely a decided woman. Quite clearly and without an ounce of ambiguity, Lacan defended Melanie Klein. He defended her mainly against Anna Freud in their hectic and endless quarrels. He was nevertheless opposed to Klein's theories for his own reasons, and as soon as her work achieved some fame in the mid–1930s, he criticized it in countless articles and seminars. You will find some of his responses to her work in Seminars I and II.

One of the strongest arches of Klein's theory is her conception of fantasy. Here I'd like to evaluate and compare it with the concept of fantasy in psychoanalysis today. Since Lacan situated the end of analysis in the traversing or crossing of the fundamental fantasy, Lacanian analysts understand the nature of fantasy as bearing upon the direction of treatment and its termination.

In 1928, in her article, "Obsessional Neuroses and the Superego," Melanie Klein states that fantasy is unconscious. She says:

> The assumption that extravagant fantasies which arise in a very early stage of the child's development never become conscious could well help to explain the phenomenon that the child expresses its sadistic and unconscious thoughts as real objects only in an attenuated form. It should, moreover, be remembered that the state of development of the ego is an early one and that the child's relations to reality are as yet undeveloped and dominated by its fantasy life.

Thus, according to Klein, fantasy life not only dominates in the child's early days but is also present prior to ego development.

On this particular point there are some variations in her theory. Sometimes she says the development of the ego starts with early fantasies, but in 1928 she distinguishes fairly well between fantasy life, which comes first, and the development of the ego. In other words, she states that unconscious fantasies have to be made conscious through interpretation, referring in particular to the discussion of "little Hans" in *Inhibitions, Symptoms, and Anxiety*, a very important landmark in Freud's work according to Klein. She reinterprets Hans' fear of being bitten by a horse, which Freud views as a manifestation of castration anxiety, as related to more precocious anxiety, originating in the superego and only attenuated by the thought of the Oedipal castration complex. Hence, she is able to oppose little Hans to the "Wolf Man" for whom some primitive anxieties, such as the wolf phobia, were never surmounted in Freudian terms. This is one of the clinical advantages of her conceptualization, which provides us, in the case of the Wolf Man, with a simple way to grasp a clinical distinction which is, in fact, far more subtle and hesitant, but also far more elaborate than Freud's initial discussion of the case.

Let me take up some of Klein's views by discussing a paper by Susan Isaacs, "The Nature and Function of Fantasy" (1943), in which Isaacs gives an accurate account of Klein's theory of fantasy. By 1943, discussion in analytic circles focused mainly on the elaboration of Freud's concept of fantasy and on the dating of fantasy in infancy. The question foremost in analysts' minds was "does fantasy predate the development of the superego?" Klein proposed a distinction between the level of castration anxiety as related to infancy and the Oedipus complex, and the level of primitive pre-Oedipal anxiety related to fantasy life. From Isaac's paper, I will extract seven main features. Actually, in her conclusion she lists thirteen different arguments. But seven will be enough here to understand her point.

First, she says that fantasy can be considered the primary content of unconscious processes. Second, she says that fantasy as such primarily concerns the body. Third, she states that fantasy is the psychical representation of the drives. Fourth, she emphasizes that the existence of fantasies is independent of one's life in the "outside world," and also independent of minds. Fifth, she says that fantasies are both psychical and bodily effects, including, for example, conversion symptoms, hallucinations, neurotic symptoms, and so on. (In other words, she conflates symptoms and fantasies.) Sixth, fantasies are the link between the drives and cancers; what she understands by the term "cancers" is projective identification and interjection. Seventh, adaptation to reality is rooted in unconscious terms. I'm not going to discuss all seven items because it would take too long. Instead, I will focus on two main points: the relationship between fantasy and the primary contents of the unconscious, and the fantasy relationship according to Klein.

Before I do so, it might be useful to sidetrack for a moment to point out that Lacan did not wait until Isaacs' article to announce a complete recasting of Melanie Klein's view. His *Les complexes familiaux* was recently published by Navarin in Paris; it was written in 1938 and is obviously directed at Kleinians as a fine introduction to the forthcoming partition between symbolic, imaginary, and real, which Lacan developed after the Second World War. In this text, he defines three complexes. The first is the "weaning complex," which is directly deducible from Klein's work. Here Lacan considers the mother the symbol of the unity or totality that has been lost forever, and this maternal "imago" (he still uses Melanie Klein's terms in 1938) must be sublimated. If it is not, the mother, at first salutary, becomes lethal. Lacan illustrates this through clinical examples of the death drive. Some primary forms of the death drive may take on less dangerous forms, even an early form of anorexia, for example. Thus he uses Melanie Klein's terms in a different way.

The second complex he defines is the "intrusion complex." It corresponds more or less to envy, which was not yet fully elaborated at that time in Klein's theory. Lacan defines it as the whole set of imaginary and aggressive relations with the other. Here the other is understood as the counterpart, the fellow man. Lacan very carefully distinguishes between the kind of aggressiveness envy involves and Oedipal rivalry (which implies the symbolic register). Lacan's intrusion complex, something we have to be very attentive to in our clinical work, is based on identification and leads to aggressive rivalry among children for their mother's love. What is interesting about the intrusion complex is that it points out the specificity of the rivalry with one's counterpart.

The third complex Lacan defines is the Oedipus complex. The Oedipal signifiers are retroactively able to organize what the two previous complexes do not achieve. In his outstanding synthesis, Lacan restates the Oedipus complex first in terms of frustration/castration—always attributed by the child to the parent of the same sex; second, in terms of the superego (he bases the superego on the Oedipus complex and not vice-versa) as a representing agency; and third, in terms of the birth of the ego-ideal as related to the father.

In Lacan's reply to Klein and to the Kleinian movement in the thirties, the castration complex is presented by Lacan as activated by a fantasy built upon a fear of mutilation which is always linked to the father (as in Freud's work). Here, contrary to Klein's approach, no reference is made to the feminine phase in both sexes. On the contrary, the paternal model as a representation of the phallus is prevalent for boys and girls.

Les complexes familiaux is one of Lacan's first psychoanalytic texts, since it followed only "The Mirror Stage," first written in 1936 as a fundamental reappraisal and re-ordering of Klein's theories. Klein's findings are considered important, but remain subordinated to a very thorough reading of Freud. I would also like to emphasize that, in this early reappraisal, Klein's reasoning is characterized as implying early anxieties versus Oedipal anxieties, a symmetry of male and female sexuality, and a harmony between fantasies and symptoms. Lacan, on the other hand, develops a dialectical relationship between the three complexes, discrepancies between fantasies and symptoms, and so forth. Triads are always necessary for Lacan to define the psychoanalytic subject, who constitutes a fourth term.

Let us turn more directly to a discussion of fantasy in Klein's and Lacan's work. Klein's view that fantasy is the primary content of the unconscious raises several questions about what she calls the "fantasy complex." Klein and Lacan both refer to Freud's 1937 article on "Constructions in Analysis." Lacan shows that Freud does not conclude, as Melanie Klein does, on unequivocal success when the patient says, "I never thought of that before." In that article, Freud says if the patient answers in that way, then you know you are on the right track. Yet Freud was not quite positive about it. He seems to lament the fact that such responses are only elicited by minor interpretations, interpretations that aim at symptoms rather than at fantasies. Fantasy then always remains opposed to symptoms in this text.

This raises the question of how to interpret fantasy on the basis of unconscious formations. How can one infer fantasy from dream interpretation? In 1956, in "Subversion of the Subject and Dialectic of Desire," Lacan says that "fantasy cannot be interpreted since it partakes of the indices of an absolute signification." That year he provides an opposition between fantasy, on the one hand, with its own inertia, and symptoms which are mobile. On the one hand, we have symptoms that can be interpreted in a Kleinian space, and on the other, fantasy as action. The more Lacan develops his theory, the more he thinks that fantasy cannot be analyzed as such: it can only be constructed.

What do we mean when we speak of the construction of a fantasy? One of the things we mean is that fantasy can be created by the analytic process. Lacan also theorizes the traversing of fantasy. He says the fundamental fantasy can be traversed at the end of an analysis, but cannot be analyzed by any means, inasmuch as it is derived from the three registers: symbolic, imaginary, and real. It cannot be fully analyzed because the real is the impossible.

In 1919, in "A Child is Being Beaten," Freud calls attention to the extreme difficulty encountered in unraveling the different stages of a fantasy. Freud distinguishes three steps in the expression of that fantasy, the second of which has to be reconstructed and cannot be provided directly by the patient. Lacan says a fundamental fantasy is part and parcel of the form of jouissance, which is always looked upon as alien by the neurotic patient, because it is the Other's jouissance. That is one of the reasons why fantasy cannot be analyzed, though it can be transformed. It can be traversed, crossed, or constructed, but it cannot be reduced or analyzed.

This constitutes a very serious disagreement between Klein and Lacan over the nature of fantasy and, in the end, this disagreement is related to opposite conceptions of the function of interpretation. Lacan's conception of interpretation is minimalist. In "Direction of the Treatment," for example, and in later texts, Lacan advises analysts not to feed their patients' symptoms with interpretation. Equivocation is the best kind of interpretation.

On the contrary, Klein's style of interpretation is experiential. But even though it is experiential, it has to be carefully distinguished at the level of content from ego-psychology's indoctrinating style. There's a certain permissiveness in Klein's style; but it remains highly informative, whereas Lacanian interpretation is always oracular in nature. This is different from analysis of resistance, for example. Lacanian interpretation doesn't interpret anything so much as it tends to stir up desire in the patient. That is what it is designed to do: arouse desire in the patient, allowing the patient to say more and more. It's not meant to explain things. Interpretation is a success when the patient comes back to see the analyst and says, "Well, I don't really see what you mean, but . . ."

In "Direction of the Treatment," Lacan speaks of the Kleinian school's misconception regarding fantasy. He says Kleinians are incapable of even so much as suspecting the existence of the signifier. According to Lacan, on the contrary, fantasy is that by which the subject sustains him or herself at the level of his or her vanishing desire, and it is designed to work in a signifying structure. Starting from this premise, the analyst's interpretative position is rendered null and void. The point is not to reveal the content of the fantasy, but to lead the subject to deliver up a fantasy which has been slowly simmering. The analytic process exhausts the patient's identifications. Only then can we catch sight of the logic of fantasy that is at work. The primary purpose of interpretation being to stir up desire, fantasy loses more and more of its imaginary content, and the subject's identifications are dismantled and discarded. Only then can the patient reach what is at the root of the fundamental fantasy. This is not merely an issue of technique—it concerns the aims of treatment.

We are now better equipped to understand why the distribution of tasks between analyst and analysand are different in Kleinian analysis and Lacanian analysis. We can also understand why Lacanian analysts may seem so silent when they're conducting sessions. It's different, of course, from Kleinian practice, but it's more in tune with Freudian practice.

Lacan indicates that fantasy shows up whenever the signifying chain comes to a dead end, to a kind of breach in its own development. (Jacques-Alain Miller discusses this point very thoroughly in his 1982–1983 seminar, *From the Symptom to Fantasy and Back.*) Acting out comes very close to enactment of the fundamental fantasy. Whenever a patient acts out, the fundamental fantasy is always at stake, even if it's not obvious at the time.

Let us turn now to the relation between fantasy and the body. Lacan is not very well known for being attentive to biological problems. Nevertheless, there is a conception of the body in Lacan's work. In the conclusion of her article on fantasy, Susan Isaacs claims that fantasy primarily concerns the body. I will try to explain Lacan's objection. Both Lacan and Klein make use of what I will call Abrahamian objects—the breast and the feces—and Lacan added other objects as well. The difference between Lacan and Klein, as I understand it, lies in the way these objects function. Let's take an example from the sixth chapter of Seminar XI where Lacan refers to one of his own objects: the gaze. He makes a very simple distinction founded on observation, "Look at a description of a dream, any dream, and you will see that it not only looks but shows. Our position in dreams is profoundly that of someone who does not see." At first this seems a bit odd, because we associate dreams with movies in which we see everything. But there is always something beyond the satisfaction of the eye in a dream. Something doesn't quite fit in with the whole picture, and Lacan calls that the "stain." A dream cannot be reduced to a whole picture because there is a stain in it.

We can draw an analogy between what Lacan says about dreams and the narration of the self. There's always, in narration, something outside the narration which has to do with the object, and not merely with the signifier. To Lacan, the interesting point in any dream is the point where there is something indicative of anxiety. The stain reveals the spot where there is a discrepancy between the subject and his or her bodily perception. That is why Lacan constructs his own object *a*'s. In Seminar XI he explains why, although he has adopted them thus far, he is not very pleased with the traditional use of Abrahamian objects.

Kleinians take the object as a given of nature. The object is viewed as natural. In the relationship between mother and child, for example, the mother is supposed to have the breast, and the child is supposed to take the breast for itself. Yet Lacan says the breast is on the side of the child, not the mother. Lacan's idea here is to show that the breast is not part of the mother's body; it is, on the contrary, the medium of the child's jouissance.

In Kleinian analysis, no chance is left for the subject to encounter castration. In other words, castration and frustration are conflated. That is why, for example, Susan Isaacs describes the fantasy of the unweaned child as "I want to devour my mother's breast and have it inside my body." Words are not necessary in this conception. Words are not necessary for the fantasy to be put to work. To Kleinians, words are only signals or signs; they are not signifiers.

The question of the relationship between fantasy and the body, far from being a simple terminological quarrel, leads to a different conception of treatment. To Klein, the object is empirical; she confuses the unconscious drive and the Abrahamian object. Diana Rabinovitch, a member of the *École de la Cause freudienne*, has published several articles in the journal *Ornicar?* comparing Kleinian analysis to Lacanian analysis. She says the "not" object of Freudian desire is, in Kleinian analysis, positively transformed into an object of knowledge. In other words, to Kleinians, either the object is there or it is missing, but it is not lost forever. This object is reduced to an object of knowledge.

Now we can better understand why Susan Isaacs concludes her article by saying that, for a child, fantasy is a means of getting acquainted with reality and of learning how to adapt to reality. And, strangely enough, though they have very different premises, Klein and ego-psychology agree here, for reality is taken as something that is given in the outer world, can be taught, and can be learned. This is light years away from Lacan's view of reality. To Lacan, reality is always—whatever we are, whoever we are, and whatever our structure is—seen through the window of our fantasy. What we may obtain by traversing our fantasy is the knowledge that the illusion of the countryside we see through that window is dangerous. We all go on seeing life through the window of our own fantasy. There is no such thing as a fantasy of reality, but Lacan proposes a different aim of analysis: "*un désir décidé.*" It means that you know more about your desire—you know what you want.

THE IMAGINARY

∞

Marie-Hélène Brousse

Today I'm going to talk about narcissism, referring to chapters 9 and 10 of Seminar I, and bringing in some material from the *Écrits*, in particular from "The Mirror Stage," "Aggressivity in Psychoanalysis," and "Remarks on the Report by Daniel Lagache." I will begin with Lacan's discussion of transference in chapter 9. Transference has two faces. First of all, it facilitates psychoanalytic work and allows us to construct the subject's history by renovation and addition. Freud emphasized a second face of transference, which seemed to him not to facilitate, but rather hinder psychoanalytic work. That is what interests Lacan in this chapter. Transference as an obstacle to analytic work is directly discussed by Freud as transference love or the transference of love. To Lacan at that time, love is always a narcissistic phenomenon. Transference love is a narcissistic phenomenon appearing in treatment which requires working through.

Let me say something first about transference and counter-transference. In a way, transference and counter-transference are dual concepts: one is based on the other. Every dual concept is, according to Lacan, marked by its origin in the imaginary, which means its origin in narcissism, to speak very approximately. Thus the problem with counter-transference is not that Lacan does not think it exists—he says that it exists de facto. His first way of defining it is as the "sum total of the analyst's prejudices," an expression found in the *Écrits*. The first definition of counter-transference, and it's a negative definition, is that it is something you have to get rid of to be able to act. It is something the analyst has to get rid of if s/he doesn't want his or her interpretations to be taken as opportunities for imaginary identification or counter-identification. To dispose of this dual point of view, Lacan constructs a model based on the game of bridge. In bridge, there are four players, and one player is given the role of the dummy; in French we say "*la place du mort*," which is rather striking. Lacan says the analyst has to put him or herself *à la place du mort* (in the role or position of the dummy/dead person), indicating thereby what the analyst has to do with his or her counter-transference.

That is the first definition of counter-transference we find in Lacan's work. But there is another one. In "Direction of the Treatment" (*Écrits*) he makes a very precise and yet general critique of psychoanalytic literature. He defines three main psychoanalytic orientations in the 1950s and at the beginning of the 1960s: geneticism, object relations, and identification with the analyst. He tries to show how each of these orientations isolates problems it sets out to solve. In comparing these three orientations, he points out that the problems they are trying to solve are the central problems of psychoanalysis. The question here is what the concept of "counter-transference" is designed to solve. Lacan believes that a real problem is being pointed to by analysts with the term "counter-transference," which means that he himself does not intend to provide a definition of "counter-transference." He does not consider the problem of "counter-transference" any more important than problems of imaginary prejudice. His orientation leads him to the view that as long as you conceptualize that problem, the main problem discussed in "Direction of the Treatment," in dual terms (transference and counter-transference), you remain in the imaginary. And thus you can't really escape from it. You remain stuck in a dynamic of projection, counter-projection, or interjection. What Lacan proposes to do is interpret the problem signalled in psychoanalytic literature as the problem of counter-transference with his two axes, the symbolic and the imaginary. When he does so, the problem changes into the problem of the analyst's desire. From the "Direction of the Treatment" on, the problem of counter-transference is no longer evoked as such. But the problem referred to by others with the term "counter-transference" leads Lacan to elaborate the concept of the analyst's desire. It's not a question of dominant terminology, but of what is at stake in transference love.

This is a good example of the way Lacan works with the analytic literature of his time. He reads it very carefully, trying to take it as a series of problems to be solved which may lead him to further develop his own theory. The analyst's desire, which is absolutely central to his elaboration of psychoanalysis, is his solution to what is referred to as "counter-transference" in the literature. It's not that he thinks counter-transference doesn't exist. He thinks it is not the proper concept with which to account for transference love. If, on the analysand's part, there is transference love, Lacan's answer is that, on the analyst's part, there is the analyst's desire. Hence, there is an opposition between transference love and the analyst's desire. It is an opposition between the imaginary register, which is natural to start with in the analysand's discourse, and the symbolic register of the analyst's desire.

Let me provide an example from my own analytic work. I have been seeing a woman patient for a very long time. She has made a lot of progress, and her position in life has changed greatly; this can be seen in her behavior, her relationships, etc. But at a certain moment she stabilized at a point which to my mind was not the end of analysis, though it gave her some satisfaction in life. At the beginning of her analysis, she was always in danger, but after five years of analysis she was no longer in danger. She had accepted a few of the constraints of the symbolic order, and had more or less found a place in that symbolic order. One day she said to me, "I want to stop. I won't come and I won't pay you. You are a bore, you are terrible."

In a way, I figured "why not?" She was doing all right. But in the end, after thinking about it, I said to myself "No, I don't want her to go. I want her to stay in analysis. I want her to go further." I asked her to keep coming once a week. I told her she still needed to work on her anger and her sexuality, which had not changed. I thought she was capable of talking about her sexual fantasies though it was very difficult for her. That was my desire as an analyst. It was not her desire at that moment, it was the analyst's.

What followed gave me reason to believe my desire was well oriented, because just then she met a man and things started to get very difficult for her. With a lot of anguish and pain, she wanted to come back for more intensive analysis. The analyst's desire is different from counter-transference. It's not that I wanted her to get married and have children. My sense was that she could go a little further in analysis. And if I thought she could, I had to encourage her to do so. The analyst's desire is not a craving or a fantasy; it is not personal or individual. It's always related to a third point which can be seen in the statement "I have to ask you to continue your analysis." It's not only that I want you to— it's that I can't do otherwise than ask you to. Because you can do it, and you say you can do it.

I felt she shouldn't leave analysis before having completed something. At the beginning of her analysis she had spoken about a momentary experience which was very strange, like a dream—not reality, but almost an out-of-reality experience. She did not really know if it had happened or not. She had a memory of it, but could say nothing about it. It played only a very small part in her life, according to her. In this memory, a man asked her to have sex with him. She said "Okay." They went to a place, but she could not even remember where it was or how everything had gone. They made love in a very peculiar way, she said, which was very important to her. Having said that at the beginning of her analysis, she never again talked about it and, in fact, refused to do so. It seemed to me that that needed to be elucidated. As long as she had not elucidated it, I felt her analysis was incomplete.

It was not counter-transference on my part. I really had no idea if it was good for her or not to continue analysis. I was not concerned with what was good for her. I thought it was going to be very difficult, unpleasant, and anxiety-producing. The analyst's desire is not the desire of the analyst as a person. As a person I had no desire regarding her, no desire for her to do this or that. The analyst's desire is related to supposed knowledge. Supposed knowledge is elaborated in the psychoanalytic setting. Not by the analysand or the analyst, but by the analytic relation: analytic discourse.

The analyst's desire is based on that. Not his or her desire as a person, but the analyst as part of the mechanism, part of analytic discourse. The only way for me to orient myself was to remember and work on what she had told me. She had been working on her relationship with the symbolic order, which means with the Name-of-the-Father, and her relationship with her mother. She had been working on her Oedipus complex a lot. This had changed her position. But she had not worked on her jouissance or her fantasy. I felt that I couldn't let her leave analysis without confronting her relation to jouissance.

Let us turn now to the subject of narcissism. Lacan tells us there are two different forms of narcissism. The first is a narcissism that is valid for every living being, animals and humans: a supposed narcissism before language. What is the second? The second narcissism, in reference to what Lacan calls the "mirror stage," is the narcissism of speaking beings. It stems from the fact that you are not only a living, but also a speaking being, that is, you have a relation to castration. Speaking beings are subject to the castration function. To speak is to sacrifice some of your jouissance, which is the characteristic of the supposedly pure living being.

In a way, we can say there are two forms of the imaginary: a pure imaginary, which is proper to animals, and a distorted imaginary, which is proper to speaking beings. Lacan elaborates the first narcissism with reference to Gestalt theory and ethology. On page 3 of the *Écrits*, he says, "The fact that the Gestalt can have formative effects on organisms is attested to by a piece of biological experimentation that is itself so alien to the idea of psychical causality that it cannot bring itself to formulate its results in these terms." There he speaks about female pigeons, and the fact that seeing the image of a pigeon has what he calls "formative effects" on the female pigeon as an organism. That's a good example of the first narcissism: a narcissism which is reduced to an image, and which emphasizes the material power of the image. But that deals with organisms, and we are not organisms, we are bodies. You have to distinguish between organism, body, and subject, which are not really the same for Lacan. A subject is the effect of language, and a body is the result of the second narcissism.

This is not chronological in any way. You can't say you were first an organism, then a body, and then a subject. The subject corresponds to the symbolic level, the body to the imaginary level, and the organism to the real. You never encounter your organism as such. You encounter it very briefly (the more briefly the better) through your bodily and subjective experience.

"This initial narcissism is to be found . . . at the level of the real image. . . . [T]his way of functioning is completely different in man and in animals, which are adapted to a uniform *Umwelt*" (Seminar I, p. 125). This first narcissistic reaction to the Gestalt, which he speaks of in "The Mirror Stage," is for animals. You have to distinguish between living beings, which includes both humans and animals, and speaking beings, which is a division within the species Homo sapiens. You can never find the first narcissism in a speaking being. You can only find it in the animal kingdom. "For the animal there is a limited number of preestablished correspondences between its imaginary structure and whatever interests it in its *Umwelt*, namely whatever is important for the perpetuation of [. . .] the species. In man, by contrast, the reflection in the mirror indicates an original noetic possibility" (p. 125). This possibility does not come from the imaginary, but from the correlation with language. It "introduces a second narcissism" (p. 125). In men, you only deal with the second narcissism. An image, for a human being, is always an image correlated with and regulated by the symbolic function.

LANGUAGE, SPEECH, AND DISCOURSE

∞

Marie-Hélène Brousse

I'm going to try to elucidate a few of the major concepts in Seminar II and I shall begin with a sentence you can find in the French edition of the *Écrits* on page 67: "The only act of carelessness which ever deceived us is a reference to language, that is to say, this experience of the subject which is the only matter of analytic work." This sentence could be put at the beginning of Seminar II which more or less marks the beginning of Lacan's systematic references to language.

I shall propose two questions which I shall try to answer. In Seminar II, Lacan says analysis changes nothing in reality but everything for the subject. How does analysis change everything for the subject? The second question is, why at the end of Seminar II does Lacan find it necessary to refer to cybernetics? What does the reference to cybernetics provide him with?

To understand the analytic operation, we need to differentiate at least three terms: language, speech, and discourse. We cannot understand what Lacan says about the analytic operation without knowing how these terms are defined. They are taken from linguistics, but like all of Lacan's borrowings, are altered. Lacan defines language as a wall and we have to consider that rather simplistic image because it defines the relationship between language and the real. Language is the wall that separates us from the real, and Lacan introduces the problem of the Other here with a very strange question about the planets: "Why don't they speak?" The planets stand for the real here, and the problem is why the real doesn't speak. Galileo says nature speaks the language of mathematics. The wall of language is to be taken as the wall that separates us from the real.

When the planets start talking, they become real. Lacan says they began talking when astrophysics began. The real is what we are separated from by language.

Saying language is a wall is not sufficient to define language. Language is not *a* structure, but rather structure itself. Lacan maintains the notion that language is structure, and that it has an effect on living beings, right up until the end of his teaching. (You can find it, for example, in *"Radiophonie."*) As structure, language is the set of pre-existing signs. In Seminar II, Lacan emphasizes that this set of signs obeys rules. This definition still does not allow one to differentiate between language as belonging to an individual or social group and as belonging to physical or physiological beings.

We have to accentuate two different aspects of language: first, it is a concrete scientific universe; science is material, and as Lacan says in Seminar II, atemporal. Lacan's second point regarding language is that there is no language without syntax, that is, no language without rules. At that level there is no question of meaning or signification, only science. Opposed to that definition of language or different from it is speech which is opposed to syntax. It is with speech that signification appears, and Lacan defines speech as the act of an individual. He even defines psychoanalysis as a speech act induced by analysis; a Freudian setting is a speech setting. The idea of psychoanalysis as an act is already implied when Lacan emphasizes the question of speech and opposes speech to language.

With speech we have semantics and signification, and the dimension of action—which is not in language—and then a third term which is discourse. Discourse is a text. Speech is not a text, but a voice. Correlated to voice, discourse is a text in which there are tears or rips where symbolic marks appear. By tears and rips, Lacan means unconscious formations and slips. Discourse is a text which is opposed to speech and to language, which is nowhere a text. The difference between language and discourse is that discourse is already organized and bears the mark of enunciation. Being a text, it is constructed. Language is not constructed. Language is defined as a set of material signs plus a syntax with no regards to organization. In a sense, that is the definition of the unconscious: no negation, no time, no reference (either to speech or discourse). Discourse and speech are opposed to language because they are already marked by signification, being on the side of semantics. You see for Lacan, syntax has to be separated from semantics, and is in a way logically prior to semantics. Signification and action appear with speech; and there is no speech without voice. Lacan distinguishes the voice from words. Of course, you only hear the voice through words, but on certain occasions, for example, in shouting, you hear only bare voice without any signification, words, or speech. Generally, however, speech is correlated with voice, one of Lacan's object *a*'s. Thus, speech is correlated with a drive object. Psychoanalysis is concerned first with drives and libido, and second with particular individual organization.

Lacan is concerned here with the training of analysts; there are certain disciplines an analyst has to be trained in, such as linguistics, mathematics, case histories, etc. Linguistics is a form of extra-analytic knowledge. It is necessary to have that knowledge because of the nature of the analyst's intention. With a knowledge of linguistics alone you cannot do anything in psychoanalytic therapy because you have only general formulas, whereas you have to find the particular formula of an individual's subjective position. One of the problems of psychoanalysis is to figure out how to use that knowledge in the analytic setting.

A message is defined as a series of signs which produces an effect on the subject, an effect of signification. The image Lacan uses is that of someone bearing a message he does not know he is bearing on his forehead—it is an example from ancient Greece of a man bearing a message on his scalp though he does not know what the message is, and the message instructs its receiver to put the message bearer to death. In a way, your position as subject vis-à-vis the message is precisely that. The message concerns your destiny. In an analysis, destiny has to pass into speech. Thus the message is not a set of significations—it is a set of signs.

Earlier I asked why Lacan refers to cybernetics in Seminar II. It has to do with the nature of the message as a pure set of signs. In Seminar II he uses 0 and 1 as his set of signs, and elsewhere he complicates it further. I will take the simpler example he provides to show how this is related to his work on language. I will simplify what he says. Let's take the symbols plus (+) and minus (−). You can speak of a structure if you have a set of at least two elements. (Later Lacan uses S_1 and S_2). You can take any two elements that are opposed. You put one after the other (e.g., $+ + - + -$) and create a rule (that is, a syntax): the signs are to be grouped by threes. Your first element is $+ + -$. Your second is $+ - +$. Your third is $- + -$. Next Lacan classifies these elements on the basis of symmetry $(+ + +, - - -)$ and asymmetry $(- - +, + + -)$. That suffices to give rise to an impossibility, because after $+ + +$, you cannot have anything but a $+ + +$ or a $+ + -$.[1]

With such a model, Lacan formulates a minimum symbolic system of material signs, saying this is precisely the way memory works. As long as you can produce possibilities and impossibilities, you can produce the real. This is a way to define memory, not in a psychological sense, but in a semantic sense—memory as a system, a series of possibilities and impossibilities. That is what Lacan calls structure.

Of course, that does not give you the individual, subjective formula, but it gives you an idea of what an analyst is looking for in the main signifiers to order them in a speech pattern. In the case of interpretation, you take your cue from material signs or signifiers. You never interpret significations. Let me give you an example. A patient of mine told me a dream. He is a musician, and he dreamt he was on a bus with his cat and his musical instrument. The bus stopped, the cat got off, and he got off to try to find the cat, leaving his musical instrument on the bus. The cat's name is "Chouchoute"; he runs after the cat, cannot find the cat, and the bus takes off with his musical instrument. This poses the alternative: either Chouchoute or the musical instrument. What I want to emphasize is the cat; the only important thing about it is its name. His association was not about cats; in French, "chouchoute" means teacher's pet. He is a music teacher and has a special relationship with a girl he is teaching whose name is similar to his cat's name. She is not in the dream, except for her name. You mustn't go into the cat's meanings, interpreting instead the signifier "Chouchoute." That allows you to focus on the lady who is currently a problem for him and music, the idea being that you have to lose one thing to get something else.

If you interpret dreams, you have to take your cue from signifiers, and get to the nonsense in signifiers. Secondly, if we are not looking for more meaning, but rather for less, by emphasizing signifiers in your interpretation, you orient analysis in the sense of the bare subject, not in the sense of ego, because the ego is closely tied to meaning. In the case I mentioned, all the meanings of "cats" are narcissistic—a cat is to him a little lover, an imaginary lover. If you avoid that you find the question of his position as a man, his subjective sexual position, which is very difficult for him to assume. Let's say you always orient yourself by the signifier, and you interpret in the sense of subjective division—less sense, nonsense. That allows you to impoverish the ego. Interpretation has to be enigmatic, that is, it has to produce less knowledge. By that, Lacan means, in the analytic setting, knowledge is to be taken as a test for knowledge and not as an application of knowledge.

The relationship of analysis to knowledge, of analytic knowledge to previously existing knowledge, is regulated by a requirement, which is formulated at that point in Seminar II and the *Écrits*, that there be an identity between the analyst's speech and his or her being.

Let's take an example from Freud's psychoanalytic work. I will take an interpretation by Freud which I consider a very good example of the identity between the analyst's speech and being. At the end of a woman's analysis, Freud said something along the lines of 'I have only one request' (and she said that she was amazed because it was precisely the words her mother used to say). 'I pray you, I beg you, never under any circumstances attempt to defend me if you happen to hear disparaging remarks about my work.' I think that is an interpretation that illustrates my point. Freud was convinced he was the scrap of the analytic movement. He was in the position of the object, the object *a* of the analytic movement. In other places, Freud presents himself in precisely that way. At the end of a meeting of the Vienna Psychoanalytical Society where everyone was speaking, Freud remained silent, no one asking him anything, and at one moment he said something like, 'Gentlemen, you treat me in a way which does not honor me. Why do you treat me as if I were already dead? You are arguing amongst yourselves about what I wrote in this article, you quote me here and there, while I am presiding, acting as chairperson, and nobody bothers to ask me what I meant. This torments me because it is what you are doing when I am still with you. I can easily imagine what will happen when I am dead and gone.' That is why he is both in the position of the dead father and in the position of the exception, having an original sin because he had not been analyzed, but meriting forgiveness because he invented psychoanalysis. This position is very close to that of the scrap, object *a*. I like this example because I think it illustrates the identity between the analyst's speech and being.

Identification

Let me turn now to the concept of identification, as it is introduced in chapters 19, 21, and 23 of Seminar II. These chapters center around the difference between the Other (A) and the other (a), "a" being in French the first letter of the word *"autre"* (other). The Other and the other correspond to the difference between the two registers we talked about last week—the symbolic and the imaginary—an important difference in Lacan's teaching. In chapter 19, he discusses that difference after talking about the third register, the real, which is not the same as reality. Reality is a mixture of the symbolic and the imaginary.

I shall first discuss a point mentioned by Lacan in chapters 19 and 21, which is the relationship between psychoanalysis and science.

The relationship between psychoanalysis and science is a very thorny issue. Psychoanalysis is neither a science nor a scientific discipline. We cannot provide proof as scientists do. But while psychoanalysis is not a science, Freud organized it in accordance with the ideals of science: objectivity and modification of reality. But the first thing Lacan says is that the subject of psychoanalysis is the subject of science. What does that mean? First, it means psychoanalysis could not have been possible before the birth of science. Freud could not have worked as he did without his scientific conception of the world. Science is an epistemological condition of psychoanalysis. But what is the subject of science if it is also the subject of psychoanalysis? The subject of science is, as Lacan shows in his reading of Descartes, a purified subject, purified of all that is pathological (in the Kantian sense of the term): doubts, feelings, and sensations.

Let us turn now to the schema found in chapter 19.

Schema L

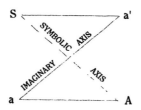

The imaginary relationship runs between a and a', between the ego and its object, that object being modeled on the ego's own image. It is a narcissistic relationship. I spoke about that last week and won't go into it here. The relationship here between S and A–S being related by Lacan to the Freudian *Es* (id)–is what is called the wall of language: the symbolic. But a patient sees him or herself as an ego. "Seeing him or herself" is a reference to the mirror stage. S/he sees him or herself through his or her images, that is, his or her identifications. The first aim of psychoanalysis is to get him or her to see that s/he is actually situated at S. Which does not mean that, in the end, s/he will be a realistic ego, but on the contrary, that s/he will know that s/he is nothing but a *manque-à-être*, a want-to-be. This *manque-à-être* is a result of the successive stripping away of imaginary identifications: I thought I was such and such, but I'm not; what am I in the end but a want-to-be? As analysts, we work on those imaginary relationships so that our analysands can get rid of them, one after the other. We can do that only if we are situated on the symbolic axis.

Psychoanalysis works only in reference to the symbolic axis. Interpretation must be organized on the basis of the combinatory of signifiers which is peculiar to each subject. What we attempt to reach is the subject as a pure effect of signifiers; here we see the relation between the subject of psychoanalysis and the subject of science. The subject as an effect of signifiers manifests him or herself as a want-to-be, that is, as desire. We work on the subject's desire, which is not the subject's needs, drives, or demands.

Neither Lacan nor Freud thinks psychoanalysis aims specifically at therapeutic results. It's not that Freud and Lacan are uninterested in alleviating symptoms—of course they are. But it is not their principal aim. Their aim does not concern the symptoms as developed in ego behaviors or attitudes. What they strive to change is the subject's position, not his or her identifications. They change nevertheless, because action at the symbolic level also has effects at the imaginary level. But it is very different from the post-Freudian theories of psychoanalysis in which the aim is to change the patient's identifications, mainly through identification with the analyst—which means the analyst is, in those models, situated at a'. Lacan certainly would not situate the analyst there, nor anywhere else on the schema for that matter. It's a schema of the structure of the analysand, not of the analytic relationship.

Last time I mentioned that Lacan uses a metaphor from the game of bridge. In the *Écrits*, Lacan says the place of the analyst is that of the dummy in bridge (*"la place du mort"*). But in "Direction of the Treatment" he says keeping your mouth shut in analysis doesn't have the same meaning as in bridge. The analyst strives to work on the analysand's identifications, making them fall away one by one, until he reaches the ultimate one: identification with death. The fact that the analyst has to be identified with the dead person or death means that s/he has to be dead to desire. And his or her desire is crucial in analysis. This does not imply the death of desire. Death is another name for the symbolic. Symbolic identification is ultimately an identification with death. There is always a relationship in Lacan's work between the symbolic order and death, for the symbol is the death of the thing. This implies an identification with the subject's want-to-be, as deduced from his or her symbolic subjective position. Identification with a signifier—the ultimate identification or meaning, after all the imaginary identifications—is a mortifying identification, which is the only way desire can arise as such, as pure subjective division.

Notes

1. [This is an extremely abbreviated account of this point in Seminar II. For a much fuller account, see Jacques-Alain Miller's discussion in his unpublished 1984–85 seminar, *1,2,3,4*. See also "The Nature of Unconscious Thought" in this volume.]

THE MIRROR
OF MANUFACTURED CULTURAL RELATIONS[1]

$$\infty$$

Richard Feldstein

X Degrees of Separation

How have strategies associated with the process of identification been appropriated by right-wing activists? How do neoconservative critics project their moral agenda upon an academic profession less concerned with dyadic superego designations like political correctness/political incorrectness than with an ethics of lack? An ethics of lack is concerned with the gap between signs and objects and how this gap is bridged. It is also concerned with the good or bad faith employed when negotiating that gap, and with the appropriation of forms of representation for a particular political purpose. An examination of the interaction of signs, signifiers, signifieds, and the objects they designate requires an investigation of the gap between the objects represented and the semiotic indicators that mark these objects. In the mirror stage, the gap marked by x degrees of separation between the person peering into the looking-glass and her or his virtual image objectified there will be foregrounded. To develop the implications of these distinctions, I will invoke a Lacanian paradigm that could easily be traded for another methodological model (semiotic, deconstructive, new historicist) to critique the neoconservative construction of the PC narrative. Since my concern is to analyze the phenomenon of *projected* political correctness, however, I use psychoanalytic and post-psychoanalytic paradigms to decipher how neoconservative theorists have constructed a mirror of manufactured cultural relations in which they reflect the aims and aspirations of their constituency. By using a cultural mirror to reflect events in a light favorable to the neo-conservative cause, PC critics have constructed stigmatized scapegoats that can only be represented *indirectly* through the intermediary of right-wing carica-ture. Those not interested in this discussion of neoconservative strategies in a postmodern age might want to skip to the next section, Gaps in the Lacanian Mirror.

Right-wing theorists have incorporated postmodern rhetorical strategies as a means of making their assault on the left more sophisticated. This incorpora-tion of postmodern tactics puts them in the improbable position of invoking an overly simplistic moral certitude that they conflate with contemporary models of ethical difference. For instance, one of the aims of poststructuralist and post-modern theory is to disrupt a Eurocentric worldview through the advocacy of "local, varied, heterogeneous 'difference[s]' [pitted] against the unifying, iden-tity-obsessed practices of the massive states and bureaucracies that characterize the contemporary West" (McGowan 586). Over the last fifteen years Republican leaders have lobbied to limit the size of the federal government by transferring power to individual states; to accomplish this goal they have parodied this local-izing impulse as a prominent part of their antigovernment stance. Although they have issued a clarion call to return to the nineteenth-century reliance on state's rights, contemporary Republican strategists have also shrouded their designs within the playful postmodern impulse to divest unified cultural, polit-ical, and discursive fields of authority, which, ironically, has enabled them to sanction their own epistemological models as unproblematically sacrosanct.

The postmodern tendency to deconstruct (or "unmake") idealized unities is further delineated in Ihab Hassan's "Toward a Concept of Postmodernism," which characterizes this tendency as indeterminacy. By indeterminacies, Has-san means

> a complex referent that these diverse concepts help to delineate: ambiguity, discontinuity, heterodoxy, pluralism, randomness, revolt, perversion, deforma-tion. The latter alone subsumes a dozen current terms of unmaking: decre-ation, disintegration, deconstruction, decenterment, displacement, difference, discontinuity, disjunction, disappearance, decomposition, dedefinition, demys-tification, detotalization, delegitimization—let alone more technical terms refer-ring to the rhetoric of irony, rupture, silence. Through all these signs moves a vast will to unmaking, affecting the body politic, the body cognitive, the erotic body, the individual psyche—the entire realm of discourse in the West. (153)

Cognizant of the contemporary debate as it has appeared on television since the 1960s, neoconservative critics have seized hold of this powerful intellectual fashion and made it part of their repertoire. Because postmodern indeterminacy has proven to have a certain historical velocity, neoconservatives have borrowed it as part of their epistemic reaction to the contemporary political scene, not to affect a cultural revolution that decreates, deconstructs, and decenters the denaturalized body politic, but precisely for the opposite purpose: to insist upon the natural relation between the sign and its referred object. In this way they have produced a discourse that recodes postmodern values as they insist that discursive systems are backed by a disinterested "objectivity" that neutrally designates its object of reference.

In the twentieth century, poststructuralism and postmodernism have analyzed the distinctions between the sign and its referred object as well as between the signifier and the signified, which intersect in these denaturalized semiotic gaps. Because neoconservative writers have had difficulty reading poststructuralist theory, there is a paucity of references in the indexes of their books on political correctness. Because postmodernism has entered the mainstream culture as a popularized discourse disseminated through numerous media circuits, it has provided neoconservatives with a text they can grasp and thus manipulate to influence public opinion. Although right-wing theorists might be unable to put postmodern principles into so many words, they seem aware that one of its basic tenets privileges the "capacity of the mind to generate symbols that intervene more and more into nature" (Hassan 153). For instance, they apparently know that in the twentieth century the mind acts "upon itself through its own abstractions," which has enabled it to "become, increasingly, immediately, its own environment" so that "we have reached the edge of a natural universe that is receding" (Hassan 153). Although right-wing critics know that contemporary theory has solidified this tendency toward symbolic abstraction, they still seek to *conserve* their vision of the past; in keeping with this mode of conservation, they have labeled this trajectory of symbolized abstraction a "mental devolution" that must be simultaneously scorned yet appropriated for their own purposes. Should we be surprised at this twofold reaction? Probably not, if we consider the prescient observation offered by William James in the nineteenth century: "Novelties are first repudiated as nonsense, then declared obvious, then appropriated by former adversaries as their own discoveries" (quoted in Hassan 148). In the twentieth century neoconservative political operatives have added their own spin to this rule of political law and juridical power. They portray postmodernism as a novelty even *as* they appropriate it to further the fundamentalist end of instating their Victorian morality in ethical gaps that have little to do with the superego's procedure of dividing the world into good and evil phenomena.

My aim here is to illustrate how neoconservative theorists have displaced the ethical space of semiotic difference with a moral forum that contrasts political incorrectness with religious correctness. To demonstrate how they affect this displacement, I shall invoke Lacan's topological imaginary to highlight the intersection where politics segues with culturally constructed identities. I wish to stress that neoconservatives would never use a psychoanalytic topology to describe their actions, so, invoking the logic adumbrated in the film *Six Degrees of Separation*, I will do it for them. In that film the female protagonist posits the following claim:

> I read somewhere that everybody on this planet is separated by only six other people—six degrees of separation between us and everyone else on this planet . . . I find that extremely comforting that we're so close, but I also find it like Chinese water torture that we're so close because you have to find the right six people to make the connection. It's not just big names; it's anyone . . . I am bound, you are bound to everyone on this planet by a trail of six people . . . How everyone is a new door opening into other worlds. Six degrees of separation between us and everyone else on this planet. But to find the right six people.

When reading right-wing criticism on the issue of political correctness, I have the feeling that if they knew which six cultural critics to consult they might be able to make a more informed critique of their adversaries. I know this is wishful thinking because they seem resistant to reading critical theory or incapable of doing so. But if undergraduates across the country can learn how to read writerly texts, then neoconservative theorists should be able to do so once they found the "right six people" to help them make their initial foray into poststructuralist criticism. Once they could chart such a theoretical path, right-wing theorists would probably reenact a typical strategy: in this instance, denigrating Lacanian psychoanalysis while appropriating it for their own ends.

Gaps in the Lacanian Mirror

In the Lacanian paradigm, the imaginary register topologizes a gap or split that can be located in the division between the child who peers into the mirror and the objectified virtual image that seems to stare back at the child. Those acquainted with contemporary critical theory know of Jacques Lacan's essay on the "Mirror Stage," which posits that when an infant peers into the mirror for the first time, s/he discovers in a "series of gestures" a relationship between the infant's reflection in the mirror and animate and inanimate background phenomena surrounding the infant (1). In Lacan's mirror, the child discovers a unified self in a series of "movements assumed in the image," movements connected to an attitude acquired when the child leans forward while anticipating in the mirror a "mirage" of maturation. This mirage manifests within a gestalt of images assembled into a form that assures the infant of an imaginary self-unity (1–2).

When the child visualizes its body in the mirror as a coherent shape, it crosses a spatio-temporal borderline. This crossing creates a transfiguration that helps it to elide the gap between the child as a biological organism and its virtual image of itself. In the mirror stage this gap is elided when these facets are reinscribed phantasmatically as one. At this mistaken site of integration, the gap between the child and its virtual image is crossed, then reformulated in an imaginary spatio-temporal union assembled in this process of specular interaction: spatial because the illusion of unity is pieced together through a projective playing with boundaries that is figured finally, in a subsequent stage, as the two-body object relation; temporal because there is a future-perfect anticipation related to the ego's imagined mastery over its own body.

The temporal logic of the mirror-stage presents the following scenario: a child peers into the looking-glass and experiences an anticipatory jubilance when piecing together a body image related to the ego's conception of itself. As the amorphous ego projects itself into a rigid body-image, it constructs the conceptual contours of subjectivity and experiences a jubilant anticipation of a future mastery that is connected to the acquisition of motor skills associated with this totalizing image of itself. This image of self-unification is constituted in part to repress anxiety-producing images of the body divided into bits and pieces. As a stage of chronological development, the dissociated body of bits and pieces would seem to precede the mirror stage, yet one can only measure part object and whole object representation in relation to each other. In actuality, the body in bits and pieces is constructed post facto from an anticipated future retroactively recognized. On this subject Jane Gallop has argued that any chronological account of the mirror-phase is reductive because its temporal logic suggests that part-object inorganization comes "after the mirror stage so as to *represent what came before.* What appears to precede the mirror stage is simply a projection or a reflection . . . [thus] the mirror stage is a decisive moment. Not only does 'the self' issue from it, but so does 'the body in bits and pieces'" (80).

Thus, in the process of identification of the ego with its virtual image, the infant not only traverses the gap of spatial difference, but experiences itself as a unity framed through temporal shifts and modifications. In this way the infant seeks to avoid paranoia associated with the fragmentation it has jubilantly transformed though the creation of an Ideal-I. The result is the founding of an anticipatory mirage of power related to the inverted image in the mirror, which tricks the infant into believing that "the turbulent movements . . . the subject feels are animating [her or] him" can be magically converted into a "mental permanence" ("Mirror" 2). This "mental permanence" symbolizes the ego by prefiguring "its alienating destination" in this fictive conversion of images ("Mirror" 2). In this way instances of self-discovery and self-recovery are, for Lacan, ironic because the child, whose turbulent movements, motor incapacity, and disjointed self-image dominates the first six to eighteen months of life, discovers itself as a fictional totality based on an ideal form whose boundaries are figured in the process of projective *form*ulation.

Implied here is an extension of the child beyond the *point* of self-construction into the indeterminate *between* of passage that problematizes any linear, chronological description of maturational development. It also prevents any notion of identificatory closure because the only guarantee one finds in the mirror is a *méconnaissance* (misunderstanding) warranted by an idealized other of otherness seen as the foundation of self-replication. This meta-other enables "one" to elide another kind of gap or rupture–that in which anxiety-producing images of the fragmented body are disavowed because such untotalizable self-differences could give rise to paranoid perceptions. In the Freudian paradigms paranoia is related to projection as a psychic defense. Freud demonstrates how the ego dismisses self-aspects that are inadmissible to consciousness by first denying and then projecting them onto another person where they seem to originate. Freud delineates this twofold process, providing us with the blueprint for self-deception wherein paranoiac perceptions are abolished within consciousness only to return in the form of hallucinations and displaced voices. Paranoid distrust is often mapped onto demonized scapegoats equated with spectral forces that are believed to haunt the subject from beyond the grave.

For Lacan, paranoia is related to the mirror-stage attempt to manufacture a future-perfect mastery, which seeks to overcome the "fragmented body" that sometimes appears in nightmares of the "aggressive disintegration" of the subject. Such fragmentation usually appears in "the form of disjointed limbs, or of those organs represented in exoscopy, growing wings and taking up arms for intestinal persecutions" ("Mirror" 4). In the mirror-stage essay Lacan explains that these persecutions are related to the "paranoiac alienation which dates from the deflection of the specular I into the social I," whereas in "Aggressivity in Psychoanalysis" he elaborates upon this proposition by claiming, "what I have called paranoiac knowledge is shown, therefore, to correspond in its more or less archaic forms to certain critical moments that mark the history of man's [and woman's] mental genesis, each representing a stage in objectifying identification" (16). In Seminar III he provides further details of this account:

> Here we are dealing with another sort of otherness. I can't repeat all I once said about what I have called paranoid knowledge, since I shall also have to take it up again constantly over this year's discourse, but I am going to give you some idea of it. . . . All human knowledge stems from the dialectic of jealousy, which is a primordial manifestation of communication. . . .What takes place between two young children involves this fundamental transitivism expressed by the fact that one child who has beaten another can say–*The other*

beat me. It's not that he is lying–he *is* the other, literally. . . . [This is only possible] because the human ego is the other and because in the beginning the subject is closer to the form of the other than to the emergence of his own tendency. He is originally an inchoate collection of desires–there you have the true sense of the expression *fragmented body*–and the initial synthesis of the *ego* is essentially an *alter ego*, it is alienated. The desiring human subject is constructed around a center which is the other insofar as he gives the subject his unity, and the first encounter with the object is with the object as object of the other's desire. (39)

In this passage Lacan ties paranoia to all "human knowledge" which stems from "the dialectic of jealousy" that is "a primordial manifestation of communication" and its interrelation to the dialectic of desire (39). Although Lacan later distinguishes the term *desire* from need and demand by equating the former with the chain of signifiers that is shorthand for the Other which structures the field of the unconscious, here he introduces the term, not to designate the desire of the symbolic Other, but to refer to an incoherent sequence of "inchoate desires" springing from the mirror stage. In the Lacanian paradigm, the mirror stage is associated with an imaginary topology that exists prior to the symbolic register and yet is retroactively constructed from it. If we take this distinction into consideration, it becomes apparent that, at this stage in his writings, when Lacan provides an account of "the body in bits and pieces," he is indicating not only a part-object logic of fragmentation but an incipient collection of dissociated impulses (here labeled as desires). Implicit in this analytic model is the notion that such incipient "desires" are related to body parts that, in their radical estrangement, summon forth contradictory wishes allied with the paranoia that attends such hybrid, disparate desires.

One of the agendas of the mirror stage is to center the dissociated circuit of body parts around the nucleus of the ego's visual image of itself. According to this logic, the emergent ego connects divergent body parts with a constellation of "desires" formed around the unified image of the ego in the mirror. In the above passage on transitivism (wherein "one child who has beaten another can say–*The other beat me*"), Lacan claims that the aggressor becomes confused with the victim because of his or her all-inclusive identification with the other. This identification is really a misidentification that alienates the child in the desires of the other in the same way that an infant before the looking-glass takes its mirror-image to be itself. The connection between the two instances–the intrapsychic and the intersubjective–rests on the proposition that "the initial synthesis of the *ego* is essentially an *alter ego*, it is alienated" (Lacan, Seminar III, 39). In other words, the "desiring human subject is constructed around a center which is the other insofar as he [or she] gives the subject his [or her] unity, and the first encounter with the object is with the object as object of the

other's desire" (Lacan, Seminar III, 39). This explains the passage from the specular to the social interaction indicated in the difference between the ego visual-
izing itself before the mirror and the subject finding itself in another subject's
desire. It also explains how paranoia is a form of projection that is further
decentered by the identificatory transition between the intrapsychic and the
intersubjective relation, which becomes infused with an aggressive edge represented above by the phenomenon of transitivism.

Imagistic Shuttle to the Other

In Seminar I Lacan ties the construction of imaginary identification to the transition from the ideal-ego to the ego-ideal. Lacan notes that Freud, when speaking about the composition of the ideal, demonstrates that, as a love object, the
ideal induces fixations upon it. More specifically, when developing the implications of these fixations, Freud outlines various types of fixed love "objects":
"one loves–first, what one is oneself . . . secondly, what one was–thirdly, what
one would like to be [and] fourthly, the person who was a part of one's own
self," which usually refers to the parents internalized as paternal imagoes
(Lacan, Seminar I, 132). The parents provide the first social relation for children
in their capacity as ideal objects. But before a parental imago is introjected, the
child enacts a ritual "with the image in which we appear likable to ourselves"
(Žižek 105). As we have seen, in the initial stages of imaginary identification,
the child visualizes itself as an idealized image bound up with the notion of
what the child would like to be at some future date. This ideal ego (*Idealich*)
gives the child a vision of completeness because it presupposes a perfect fit
between the child and his or her virtual image (Lacan, Seminar III, 137).

Unified gestalt, idealized image, transcendental possibilities–these are the
immediate and delayed effects emanating from the child's union with the looking-glass form. Lacan's emphasis on the *constructed* form in the mirror is
important if one is to understand how the child transfers narcissistic libido (in
the imaginary relation) to object libido (usually associated with the symbolic discourse binding the subject to language). For the child shuttles from specular
narcissism to the intersubjective object relation *via the constructed image*,
which creates an imaginary connection between the future subject and his or
her object world. In its capacity as intermediary shuttle between the subject and
the object world, the imagistic model of the child serves as a prompt to release
sexual behavior related to the form as it appears from an external position. In
this way, the image enables the initial discharge of narcissistic libido bound up
with the object's bodily outline, which is, at this stage of development, nothing
more than a constructed self-image that in*forms* the child's representations and
produces an adequation of the ego with its developing form.

But we can also discern another dimension to mirror-stage phenomena connected to the transformation of the ideal-ego to the ego-ideal. The ego-ideal, sometimes equated with the superego, induces an identification of the subject with the parent of the same sex via the image proffered as its ideal. In the chapter entitled the "Ego-ideal and Ideal Ego" in Seminar I, Leclaire describes the ideal ego as the seat of idealization of the self-turned-object viewed in the mirror, "which has been ennobled, elevated" by the ego that has established an intrapsychic tie between itself and its image (134). In the transition from the ideal ego to the ego-ideal, however, the resulting "idea" or "form" goes beyond the ego, since it is taken over by another structural agency. As we have seen in the process of transitivism, the structuration of the ego-ideal (the *Ichideal* in German) implies an estrangement of the self from the other because the ego-ideal seems to be "imposed from without" (Lacan, Seminar I, 136). The ego-ideal takes on the appearance of a foreign, external entity that requires the subject to fulfill the dictates of its idealized mandate, which becomes aggressive, if not savage, once the carrot proffered by the ego-ideal is rejected. In *The Ego and the Id*, Freud describes the ego-ideal/superego as "sadistic" in its capacity to induce feelings of guilt and shame. In *Lacan: The Absolute Master*, Mikkel Borch-Jacobsen explains that, for Lacan, this "other-me" refers to an "obscene and savage" agency that establishes a dual relationship between the subject and its conscience:" a relation of non-relation—of violence, hatred, and guilt" (32). In "The Wolf! The Wolf!" Lacan describes the superego this way:[2]

> The super-ego is an imperative . . . consonant with the register and the idea of the law, that is to say with the totality of the system of language, in so far [as] it defines the situation of man [and woman] as such . . . not just [as] a biological individual. . . .
>
> The superego has a relation to the law, and is at the same time a senseless law, going so far as to become a failure to recognize (*méconnaissance*) the law . . . the superego is at one and the same time the law and its destruction . . . [and] it ends up being identified with what I call *the ferocious figure*, with the figures which we can link to primitive traumas the child has suffered, whatever these are. (Seminar I, 102)

In another chapter, aptly named "The Nucleus of Repression," Lacan refers to the superego as a "toxic" product that produces other "toxic substances" that induce a "schism" around the issue of the "reproductive cycle" (Seminar I, 196). That is why there have traditionally been prohibitions against masturbation and other sexual "transgressions" from the perspective of the superego. This perspective, Slavoj Žižek explains, is equivalent to "the very place *from where* we are being observed, *from where* we look at ourselves so that we appear to ourselves likable, worthy of love" (105). Thus, if we are to appear worthy in the eyes of the ego-ideal/superego, we are forced to follow this psychic agency's dictates no matter how savage the punishment be if we do not accept its imperialistic degrees. For instance, in *The Dead Father* Donald Barthelme presents a comic description of the superego:

> The death of fathers: When a father dies, his fatherhood is returned to the All-Father, who is the sum of all dead fathers taken together. (This is not a definition of the All-Father, only an aspect of his being.) The fatherhood is returned to the All-Father, first because that is where it belongs and second in order that it may be denied to you. . . . Fatherless now, you must deal with the memory of a father. Often that memory is more potent than the living presence of a father, is an inner voice commanding, haranguing, yes-ing and no-ing–a binary code, yes no yes no yes no yes no, governing your every, your slightest move-ment, mental and physical. At what point do you become yourself? Never, wholly, you are always partly him. That privileged position in your inner ear is his last "perk" and no father has ever passed it by. (144)

In Barthelme's wry explanation of the transfer of authority from the father to the dead father, the latter is represented by the superego–the introjected psychic apparatus symbolizing phallic power. In the superego, the memory of the actual father is inscribed in a system of binary codes that structures the ego to do its bidding. Barthelme's mythic All-Father is representative of the phallogocentric structure of society comprised, in part, by the memory of the biological father after it has faded into a shadow subsumed by the symbolic's binary code of good/bad, right/wrong, and, in the case of right-wing notions of PC, correct/incorrect. Once you identify with the superego, "you are always partly him" because his "privileged position in your inner ear is his last 'perk.'"

In an earlier chapter of *The Dead Father*, Barthelme offers the following passage on the nature of the superego's degree to prevent patricide or any less threatening opposition to the father: "You have rapped the Father, he said between moans. Again. You *should not* rap the Father. You *must not* rap the Father. You *cannot* rap the Father. Striking the *sacred* and *holy* Father is an offense *of the gravest nature*. Striking the noble, wise, all-giving Dead Father is" not permitted (55). Less funny is the Koranic law that decrees, "with respect to the person who is found guilty of theft–*the hand will be cut off* (Lacan, Seminar I, 197). If we do not render unto the superego what is the superego's and sanction psychic repression as it occurs in its interaction with other agencies, aggressive and paranoid behavior manifests as a result of such defiance. Witness the Santa Claus phenomenon before it was appropriated in the 1940s by corporate America. Before the 1940s the patron saint embodying the dead father was internalized as a paternal voice of the superego. Earlier versions of the Santa Claus/Saint Nicholas combinatory not only rewarded "good" children with presents, but punished them after they had been spied upon; if they entertained "bad thoughts," Claus disciplined them by placing coal in their stockings. Because the Claus punished children as well as rewarding them, Governor Al Smith was led to declare, "Nobody shoots at Santa Claus" (*The Writer's Toolkit*). In any of the examples above, such calibrated rewards and punishments encourage an aggressive "paranoid symptomatology" invested with the self-reflexive ability to read one's mind and erase from it (into the repressed recesses of unconscious oblivion) thoughts that have been censored.

Unlike the ideal ego, the ego-ideal is associated less with the image in the mirror than with the censorious, self-observing voice of conscience. While the ideal ego is established along the plane of projection wherein the child casts the fantasy of the whole gestalt onto the image found in the mirror, the ego-ideal/ superego is introjected as the speech of the other, which sounds the call of conscience associated with the internalized laws and strictures of society. Through the secondary identification of the child with the superego, this "blind-repetitive agency" takes on the vocal attributes of censorship originally associated with parental authority (Lacan, Seminar I, 198). Superimposed over the ideal ego, the punitive superego creates the social tie that binds one to the "'masochistic-moral' character of paranoia," which drives the subject toward a split identification with and rejection of the dictates of conscience (Borch-Jacobsen 30). While, on the one hand, the subject can identify with those who oppose the paternal dictum, on the other, the superego is introjected and activated as an autodetermined, self-punishing supplement of "repressive constraints," whose prohibitions regulate the subject as if s/he were on automatic pilot (Borch-Jacobsen 31). It is in the transition of influence from the intrapsychic ideal ego to the intersubjective ego-ideal that the paranoia of self-punishment is yielded as a result of the superimposition of the latter over the image of the former. This considered, we can now turn our attention to a study of cultural phenomena, right-wing fantasy, and the neoconservative projection of moral *right*eousness upon the mirror of manufactured cultural relations.

In the Cracks and Margins of the Cultural Mirror

In Chapter 1 of *Male Subjectivity at the Margins*, Kaja Silverman stresses that any attempt to impose a hierarchical grid on society rests upon the successful assignment of stereotypical identitarian categories to members of the mass culture. Silverman states that "*hegemony* hinges upon [an] identification . . . [that] comes into play when all the members of a collectivity see themselves within the same reflecting surface" of an imagistic construction whose cultural parameters Louis Althusser sketched in applying Lacan's paradigm of the mirror stage to the manipulation of mass consciousness (24). Following Althusser's lead, Silverman asserts that "social consensus is not a matter of rational agreement, but of imaginary affirmation . . . that is synonymous with the very constitution of the subject" (34). Like Althusser, Silverman extends the mirror stage beyond the Lacanian intersubjective model to what I am designating as the post-psychoanalytic paradigm of cultural relations.

One way to describe post-psychoanalysis is to recognize it uses psychoanalytic principles in the service of cultural criticism, which critiques gender, class, race, ethnicity, age, and the heterosexist axes of power relations. Having developed during the last twenty years in the politically charged environment of the academy, post-psychoanalysis presents us with a cultural discourse that is disconnected from clinical relations. As I will develop in my next book, *Post-Psychoanalysis*, this politicized discourse is less concerned with the psyche of a particular analysand than with the cultural construction of ideological power relations in society. Such relations assume, as if they were generated as a prompt in a rigid computer logic, the following "facts" about the subject: that for most Anglo-Americans, images of fantasy tend to be white and all too often male, except when stereotypical examples are evoked, like a nurse or flight attendant; that colonial attitudes are still in circulation in many segments of society; that the construction of gender is all too often reduced to sexual difference which is biologically determined; that privileging people who can afford to pay for psychoanalysis does not call into question the class bias of this therapeutic practice. For the purpose of critiquing dominant cultural formations in *Projected Political Correctness*, however, I will interweave a description of Lacan's mirror-phase assumption of identity with an analysis of the post-psychoanalytic mirror of manufactured cultural relations. These textually allied tools will help us to visualize the process of imaginary interpellation, wherein the biological organism becomes a subject and the subject identifies itself as part of a recognizable cultural consensus.

Turning our attention back to the issue of political correctness, we find right-wing critics busily defending themselves against multicultural theories that mine the cultural field for foundationalist fables encouraging a predictable repertoire of fundamentalist identities. Neoconservatives excoriate multiculturalists because even a passing glance in the cultural mirror calls into question idealized images of biological formation that right-wing icon peddlers have projected upon the American public. Conversely, part of the multiculturalist agenda involves deconstructing all substantializing views of identity formation while denouncing any stable, unified, and agreed upon cultural identity as conventionally constituted in a totalizing frame of reference fraught with contradictions. For instance, in *Nation and Narration*, Homi Bhabha details how an account of radically incomplete communal identification might be approached to map cultural relations as instances of ideological misrepresentation:

Freud uses the analogy of feuds that prevail between communities with adjoining territories—the Spanish and the Portuguese, for instance—to illustrate the ambivalent identification of love and hate that binds a community together: "It is always possible to bind together a considerable number of people in love, so long as there are other people left to receive the manifestation of their aggressiveness." The problem is, of course, that the ambivalent identifications of love and hate occupy the same psychic space; and paranoid projections "outwards" return to haunt and split the place from which they are made. So long as a firm boundary is maintained between the territories, and the narcissistic wounded is contained, the aggressivity will be projected onto the Other or the Outside. But what if, as I have argued, the people are the articulation of a doubling of the national address, an ambivalent *movement* between the discourses of pedagogy and the performative? What if, as Lefort argues, the subject of modern ideology is split between the iconic image of authority and the movement of the signifier that produces the image, so that the "sign" of the social is condemned to slide ceaselessly from one position to another? It is in this space of liminality, in the "unbearable ordeal of the collapse of certainty" that we encounter once again the narcissistic neuroses of the national discourse with which I began. The nation is no longer the sign of modernity under which cultural differences are homogenized in the "horizontal" view of society. The nation reveals, in its ambivalent and vacillating representation, the ethnography of its own historicity and opens up the possibility of other narratives of the people and their difference. (300)

Although Bhabha uses the feuds between the Spanish and Portuguese as a model of hostility generated between two countries, his example is applicable to the divisions between ultraconservative policymakers and multicultural critics in academia today. Bhabha proposes that the same "psychic space" of iconic signification can be traversed by those who hold an opposing or ambivalent set of identifications, which means that those marked as idealized love objects and detested scapegoats can coexist within the same frame of reference as competing representations.

But how is this done? When those who disseminate dominant ideological perspectives to members of the postwar culture face a cultural dissensus, they set about imposing their viewpoints on society by employing psychic maneuvers like splitting and projection to accomplish their goals. From Bhabha's example above, we can determine that modern ideology is "split between the iconic images" linked to the ideal ego and the ego-ideal that displaces it when appropriating, reconfiguring, and supplanting the image of the ideal ego with its own. As we know, the ego-ideal/superego is associated with the *voice* by Freud and Lacan, and "with the signifier that produces the image" by Bhabha, who explains that "the nation is no longer the sign of modernity under which cultural differences are homogenized in the 'horizontal' view of society." Because cultural configurations have a vertical dimension, he declares that the liminal space submerged in the surface of the mirror of intersubjective relations must be recognized as contributing to the acculturation process.

Judith Butler reminds us, however, that if we map the horizontal and vertical vectors of a particular cultural paradigm, we should avoid linking a "discrete, sequential coexistence along a horizontal axis" with a vertical plane that unearths fraudulent foundational images, which are "summarily ranked, causally related, distributed among planes of [vertical] 'originality' and 'derivativeness'" (13). Instead, when peering into the cultural mirror, we find unreflective cracks on the surface that are indentations without vertical or metaphysical depth. Bhabha instructs us that the unidimensional, "homogenized" version of the nation state graphed upon a "horizontal" axis does not reveal the "chinks and cracks of the power-knowledge apparati," which Teresa de Lauretis locates in "the blind spots, or the space-off, of its representation" (25). De Lauretis borrows the term "space-off" from film theory to point to "the space not visible in the frame but inferable from what the frame makes visible" (26). Thus, the "space-off is, in fact, erased, or, better, recontained and sealed into the image by the cinematic rules of narrativization . . . [so that it exists] concurrently alongside the represented space" (26). While de Lauretis employs this terminology to describe the attributes of gender in the construction of subjectivity, in a post-psychoanalytic paradigm of cultural identification we detect strategies of idealization, aggression, and projection used by right-wing spin doctors to reconfigure the frame of reference itself. This referential borderline allows for the reflection of "respectable" attributes while aspects of otherness are often devalued as politically subversive, usually excluded from the domain of iconic and discursive representation, and frequently projected "outwards" before returning "to haunt and split the place from which they are made" (Bhabha 300).

I have argued that the mirror of manufactured cultural relations both legitimates and excludes icons of the body politic according to ideological standards of gender, race, ethnicity, class, and age. Certain representations—whether they be political, historical, social, and/or psychological—can be visualized within sanctioned contexts, while others are discredited or not reflected in the social field. Beginning in the 1980s, media-savvy propagandists associated with the Reagan administration began to equate right-wing fantasy with mythologized images manufactured for public consumption, so that Americans were induced to envision themselves as part of this constructed ideological hall of mirrors. To accomplish this feat, neoconservatives propagated the notion that televisual images accurately reflect the illusion of individual identities ("rugged individualism" is one example) against a background of "shared signifiers"; together, imagistic figure and signifying ground fortify the subject's participation in an orchestrated group fantasy. In this way, those who found themselves in the cultural mirror as "individuals" were confirmed and reconfirmed by such shared fantasies. In other words, those who saw themselves mirrored by this process found a *place* for themselves as subjects as well as a *position* in the social array of sanctioned sites guaranteed by the dominant social fantasies produced for the masses.

Moderate Republicans, ultraconservatives, middle-of-the-road liberals, as well as more progressive political forces continue to vie with each other to mirror their version of corporeal identities against (depending on the group) mythic or historical backdrops that convey images, values, and tastes that are declared desirable. To establish such "acceptable" backdrops for their iconic depictions, these political groups carefully select meaningful props that signify specifiable values in carefully planned photo-ops calculated to influence public opinion. Contentious attempts to sway the public through the introduction of stereotypical images set against signifying backgrounds spur members of the mass culture to find their likenesses in instances of identification that are validated as integral to society.

Let us look at a specific example to illustrate the process. Nowhere is this competition to sway the public more clearly demarcated than in the abortion debates that have pitted conservatives against liberals. Both groups have proffered images for consumption that have been produced, marketed, and distributed on a repeated and predictable basis. In their dissemination of televisual propaganda, right-wing fundamentalists have presented images of traditional women who celebrate domesticity in a patriarchal family setting. These male-identified women are invariably visualized against a hypermoral background of biblical proportions. To counter impressions that promote domestic servitude, progressive feminists have produced, valorized, and circulated in the American mass market images of independent working women who can fend for themselves. In this way, they have disinvested traditional images of women of their negative value–bearing form; through a feminist perspective, images depicting women as domestic servants that labor against a fundamentalist ground of mythical signification are denigrated as misogynist. Feminist critics take this tack, in part, to emphasize that gendered subjects marked by race, ethnicity, class, and age cannot be degendered by an ahistorical macroperspective passing itself off as an idealized cover-fantasy.

To counter such tactics, right-wing imagemakers flood the media with hyperreal images that are obscene in their brash and repetitive quality. In this manner they reinforce valorized notions of mainstream Americans that can be found in the viewfinder of predictable images *and* the backdrop of determinant signifiers. This gestalt enables some members of the public to discover discrete *types* that mirror them. These people confuse the *type* with the *person*, believing that the mirror of manufactured cultural relations objectifies them within the purview of the American context. Through the distribution of images coded as recognizable stereotypes, right-wing opinion shapers have promoted icons of "mainstream citizens." These icons have been hurled into motion in an ongoing saga that narrativizes them as desirable representatives of an "authentic" American lifestyle.

In this dominant fiction, Americans who do not answer the clarion call of mythic interpellation are cast as outsiders. In the process neoconservative critics project "dissident" radical groups beyond the boundaries of their fundamental(ist) fantasy, which is demarcated at the nexus of desire and law. In such textual dispersions, leftist radicals are typecast as "subversives" who are unable to find a subject position within the mirror of manufactured cultural relations; instead they are marginalized to the extent that, when the cultural mirroring process occurs, they cannot find themselves reflected within the gestalt—in the foreground or backdrop of shared cultural signifiers offered by mainstream politicians and the media. Since the late 1980s we have seen how neoconservative writers and their right-wing religious allies have cast proponents of multiculturalism as un-American scapegoats who pose a threat to students in their classrooms. To political conservatives intent upon consolidating a stable image of themselves and their followers, heterogeneous multiculturalism itself has become a symbol of the very chaos that the fundamental(ist) fantasy of neoconservatism was designed to overcome.

We have already seen how the child seeking itself in Lacan's mirror finds an idealized form that is fictive by design. Right-wing fundamentalists maintain the opposite viewpoint, however, when they assert a version of identity politics that promotes socially constructed images that they claim are absolutely accurate. Some consumers internalize these snapshots of themselves because they experience a cultural urgency to overcome the proliferating and contradictory demands of contemporary life, demands that leave them feeling fragmented and confused about their role as citizens. So they accept the juridical images of cultural law and order placed in circulation by right-wing practitioners, who promise them a corporeal unity incapable of disintegrating back to the part-object logic associated with the body of bits and pieces. The "truth" of such imagery is based on cultural givens that are, in actuality, hotly contested, not only because they pledge to harmonize the discordant elements of postmodern life, but because they purport to transform the radical incompleteness of life-terminated-by-death into the transcendental promise of heavenly transport based on the moral worthiness of a select group of people. How do right-wing mythologists produce such conceptual hocus-pocus? By suturing images for consumption onto neoconservative master narratives that hold out the hope of making the unimaginable and enigmatic imaginable and clear and of deciphering the untranslatable aspects of life by grounding them upon the bedrock of ideological fundamentalism. In this manner they deny the entire heterogeneous social field of signification, replacing it instead with their micropolitical theories generalized into macropolitical "facts," which generate the presumed universality of a *Truth* that is applicable to everyone.

I have indicated that in this attempt to reassert a hegemonic fundamental fantasy based on the reactive design of identity politics, neoconservatives have denied diversity while consolidating a self-shaping dynamic to which many of their followers pay obeisance in lockstep fashion. Those who have followed the paper trail left by neoconservative think tanks have determined that politicians in league with right-wing religious factions have, with rare exceptions, offered the electorate a unified front on each succeeding issue brought before public consciousness. Although neoconservative politicians and religious leaders do occasionally reveal the particularity of their desires, they have been very successful in speaking with a united voice on the salient issues of the day. More importantly, they have managed to delineate a pseudo-unified image of themselves by adhering to the choreographed scripts presented wholecloth to them by neoconservative think tanks. Neoconservatives have also mounted a concerted protest against competing groups that mirror a divergent set of American values; as we have seen, these attempts are disparaged as illegitimate, and, in certain instances, as un-American. For the last fifty years, right-wing imagemakers have peddled the illusion of a unified leftist front that has infiltrated American society only to topple it. These imagemakers have sold this scenario as a mythic certainty of consciousness while encouraging public fears of contradiction, multiplicity, and heterodoxy that undermine any totalizing image of society in which Americans can find themselves *placed*—their positions reinforced, their images signified as legitimate, and their values idealized as patriotic— within a conventional gestalt of intersubjective relations.

To institute the grand fiction of their fundamental(ist) fantasy, neoconservative power brokers must regulate any aspect that remains at odds with the matrix of intelligibility they establish; to accomplish this objective, they must split off discordant elements, then project them onto vilified scapegoats, who return as the embodiment of these disavowed traits. Catherine Clément, quoting Lévi Strauss from *Sociologie et anthropologie de Marcel Mauss*, describes this process in the following manner:

> The same goes for women as for madmen: in a *manifest* position of exclusion, they keep the system together, *latently*, by virtue of their very exclusion. Crisis signifies that as well. "In every society it is inevitable that a percentage . . . of individuals find themselves placed . . . outside of the system or between two or several irreducible systems. The group asks and demands of those people to figure certain forms of unrealizable compromise, on the level of the collectivity, to figure certain imaginary transitions, to embody incompatible syntheses. . . . Their peripheral position in relation to a local system, does not keep them from being by the same token, an integral part of a total system." (134)

What Clément states about women is true for the mythic construction of those "nefarious" politically correct "monsters," whose "integral" value lies in their posing a threat to society. As we have seen previously, some reactionaries equate PCers with "madmen" in order to sequester them in the Siberian margins of reference, to project them beyond the very frame itself, or to suppress them in the unreflective, opaque cracks within the reflected surface. Thus, monoculturalists manufacture the scapegoated other through an oppositional process that is not dialectical but imaginary, since it is brought into being at the level of sadistic fantasy that cannot be owned by right-wing reactionaries intent upon disavowing aspects of their own personality.

We have seen that when the subject identifies with the punitive superego in the mirror of intersubjective relations, there is usually a counter-identification that reflects some degree of ambivalence. Since the belief in a unified field grounds the certainty of neoconservatives who believe they know the incontrovertible Truth, these theorists must disavow any counter-identification existing within the margins of consciousness that might affect their behavior through its return in repressed phenomena. Neoconservatives who consider themselves purists at heart are forced to disidentify with any rebellious counter-identification that surfaces as a dissident counter-image. To disavow these images, they project denied self-aspects onto left-wing critics, who reject the hypermoral "paranoia of self punishment and the paranoia of righteousness" as "determined . . . by arrested development of the personality at the genetic stage of the Superego" (quoted in Borch-Jacobsen 31). Thus, certain mirroring aspects are so unacceptable for neoconservative purists that they must first deny them and then project these facets onto elements of the body politic which become tabooed—*unable to be mirrored against the shared gestalt of fundamental(ist) cultural fantasies.* In this way, psychic projection becomes a means of excluding traumatic desires that would otherwise implode unregulated fantasies and revive anxiety associated with the body of bits and pieces. In order to avoid this inevitability, superegoistic desires gain ascendancy to regulate anxiety related to unformed aspects of the ego's body image that threaten to deform a unified conception of the self. Such regulatory desires create a psychic "space" for selective amnesia, which enables right-wing strategists to sell their emotionally charged, high-voltage fantasies to members of the general public interested in making an identitarian leap of faith.

Boys to Men to Gods

I have emphasized mirror-stage phenomena because, while Freud ties projection to paranoia and the process of demonization associated with it, Lacan links projection with paranoia and the instance of primary identification enacted before the looking-glass. In the sketch of post-psychoanalysis presented in this chapter, we have seen how a subject's experience before the mirror is appropriated politically to reinforce a process of cultural mirroring that recurs, not just in infancy, but throughout one's life. The importance of these instances of secondary identification are based on the premise that from time to time people feel compelled to reconfigure themselves against a backdrop of shared signifiers that present them within a communal context. Because of this conflation of primary and secondary identifications, image-crafters are able to engage icon-consumers in a multifaceted specular interaction: (1) to manipulate their constituency to do their bidding, politicians of various persuasions seize control of powerful media institutions to circulate stereotypical images as prompts for identification; (2) to induce consumers to identify with the images manufactured for them, politicians plant ideological signifiers in the background gestalt offered for identificatory consumption; (3) to identify with one or more of the stereotypes distributed for mass consumption, members of the community must deny their difference from these imagistic prototypes as they place themselves within the frame of reference that incorporates them; (4) to identify with these image-types, subjects must reconfigure themselves within the selection of pictorial role-models presented by politicians and broadcasters who seek to influence public opinion.

Differences manifest when divergent political groups vie with each other to establish media profiles for the disbursement of propaganda to specified target groups. We know right-wing imagemakers project upon the public images which support the fiction of a self-shaping, self-aggrandizing individualism that reinforces the single-vision pretense of identity formation. Such purveyors of iconic myths deny the basic formulation of the mirror stage: that the construction of the figure in the mirror leads the ego to misread its imagistic correlate because the inaugural act of identity formation is established from a false unity that denies the experience of fragmentation associated with the body of bits and pieces. Turning this theory on its head, neoconservatives induct their constituency into the cultural mirror by elevating idealized images of the ego and superego as prompts for the status quo to revere. As these exalted pictures circulate through our image-dominated consumer society, media-savvy neocons "bestow" upon the body public contextualized images that promote identity positions. These select positions reinforce social institutions guaranteed by juridical structures that bolster right-wing values.

As I have previously indicated, neoconservatives have inscribed a hyper-moral metaphysics of substance in the cultural mirror as part of a repressive juridical gestalt presented for identificatory consumption. In this staged spectacle where desire intersects with the law, an imagistic never-neverland is established for gay men, lesbians, feminists, people of color, Marxists, and "politically correct" academics. They find themselves inscribed in "the margins of hegemonic discourses"—in the "social spaces carved in the interstices of [sanctioned] institutions and in the chinks and cracks of the power-knowledge apparati" (de Lauretis 25). Although liberals are begrudgingly graphed within neoconservative lines of demarcation, "members of the radical fringe" are first effaced, then reinscribed as two dimensional parodies of themselves. In response to this effacement, the task of cultural critics is twofold: to expose right-wing tactics that reduce perceived adversaries to cartoon scapegoats and to deconstruct nonhistorical subject positions promoted to disseminate right-wing propaganda.

To this end, postmodern and poststructuralist critics have argued against the possibility of a subjective individualism that maintains one's identity can be somehow separate from the internalization of cultural representations. Such internalized representations become the backdrop of narcissistic fantasies that foreground the grammatical subject as the center of image-clusters coded with cultural data. This model, with its emphasis on the permeability of psychic space, deconstructs any reductive binary grouping of inner and outer phenomena, replacing it instead with a performative model of representation. This performative paradigm emphasizes the circulation of introjected and projected desires *between* the subject and its object word, which is mediated by the symbolic Other—a third term introducing a pre-given structural site into the equation that proceeds the birth of the subject.

In the symbolic language system we find no originals, only semiotic duplicates where signs refer to objects. In the semiotic field of representation, the notion of the original or a "pluralism of originals" generated by right-wing fantasy is traded for a "pluralism of copies," which are produced, advertised, sold, and consumed as copies and "copies of copies" whose presence is based on ethics, not morality (Crimp 172–173). I have previously suggested that, in the symbolic register, this ethical dimension is utilized to negotiate the referential gap between the sign and its object and the signifier and the signified. In the symbolic register, the only pretense toward originality is established through a ghostly absence associated with the violence of representation in which semiotic designators displace their animate and inanimate designates. In the mirror of imaginary identification, however, this representational gap is depicted differently: by the space between the ego and the virtual image providing it with the contours of visual coherence.

It becomes evident that in the mirror of manufactured cultural relations the violence of representation irremediably stymies any humanistic perspective of presence. Recognizing that the idealization of identity positions is an ideological ploy, feminist critics have foregrounded gender distinctions because women have traditionally been underrepresented, misrepresented, or not represented at all in the scopophilic lens of cultural production. Aware that masculine ideals have traditionally been equated with universal truths, feminist theorists have insisted upon marking the subject with the specifics of gender, race, ethnicity, class, and age as a means of historicizing the construction of subjectivity. In the cultural mirror wherein images are produced for intersubjective consumption, feminists, Marxists, multiculturalists, and proponents of queer theory have framed within historical boundaries the neoconservative iconography that connects universal assumptions about the subject with juridical structures determining its position within society. It is not for nothing that theorists like Michel Foucault, Judith Butler, and Teresa de Lauretis have politicized the *production* of subjectivity, tying it to the economic influences and cultural factors that determine it. For her part, Judith Butler reminds us that "politics must be concerned with this dual function of power: the juridical and the productive" because the law produces a dense discursive texture, then conceals its legal underpinning beneath clichéd precepts that reinforce the subject's assumed identity-to-itself. In the United States women are unfailingly inscribed within this tangled web of deception, which is legislated by a marketplace autologic that simultaneously produces and restrains them in accordance with repressive structures of power (Butler 2).

In this way gender becomes a stratified mark that designates the subject within the aforementioned categories of class, race, ethnicity, and age. These related categories are part of a cultural construction the attributes of which are projected upon sexed subjects of desire. As such, this cultural production gives testimony to a radical incompleteness between the biological attributes of the subject and the cultural traits used to render them. When reconceptualizing a model of gender distinctions applied to sexual difference, Judith Butler explains that gender is something people "have" rather than something people are said "to be" (7). In Butler's analysis, the "universal subject" appears within the field of representation equated with—depending on the paradigm presented—masculinity as the privileged gender or the symbolic as the phallogocentric structure of representation itself. When fleshing out a sketch based on the former premise, Butler depicts Simone de Beauvoir's belief that the feminine gender is indicated by particular attributes while masculinity is equated with universality itself. Butler goes on to demonstrate that, for de Beauvoir and Wittig, femininity comes into focus as an absence, lack, or expression of masculine otherness-to-itself that is projected onto women.

For Irigaray, however, both the subject and the process of symbolization reveal a system of masculine representation produced in the "between-men" phallogocentric system (*je, tu, nous* 45). Thus, whether feminists critique the equation of femininity with the otherness of men, which has been projected onto women in the masculine confusion of femininity with the displaced aspects of male subjectivity, or, whether the subject/other binary is considered as a manifestation of the logocentric economy of representation itself, the pretense of a neutral model of representation is undermined. In this way images of objectivity and paradigms of originality are contested. To reveal the partisan nature of universal values proposed by neoconservatives, feminist critics have demonstrated how claims of subjective originality can be deconstructed at the intersection of "differentials which cannot be summarily hierarchized either within the terms of phallogocentrism or any other candidate for the position of 'primary condition of oppression'" (Butler 14).

Whether multicultural critics analyze advertising images that repeatedly target young people to the exclusion of the elderly, examine the barrage of mass produced icons printed for quick consumption in newspapers and magazines, or witness the marginalization of people of color from the televisual circuits that process information today, many cultural critics have taken measures to offset the obvious bias displayed in the dissemination of information. Two of these measures include recognizing the performative nature of representation and discerning who controls the agenda that enables the performance in the first place. To avoid such visual colonization, multicultural critics have called attention to performative discursive patterns set in motion to politicize the exchange of information. These critics have also called attention to the fictional basis of subjectivity, which substitutes the heterogeneous subject-in-contradiction-to-itself for the pure presence of subjective neutrality and unification. Rather than celebrate totalized images that provide "one" with the illusion of an unproblematic identity position, postmodern and poststructuralist readers of the multicultural text explore the exclusions, contradictions, and convergences that appear *among* gender, race, ethnicity, class, and age as well as the cultural coordinates and displacements *within* each rubric.

In a culture of mercurial changes and rapid slippage between the terms of representation, contemporary critics use deconstructive tactics to emphasize how fictional identities coincide with themselves. While neoconservatives constitute wannabe identities in the cultural mirror to "eliminate the productive tension" that exists between cultural coordinates such as gender, class, race et al., multicultural theorists seek to "heighten that tension, even to rediscover it and to bring it back into focus" (Huyssen 221). In this way, a paradigmatic shift occurs, blunting the influence of the superego and its dyads of judgment that foreclose upon experience. The sway of this repressive psychic agency is diminished as a result of this shift, as is its project to colonize the site of consciousness. Instead, the obsession with judging people against moralistic ideals is displaced by an ethical dimension of lack created in the displacement of the thing by the semiotic stand-in, whose intention is not to restore the subject to a place of visibility, presence, and agency, but to emphasize subjective discontinuity in the decolonized structure that affirms its sociopolitical difference-to-itself. This paradigmatic shift has not been achieved to affect yet another dichotomy (this one pitting identity politics against the subversion of identitarian unities), but to recognize that an emphasis on self-difference is crucial to offset the will-to-know, which asserts itself even as cultural critics write about not knowing, so strong is its impetus to reverse the counter-tendency toward discontinuity, disintegration, and deconstruction. For even cultural theorists who subvert the illusion of substantial identity formations recognize that somewhere the desire *to know* how to implement their strategies manifests in such a way as to influence their own projects.

Their strategies remain in stark contrast, however, to the neoconservative mirror-phase sleight-of-hand that postulates the subject as anterior to any knowledge of itself. Neoconservatives ground their global/natural representations in universal/spiritual images proffered for graphic consumption by the American public. In this way right-wing critics combine global phenomena with regulatory images guaranteed by the metaphysical assemblage standing behind the mirror as a neutral, founding source that enables the subject to arrive at some "greater" reality. But if one looks closely, the only warrant guaranteeing this metaphysical colonization of unconscious sites subject to repression is the ego-ideal associated with the father, the phallus, the logos, and the phallogocentric desire to possess suprahistorical information about the object world and the subject's unproblematic relation to it.

Writing about this phenomenon, Luce Irigaray explains in *je, tu, nous* that patriarchal traditions were further solidified when men seized "hold of the oracle, of truth" and thus became "the gods-men" who severed the oracle and truth "from their earthly and corporeal roots" (17). In this way a "new logical order was established, censuring women's speech and gradually making it inaudible" (Irigaray 17). But there was another aspect to this appropriative exploit: the privilege accorded to men in general and the father-son genealogy in particular. Thus, in any neoconservative bid to establish a metahistorical site of universal proportions, there is an equation of the ideal ego/ego-ideal with the father's name and its sanction by "the gods-men." These psychic agencies and the personified figures that symbolize them are in turn sutured to the signifying ground of the mirror-gestalt and the formative images that emerge from it like televisual wavelengths from the indistinct background of channel-surf. As Irigaray has shown us, the meta-image whose contours cohere into the phallic privilege is coded by the logocentric binary, which has gained ascendancy in direct proportion to the suppression of mother-daughter genealogies. It is likely that the father-son line of succession has been established so that the economy of gender, law, and power could be perpetuated in such a way that patriarchal privileges would be retained throughout *his*tory. In the following quotation from Irigaray, notice the interlinkage of familial privilege with the *form*ation of the masculine genealogical line of succession:

> The difficulties women have in gaining recognition for their social and political rights are rooted in this insufficiently thought out relation between biology and culture. At present, to deny all explanations of a biological kind—because biology has paradoxically been used to exploit women—is to deny the key to interpreting this exploitation. It also comes down to remaining with the cultural naïveté that dates back to when the men-gods established their reign:

only that which manifests itself in the form of a man is the divine child of the father, only that showing an immediate resemblance to the father may be legit-imized as a valued son. The deformed or the atypical are to be hidden in shame. And as for women, they have to reside in darkness, behind veils, indoors; they are stripped of their identity insofar as they are a non-manifesta-tion of forms corresponding to male-sexed chromosomes. (*je, tu, nous* 46)

In this passage Luce Irigaray demonstrates how social and political rights are constituted upon a divine paradigm that privileges the god/father/son suc-cession, whose parallel includes god-the-father, god-the-son, and the holy ghost as the metaphysical guarantee of the other two positions. The most salient point of reference here, however, distinguishes the formation of the son in the father's image. In other words, when the father looks at his son, he is really searching for a manifestation of his own image. If "deformed" or "atypical" traits become predominant, the son is cast out of the loop because he is unable to mirror the image projected upon him by his father, who wishes to perpetuate the god/father/son lineage as a triadic hybrid reflecting the idealized aura of masculinity.

In this androcentric model of genealogical succession, the mother-daugh-ter link is suppressed, and, in many cases, eliminated altogether whenever the gods are summoned to ratify the rites of passage from generation to generation. As we have seen, this covenant is partially engendered by mirror-phase phenom-ena, which warrants the masculine form as the universal designate, much in the way that the Bible grants as primary the relationship between Yahweh and Adam. For Yahweh creates Adam first, and then, almost as an afterthought of anatomical destiny, makes Eve from him—from a spare rib, as if Yahweh were ordering take out. As Mary Wollstonecraft reminds us in *A Vindication of the Rights of Women*, Eve stands in relation to Adam as he does to God: as a direct descendent that enables the birth of the second term. This secondhand genesis gives us the precedent for mirror phenomena that replicates the patriarchal myth in which women and other marginalized groups are commodified, then exchanged in our Anglo, between-men culture.

The Commodity Exchange in the Cultural Mirror

In the back and forth interchange that constitutes the projective-introjective dynamics of the mirror stage, it is important to recognize that the subject does more than internalize an image from the looking-glass. This point of distinction becomes especially significant if we consider that the objectification of the self in the mirror enables the transfer of images into commodities that circulate between producers and consumers. When reading Lacan on the objectification

of mirror phenomena, John Muller and William Richardson delineate a proliferating pattern of outward expansion that projects the ego into an imagistic
envelop. Following the concepts developed by classical psychoanalysis, Muller
and Richardson identify the amorphous ego (or *Ich* in German) as a psychical
apparatus closely allied with the perception-consciousness system (*Pcs.-Cs.*),
which perceives itself as a unity only after it projects its desire upon the love
object known as the ideal ego. Because the ego takes on the idealized attributes
of an objectified image that is initially external to itself, its properties resemble
those of the object. The objectification process that shapes the ego's body-image
permits it to adopt a compensatory introjective logic of permanence, identity,
and substantivism as it takes in "a tensile strength that eventually becomes rigid
and armorlike" (Muller and Richardson 30–31). It is no coincidence that the
rigidification of boundaries in the construction of the idealized image in the mirror stage provides the basis for 'the inertia characteristic of the formations of
the I' . . . that is, its defense mechanisms" (Muller and Richardson 30–31). Eventually, this projective-introjective interchange leads to the "square of identification" comprised of the "subject-ego-others-things" wherein "things are treated
narcissistically as reflections of the ego" (Muller and Richardson 34).

In the process of objectification, the ego becomes identified with the imagistic other, which takes on the properties of an object as value is ascribed to it
as one of many objects. How is this value established? Since time immemorial
people have argued that there is an inherent value that fuses the immortal soul
with the finite body. If one accepts this theological model, body and soul retain
a value that cannot finally be calculated as an effect of the exchange of commodities. All economists describe use value as an attribute of a utilitarian object
(a heavy coat provides warmth in the winter); yet as soon as they discuss the
use value of the labor force, the distinction between use and exchange value
becomes less distinct: "the use value of labour power is its ability to produce
new value by being turned into labour in production . . . [which] derives from
the development of commodity relations, value and money" (Foley 504). Contemporary theorists like Gayatri Spivak, however, have maintained that use
value "can be shown to be a 'theoretical'–as much of a potential oxymoron as
'natural exchange'" (309). For critics like Spivak, the problem with distinguishing use value from exchange value, which is derived from the desirability of
objects within the culture, is obvious. When the human image circulates in the
system of exchange as a commodity manufactured within the cultural mirror, it
retains "nothing in common as regards [its] substance: anything can be
exchanged for anything else" (Giddens 12). As subjects determined by discursive structures, we internalize social, political, and religious values through the
introjection of representations that we appraise and reappraise.

Such appraisal is not based on any inherent merit, but upon the ascribed
worth of the commodified object as it is measured against other objects of

exchange, whose significance is determined in a dialectical process that weighs each imagistic object upon the symbolic scales of culturally assigned values. In this way the use value of a particular object is inscribed in the retroactive determination of its significance. The imagistic object is produced in the cultural mirror of social relations as one object is seen or not seen as equivalent to another, depending upon an intermediary force—desire (Muller and Richardson 33). As mediating desire codes the object found in the mirror, it saturates images with an ideological quotient of desirability, which emanates from the centrifugal force of collective engagement. As Lacan observed, once the subject identifies with the other, the object of desire becomes the object desired by someone else. Because objects attain a desirability factor, each object takes on a plus or minus value, which confers or withholds merit depending on who does the judging and the cultural system selected to judge.

How does an object attain a quotient of desirability within the mirror relation? By the judgment appended to the image rendered against the backdrop of signifiers indicating the estimated value of the image advanced by those empowered to shape public opinion. Values are also determined by what is included or excluded in the mirror image and by its frame of reference, which provides a cultural context for the objectification of merit mirrored to the public. Because of these factors, one must vigilantly scrutinize images manufactured for iconic consumption, especially if we consider that, in our technological market culture, this process of imagistic germination and gestation makes the conception of the ego projected into its bodily envelop more concrete as time goes by. In its incremental reception of self-representations, the ego adopts "objective" correlates which, as they are internalized, weigh it down under the onus of external opinion.

In the introjective and projective cycles of identity formation, categories of gender, class, race, ethnicity, and age become valued or denigrated factors within the matrix of cultural opinions set up by groups that have an agenda for the American public. Such agendas are packaged for promotional merchandising and iconic distribution to our desire-infused economy. In the competition to influence the formation of public sentiment, members of the mass culture are implicitly instructed to square themselves with images promoted by special interest groups in the construction of group identities. In this techno-culture of aesthetic production and mass consumption, one group is not inherently superior to another; superiority and inferiority are sutured into the gestalt that reckons self-worth, as self-worth is designated by the desires of others whose self-presence stands in for a semiotic absence. Because discursive references figure a "being there" that enables the subject to see itself front and center, it accrues influence in direct proportion to the avoidance of an experience of "not being there"—of being dispersed in the cultural mirror that is *fun-*

damentally empty, since it is primarily a product of iconic and lexical signifiers determined by market forces that help to determine its characteristics.

The cultural mirror is filled with objectified images whose desirability increases or decreases in an exchange mediated by money, which is not, however, the only arbiter of value in the commodity system. For the categories of time and space also help to set the standards of production practices that transform the identity of workers who recognize themselves as having positions within the institutionalized structure. As Mumford notes, "the clock, rather than power-machinery as such, is the prime element in [the] modern mechanical culture," time as it is allied with space to place constraints on the mobility of laborers in the workplace (quoted in Giddens 12). Giddens concurs with Mumford that commodified time and space are "integrally related to the coordination of activity involved in labour discipline in the workplace" (Giddens 12). In other words, time and space are mapped upon the subject as visible tokens announcing the divide between labor and management. Although both groups are dependent upon the clock to quantify time spent on the job and both are placed spatially in accordance with their status at the worksite, members of labor and management internalize different spatio-temporal gestalts which, like images in the cultural mirror, are internalized and brought home at night.

But there is another, less obvious aspect to the steering activity of time and space upon the subject. Giddens explains that "the 'substance of time-space' has become overshadowed by time as quantified form, and space as quantifiable extension" (12). We have already seen how this dynamic operates in the mirror phase transaction: when the dependent infant who cannot walk raises its head to find an image to appropriate as its ideal ego, it reconfigures space insofar as the infant is able to project itself through a future-perfect temporal dimension. This temporal projection establishes a "quantifiable extension" of its spatial dimension, which enables the child to fictionalize its body image as a totalized unity based upon two factors: its capacity to thrust itself into an idealized future of projected mastery and its capability to center its physical form upon the historical stage where the human being is objectified. As Lacan states, "the mirror stage is a drama whose internal thrust is precipitated from [motor] insufficiency [in the infants inability to move rapidly through space] to [the temporal] anticipation" of a future mastery dependent upon an unfragmented body-image ("Mirror" 4). In Lacan's mirror, this image coheres in space only to the degree that the infant can anticipate its mastery over itself at some future time.

This dynamic enables the subject produced in the cultural mirror to circulate in an exchange of desires factored in terms of financial considerations as well as the time-space quotient that under-codes the interchange of commodities. We already know that each object located in the mirror of manufactured cultural relations is assigned a plus or minus factor of desirability in a system that venerates the exchange, extracts an excess of surplus value as its end product, and generates massive confusion pertaining to the "relations between people with [the] relations to things" (Foley 87). In this way desire is tied to the production and circulation of subjects in accordance with the laws of the marketplace, where small segments of society attain a privileged position, where the majority become the proles who form the lower-middle class, and where scapegoated "others" are devalued as less-than-human. To sell the American public images of themselves which are sewn into the gestalt of cultural relations, an intermediary step must be layered into the iconic network to accomplish this goal. This intermediary step is predicated upon the internalization of numerous variables: the objectification of self-images that reinforce mass-produced generic identities and cultural stereotypes, the codification of image-generated desires as the desires of others, the wholesale distribution of the spatio-temporal dynamic used to police the workplace, the launching of promotional campaigns to influence the mass-production of images for iconic-consumption, and the polysemantical organization of institutional relations that operate systematically upon the exchange process. These are a few of the factors that combine to form the parallel modes of transfiguration capable of altering the ways we view ourselves.

In America various forms of production, dissemination, and consumption of images are mobilized to establish perceptual identities within institutional relations. Such images of the body politic couch ideas and values that are internally configured in the background commentary of the visual gestalt sold daily to Americans daily in overly simplistic sound bites. I use the word commentary here because, even in instances of primary identification wherein the infant traces its image in the mirror, the background gestalt contains icons that are "potential signifiers," whose meaning is realized retroactively at some future date. In the array of subsequent identifications constituted from images graphed onto the screen of lived experience, the iconic likeness used to identify one's body with oneself does not always remain separate from the narrative that inscribes events within its discursive structure. Because the process of identification is mapped onto a narrative accounting of events, the narrative becomes more than a formal construction of structural elements that orders relations between subjects.

Just as a narrative progression can be interrupted by temporal digressions that undermine the forward motion of its textual impetus, so too does the insertion of self-reflexive images in the diachronic unfolding of sequential events divert attention to image-prompts which enable the subject to verify itself within the narrative. This dynamic becomes easier to understand if we pause to consider the habitual behavior of Americans who ritualize the process of getting dressed in the morning. While many people examine the arrangement of their clothes after they get dressed each morning, most of them do not look down at their shirt or pants or dress or shoes and say, "This piece of clothing looks good or that piece of clothing looks bad." Instead of staring directly at each item of clothing to determine how it fits upon the body, most people turn their gaze toward the mirror to evaluate how their clothes enhance or detract from their appearance. Just as they interrupt their morning activities to view themselves in the mirror each day, so too do they ferret themselves out in instances of reflexive perception while engaged in the narrative activity of life. They detect themselves in the eyes of other people, in the way others treat them, in the other's gestures, body movements, and expressions. That is to say, *through indirection they find direction out* by interrupting the narrative trajectory of events with digressions that enable people to imagine themselves within the mirror of social interaction. In moments of narrative pause they recognize themselves in order to establish the parts they play in the episodic transformations that validate their positions in the spatio-temporal dynamic.

This narrative model gives the public a circuitous means of imagining itself, which parallels the tactic of foregrounding self-images to compare with the pictorial prompts manufactured and distributed for icon-consumption. The latter convention provides the subject with the opportunity to recognize itself in a constellation of marketed images, but we have seen that the subject can also locate its reflection in digressions that interrupt the sequence of structured events. Still there is another, more elliptical means of establishing and reestablishing one's reified identity: when cultural narratives become tiresomely repetitive and reliably predictable, the subject does not have to suspend the narrative progression to play peekaboo with itself, so recognizable is the clichéd iconography that acts as a default in the narrative accounting. When this is the case, the subject assesses her or his role by merely reading the narrative scripting of events to determine how s/he appears in the eyes of others. When the pattern of interaction becomes so familiar as to be predictable, the subject anticipates the script and her or his place within its inscription. This holds true for the televisual narrative as well, because, in our capitalistic society, both the dissemination of predictable narrative patterns and the production of images for consumption become part of the *narrative* exchange process wherein the subject discovers a momentary mythic certainty of consciousness.

Mapping Images onto the Narrative of Political Correctness

The theoretical model developed above enables us to determine how neoconservative mythologists have stylized narrative scenarios to induce icon-consumers to find themselves in texts produced for their reception. The implementation of this model prompts those who are suspicious of its declared purpose to pose an important question: what specific narratives are fashioned for our textual economy? To answer this question, I will turn to the poster boys of right-wing propaganda—George Will, Dinesh D'Souza, and Roger Kimball. In their reductive moral narratives of good versus evil, they have assumed the roles of protagonists who believe it is their business to defend the American public against indoctrination from the "communist fascist feminist deconstructionist multiculturalists," whom they cast as the overdetermined antagonists of their political satire (Berubé 130). In this yarn of grand "epic" proportions, these self-appointed guardians of high culture and transcendental values see themselves besieged by a group of "card-carrying multiculturalist[s]," whose "strident denunciations" and "ideological bias" are cast as un-American traits in morality plays neoconservative commentators produce for their target audience. If we study the specifics of the PC narrative, it becomes apparent that, in the protagonist/antagonist dichotomy, the former position is assigned to right-wing moral custodians who appropriate the narrator's privilege for themselves to relay their suprahistorical version of universal truth to the public.

Another element they factor into their moralistic fairy tale is the PC-storyline that produces headlines like these: "MLA critics have instituted censorious speech codes at colleges and universities across the country." According to this highly partisan claim, Multicultural Leftist Academics have censored students who repudiate "special privileges" for gays and lesbians, who deny people of color basic rights that Anglo-Americans have enjoyed for centuries, and who bar women from the circle of distributed political influence. In D'Souza's version of the PC narrative, students have felt so intimidated by their professors' political views that they have refrained from confronting them for fear of being sent to "sensitivity classes" where they would be indoctrinated in the requisite PC think of the 1990s. How does D'Souza backup such farfetched assertions? By making insupportable claims. With cosmic superiority oozing from his pen, he asserts opinions disguised as unequivocal facts. These "facts" support the premise of widespread student dissatisfaction based on a scant selection of interviews with neoconservative students, whose reactionary perspectives are made to stand for that of the college population as a whole. By examining such tactics, we can determine that all of D'Souza's observations are grounded in a narrative ruse enabling him to read minds as if he had the omniscient powers of a political Messiah.

The last of these claims reveals how the narrative of political correctness is sustained by right-wing ideologues who pretend their point of view is apolitical, if not neutral, even when it is advanced solely for the purpose of striking out against their adversaries. The "political correctniks" they demonize are always subjective, ideological, dogmatic antagonists who repeatedly block any advancement within the profession "according to merit" (Kimball 65). On the other hand, the "judicious," "objective," and "level-headed" neoconservative protagonists defend the ideals of disinterested criticism, universal human interest, and transcendental values. Such ideals are exalted by these fundamentalist politicos even as they demean the "agents" of political correctness as ideological profiteers who have infiltrated our society for the purpose of toppling it. This comedic depiction becomes even more preposterous when neocon artists portray themselves as objective and apolitical *as* they fabricate tales of political inequality on campus when, in fact, they have gained an enormous amount of power outside the university. At the time of writing, Republicans constitute a majority of governors, senators, and representatives in the House, yet they cry foul because their attempts to organize students on colleges and universities across the country have met with stiff resistance. Although they exercise increasing power in government circles and in the media (on talk radio in particular), their inability to consolidate a base at the university has left them so embittered they have declared war against the "activist fringe" that opposes them there. Here is George Will on this issue:

> Such skirmishes in the curricula wars occur because campuses have become refuges for radicals who want universities to be thoroughly politicized as they are. Like broken records stashed in the nation's attic in 1968, these politicized professors say:
> America is oppressive, imposing subservience on various victim groups. The culture is permeated with racism, sexism, heterosexism, classism (oppression of the working class), so the first task of universities is "consciousness-raising." This is done with "diversity education," which often is an attempt to produce intellectual uniformity by promulgating political orthodoxy. (259)

Part of Will's strategy is obvious: to link the long-haired radicals of the 60s with the "politicized professors" who currently work in the factories of "junkthink," where they supposedly entertain a comprehensive plan to impose their rigid belief system upon others. Neoconservatives like Will often try to inoculate right-wing critics against charges of racism, homophobia, and elitism, which they deny when pretending to mirror universal truth for the public. To accomplish this goal, George Will ("America's favorite reactionary nerd") invariably takes the offensive, anticipating the critique that will be used against him and his ultraright allies (Kavanagh 318). To this end, Will recontextualizes narrative details by anticipating any damaging criticism, suturing it within a lexicon of his own right-wing making, and casting scorn upon those who would criticize him.

Against the charge of unfairly appropriating universal truth for their own political gains, right-wing critics like Will and Kimball must first establish that values can indeed be considered universal. To establish this claim, Roger Kimball scoffs at the "dollops of deconstructivist or poststructuralist theory" who contend that there are no global, let alone universal, truths that guarantee fundamental value-systems. In the narrative of political correctness this argument crystallizes around the issue of the canon, which supposedly houses great literature inscribed by "masters" with a direct hotline to universal truths that preserve the "classical heritage of mankind" (Howe 160). These "masters" have become literary monuments erected to the white male tradition. Although it seems quite suspicious that Anglo male writers have traditionally been lauded as the only ones capable of generating millennial "staying power," right-wing theorists assure us that canonical literature has an ever widening comprehensiveness reflected in its

> ability to speak to us *across* the barriers of time, geography, social system, religious belief, to say nothing of the currently favored barriers of sex, class, race, and ethnic origin. "Transcendent," like "universalist," is a naughty word for the politically correct multiculturalist largely because, if taken seriously, it suggests that the qualities that unite us as human beings are more important than the contingencies that separate us as social and political agents. (Kimball 69)

Notice how Kimball pretends to be a "custodian of Western culture" who protests against "the irruption of politics into something that has always been political" (Gates 195). Enacting a compulsive pattern of defensive self-promotion, Kimball never tires of launching preventative strikes against the reviled PC enemy. Through such strategies he hopes to snooker the public into believing that God is a cultural neoconservative, that right-wing mythmakers have the ability to transcend petty political concerns, and that they can conflate themselves with the omniscient narrators who detail the PC chronology cooked up by think-tank Republicans. As Jon Wiener states in *Professors, Politics and Pop*, groups like the John M. Olin Foundation have poured "millions of dollars into universities in an effort to reshape the curriculums" and bestowed large sums on the likes of D'Souza, Kimball, and Martin Anderson so they could continue to churn out their propaganda (99). That is why many neoconservative storylines state the same objectives, present identical narrative details, and invite the public to find themselves within a repetitive fantasy of intersubjective relations. This is often accomplished in sound-bit jargon disseminated as an ideological narrative that passes itself off as a full-fledged research tract. These tracts are given the stamp of authenticity because their work appears in hardbound books published by presses that, interested in increasing their profits, lend their names to sanction such prescripted propaganda as credible.

In these quick-read, scantily researched texts, neoconservative authority is reinforced by a narrative omniscience that purports to be objective in relating events to readers. The most obvious appropriation of the omniscient narrator occurs in D'Souza's work when he writes about the Afrocentric menace whose "black supremacist" policies are dividing the American masses against themselves. As D'Souza puts it, a "liberal education should be about integration, about bringing groups together"; however, the Afrocentric professorate have instituted the big chill of "a new separatism on campus, what some have called a new segregation on campus" (30). When fabricating this narrative, D'Souza invokes an Orwellian doublethink in which "'diversity' really means strict intellectual conformity, and 'tolerance' is reserved exclusively for those who subscribe to one's own perspective"—one that precludes all middle Americans who believe in God, country, family, and that idealized slice of corporate pie (64). In this upside-down world where deceptive stereotyping is the norm, neoconservative mythmakers like D'Souza pit their religious idealism against academics whom they parody in malicious distortions that form the theoretical particulars of their promotional campaign. For instance, look at what D'Souza has to say on the issue of racial separatism:

> I'm a native of India. I was raised in Bombay. I came to this country in 1978. I became a citizen last year. I'm a first-generation immigrant to the United States. I think that America is becoming a multiracial society and *the whole issue is transcending black and white.* We are going to have four or more groups, whites, blacks, Hispanics, and Asians in this diverse culture [notice how he leaves out Native Americans]. It's *very* important to have a fair set of rules to arbitrate the differences among these groups. And the problem is that universities and to some extent society at large are moving away from *a fair or neutral set of principles* and are engaging in a politics of expediency, of racial rationing, of racial preference. I think this is a formula for division, for Balkanization, and ultimately for racial hostility. (my emphasis, 35)

D'Souza, who came to this country after the great civil-rights conflicts of the 1950s and 1960s, proves here that he has a selective memory. He gives weight and gravity to the ornamental ideal that America is "the home of the brave and the land of the free"—an old cliché that has been belied by the treatment of, among others, African-Americans, Native Americans, and women in our country's brief history. D'Souza has forgotten that African-Americans were brought here like cattle, dragged from their homelands, torn from their families so they could toil in the fields as slaves in a foreign land. He has also blotted from memory the fact that Native Americans were either slaughtered in the name of westward expansion or rounded up, then herded into societal cages euphemistically called reservations. And D'Souza denies that all women—Asian-American, Native American, Hispanic American, African-American, and Anglo American—were legally disenfranchised, kept from voting until the early half of this century. Such inequality considered, it makes one wonder how free D'Souza's America really is and how brave were those who committed such acts of enslavement.

In *Moving the Centre*, Ngugi wa Thiong'o provides a category for people like D'Souza who are quick to deny that the "wealth of the West is rooted in the poverty of the rest of us," that, in fact, "Western Europe and North America accumulated capital through the slave trade, slave labour and colonial labour"

(118). According to Ngugi, such a deep-rooted and pervasive pathological denial can only be accomplished through the implementation of ideological methods of persuasion: (1) an "obscurantism" that not only hides the economic advantages of the few in society who rule the many, but that inverts the terms of gratitude so workers actually feel guilty when they recognize the capitalistic engine could not run without their labor power; (2) a strategy of "divide and conquer" wherein workers are pitted against other workers who defend their job security against those whom they could join in solidarity; (3) a form of "political domination" that is virtually transparent in countries like South Africa but camouflaged in the Euro-American orbit where ideological brainwashing is implemented to convince workers to betray one another; (4) finally, as a result of these three stratagems, an "exploitation" increases profit and accumulated wealth for both the empowered elite and those crossover figures who support their cause; (5) unfortunately, this leads to a cycle of "oppression" built on an institutionalized racism that pits "the whites of European stock" against "the dark races of the earth" (Ngugi 116–120). But there is an exception to this rule, and D'Souza fits the case:

> The Western bourgeoisie has its allies among the dominated nations of Asia, Africa and South America. This is because they have brought up, from among the colonies, semi-colonies and neo-colonies, a native elite imbued with an almost pathological self-hatred and contempt through years of racist cultural engineering. Racism has thus produced an elite endowed with what Frantz Fanon once described as an incurable wish for the permanent identification with the West. (120)

These turncoats are like Gulliver in Book 4 of *Gulliver's Travels*, for in that segment he visits the land of the Houyhnhnms, undergoes a cross-species identification, identifies with the perspective of the Houyhnhnms, and sees himself as a Yahoo, which leaves him intolerant once he encounters human beings again. For after he returns home to his family, Gulliver prefers the smell of horses to humans, suffers to eat with his wife and children in the same room, but enjoys conversing with horses at "least four hours every day" (Swift 234). While Gulliver undergoes a cross-species identification that leads him to detest members of his own species, D'Souza undergoes a cross-racial identification that leaves him white-identified. Because of this cross-over identification, he can comfortably fight on the side of a Euro-American elite that has traditionally oppressed people of color. Moreover, this cross-racial identification enables him to entertain a comforting fantasy of solidarity with whites who use him as a lever to divide and conquer their enemies. Isn't it obvious that, because D'Souza is a person of color, it becomes more difficult to accuse him of racism? For as the white powerbrokers in South Africa are fond of saying, when people like D'Souza attack others of his own race, it is a black on black affair. This is a most useful diversion to give cover to ambitious white social engineers.

When one looks beneath the cover of D'Souza's camouflaged opinions, it becomes readily apparent that he is really pushing his readers toward a perceptible goal that has little to do with objectivity, universality, or neutral reportage. Instead he is a huckster selling a fictive text that reinforces the right-wing narrative pushed by the neoconservative minority in the last fifteen years:

> I'm in favor of a multicultural curriculum that emphasizes what Matthew Arnold called the best that has been thought and said. Non-Western cultures have produced great works that are worthy of study, and I think young people should know something about the rise of Islamic fundamentalism. To do so, it's helpful to be exposed to the Koran. Young people should know something about the rise of Japanese capitalism. Is there a Confucian ethic behind the success of Asian entrepreneurship in the same way we hear about Max Weber, the Protestant ethic, and the spirit of capitalism? (31)

Is there any wonder that a man selling the American dream of making millions of dollars would foreground "entrepreneurship," the "rise of Japanese capitalism," and "the Protestant [work] ethic" as distinguishable signs that celebrate "the spirit of capitalism"? In this amalgamation of corporatist dogma, multiculturalism becomes a code word for fast-capital allied with religious foundationalism, in this case, with the celebration of "Islamic fundamentalism" (31). For D'Souza's brand of multiculturalism venerates a reactionary professionalism that marries international capitalism with a market-driven fundamentalist politics, whose purpose is to influence American consumption habits by targeting specified markets to placate consumers.

In this regard D'Souza takes a page out of Pat Robertson's book, for Robertson markets himself as a minister while he sells products to members of his flock, a ready-made audience if there ever was one. In fact since 1990 Robertson has amassed a business empire that grossed over one hundred million dollars (Primetime). In 1990 the nonprofit Family Channel was sold to a company Robertson had formed with the backing of TCI Cable, the telecommunications octopus which desired that the Robertsons retain controlling stock of a new company created to buy the Family Channel. For a stock certificate of $183,000, TCI gave Robertson controlling interest in this new company, an investment that has recently skyrocketed, enabling the Robertson family to gross over one hundred million dollars! Later, CBN recognized that the Family Channel was making so much money it had to be sold to preserve CBN's tax-exempt status: It "got a good deal, cash, stock and other benefits now worth 'in excess of an astounding $600 million dollars" (Primetime). With this money, Pat Robertson, who often rails against the Hollywood elite, bought the MTM (Mary Tyler

Moore) Studio as well as the Ice Capades (Primetime). As if this were not enough, Robertson has now entered into another corporate venture–KaloVita–a company which markets "vitamins, cosmetics and discount shopping coupons" to a gullible public which believes that Robertson is more interested in the immortal soul rather than the ol' mighty dollar.

Although he is a religious leader, Pat Robertson has been able to profit from his business dealings because the narrative framing the American Dream connects corporate capitalism with religion and politics. Earlier in this book we saw how right-wing critics linked Marxism with other terms they sought to stigmatize: liberal, political correctnik, multiculturalist, Afrocentrist, and victim. By evoking one term, neoconservatives hoped to delegitimize the others that followed in its wake. In this way they tried to dissuade the American public from identifying with those cardboard caricatures who were associated with them. Neoconservative imagemakers have succeeded to some extent, though there is still a shrinking population of self-professed liberals in this country. But they have had success in this regard by framing these terms within the two operative metanarratives they have summoned to contextualize their project.

For the demeaning caricature of the politically correct academic is but one facet in a larger adversarial metanarrative. After the Second World War a marriage of sorts was established between the two predominant American metanarratives–the Christian promise of Christ's return and the corporate fable of capitalism's triumphant ordering of world relations. The overriding metanarrative which has structured Christian thought since Christ's crucifixion is the promise of a second coming ushering in a new millennium. This moment of ahistorical transformation will occur after a religious war to end all religious wars, a global conflict between the forces of good and evil that, ironically, will give way to an unprecedented period of love and peace. This legendary site of after-world identity-formation is a most unlikely candidate to be paired with the narrative of international capitalism, which has emerged in its technological incarnation in the latter part of the twentieth century. The customary codes of fast-capital present an improbable corollary to the Christian myth of the paradisal completion of history in the not-distant future. Why, one might ask, is it improbable? Because, throughout the twentieth century it has been common knowledge that "godless" capitalism would sell whatever it could to whoever would buy its mass produced products. And that includes the sale of worldly identities which defy intergenerational Christian codes of conduct traditionally evoked to insure the smooth transition of theological influence. For international capitalism thrives on the principle of planned obsolescence, which requires the recreation of goods and value-invested identities that have need of these particular goods every so many years. Because capitalism must repeatedly sponsor new fantasies that depend on the production, circulation, and consumption of the latest goods from secular heaven, it is peculiar, to say the least, that its metanarrative would join at the neoconservative fork in the road with a corporate crossover which, in the last stages of the twentieth century, would act as its co-guarantor.

Considering that money constitutes the heart and soul of a commodity system, it seems surreal that neoconservative fundamentalists would be so pro-business. Yet that's the case. In fact, it is one of the most predominant aspects of McReaganism, this unholy match of opposing positions inaugurated as a means to accomplish conservative ends. How else could we explain the inexplicable reliance of neoconservatives on postmodern hyperreal sound-bite technologies? Or the outrageous contradictions posed by the National Association of Scholars, who deny that "the traditional curriculum 'excludes' the contributions of all but males of European descent" as they back the male-whites-only canonical list offered by Charles Sykes and Brad Miner in *The Nation Review College Guide* (quoted in "Is the Curriculum Biased?"). Many people in the academy have come to expect such inconsistencies, for how else could one explain the National Association of Scholars pretending, at one moment, to be "in favor of ethnic studies, the study of non-Western cultures, and the study of special problems of women and minorities," while, in the next, it criticizes multicultural studies as an attempt to add "inferior works" to the curriculum ("Is the Curriculum Biased?"). These examples of double-talk show in microcosm how the overarching metanarratives of fundamentalist neoconservativism brought forth during the age of Reaganism are at odds with themselves yet are presented as if they had no contradictions.

Right-wing critics reinforce these white, middle-class metanarratives over and over again to exploit the racist and sexist social arrangements currently in existence in America. The metanarratives linking multinational capitalism with fundamental(ist) social fantasies privileging those who are currently politically empowered acquire even more influence once the conservators of past traditions couple them with media images disseminated to their target audiences. As we have seen, this happens because the production of manufactured cultural images can be packaged in such a way that icon-consumers will ignore their contrived, made-up character. By ignoring the fabricated aspect of the manufactured image and the ideological identity between narrative occurrences, members of the public can better identify with the programmed narrative agenda which contextualizes images distributed for group-identification. If the combined metanarrative of Christian-capitalism is eventually accepted by enough people as the "natural" locale of identity-formation, triumphant neoconservatives will be able to sell mercantilized images that insure a transcendent metareality guaranteeing the ego-ideal as the God of commercial relations. In this way, a commodified deity can be appropriated for political as well as religious purposes by groups that decry the apocalypse-now of postmodern times, yet are doing everything in their power to insure that a telecommunicational Creator guarantees the paradisaic project of right-wing information-processing.

Notes

1. This excerpt, which includes sections of psychoanalytic theory that my book, *Projected Political Correctness*, does not, has been reprinted with the permission of the University of Minnesota Press.

2. At this juncture, I have chosen to equate the terms *ego-ideal* and *superego*, as did Freud in *The Ego and the Id*; this will enable us to understand Lacan's distinction between the ideal ego and the ego-ideal, two developmental models that emphasize the distinction between the love-object and the dreaded figure of prohibition. Laplanche and Pontalis point out in *The Language of Psycho-analysis* that, although "the super-ego is considered to be indistinguishable from the ego-ideal," in *The Ego and the Id*, "the super-ego's relation to the ego is not exhausted by the precept: 'You ought to be like this (like your father).' It also comprises the prohibition: 'You *may not be* like this (like your father)—that is, you may not do all that he does; some things are his prerogative.'" For other psychoanalytic theorists like Nunberg, the "ego-ideal and the prohibitive agency are quite separate." He makes a distinction between the motives they induce in the ego— "Whereas the ego submits to the super-ego out of fear of punishment, it submits to the ego-ideal out of love." Regarding their origins, Nunberg states that "the ego-ideal is said to be formed principally on the model of loved objects, while the super-ego is formed on that of dreaded figures." For Lacan, however, the ideal ego originates in the narcissistic formation of the mirror phase while the ego-ideal remains distinct from it until one psychic agency is graphed over the other. As Bruce Fink explains, Lacan later notes the difference between the "ego (the imaginary other [ideal ego] and the Other as desire [ego ideal])," which he distinguishes from "the Freudian superego (the Other as Jouissance)" (*The Lacanian Subject*). This distinction is useful when one considers the relationship between the gaze and the ideal ego, which coheres in the mirror as a result of the identification between the ego and its virtual image in the looking-glass.

Works Cited

Barthelme, Donald. *The Dead Father*. New York: Penguin Books, 1975.

Berubé, Michael. "Public Image Limited: Political Correctness and the Media's Big Lie." *Debating P.C.: The Controversy over Political Correctness on College Campuses*. Edited by Paul Berman. New York: Dell, 1992.

Bhabha, Homi K. *Nation and Narration*. Edited by Homi K. Bhabha. London: Routledge, 1990.

Borch-Jacobsen, Mikkel. *Lacan: the Absolute Master*. Translated by Douglas Brick. Stanford: Stanford University Press, 1991.

Butler, Judith. *Gender Trouble: Feminism and the Subversion of Identity*. New York: Routledge, 1990.

Clément, Catherine. "Warnings." *New French Feminisms: An Anthology*. Edited by Elaine Marks and Isabelle de Courtivron. New York: Schocken Books, 1981.

Crimp, Douglas. "The Photographic Activity of Postmodernism." *Postmodernism: A Reader*. Edited by Thomas Docherty. New York: Columbia University Press, 1993.

de Lauretis, Teresa. *Technologies of Gender: Essays on Theory, Film, and Fiction.* Bloomington: Indiana University Press, 1987.

D'Souza Dinesh and Robert MacNeil. "The Big Chill? Interview with Dinesh D'Souza." *Debating P.C.: The Controversy over Political Correctness on College Campuses.* Edited by Paul Berman. New York: Dell, 1992: 29-39.

Feldstein, Richard. *Projected Political Correctness.* Forthcoming from University of Minnesota Press, 1995.

Fink, Bruce. *The Lacanian Subject: Between Language and Jouissance.* Princeton: Princeton University Press, 1995.

Foley, Duncun. *A Dictionary of Marxist Thought.* Edited by Tom Bottomore. Cambridge: Harvard University Press, 1983.

Freud, Sigmund. *The Ego and the Id. The Standard Edition of the Complete Psychological Works of Sigmund Freud,* vol. 19. Edited by James Strachey. 24 vols. London: Hogarth, 1953-74: 3-66.

Gallop, Jane. "Where to Begin." *Reading Lacan.* Ithaca: Cornell University Press, 1985.

Gates, Henry Louis, Jr. "Whose Canon is it, Anyway?" *Debating P.C.: The Controversy over Political Correctness on College Campuses.* Edited by Paul Berman. New York: Dell, 1992: 190-200.

Giddens, Anthony. "Modernism and Postmodernism." *Postmodernism: A Reader.* Edited by Patricia Waugh. New York: Edward Arnold, 1992.

Hassan, Ihab. "Toward a Concept of Postmodernism." *Postmodernism: A Reader.* Edited by Thomas Docherty. New York: Columbia University Press, 1993.

Howe, Irving. "The Value of the Canon." *Debating P.C.: The Controversy over Political Correctness on College Campuses.* Edited by Paul Berman. New York: Dell, 1992: 153-171.

Huyssen. Andreas. *After the Great Divide: Modernism, Mass Culture, Postmodernism.* Bloomington: Indiana University Press, 1986.

Irigaray, Luce. *je, tu, nous: Toward a Culture of Difference.* Translated by Alison Martin. New York: Routledge, 1993.

Kavanagh, James H. "Ideology." *Critical Terms for Literary Study.* Edited by Frank Lentricchia and Thomas McLaughlin. Chicago: University of Chicago Press, 1990.

Kimball, Roger. "The Periphery V. The Center: The MLA in Chicago," 61-84. *Debating PC: The Controversy on College Campuses.* Edited by Paul Berman. New York: Dell, 1992.

"Kingdom of Pat." *Primetime Live*. ABC. WPRI, Providence. October 27, 1994.

Lacan. Jacques. "Aggressivity in psychoanalysis." *Écrits: A Selection*. Translated by Alan Sheridan. New York: Norton, 1977.

———. "The mirror stage as formative of the function of the I." *Écrits: A Selection*. Translated by Alan Sheridan. New York: Norton, 1977.

———. *The Seminar of Jacques Lacan: Book I: Freud's Papers on Technique, 1953– 1954*. Edited by Jacques-Alain Miller. Translated by John Forrester. New York: Norton, 1988.

———. *The Seminar of Jacques Lacan: Book III: The Psychoses 1955–1956*. Edited by Jacques-Alain Miller. Translated by Russell Grigg. New York, Norton, 1993.

Laplanche, J., and J.-B. Pontalis. *The Language of Psycho-Analysis*. Trans. Donald Nicholson-Smith. New York: Norton, 1973.

McGowan, John. "Postmodernism." *The Johns Hopkins Guide to Literary Theory & Criticism*. Edited by Michael Groden and Martin Kreiswirth. Baltimore: Johns Hopkins University Press, 1994: 586–587.

Muller, John P., and William J. Richardson. *Lacan and Language: A Reader's Guide to Écrits*. New York: International Universities Press, 1982.

National Association of Scholars. "Is the Curriculum Biased?" A Handout Circulated at Rhode Island College.

Ngugi, wa Thiong'o. *Moving the Center: The Struggle for Cultural Freedoms*. Portsmouth: Heinemann, 1993.

Silverman, Kaja. *Male Subjectivity at the Margins*. New York: Routledge, 1992.

Six Degrees of Separation. Directed by Fred Schepisi. With Stockard Channing, Will Smith, and Donald Sutherland. Metro-Goldwyn-Mayer, 1994.

Spivak, Gayatri Chakravorty. "Can the Subaltern Speak?" *Marxism and the Interpretation of Culture*. Edited by Cary Nelson and Lawrence Grossberg. Urbana: University of Illinois Press, 1988.

Swift, Jonathan. *Gulliver's Travels*. Edited by Louis A. Landa. Boston: Houghton Mifflin, 1960.

Wiener, Jon. *Professor, Politics and Pop*. London: Verso, 1991.

Will, George F. "Radical English." *Debating P.C.: The Controversy over Political Correctness on College Campuses*. Edited by Paul Berman. New York: Dell, 1992: 258– 61.

The Writer's Toolkit. Version 2.01. Systems Compatibility Corporation, 1991.

Žižek, Slavoj. *The Sublime Object of Ideology*. London: Verso, 1989.

PART IV

REAL

THE NATURE OF UNCONSCIOUS THOUGHT OR WHY NO ONE EVER READS LACAN'S POSTFACE TO THE "SEMINAR ON 'THE PURLOINED LETTER'"

∞

Bruce Fink

Thirty-five years after the publication of Lacan's "Seminar on 'The Purloined Letter,'" some of the notions contained therein seem to be fairly widely understood, most notably the structural repetition of scenes within Poe's text and the feminizing effect of possessing the letter. The letter is seen to take on a degree of autonomy: it determines characters' positions, reversing in successive scenes who can see, who cannot, and who takes advantage of the conjuncture thus constituted.

But what has been made of all the diagrams and mathematical-like symbols mobilized in what Lacan refers to simply as the "*suite*"? Most readers,[1] I would venture to say, have not found the postface exactly to their liking, lacking as it does the literary appeal of what precedes it in the *Écrits*. It presents, however, certain developments which go well beyond what we find in the body of the original text. For here Lacan begins to deploy his characteristically psychoanalytic epistemology which turns habitual Anglo-American ways of thinking about knowledge, language, and reality on their head. I will use Lacan's inventions in this postface, already sketched out in Seminar II, *The Ego in Freud's Theory and in the Technique of Psychoanalysis*, as a congenial explanation of the workings of the symbolic order as it functions in the unconscious.

It seems to me that there is no other text in the Lacanian opus that so clearly goes beyond the work on the symbolic order done by structuralists such as Lévi-Strauss and Jakobson, and even well beyond Lacan's own prior work on language, metaphor and metonymy, and the creation of meaning. The ideas presented in this afterword show the symbolic order or signifying chain to be still more autonomous than previously imagined, usurping even more of the functions usually assigned to the ego and the subject, and yet at the same time point to the limits of the symbolic order: the latter is shown to revolve around something else, to be centered or decentered in relation to someThing which is not of the realm of meaning, being neither sign, symbol, nor signifier.

Even without yet introducing the notion of subjectivity, the limits Lacan traces here of the symbolic order already in and of themselves prove that Lacan is not a structuralist: while extending ever further the impact of structure and otherness in the activity of speaking beings, Lacan, at the same time, through his notion of that someThing that is not symbolized and in fact resists symbolization, points to the limits of structure, suggesting there is something "above and beyond" structure, something "outside of" and radically different from or in excess of structure, and which nevertheless can be seen at work "within" structure itself.

A certain amount of mathematical gymnastics is required to follow Lacan's argument in his postface to the "Seminar on 'The Purloined Letter,'" and it should be viewed as neither superfluous nor gratuitous. For it is perfectly in keeping with Lacan's view of the nature of "unconscious thought processes": they are logico-mathematical in nature and involve various degrees of cyphering. The section below presents a vastly simplified model of the "language" Lacan develops which should ultimately suffice to follow the more conceptual discussion in the section entitled "Randomness and Memory." "Recreational Mathematics" lays out the complete model in all its complexity.

Heads or Tails

The model Lacan provides in the postface under consideration here involves a certain technicity which I will attempt to lay out as clearly as possible through the use of a simplified example.

We assume at the outset that, in flipping a well-balanced, unloaded coin, there is no way to predict, at any one toss, whether the result will be heads or tails. Following Lacan's non-arbitrary choice of "+" and "−" for heads and tails, a random string of toss results can be broken down in a variety of ways. Consider, for example, the following chain:

```
1 2 3 4 5 6 7 8 9   Toss Numbers
+ + − − + − − − +   Heads/Tails Chain
```

The "toss numbers" refer to the first toss of the coin, the second toss, the third toss, and so on, while the "heads/tails chain" presents the result of each toss: "+" stands for heads and "–" for tails.

The rationale for referring to this string of toss throws as a chain, whereas their results are a priori altogether independent (the second throw having the same 50/50 chance of showing up heads or tails whatever the result of the first throw), derives from the fact that we proceed to group the signs by pairs along the chain. There are four possible pair combinations: $++, --, +-,$ and $-+$.

$$
\begin{array}{lllllllll}
1 & 2 & 3 & 4 & 5 & 6 & 7 & 8 & 9 \\
+ & + & - & - & + & - & - & - & + \\
& 1 & & 3 & & 2 & & 2 &
\end{array}
$$

Toss Numbers
Heads/Tails Chain
Numeric Matrix Category

Let us assign the pair $++$ the number 1 (see the "numeric matrix category" line above). This is the first level of coding we are going to introduce, and it marks the origin of the symbolic system we are creating here; I will refer to this first level as our numeric matrix. The two alternating combinations ($+-$ and $-+$) will be designated by the number 2. And the pair $--$ will receive the designation 3.

$$
\begin{array}{c|c|c}
1 & 2 & 3 \\
\hline
++ & \begin{array}{c} +- \\ -+ \end{array} & --
\end{array}
$$

However, a still more chain-like aspect will result if we group the toss results by *overlapping* pairs.

$$
\underset{\underset{3}{1}}{+} \; \overset{\overset{2}{2}}{+} \; - \; - \; + \; - \; - \; - \; + \qquad \text{Heads/Tails Chain}
$$

In the above chain, we see that our first element is $++$, a 1 combination; taking the second and third toss results, we have $+-$, to be noted 2; the third and fourth ones, $--$, a 3 combination, the fourth and fifth ones, $-+$, a 2, and so on.

Following Lacan's notation (in *Écrits* 1966, p. 47, footnote 1) we can write these figures just below the heads/tails chain; here, each numeric matrix category (1, 2, or 3) refers to the plus or minus sign directly above it, taken in conjunction with the plus or minus sign immediately to that sign's left.

$$
\begin{array}{ccccccccc}
+ & + & - & - & + & - & - & - & + \\
& 1 & 2 & 3 & 2 & 2 & 3 & 3 & 2
\end{array}
$$

Heads/Tails Chain
Numeric Matrix Category

It is already clear at this point that a category 1 set of tosses ($++$) cannot be immediately followed in the lower line (that is, that of category numbers) by a category 3 set, as the second throw in a category 1 is necessarily a plus, whereas the first throw in a category 3 must be a minus. Similarly, though a category 2 can be followed by a 1, 2, or 3, a category 3 cannot be immediately followed by a category 1, for the former ends in a minus while the latter must begin with a plus.

We have thus already come up with *a way of grouping tosses* (a "symbolic matrix") *which prohibits certain combinations* (*viz.*, 1 followed by 3, and 3 followed by 1). This obviously does not in the least require that a heads toss be followed by any one particular kind of toss: in reality, a heads may still just as easily be followed by another heads as by a tails. *We have generated an impossibility in our signifying chain*—we have not determined the outcome of any particular toss. This amounts to a grammatical rule, akin to i before e except after c (except that the rule we have just created knows no exception); note that most rules of spelling and grammar concern the way letters and words are strung or *chained* together, dictating what can and cannot precede one letter or term and what can and cannot follow it.

Suppose now that we know the first pair of tosses fell into category 1 and the third pair was a category 3. The series can be easily reconstructed: $+ + - -$, and we can have no doubt that the second pair of tosses fell into category 2. If we suppose anew that we began with a 1 (that is, a category 1 pair) and that position four (that is, the fourth overlapping pair) was occupied by a 1, there are clearly only two possibilities open to us:

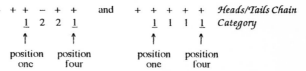

And in neither of them is a category 3 combination visible: a type 3 combination is, in fact, *impossible* here. It is also clear that, if there are not simply 1s in the "numeric chain," there must be *an even number of 2s* if we are to ever find a 1 in the chain again after the first one, the first 2 introducing a minus sign $(+ -)$, while the second (or even numbered 2) moves the chain back to positive from negative $(- +)$.

```
+  +  -  -  +  -  +  +
1  2  3  2  2  2  1 =  four 2s.
```

```
+  +  -  -  -  +  -  -  +  -  -  -  -  +  -  +  -  -  -  +  +
1  2  3  3  2  2  3  2  2  3  3  3  2  2  2  2  3  3  2  1  =  ten 2s.
```

Here the chain prohibits the appearance of a second 1 until an even number of 2s has turned up. In this sense we may say that *the chain remembers or keeps track of its previous components.*

The example found in Lacan's post-scriptum is far more complicated than the one I have provided here, as it groups the coin tosses into triplets instead of pairs, and proceeds to superimpose upon them a second symbolic matrix. The simpler 1, 2, 3 matrix described above (1) results in impossibilities related to the *order* in which the category numbers can appear as well as to *which* of them can appear if certain positions are pre-defined, and (2) records within itself or "remembers" its previous components. Thus, we have at our disposal a simple symbolic coin-toss overlay which suits our needs. For it not only comports an elementary though consequent grammar, but a built-in memory function as well, primitive as it may be.

Still we should not lose sight of what Lacan claims in Seminar IV on *Object Relations*: "A minimum of terms is necessary to the functioning of a symbolic system . . . [and] it is certainly not only three" (p. 261), a similar point being stated rather differently in the *Écrits*: "A quadripartite structure can always be required—from the standpoint of the unconscious—in the construction of a subjective ordering" (p. 774).

Which suggests that our three-sign system (1, 2, 3) is *not* ultimately adequate. This is why, in the next section, I provide a long and detailed explanation of the workings of the *numeric* matrix found in the afterword to the "Seminar on 'The Purloined Letter,'" as well as of Lacan's laconically laid out second *alphabetic* overlay, bringing out the pertinent features one finds therein of this four-sign system (along with a couple of typographical errors in the French text). The reader particularly averse to mathematical presentations may wish to proceed directly to the section entitled "Probability and Possibility" below, skipping "Recreational Mathematics" for the moment, coming back to it only after having gleaned the essential elements of the concept of structure I develop further on. I should nevertheless mention that while the 1, 2, 3 matrix outlined above suffices to illustrate *some* of what Lacan is up to here, certain constructions in later sections remain somewhat opaque without the fuller version presented immediately hereafter. I have tried to make the presentation which follows as simple and straightforward as possible.

"Recreational Mathematics"

Lacan's exposition of his two matrixes is laconically confusing, but his moves can nevertheless be laid out rather simply:

Step One: Coin tosses are grouped by threes, each grouping falling into one of the following categories:

1 (identical)	2 (odd)	3 (alternating)
+ + +	+ + − − − +	+ − +
− − −	+ − − − + +	− + −

Lacan refers to the triplets falling under categories 1 and 3 as "symmetrical," and to those falling under category 2 as "asymmetrical"–thus, the appellation "odd" for these latter. This will be important further on.

Taking a string of toss results, we group and label them as follows:

The first three toss results (+ + +) fall into category 1; the next *overlapping* group of three (+ + –) falls into group 2; the third (+ – +) is of type 3; etc. I will abbreviate this as follows:

$$+ \quad + \quad + \quad - \quad + \quad + \quad - \quad - \quad + \quad - \quad - \quad - \quad - \quad -$$
$$1 \quad 2 \quad 3 \quad 2 \quad 2 \quad 2 \quad 2 \quad 3 \quad 2 \quad 1 \quad 1 \quad 1 \; ...$$

The reader will easily observe that one cannot move directly from a 1 to a 3 (or from a 3 to a 1) without a 2 intervening to begin (or remove) alternation of signs. All other direct succession combinations are possible. Lacan provides the following graph (called 1–3 Network, p. 48 of the *Écrits* 1966) to visualize all the allowable moves:

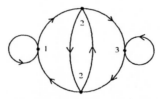

(Note that this same graph applies in all respects to the simplified two-sign toss-grouping matrix described in the preceding section.)

Step Two: We now lay a symbolic matrix upon this numeric one:

Greek Letter Matrix I

α	β	γ	δ
1_1, 1_3	1_2	2_2	2_1
3_3, 3_1	3_2		2_3

Here the blank space between the pairs of numbers must be filled by a third number. Each Greek letter thus regroups the first-level groupings by *threes*, e.g., α covers the cases where we find two 1s (under the plus/minus line) *separated by another number.*

$$+ \quad + \quad + \quad + \quad + \quad - \quad - \quad - \quad + \quad - \quad - \quad - \quad - \quad -$$
$$\underbrace{1 \quad 1 \quad 1}_{\alpha} \quad 2 \quad 2 \quad 1 \quad 2 \quad 3 \quad 2 \quad 1 \quad 1 \quad 1 \; ...$$

In this case, the middle number must be a 1, for, as we saw above, it cannot (a) be a 3, it being impossible to go directly from a 1 to a 3 configuration—there must be a 2 in between—nor (b) a 2, as we need two 2s in a row to be able to return to a 1 (one 2 alone is not sufficient). If we fill in the blanks correctly, we can provide a more detailed table than that provided above:

Greek Letter Matrix II

α	β	γ	δ
111, 123	112, 122	212, 232	221, 211
333, 321	332, 322	222	223, 233

The most important things, however, for us to keep track of, for the moment, are the first and third numbers in each triplet.

Lacan does not say this in so many words (or not explicitly enough, at any rate, to be easily understood),[2] but any other way of regrouping these first order symbols reduces the rest of what follows to sheer nonsense. The strings of numbers must be regrouped in the following way: considering once again our toss-result line (that is, the +/− line) and the number coding line (second line), first we group the first and third numbers, then the second and fourth, then the third and fifth, and so on, adding a symbol below each linked pair to represent it:

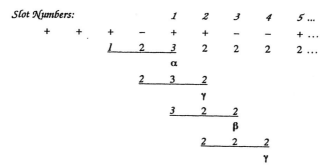

I will abbreviate this schema as follows:

$$
\begin{array}{cccccccccccc}
+ & + & + & - & + & + & - & - & + & - & - & - & - & - \\
1 & 2 & 3 & 2 & 2 & 2 & 3 & 2 & 1 & 1 & 1 \\
& \alpha & \gamma & \beta & \gamma & \gamma & \delta & \gamma & \alpha & \delta & \alpha
\end{array}
$$

Note that in defining his Greek letter matrix, Lacan says that an α goes from a symmetrical three toss grouping (that is, category 1 or 3) to another symmetrical one, a β goes from a symmetrical to an asymmetrical (that is, category 2), a γ from an asymmetrical to another asymmetrical, and a δ from an asymmetrical to a symmetrical. I will come back to this point further on.

What must be pointed out next is that while any one letter may follow *directly* upon any other (this can be checked by inspection of Greek Letter

Matrix II), any one letter may not follow *indirectly* upon any other. The case we will look at here, to begin with, is the determination of or limitation imposed upon the *third* position.

Suppose we begin with the letter α; the next letter can be α, β, γ, or δ, but we always get an α or a β in the third slot. Why so? The four possible α combinations (*viz.* 111, 123, 333, 321) all end in either 1 or 3. As the last number of these triplets will become the first number of the third-slot triplets, and as α and β are the only letters to comprise combinations beginning with 1 and 3, only α and β can fill the third slot.

This whole reasoning process can be repeated if, instead of α, we begin with the letter δ, for all δ combinations also end in 1 or 3.

On the other hand, all β and γ combinations *end* in 2, and as only δ and γ combinations *begin* with 2, only they can fill slot 3 if there is a β or a γ in slot 1.

This accounts for Lacan's emblematically laconic formula (*Écrits*, p. 49):

AΔ Distribution

$$\frac{\alpha,\delta}{\gamma,\beta} \quad \longrightarrow \quad \alpha,\beta,\gamma,\delta \quad \longrightarrow \quad \frac{\alpha,\beta}{\gamma,\delta}$$

Times: 1   2   3

We see on the top line that, in the case of α and δ, regardless of what letter we put at time 2, we still get α or β at time 3; and the lower line shows that, in the case of γ and β, every letter we try at time 2 gives us γ or δ at time 3.

Which is to say that the third slot is already to some extent determined by the first—the first "bearing within itself" the "kernel" of the third. Before developing this notion further, let us examine Lacan's *four-time* schema on page 50.

Looking first at Table O, with slots numbered in the top line, and a sample number line (coding the coin toss results) provided in the second line down:

Table O

Slot Numbers:			1	2	3	4				
sample number line:	2	1	1	1	1	2				Greek letter lines:
			δ	α	α	β	γ	γ	δ	1
				γ				α		2
			β	δ		δ	β			3

Lacan *does not* claim that the only way to get from δ in slot 1 to β in slot 4 is by inserting two αs between them. There are in fact a number of different ways to get from δ to β; Lacan's point here is that *none of them* include the letter γ (Greek letter line 2), a fact one can check by trying all the various possible combinations (a fastidious task at best), or by simply noticing that, as all δs end in 1 or 3, a γ is not possible in the third slot (we saw above, in the AΔ Distribution, that only α and β can follow δ in the third slot), and that a γ in the second slot automatically means that the slot–4 triplet will begin with a 2, whereas no β begins with a 2.

Greek letter line 3 of the table shows that if you try to put a β in slot 2, you never get to β in slot 4 (for a β puts a 2 at the beginning of the slot–4 triplet and no β begins with a 2); and that if you should be so foolhardy as to try to put a δ in slot 3, you come up against what we already saw in the three-time example: a δ can never be found in slot 3 if there's a δ in slot 1.

The rest of the Greek letter line to the right of δααβ shows us the excluded terms for the series βγγδ, which works exactly like the left-hand side.[3]

On the following pages, Lacan mentions other syntactic features of the Greek letter overlay: for example, if one comes across two βs following one another without a δ in between, they must either be immediate successors (that is, ββ) or be separated by one or more αγ pairs (e.g., βαγβ, βαγαγβ, βαγα . . . γβ). What is more immediately pertinent for us here is to note that, whereas it is theoretically possible for a random series of coin tosses to indefinitely reproduce αs or γs—here are two sample series:

$$+ \quad + \quad + \quad + \quad + \quad + \quad + \quad + \quad + \quad + \quad + \quad + \quad +$$
$$1 \quad 1 \quad 1 \quad 1 \quad 1 \quad 1 \quad 1 \quad 1 \quad 1 \quad 1 \quad 1$$
$$\alpha \quad \alpha \quad \alpha \quad \alpha \quad \alpha \quad \alpha \quad \alpha \quad \alpha \quad \alpha$$

$$- \quad - \quad + \quad + \quad - \quad - \quad + \quad + \quad - \quad - \quad + \quad + \quad -$$
$$2 \quad 2 \quad 2 \quad 2 \quad 2 \quad 2 \quad 2 \quad 2 \quad 2 \quad 2 \quad 2$$
$$\gamma \quad \gamma \quad \gamma \quad \gamma \quad \gamma \quad \gamma \quad \gamma \quad \gamma \quad \gamma$$

—no random series whatsoever could possibly endlessly produce δs or βs in this way, for δs always go from even numbers at the beginning of triplets to odd numbers at the end (e.g., 223) and must thus exhaust themselves after two repetitions, and βs do just the opposite (going from odd to even) and similarly exhaust themselves. In other words, they can only replenish themselves through the interpolation of other letters—and in fact every β couple requires at least *two* other successive letters before it can come up again. The same is true for δ couples.

Probability and Possibility

One of the conclusions that can be drawn from Lacan's second order matrix is that, try as one might, regardless of how loaded the coin used may be or how much one cheats, some of the letters defined, namely β and δ, can *never* turn up more than 50 percent of the time. Whereas with a lot of luck or a little coin loading, α, like γ, *could* turn up more than half the time. While this two-tier symbolic matrix was designed in such a way as to give each Greek letter *exactly* the same probability of showing up as the others,[4] a restriction in terms of possibility and impossibility has arisen, as it were, ex nihilo.

Probability and possibility are not one and the same thing. Hence, Lacan's assertion that prodigiously propitious combinations of coin tosses *could* lead α or γ to utterly overrun the series, while even the most preposterously propitious combinations *could never* lead β or δ to do so, points to a significant result of the combinatory, surpassing all considerations of probability.

But the most important outcome, to my mind, is the *syntax* produced which allows certain combinations and prohibits others. We see here that the laws generated by our numeric overlay (barring direct moves from 1 to 3 and from 3 to 1) blossom into an intricate apparatus with the introduction of the alphabetic matrix. I will explore the similarities between this kind of apparatus and language further on. The grammar generated here can be represented on a graph similar to the 1–3 Network (see *Écrits* 1966, p. 57).

Randomness and Memory

Now what is the point of Lacan's ciphering? As I mentioned above, Lacan is interested, in Seminar II and the postface to the "Seminar on 'The Purloined Letter,'" in constructing a symbolic system which brings with it a syntax—a set of rules or laws—which is not inherent in the "pre-existing reality." *The resulting possibilities and impossibilities can thus be seen to derive from the way in which the symbolic matrix is constructed,* that is, the way it ciphers the event in question. It is not so much the fact of ciphering, in this particular instance, as the method of ciphering which gives rise to laws—syntactic laws— that were not "already there." The method of ciphering Lacan employs here is by no means the simplest imaginable, and a far simpler method yields no syntax whatsoever; but his method seems to significantly mimic the ciphering of natural languages.[5]

Let us note another feature of the symbolic system Lacan develops. I have shown above that the numeric chains "keep track of" numbers, that in a certain sense they *count* them, not allowing one to appear before enough of the others, or certain combinations of the others, have joined the chain. This keeping track of or counting constitutes a type of memory: the past is recorded in the chain itself, determining what is yet to come. Lacan points out that "the remembering [*mémoration*] in question in the unconscious—and I mean the Freudian unconscious—is not the same as that assumed to be involved in memory, insofar as this latter would be the property of a living being" (*Écrits* 1966, p. 42).

The implication here is twofold: in the first place, grey matter, or the nervous system as a whole, is incapable of accounting for the *eternal and indestructible nature of unconscious contents*. Matter seems to behave in such a way as to necessarily lead to a gradual decay or decrease in the amplitude or quality of impressions. It cannot be the guarantor of their ever-lastingness. And in the second place, rather than being remembered by the individual (in an active way, that is, with some sort of *subjective* participation), things are "remembered" for him or her by the signifying chain. As Lacan says in the main body of the "Seminar on 'The Purloined Letter'": "Such is the case of the man who retreats to an island to forget, what? he has forgotten—such is the case of the minister who, by not using the letter, winds up forgetting it. [. . .] But the letter, no more than the neurotic's unconscious, does not forget him" (*Écrits* 1966, p. 34).

We see here a clear connection between the letter (or signifying chain) and the unconscious. The unconscious *cannot* forget, composed of "letters" working, as they do, in an autonomous, automatic way, which preserves in the present what has affected it in the past, eternally holding onto each and every element, remaining forever marked by all of them. According to Lacan, we find that, "For the moment, the links of this [constituting order which is the symbolic] are—as concerns what Freud constructs regarding the indestructibility of what his unconscious conserves—the only ones that can be *suspected of doing the trick*" (*Écrits* 1966, p. 42), that is, of guaranteeing indestructibility.

The Unconscious Assembles

This characterization of unconscious thought was by no means a passing fancy of Lacan's, representative at best of his "structuralist" years. In his twentieth seminar, *Encore*, Lacan says that, in his vocabulary, "the letter designates an assemblage . . . [or rather] letters *make up* assemblages; not simply *designating* them, they *are* assemblages, they are to be taken as functioning as assemblages themselves" (Seminar XX, p. 46). He goes on to add that "The unconscious is structured like the assemblages in question in set theory, which are like letters" (p. 47).

Freud leads us to wonder whether the expressions "unconscious thought" and "unconscious idea" are not simply oxymorons: "The process of dream-work is something quite new and strange, the likes of which have never before been known. It has given us our first glimpse into those processes which go on in our unconscious mental system . . . we hardly dare call them 'thought processes'" (*New Introductory Lectures on Psycho-Analysis*, Lecture XXIX).

Freud has accustomed psychoanalysts to the notion that "thinking," as we commonly understand it, plays a far smaller role in the determination of human action than previously thought. We may believe, feel, and claim that we have done A for reason B; or when we seem unable to immediately explain our behavior, we grope around for ad hoc explanations: rationalizations. Psychoanalysis seems, in a sense, to intervene by asserting the existence of reason C which we hadn't even considered or had been deliberately ignoring. Not to mention the flood of ulterior motives D, E, and F which slowly but surely "raise their ugly heads" in the course of analytic work.

But this is to liken unconscious thought processes to conscious ones, whereas Lacan insists, instead, upon a dichotomy. Conscious thought is grounded in the realm of meaning, in a striving to make sense of the world. Lacan proposes that unconscious processes have little if anything whatsoever to do with meaning. We can, it seems, completely ignore the whole issue of meaning, that is, the whole of what Lacan calls the signified or signification, in discussing the unconscious.

According to Lacan, the unconscious is structured like a language, and a natural language (unlike speech) is structured like a formal language. As Jacques-Alain Miller says, "the structure of language is, in a radical sense, ciphering,"[6] the type of ciphering or coding Lacan engages in when he superimposes numeric and alphabetic matrices on chains of pluses and minuses (altogether akin to the type of ciphering used in the machine language "assembler" to go from open and closed circuit paths to something resembling a language with which one can program). To Lacan's mind, the unconscious consists in chains of mathematical-like inscriptions, and—borrowing a notion from Bertrand Russell, who in speaking of mathematicians said that the symbols they work with *don't mean anything*—there is thus no point talking about the meaning of unconscious formations or productions. While Lacan provides a variety of glosses on the nature of truth in psychoanalysis, at his most mathematical he insists that

> there is no such thing as a truth which is not 'mathematicized', that is, written, that is, which is not based, qua Truth, solely upon axioms. Which is to say that there is truth but of that which has no meaning, that is, of that concerning which there are no other consequences to be drawn but within [the register] of mathematical deduction (Seminar XXI, *Les non-dupes errent,* Dec. 11, 1973).

The kind of truth "unveiled" by psychoanalytic work can thus be understood to have nothing whatsoever to do with meaning. and while Lacan's mathematical "games" may seem to be merely recreational, his belief was that an analyst gains a certain agility in working them through, in deciphering them, and in discovering the logic behind them. It is the kind of deciphering activity required by any and every encounter with the unconscious. Language in the unconscious, and as the unconscious, ciphers. Analysis thus entails a significant deciphering process.

Consider, for example, Lacan's enthusiasm in Seminar XI, *The Four Fundamental Concepts of Psychoanalysis*, over Serge Leclair's reconstruction of the assemblage "Poordjeli" as the key to the whole configuration of unconscious desire and identification in one of his patients. Though letters themselves are not decomposed in this example, it is clear that, while we can provide glosses "accounting for" specific elements, the assemblage as a whole—for example, the order of its components and the logic of its construction—remains as impenetrable as a dream's navel. According to Lacan, Leclaire was able to

> isolate the unicorn sequence [Poordjeli], not, as was suggested in the discussion [following his talk], in its significant dependence, but precisely in its irreducible and insane character as a chain of signifiers (Seminar XI, p. 192).

Here, as elsewhere in the same seminar, Lacan notes that interpretation does not so much aim at revealing meaning as at "reducing signifiers into their non-meaning (lack of meaning) so as to find the determinants of the whole of the subject's behavior." Interpretation brings forth an irreducible signifier, "irreducible, signifying elements" (Seminar XI, p. 226). What must be glimpsed by the analysand, beyond the meaning inherent in interpretation itself, is "the signifier—which has no meaning, and is irreducible and traumatic—to which he, as subject, is subjected" (p. 226).

Knowledge Without a Subject

> Once the structure of language is recognized in the unconscious, what sort of subject can we conceive of for it? (*Écrits* 1966, p. 800).

> There is perfectly well articulated knowledge for which no subject is, strictly speaking, responsible (Seminar XVII, p. 88).

Now this way of conceptualizing the unconscious apparently leaves *no room for a subject of any kind*. There is a type of structure automatically and autonomously unfolding therein, and there is absolutely no need to postulate any kind of consciousness of this automatic movement (Lacan, in any case, breaks with the association made by so many philosophers of subjectivity and consciousness). The unconscious contains "indelible knowledge" which at the same time is "absolutely not subjectivized" (Seminar XXI, *Les non-dupes errent*, Feb. 12, 1974).

The unconscious is not something one knows, but rather something which is known. That which is unconscious is known *unbeknownst to* the "person" in question—it is not something one "actively," consciously grasps, but rather something which is "passively" registered, inscribed, or counted. And this unknown knowledge is locked into the connection between signifiers—it consists in this very connection. *This kind of knowledge has no subject, nor does it need one.*

And yet Lacan speaks constantly about *the* subject—the subject of the unconscious, of unconscious desire, the subject in its phantasmatic relation to object *a*, etc. Where can the subject possibly fit in?[7]

Notes

1. One must, of course, mention the exception: Jacques-Alain Miller. I am highly indebted to his discussion of it in his 1984-85 Seminar, *1,2,3,4*. The present talk was prepared in 1988, and I was as yet unaware of John Muller and William Richardson's discussion published in *The Purloined Poe*, Baltimore: Johns Hopkins University Press, 1988.

2. In the first publication of Lacan's "Seminar on 'The Purloined Letter'" (*La Psychanalyse*, 2, 1956), things are spelled out a bit more clearly. There Lacan writes that "Consideration of the 1–3 Network alone suffices to show that, in accordance with the terms whose succession it fixes, the middle [term] will be unequivocally determined—otherwise stated, the said group will be sufficiently defined by its two extremes. Let us thus posit the following extremes (1) and (3) in the [(1)(2)(3)] group" (p. 5). Yet in more clearly stating how the terms are to be grouped, Lacan lapses into inaccuracy: fixing the extreme terms does *not* in all cases unequivocally determine the middle term (e.g., as we saw in the Greek Letter Matrix II, the blank in the 2__2 configuration can be filled by 1, 2, or 3.

3. Note here, however, that this latter series cannot follow directly upon the former without the interpolation of a second β, for two γs in a row necessitate two 2s in a row, and they can only be generated here by two βs. Cf. the α,β,γ,δ Network on p. 57 of the *Écrits*, reproduced further on in this paper.

Important note: there are mistakes in this part of Lacan's *Écrits* and they can be extremely misleading.

The table one finds directly above this one on page 50 of the *Écrits:*

Table Ω

Slot Numbers:			1	2	3	4				
sample number line:	1	2	3	3	?	?	?	?	?	Greek letter lines:
			α	δ	δ	γ	β	β	α	1
				δ				β		2
			α	γ			γ	α		3

is misleading in that (1) there is clearly a typographical error here, and (2) while the toss-result and number coding lines run left to right, and thus the Greek letter line normally would as well, Lacan seems to be running the latter right to left here. We saw above, for example (and Lacan mentions this explicitly), that one can *never* find a δ in slot 3 if there is an α in slot 1—but the table above seems to suggest that this is altogether possible.

Note that this typographical error also appears in the simpler table found in Lacan's 1956 version:

α	δ	δ	γ	β	β	α
δ	δ	δ	β	β	β	

Now if we run the chain in the other direction, we see that it works just fine:

Table Ω (modified)

Slot Numbers:			1	2	3	4				
sample number line:	1	1	1	2	2	2	3	3	3	**Greek letter lines:**
			α	β	β	γ	δ	δ	α	1
					δ			β		2
			α	γ			γ	α		3

The reader may notice that I have not reversed the excluded terms on the lines below the Greek letter-code line, they being patently nonsensical as they stand in the French *Ecrits'* table: before modification, Table Ω suggests, for example, that we can use two δs to get from α to γ, and on the line below goes on to suggest that δ can never be a part of any such progression.

So either Lacan intended to run this series of Greek letters from right to left instead of left to right but didn't catch the erroneous inversion of δ and β in line 2 (which could perhaps explain some prohibited combinations Lacan provides at the bottom of p. 51), or else the inversion took place in line 1 itself where the doubled δs and βs were reversed. [One could also imagine that the extreme terms, α and γ, were inadvertently inverted. The two series which work, in any case, are α β β γ δ δ α and the same series read right to left: α δ δ γ β β α (which, for all intents and purposes, is equivalent to γ β β α δ δ γ).] Which amounts to the same thing for our purposes, and the version to which I will refer is that presented in the modified table above.

This table should by now be fairly easy to understand: δ cannot be used in an α-γ four-step combination; α cannot figure in slot 2 nor γ in slot 3; β is excluded from γ-α four-step combinations, γ being barred from slot 2 and α from slot 3. The reasons for these exclusions can be deduced in the same way we deduced those listed in Table O. (Note that the two four-step series here can in fact follow immediately upon one another. Cf. the α,β,γ,δ Network, *Écrits* 1966, p. 57.)

4. Though there was an imbalance in the first level matrix—

1 (identical)	2 (odd)	3 (alternating)
+ + +	+ + − − − +	+ − +
− − −	+ − − − + +	− + −

—there being twice as many possible 2 combinations as 1 or 3 combinations, the second level matrix set out to rectify this:

α	β	γ	δ
1_1, 1_3	1_2	2_2	2_1
3_3, 3_1	3_2		2_3

If we take this matrix at face value, we are inclined to think that wherever we find a 2, the combination which includes it is twice as privileged as non-2 combinations; thus a letter which does not subsume 2 combinations should have twice as many ordinary combinations as one which does (α, for example, subsumes twice as many triplets as β). And if a triplet includes two 2s, it seems it's twice as likely to show up as a triplet with one 2.

Probability in fact bears out this calculation, but not exactly in this way. First we return to our Greek Letter Matrix II where we listed the entire combinatory:

α	β	γ	δ
111, 123	112, 122	212, 232	221, 211
333, 321	332, 322	222	223, 233

Normally there would be 27 triplets possible for such a three-slot, three-number combinatory (3^3), but 12 of them have been eliminated here because of our 1–3, 3–1 restriction (i.e., 1 and 3 cannot be immediate successors), and because 3 cannot be immediately followed by a 2 and then 3 (two 2s necessarily being interpolated between two 3s); nor can 1 be immediately followed by 2 and then 1 again.

To give an example, the triplet 111's probability must be calculated as followed: the first 1 has one chance out of four of turning up (1/4); the second 1, however, occupies a slot which only 1 or 2 can occupy, 3 being barred here; now 2 can show up just as often as 1 (in the case of the 1–combination + +, a + can just as easily follow a −), and thus 1's probability is 1/2 here; the third 1, as it also follows directly upon a 1, also has a one in two chance of showing up. We thus have 1/4 X 1/2 X 1/2 = 1/16.

In fact, all but one of the triplets in the completed matrix have a probability of 1/16. The 222 triplet under γ, however, has a 1/8 probability, thus balancing out the seemingly unequal distribution of triplets. This can be checked with a flow chart which, starting with two branches (+ and −), is extended by splitting each branch continually into two, adding a plus to one branch and a minus to the other. One finds that 222 combinations come out twice as often as any other, and that the various Greek letters have, in effect, exactly the same probability of turning up.

5. To hone in as closely as possible on what exactly it is that gives rise to Lacan's syntax, let us look in some detail at what we *put into* this model as we constructed it:

We *assumed* the "real" event in question—the tossing of a coin—to be *random*, that is, we presupposed that the coin was not loaded. But what does it mean for a coin *not* to be loaded? Generally speaking, it means that it is exactly as likely to turn up heads as tails. How is this determined? By throwing it over and over, and counting the number of times each possibility turns up, an acceptable coin being one which, out of 1,000 tosses, gives us 500 heads and 500 tails. Which is tantamount to saying that it is our already existing symbolic system which determines whether the event in question is considered *random* or not. The qualification "random" is thus attributed through use of a symbolic matrix involving a rudimentary form of probability theory. Therefore, nothing is to be taken to be random without having first satisfactorily undergone the test of a symbolic system. (In fact one's results virtually never show exactly 50 percent heads and 50 percent tails—randomness is more of a limit, something a coin or an event approaches as the number of throws goes to infinity. That is why we generally rely on the proper "weighting" of the coin, which once again can never be more perfect than our system for measuring weights.)

Which is to say that the "raw event" with which we began was already symbolically determined, and that symbolic matrices are never "innocent," that is, never lacking in incidence on our supposedly "pregiven reality." The event is thus retroactively constituted as random by the signifier (i.e., by the words we use to talk about it).

There is no ideal coin which weighs exactly the same amount on both sides of an imagined plane through its middle, and which thus provides "absolutely random" results. Perhaps a computer can provide perfect 50/50 results (though only after even numbers of "throws": that is, heads or tails generations). In any case, the point is simply to recognize the symbolic inputs we supplied at the outset.

For our purposes, virtually any coin will do, as will virtually any other method for choosing pluses and minuses. We can begin from almost any series of pluses and minuses, and by *grouping them* in certain ways—*chaining them together symbolically*—rules are generated concerning the order of the symbols used to group them. The syntax seems to already be there *in statu nascendi* in the grouping strategies adopted—for indeed, *if the groupings do not overlap, syntax disappears:*

$$\underset{1}{+\ +}\quad \underset{3}{-\ -\ -}\quad \underset{2}{+\ -}\quad \underset{2}{+\ -}\quad \underset{2}{-\ +}\quad \underset{1}{+\ +}$$

no rules arise as to which symbol can or cannot follow another symbol, and the symbols are totally independent of one another in terms of what signs they cipher. For example, the 3 in the above chain no longer ciphers half of what the preceding 1 had ciphered, and can thus easily follow that 1 immediately without an intervening 2. In the overlapping system, a chain is formed—

while in the non-overlapping system, no links are established between the units to be grouped: they remain utterly independent.

Overlapping means that there is no *one-to-one* (or even two-to-one) correspondence between elements of the event to be ciphered or symbolized (the series of pluses and minuses) and the symbols employed. Instead of a situation whereby each set of two signs would be designated by one and the same symbol (it would be its sole and unique referent)—

$$\underline{+\,+} \quad \underline{-\,-} \quad \underline{+\,-} \qquad \text{Situation A}$$

—more than one symbol is used to designate each set of plus or minus signs. In the example below, 3 symbols represent the two plus and two minus signs, *over-representing* or overdetermining them, so it might seem, in that 2 symbols sufficed for the same job in "Situation A" above.

$$\left(+\left(+\right)\left(-\right)-\right) + \; - \qquad \text{Situation B}$$

If, however, we consider that the symbol 2 designates *two different combinations*, $+\,-$ and $-\,+$, we see that the overlapping is necessary to *completely represent* the plus/minus series, that is, to distinguish a $+\,-$ combination from a $-\,+$.

Situation A

$$\underline{+\,+} \; \underline{-\,+} \qquad Series\ 1 \qquad \left(+\left(+\right)\left(-\right)+\right) \qquad \text{Situation B}$$

$$\underline{+\,+} \; \underline{+\,-} \qquad Series\ 2 \qquad \left(+\left(+\right)\left(+\right)-\right)$$

The overlapping symbolization system is able to distinguish between series 1 and 2, while the non-overlapping system is not.

Had we, however, assigned different numbers to the two different combinations $+\,-$ and $-\,+$, no such problem would have arisen in the first place, and it seems that it is the *double meaning* (or two different referents) of the symbol 2 that gives rise to two situations: Situation A, under- or ambiguous representation, and situation B, complete representation.

Thus, if we no longer assign two different combinations to the same symbol, we *can* exhaustively represent the plus/minus series with a non-overlapping string of letters that generates no discernible laws or syntax. *Syntax therefore seems to arise only from a specific way of applying the symbolic matrix to the series,* and the elaborate grammar of Lacan's second symbolic matrix stems, *not so much from the symbolic material or stuff itself* as from this specific mode of application.

But to what extent is the plus/minus series an appropriate model of "reality"? For, after all, Lacan's model takes on value in that it seeks to establish a sort of analogy between the "random events" of a child's early experience, say, and the random chain formed by the string of pluses and minuses. Were a child a binary/analogue computer, such an analogy might suffice, but as a child's experience is not symbolized at all at the outset, that which is to be symbolized apparently bears no resemblance to the clean-cut alternation of pluses and minuses.

But consider Freud's grandson's *Fort-Da* (absent-present) game whereby the first two words the child speaks seem, in Freud's interpretation, to symbolize the comings and goings of his mother, a considerable event in the child's life. Two terms ("gone" and "here")—which are interdependent in that the mother can only be designated as "here" by the very possibility of her being "gone" and vice versa—code or cipher her appearances and disappearances, constituting "the simplest symbolic sequence, a linear series of signs connoting the alternative, absence or presence" (*Écrits*, p. 141).

Lacan's model, on the other hand, presupposes such a first-level coding. It can perhaps be seen as making up in its symbol application strategy what it lacks by way of a "complex reality" to begin from.

We can, as we have seen, cipher the "reality" of coin tossing in a way which *seems to add nothing* to the initial event, but in any case adds another level of meaning to the integers (1, 2, and 3) we used to cipher it.

The α,β,γ,δ language provides a method of ciphering which assigns double meanings/referents (and sometimes quadruple ones) to all symbols, thus requiring overlapping for complete representation—a form of overdetermination. In this respect, his symbolic matrix seems to quite closely mimic natural languages which regularly assign more than one meaning to the same word, and generally require a surplus of words to precisely represent anything.

6. *1,2,3,4*, class of Feb. 27, 1985.

7. For a partial, but by no means adequate, answer, see my paper "The Subject and the Other's Desire" earlier in this volume. See also my *The Lacanian Subject: Between Language and Jouissance* (Princeton: Princeton University Press, 1995).

AN OVERVIEW OF THE REAL,
WITH EXAMPLES FROM SEMINAR I

∞

Ellie Ragland

Throughout his teaching, Lacan tried to bridge the gap between psycho-analysis and philosophy, seeking to answer the question of how body is joined to mind, how, in fact, they are intertwined in their formation and are, finally, not truly separate entities. One of the most difficult categories he elaborated during his teaching is that of the real, which does not refer to reality, objects in the world, the body, or some phenomenological thing-in-itself. Lacan's development of this category parallels his continual reworking of theories of the "object," work which culminates in his break with philosophical traditions of thought categorized as epistemology, ontology, classical logic and classical psychoanalysis.

Jacques-Alain Miller's periodization of Lacan's teaching in three phases— the 1950s and early 1960s, 1964 to 1974, 1974 to 1981—establishes a basis from which to work with Lacan's evolving theory of the real.[1] Although Miller has since given other divisions to help us work with the complexities of Lacan's return to Freud, the periodization established over a decade ago remains illuminating. In the first period of his teaching in the 1950s, Lacan described the real as concrete and already full, a brute, pre-symbolic reality which returns to the same place in the form of need, such as hunger. Moreover, as early as Seminar I he defined *repression and its return* to the same place as the same thing.[2] In "repression in the true sense of the word—because repression is not repetition, repression is not negation—there is always interruption of discourse. The subject says that the word escapes him" (Seminar I, 268). In other words, the real enters discourse as a sign that something that has been *re*-pressed still functions.

In his recent book, *Validation in the Clinical Theory of Psychoanalysis*, Professor Adolf Grunbaum shows no awareness of Lacan's thorough reworking of the concept of repression in his return to Freud.[3] Attacking Freud's contention that repression is the cornerstone on which the whole structure of psychoanalysis rests, Grunbaum argues that Freud failed to prove a causal relation between the alleged repression and the pathology. On this and other grounds, Grunbaum dismisses the validity of any claim to a scientific underpinning of psychoanalysis.

Although one may think of Lacan's early concept of the real as the "object" of hunger—that is, the breast, the bottle or the mother—such images are, in his teaching, imaginary objects, both more and less than the real object which, in and of itself, is no-thing. That is, the object does not exist as such in a visible empirical form, but is, all the same, an absolute density. Indeed, if the first real *object* of the drive is the attempt to satisfy hunger, the real enunciates itself from the start as the *place* of a hole constituted *in* the compact space we call being.[4] Insofar as each experience of hunger pivots around the necessity of calling for more—*Encore*—pleasure will, by necessity, find its roots in displeasure, in disappointments in the first gifts of love.

In the 1960s and the early 1970s, the second period of his teaching, Lacan's concept of the real resembled his 1950s concept of the imaginary. By the third period, as he gradually differentiated one order from the other—"the tripartition of the symbolic, the imaginary and the real . . . those elementary categories without which we would be incapable of distinguishing anything within our experience" (Seminar I, 271)—he was able to attribute a series of properties to the real, as well as a structural causality. The past returns *as if* from the future, introducing conflict into symbolic reality.[5] That is, the repressed unconscious returns as contradiction, which means, simply, that "authentic speech has other modes, other means, than everyday speech" (Seminar I, 267). The structure of conflict that characterizes the real is the following: Individuals seek the satisfaction—itself an *object* sought—in things and *in* others.

Yet the aim always misses its ultimate goal—an ongoing consistency of jouissance—because the "object" sought is the impossible jouissance of Oneness. Topologically speaking, a subject is pulled towards a totalizing (re-)union by which he or she hopes to stop up the hole in the real via the path of identifying with ideal figures and traits found in the other, traits reminiscent of the primordial jouissance first attached to the mother as *das Ding* (Seminar XX, 9-18). But to understand Lacan here, one must realize that his is a critique of Melanie Klein's imaginary articulation of the mother's body which he calls a mythologization of *das Ding*. Moreover, *das Ding* will always be represented by a void space in being—denoted by object *a*—precisely because it cannot be represented by anything else. That is, the effects of loss create a void which is not nothing, but functions to empty the *real* material of the partial drives into language and onto the body at the point where the mother is taken as the goods, the only Good.[6]

In Aristotelian terms, Lacan's real is a paradoxical order. It is at the same time the first and final cause, made up of the same material it seeks both to avoid and to (re)possess. Although Lacan adhered to Freud's idea that the real appears as conflict, he speaks of impasse rather than conflict. When one fails to get "it"—what a person thinks will fill the void—conflict appears as a *real* gap between the aim of the drive and its object. And even when a person does get something he or she wants, the wish to have another *object,* or more of the same, quickly shows up, revealing that satisfaction depends only contingently on the object desired.

Referring to the "Three Essays on Sexuality" where Freud describes the object as always "refound," Lacan stresses that if it is *re*found, it must have been lost.[7] But if one conceives of the object as Freud did, Lacan adds, it is not real, but imaginary or phantasmatic. If, however, as Lacan teaches, the *object* one seeks does not exist as such, but has effects all the same, one can say, as Miller does, that it "responds."[8] And the thing that "responds" is the subject at the point of excess in jouissance where it is an object, seeking to fill up the literal void in its own being. The subject "as barred subject—as lack-of-being—is this hole at the heart of the symbolic: S(Ⱥ). As being, the subject is *nothing but* the subtracted bit which Miller writes as the residue that falls out between the "I think" and the "I am" of the Cartesian cogito:[9]

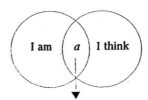

The equivalence of the subject and object *a* lies there.[10]

Miller argues in *"De la nature des semblants,"* that when object *a* is taken as an "equivalency of the subject and object," it is a semblant.[11] A person is not a "self," a totalizing concept of the person that denies the reality of how human subjectivity is structured in the first place, and how it functions thereafter. A person is, rather, the semblance or seemingness that tries to stop up the hole in being, a monkey chasing its own tail. In *"Extimité"* Miller describes the object that fills the void as a logically deduced consistency.[12] One could say that in this object which does not exist, but which contains the essence of being, Lacan has pinpointed what medieval theologians sought in material objects, and what religions, alchemy and mythologies have sought in the concept of spirit. The topological structure of object *a* refers to an "outside of the body," says Miller, that marks a particular conjunction of inside and outside, there where one's most intimate cause is *extimate*, not hidden. At the simplest level, if the telephone rings, interrupting the pleasure of two people talking in a momentary "union" of joined voices and gazes, the law of discontinuity wins the day. Pleasure quickly turns to displeasure. An imaginary consistency, whose roots are in the real of the drives, is broken. The structure of the displeasure finds its cause in the logic of the cut which already marked the drives as a *demand* for love, for more, for a continuity in the moment, a demand organized around the experience of loss.

The real is not an object *a*, then, although object *a* is real. The real appears, nonetheless, in whatever concerns the radical nature of loss at the center of words, being and body precisely because we are only "beings" at all under the sign of sexuality where *being* is first constituted in a real moment of which no "being" has memory, but to which each subject tries to give voice in words, images and symptoms. This "origin" in the real of the body places its roots in what Lacan called the *a*-sexual, that is, in the objects-cause-of-desire that give rise to the oral, anal, vocative and scopic partial drives. The real is at the beginning, then, the first agent ordering the life game around the time of loss, between the *Fort!* and the *Da!* But this early experience is foreclosed from consciousness because loss of the desired object (the *Da!* of the presence and the *Fort!* of the absence of the objects-cause-of-desire) constitutes the subject as an object framed by itself. The subject lives in the blind spot between his objectal *being* and the language that seeks to represent this. Put another way, repression is repression of the fact that we are first and foremost creatures of jouissance. Moreover, jouissance marks language (the nominal) as an essence that bespeaks a "beyond" *in* language itself, conveying the "sense" of a meaning that is always more (or less) than the words spoken.

In the second period of his teaching, Lacan defined the real as "it" or *das Ding*, reinterpreting the Freudian theory of the mother as the primary object of satisfaction. Lacan's innovation here lies in his discovery that the pre-Oedipal attachment to the mother does not concern her as a good or bad object, or even as a body. She is the object of focus, rather, because her voice, gaze, breast and care of the feces are the first anchoring points of jouissance around which an imagined continuity in being is constructed. The real of the cut—that is, the loss of this imagined continuity—produces discontinuity and inconsistency that places loss (S[Ⱥ]) squarely at the center of all language and all human relations. Woman becomes the surface onto which illusions about the mother qua imagined guarantee are projected.[13] This is a radically different meaning of the real than the one Malcolm Bowie gives in his *Lacan*, where "the real is the order outside the signifying process that is found in the mind as trauma and in the material world as intractable materiality and 'primitive undifferentiated All.'"[14] Bowie has not yet grasped the extent to which mind is constituted *from the outside*–imposed by the linking of language to images that structures the corporal real in its own meaning system, that of jouissance. Mind is constituted, then, in three orders–the imaginary, the symbolic and the real–that are ordinarily knotted together by the function of metaphorical substitution away from the mother qua primary object, in reference to the signifying *function* of a father. It would not be possible for the real to be *outside* signifying process, yet *in* the mind. This was, nonetheless, the premise of the early Lacan. It is not surprising that keen readers of Lacan, like Bowie, would confuse the Lacanian real with the "material" of the world, a primordial *Geist* infusing nature. And Lacan shows that the real is precisely not the world, but one of the orders of the signifying chain. In other words, the real is constituted at the level of flesh, and lies right in the middle of thought.

Before Freud, no one had fathomed the part played by the libido in everyday life. But Freud could not understand how it was constituted. Lacan translated the Freudian libido as jouissance which he configured as an *essence* sought in identification with another whose identificatory traits are familiar. The paradox Lacan uncovers that Freud could not explain was why the primary process quest for pleasure does not, in fact, produce pleasure. The *real* impasse imposed between the aim and its goal is repetition. Pleasure and displeasure split at the limit point where the familiar produces the jouissance that constitutes displeasure.[15] But Miller has emended Lacan's spreading of jouissance throughout language to argue, rather, that everything defends against jouissance, most particularly language. Indeed, what Freud called the psychoneuroses of defense are defenses against jouissance. Lacan locates the leftover remainder of the castrating experience of the alienation of being in language– object *a*–at the point of the divide.

In his second period of teaching, Lacan moved away from any correlation of the real to biology or need. Even though he had rethought the Freudian idea of complexes and instincts in terms of constellations of imagos as early as the 1930s,[16] by 1960 he had elaborated a theory of the imaginary body–a kind of meta-body–imposed on the real of the biological organism. The parts of the body are signified, that is. Thus, body image is given by the signifier. This linkage of the real and imaginary necessarily constructs the body's *vitality* around the primordially repressed, pre-specular objects that cause the desire around which fantasies coalesce: "The mamilla, faeces, the phallus (imaginary object), the urinary flow. (An unthinkable list, if one adds, as I do, the phoneme, the gaze, the voice–the nothing.)"[17] Subsequently, humans try to fill the hole of loss in being that appears in anxiety, demonstrating in their various forms of desperation that *something* in being does not work. The utility of the heterogeneous objects on which enjoyment depends, lies in their function of calming anxiety. In this sense, one can speak of "objects" as fetish objects, objects around which illusions and idealizations circle.

In this second period, Lacan described the real as the traumatic material of unassimilated memories and meanings that blocks the *dialectical* movement of symbolization, blocks the route to exchanging one's *savoir* with another person. Although the exchange of the "forms" that constitute one's *savoir* is generally called *communication*, nothing short of the category of the real can explain the truth everyone knows. Most communications are failed communications, miscommunications, or outright polite—that is, "social"—lies. The real resides at the points of such impasses in language exchanges—in the universal passions of love, hate and ignorance—seeming to lie outside subjectivity, language, fantasy and the dream. But it *functions* anyway. It is what we are used to, Lacan said in *Television*, and it surfaces in matters of sex, symptoms, object *a*, the aim of the drive that seems "attached" to the organ thought to produce it in the first place. The voice has the *semblance* of producing language, the eye, the gaze. But what is *actually* re-presented to produce a dialectic between signifiers is the emptiness of the object. In this "logical" time, the drive seeks to replace whatever first gave rise to desire *as the desire* for a consistency in jouissance. Hence, desire is the desire to be rid of the intimations of lack and loss.

The subject qua object, response of the real, is identified with the "cut," the name Lacan gives the mark or *letter* inscribed on the body at the place where the object that *causes* desire seems to be inseparable from the organ to which it is appended. At such points, the object *a* "bespeaks" the loss of jouissance: J(Ⱥ). Lacan named these points of identification, bifurcated between body parts and loss itself, unary features.[18] Such effects tie the "divine details" of unconscious identification (Dora's identification with her father's cough and with Frau K's beautiful white body, for example) to a concrete void place *in* a subject's signifying chain.[19] Put another way, sexual trauma—"the actual landscape of an interiority," as Miller says in *Donc—constitutes* the space of the void (June 22, 1994). In the first chronological time of constituting the landscape of interiority, the trauma consists of an encounter with the originary father, the father of jouissance. In the second traumatic moment, this originary time takes on its traumatic value in a separation of the symbolic from the real.[20]

Trauma does not automatically mean literal abuse or incest, then, but the confrontation of the body—the *a* part, the sexual—with the internal excitations that Freud called drives. Drives are, moreover, structurally traumatic because they enact the failure of the pleasure principle. Surprisingly, repetition is, in this sense, a drive: a return of the real into the symbolic.[21] And the real, or the unconscious, is absolute, solid, compact, radically Other. Thus, its repression constructs reality around the misrecognition of its own basis in fantasy.

Since there is no evident correspondence between the objects one later desires and primordially repressed Ur-objects that first caused desire, the place of the object is, perforce, empty.[22] Lacan's real—unlike Heidegger's *Dasein* which is innate, there prior to any investigation—sets the terms of the a priori condition of the signifying chain and then serves as a link in the chain. But since these are different functions, the first bearing on the object *as* symbolic, a signifier—as in the signifier "mother"—and the second concerning the real object as *semblant*, as the thing itself, they are not commensurate functions. Paradoxically, the second function, the real of the flesh, passes through the imaginary and symbolic, looping jouissance effects to words, bringing discontinuity into the symbolic. But in this sense, bits of the real *are* graspable in fantasy, repetitions, and words, coating language with what Lacan has called the *irréel* which is not "unreal." And since the real always returns—disruptively—to infer a piece of trauma into language, this order determines that there be no ontology of identity. It also drives us to depend on each other for structural reasons, not because of any "human" essence of fundamental good will. Each subject is destined to fill up the lack-in-being with jouissance taken from another.

Miller has clarified Lacan's shift away from the thingness of the object here, which is *no* thing-in-itself. Although its logically inferred consistency is *in the imaginary*, the object *a* itself is a *real* semblance, not an imaginary lure. Miller has further clarified Lacan here by making a distinction between the object of a pre-symbolic real—where the body is first constituted imaginarily—and the object of the post-symbolic real, which is the formal envelope covering over the palpable void *underlying* the objects a subject invests with emotion and meaning. That is, the object qua void is hidden behind what the subject forecloses: knowledge of the Other's desire, the radically absent Other. This structure is perfectly exemplified in Lacan's Seminar on Edgar Allen Poe's "The Purloined Letter."[23]

Between jouissance and the Other, a part of the real remains—the left-over excess in jouissance Lacan named object *a*—as an inert presence in every act, as an irreducible inertia that will not dissolve. A piece of the real constitutes a barrier to jouissance at which point one finds the limits of the pleasure principle. *Something* is present in the incomprehensible repetitions that mark the reality principle with a part of the death drive. But although the return of the real into language destroys imaginary projections of *supposed* symmetries and reciprocities, most subjects cling to the real in their lives, to the impossible to bear, choosing the death route of loving their symptoms—the familiar—more than themselves. Here the subject qua object is a death kernel, a piece of psychotic nonsense, a sign of bad faith.

In the 1970s, the concept of the object per se was not at issue for Lacan. He focused, rather, on the impossibility in the goal of maintaining consistency. The idea of Oneness itself is an illusion, an imaginary belief, that depends on the lethal jouissance of inert beliefs and fantasies. Yet these *fixions* insist and persist in each subject's language, despite the fact that they are continually subverted by the "truth" of the real discontinuities that intervene in any person's efforts at wholeness and Oneness. Paradoxically, Lacan's *final* scripting of the real has more in common with Freud's last attempts to explain the difference between the sexes than it does with the explanations of the real Freud gave between 1897 and 1914, in which he defined mechanisms of the unconscious in terms of biological first causes.

In 1920, Freud concluded that we cannot know ultimate psychic reality—that is, the real—but in 1921 he located a real beyond the pleasure principle. He found the point of this real in the compulsion to repeat that makes of Thanatos a libidinal survival "instinct," paradoxically located at the heart of Eros.[24] Stymied as he was in figuring out what produced this resistance to change, Freud concluded that "castration anxiety" and "penis envy" are the barriers to psychoanalytic cure. Lacan taught that psychoanalysis begins at the point where Freud found a dead-end, where the *non-rapport* between the sexes—the asymmetry or fundamental differences which constitute the masculine in culture or the feminine in culture—is a reality.[25] "Castration anxiety" points, not to male fear of actually losing his penis, but to the unbridgeable gap between the sexes which structures each subject's fundamental fantasy around a confusion between *having* and *being*. And "penis envy" points, not to actual envy (desire of/for) an organ, but the desire to eradicate the lack-in-being.

Even though no signifier is adequate to define gender, men mistake the symbol that represents them as different—the phallus—for the norm or standard that defines the social, against which the feminine is measured as the same, the natural, the real. In this sense, the patriarchy means that which marks the social by a third term, the difference between the infant and mother represented by the *phallic* symbol. Thus, woman is defined "beyond" the social, in the real. Yet each subject must lose his or her attachment to the primary object in the real—the mother as *das Ding* splayed into partial objects-cause-of-desire—if he or she is to "live" the domain of the social as lacking, that is, capable of reciprocity and exchange. But this is no easy task since no subject is "identified" as an imaginary whole within the binary categories of sexuation—masculine or feminine.

In the alignment of the different functions, each subject must come to terms with what it means to lose something in the divide *in the real*. Yet, the divide is constituted by the repression of the trauma caused by having to account for who one *is* on the basis of difference (castration) and not sameness (the real). Lacan formalized this as the logic of alienation (or castration).[26] He was able to make this determination on the basis of his early work with psychosis wherein he discovered the lack of a key signifier, the one that signifies the sexual difference as a difference.

In the third period of his teaching, Lacan argued that the impossibility of aligning anatomy and sexuality in terms of a wholeness of being, produces symptoms around the sexual divide for everyone. Put another way, sexuation is not sexuality. Sexuation concerns the psychic identification taken on in reference to the phallus and castration, while sexuality is commensurate with the drives. In this third period, Lacan linked jouissance to object *a*. When the subject qua object *a* appears in the signifying chain, the real of that subject surfaces as an impossibility, an impasse, a meaning that is not dialectized. Given the concreteness of the return of repressed material—the real—into the symbolic, one cannot view the real as a transcendent positive entity beyond the symbolic, then. It is an order between *being* and *thought*

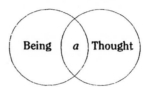

that links the excess in enjoyment—object *a*—to the subject's ultimate worth, there where the stakes are recognition, not erudition (*Donc*, June 22, 1994). The subject *as object* is a response of the real, a positive "essence" of being (or nothingness) with which one seeks to stop up the hole in its own universe with the material of being-in-the-partial-drives. Movie stars or rock stars send the same message: "I am the desired object of the sexual gaze." Opera divas deliver the message "I am *the* voice," superwoman mothers, "I am *The* mammela," while prancing machos reek of "I *am* the phallus," and so on. When imaginary consistency breaks down, the subject behind the mask appears as a *failure* to re-present itself as a being of continuity, revealing, rather, the emptiness, redundancy, non-sense, and fetishistic excess that *is* the subject.

Thus, object *a* places a piece of the real in the symbolic at the point where a subject is an absolute, a morsel of being or nothingness—an effect of jouissance—that rushes in and out of the hole in the symbolic (S[Ⱥ]) that appears most starkly in anxiety, and less obviously as a palpable yearning or nostalgia.[27] The void of loss is first covered by the illusion of (the phallic veil over) having possessed "the thing in itself" that was always already radically lost, the mother as a guarantee of the positivized essence of Woman (Ⱡⱥ). Later, when experiences of loss produce anxiety, subjects cling to any rationalization that offers a seeming consistency to the Other from which he or she expects a continuity in events, memories, beliefs, thought, love, and so on. Put another way, "beyond the phallus" lies the object *a*.

Post-structuralist theorists have either dismissed the Lacanian real or attacked the category as a simplistic literalism, misunderstanding that when

Lacan says that "there is no sexual relation" he means that no signifier gives a just ratio of a harmonious *relation* between the sexes, least of all the phallus. Given that most subjects accept the division between language and jouissance that constitutes repression, but seek to fill up the concrete gap created in the split with the beloved other taken as one's very "soul," it makes sense that the sexual "relation" itself is marked with the paradoxes inherent in the divide between the masculine and feminine in sexuation. The *cause* of *conflict* is locatable within structure, then, not at the imaginary level of alternating idealization or blame of the partner. Although people never quit trying to bridge the gap of a signifier lacking in the symbolic through love and sexual relations, conflict is the real in all relations, whether admitted or denied.

Not only have post-structuralist theorists misunderstood Lacan's formula— "there is no sexual relation"—they have also taken Lacan's account of the inexistence of a fundamental signifier for Woman as a rejection of women. Woman is certainly "positivizable" as a signifier and in the partial objects that cause desire. Lacan's point is that there is no essence of Woman, no "eternal feminine" soul—that is, no positive of the existence of Woman qua Woman, no feminine "nature." Marie-Hélène Brousse has written that there is no feminine jouissance in the real because there is only the sense of nothingness or beingness that makes of any subject a response of the real. On the other hand, Lacan marked feminine jouissance *beyond the phallus* as a supplemental one, to which some women have access (Seminar XX, 73-82).

Lacan symbolizes the lie in essentialist myths about Woman by striking a bar through the definite object in *the* Woman (*L∌a*). This particular loss—Woman qua embodiment of an essence—is the one that gives rise to a hole in the social order itself, a malaise that marks being with the real of loss. That is, the category of the real can never be detached from Woman, given that the real body of the first caretaker, usually the mother, gives rise to the drives. The real emanates from a quite palpable void at the heart of being and thinking, then (that some people only encounter in anxiety). This void bespeaks a beyond *in* language and culture that people usually "think" imaginarily, attaching their hopes and fears, their praise and blasphemy, to Woman.

When one encounters the real caused by the inexistence of *La femme*, as theorized by Lacan in Seminar XX, one has encountered the same kind of structural impasse as the incest taboo—a beyond *within* culture from which myths arise. In trying to decipher the Freudian "myth" of libido, Lacan ended up redefining myth. "In *Television*, he gave a definition of myth as something which gives an epic form to what operates from structure (structure being the Borromean unit which symbolizes the operation of body and mind in the imaginary, symbolic and real). He said that libido is appended meaning for the libido itself, for which jouissance is the Lacanian word. With the difference that libido is a myth. And Lacan tries to make of jouissance the sexual conflict. . . . Let us try to look at jouissance as an effect of signifieds."[28]

Although Lacan's psychoanalytic turn accounts for the proximity of the feminine to the real, a proximity which places women closer to an awareness of loss than men, Lacan finds a paradox here. The confusion of Woman with the mother taunts all subjects with a burden that only makes sense if one understands the incest taboo as a structural necessity, a prohibition against precisely what any child desires: to be One with its mother. If myth always works from structure, then the structure of the Oedipal myth seeks to express the taboo against a fusion in the real of jouissance which, when it occurs in the pre-Oedipal and Oedipal moments, produces psychosis. There is normally a foreclosure of the signifier for Woman in the human species, then (except in psychosis).[29] Jacques-Alain Miller has developed Lacan's category of the real to suggest that the essence of woman is canceled by language at the point where a confusion between Woman and mother arises, there where she seems antithetical to herself. Woman does not exist as an essence, then, precisely because Woman and the mother are not the same.

Lacan divorced the real from reality, the real telling of the impossible contradictions we all experience daily, of the inadequacy of language to *re*-present the real of sexuality. But it is important to remember that sexuality is not the same as sexuation wherein one identifies as masculine or feminine. Sexuality is omnipresent in the drives wherein each subject seeks to make himself or herself seen, heard, fed, cared for. Lacan moved the real away from the medieval notion that an essence dwells in objects, away from the theological idea that spirit resides in being as an incarnation of the divine, away from the phenomenological notion of the real as unknowable, to a re-examination of the Freudian theory of the libido. Discerning a meaning system at work in the jouissance effects of the drives, Lacan was able to account for the *constitution* of the object in a writing of pleasure and displeasure, being and nothingness, the vulgar and the sublime, all masquerading around the irreparable gap constituted in an asymmetrical division of the sexes.

Much of Lacan's elaboration of the real in the third period of his teaching can be deduced from Seminar I if one follows his careful efforts to distinguish neurosis from psychosis via the concept of the real. From the beginning of Seminar I, Lacan addressed the question of what the real is in Freud, never losing sight of the fact that psychoanalytic practice in his wake has incorrectly interpreted this basic category. American psychoanalysts in the 1950s took Freud's idea that analysis allows a homeopathic discharge of a subject's subjective understanding of the world—a catharsis (or abreaction) supposed to produce a new equilibrium—in the wrong direction. The *transformation* of the analysand's view of the world, anchored as it is in fundamental fantasy, has been taken for the real (Seminar I, 14).

The article, "*L'analyse et son reste: Le testament de Freud,*" takes up one of the problems Freud sought to solve in "Analysis Terminable and Interminable," a text which Lacan, in Seminar I, calls Freud's testament (Seminar I, 15).[30] Referring to the "kernel of truth" that *remains* as the rock of castration—the left-over remnants of castration anxiety in men and penis envy in women—Freud wrote that a man will retain the anxiety that causes him to seek and reseek the assurance that he lacks nothing, either in relation to a lover or within a group of male competitors. And no woman can be completely cured of feeling lacking insofar as she is, by definition, the Other sex, Other to the symbolic order, even when she is a "full" participant in the professional and social interstices of that order. She is still confused with Woman, taken first and foremost as mother, the foundation on which the social depends even as that foundation is covered over, if not forgotten by the institutions erected on it. In "Analysis Terminable and Interminable," Freud wonders if psychoanalysis can ever transcend the impasses left by this reminiscence, this *Stück* that remains as a piece of the real even after an analysand's symptoms, anxiety and inhibitions have disappeared.

Lacan translated the Freudian concept of a remainder or *Stück* as object *a*. Jacques Alain Miller has noted that the development of psychoanalysis since Freud's death has continued, in the spirit of Lacan, to clarify the logic of analysis—beginning, middle, end—such that one now knows that at the end, each analysand will have resolved what he or she can do with the *Stück* that remains as a result of the sexual non-rapport. In other words, the conclusion of the treatment is concomitant with the solution one evolves for working with the real of this remainder at the level of the drive.[31]

In "The End of the Treatment," Anne Dunand writes that psychoanalysis

> deals with the transmission of its method. By method, I mean the structure of the experience itself, the passage from one way the subject has of relating to the object, of complementing his want-to-be with the desire for an object, to the position in which he recognizes the analyst as the ectopy of the object . . . until he discovers that this object is only the logical consequence of what was left over of jouissance after it had been chased into particular relations, erotic relations of his own to his own body. . . We have to be precise in indicating that the object here is not a person or a relation to a person. A person, or a relation to a person, can be described in terms of significant traits. The object that causes desire, not being a person, is what is left of the subject after it has gone through the sieve of language. In this case, the object is an unsatisfied part of whatever the subject may wish for.[32]

Lacan attributed the *constitution* of this remainder to the unnatural creation of a divide between the sexes that creates a real impasse, even arguing that this fundamental difference organizes culture around an impasse in the real. And following Freud's own unanswered questions, Lacan argued from Seminar I on that the real is not the end product of the transformation of a fantasy through talking, as post-Freudians thought, but rather, something that was present in the unconscious *before* the transformation of the fantasy; that is, something that does not disappear even after the symptoms have disappeared. From Seminar I on he argues that the real is, quite to the contrary, *something* as in the case of the Wolf Man for whom the genital plane was not symbolized at all. Basing his first comments on the real in Seminar I on Freud's Wolf Man case, Lacan speaks of the effects produced by the *lack* of a basic symbolization, one that links the real of anatomy to the images that constitute a fixion of being through an imaginarization of the body. Freud noted the absence of words in the Wolf Man's discourse at the point where no image represented the genital plane. Even when the real has not been signified, Lacan argued, it *functions*. But it functions as a non-affirmation (a non-*Bejahung*), marking the radical *lack* of a symbolization to delimit jouissance.

The symbolization in question concerns desire as a limit. Lacan took up Freud's discovery of an unconscious in dreams and in the psychopathology of everyday life, to argue that desire—the hidden secrets at the heart of thought— is not only unconscious at the level of cause, it is also timeless, that is, absolute. The *particular* conditions that give rise to desire, then, are neither the tame, philosophical undecidable, nor the innocent nothing of the empty Heidegerean vase. On the contrary, the unsymbolized real returns with a vengeance into the symbolic. And it returns because, even though it has been foreclosed— that is, not symbolized—as knowledge, it has still been "seen," even if it is the radical foreclosure of castration that marks psychosis. Miller has explained the real as that order of knowledge from which one chooses, responds or decides, even to the point that psychosis is chosen. When a child first encounters the real of sexual difference, the consistency of his or her belief in a fundamental unity between body and being is shaken. Lacan's teaching shows that images of the body (the imaginary) are quite literally woven together with language (the symbolic) and the experience of the body (the real) in an interpretation of castration; the fact that there is one symbol that marks sexual difference as difference itself. Psychosis is, in fact, the unconscious foreclosure (*Verwerfung*) of the reality of this difference. In consequence, the imaginary order of projective "self" representations is lacking. Without the cushion of the imaginary—which makes language function metaphorically (that is, substitutively)—psychotics live the symbolic order of language via the unimpeded force of the drives. The resulting petrification means that would-have-been dialectical judgments have been sacrificed to a holding-in-place of the foreclosed knowledge of the central difference from which all other differential judgments ensue (Seminar XX, 125).

In Seminar I, Lacan interprets Freud's Wolf Man case in seeking to make sense, not only of the phenomenon of hallucination, but also of the fact that the real constitutes a knowledge. Although Lacan will not say "knowledge is an enigma" until twenty years later (Seminar XX, 125), he makes it quite clear in his discussion of the Wolf Man that hallucinations are not caused by a brain dysfunction, nor by a loss of reality. Rather, a hallucination is a particular knowledge already possessed by the psychotic subject, but which he will *never* be able to assimilate into his thought. This permanent deficit in knowledge—the lack of the imaginary plane (which may, nonetheless, be supplemented by studied imitation of others)—attaches language directly to the real of the body. This dysfunction in the real drenches the body in its own foundation in the drives. Having foreclosed the structure of difference from which judgment arises as a dialectic for most subjects, the psychotic clings to the drives for dear life. Imaginary forms are soldered (holophrased) to the real of the body rather than represented at a distance as a function of the triadic Oedipal structure. Bombarded by the drives, the psychotic subject lacks the imaginary covering of *méconnaissance* that constitutes the master discourse as a set of consistent identifications that make up the fictions of the ego.

In the analysis of neurosis, the knots of the real that produce impasses in the analysand's language can be cut into and undone. The *impossible* of the sexual non-relation—the "what does not cease to not write itself" of the real—can be reconstituted in the *contingent* mode of the "what ceases to not write itself" that makes a sexual relation possible. In other words, an encounter in the real of love *can* enable a subject to pass from his or her impasse of fixation in sexuation, to the contingent mode of the possible (Seminar XX, 132). And by the *real* of love, I am referring to Lacan's reconceptualization of the object as early as Seminar IV when he taught that the object is *what* one seeks in love, that it cannot be dialectized, and, most surprising, that it was first constituted *by the symbolic order*.[33] I would suggest that *it*—the Freudian "thing," the sexuality of the drives—cannot be dialectized because it cannot be detached from the (partial) drives (oral, anal, scopic, invocatory). It is only detachable from the drives in psychosis where Lacan first discovered two object functions beyond the breast and the feces; that of the gaze (in paranoia) and the voice (in schizophrenia).

The foreclosure of sexual difference in psychosis reveals a knotting together of the orders with the non-dialectizable object, rather than with the dialectic of the signifier (Seminar I, 58–59). What is foreclosed from the real returns in the symbolic, but in the disconnected forms of hallucinations, not as the fantasies which hold systematic belief in place. Thus, the hallucinations seem *alien* from the psychotic subject's knowledge as well, bringing in their wake a delusory strangeness that makes no sense to the person undergoing the hallucination. Hallucinations arise from the psychotic subject's too great proximity to the real, then, and bear the mark of "too much" jouissance, too little distance from the object-*cause*-of-desire, and omnipresent anxiety, rather than the bittersweet yearning that marks a finitude in desire, as symbolized in Lacan's formula for fantasy: ($ ◊ *a*).

In his interpretation of the Wolf Man case, Lacan distinguishes between fantasy and hallucination. Fantasy can only occur at all as a subject function insofar as sexual difference is registered as a *difference*. The Wolf Man, for example, held the delusional conviction that he had cut his finger so deeply that it was hanging solely by a little piece of skin.[34] Such an image belongs to the *real* of unsymbolized material, not the secrecy and repression of fantasy. In this context, one can describe hallucinations as emanating from the foreclosure of the basic *symbol*ization (the symbol being the lowest common denominator of representational forms) of sexual difference whereby a child first links together his biological genital organs in an interpretation of himself or herself as masculine or feminine. In psychosis, neither side of the divide is chosen. As Judge Schreber's delusion demonstrates, he was both God and the Wife-of-God. One cannot doubt that there is all the difference in the world between an hallucinatory experience—Son of Sam's voices, the terror of believing oneself eaten alive by an eagle destroying her young—and the comfort of distance that typifies the ordinary experience of language as metaphorical, that is, substitutive.

Shortly after discussing the real in relation to the Wolf Man in Seminar I, Lacan approached the question of what the real is from another angle. Referring to a patient analyzed by Ernst Kris, he stressed a different kind of lack, the difference, indeed, between neurosis and psychosis. With Kris' analysand there is no foreclosure of a signifier linking the genital organ to "identity" (sexuation). This patient has no image of what Lacan called the real father of jouissance (Seminar I, 60). Kris' patient came to him, troubled by the symptom of being hampered in his profession: he could not produce articles. It had been his custom to discuss his ideas with a friend he considered a brilliant scholar, or with hired tutors. Although he always ended up wanting to borrow the ideas of his interlocutor after these conversations, he could not publish his understanding of what had been said because he was convinced that he was a plagiarist.

Lacan did not adhere to the Freudian hermeneutic approach, that is, interpreting a patient's dreams, "story" or fantasies. Indeed, he severely critiqued this method of analysis precisely because the analyst does not know what they mean. Kris, nonetheless, hit the nail on the head in this case, Lacan maintained. And we know that only because of what follows in the response of the patient. After working with Kris in analysis for a period, the aspiring scholar finally got together an article he hoped to publish only to have his hopes dashed upon finding a book in a library that seemed to have developed the whole of his own thesis. He was a plagiarist *malgré lui* (in spite of himself), Lacan quipped. Kris agreed with the patient's own interpretation of himself, in other words.

Praising Kris for having given an accurate interpretation—that is, one which elicits a response "both paradoxical and full of meaning" (Seminar I, 60)— Lacan suggested that Kris had demonstrated the crystallized form of neurosis, obsession in this case. In neurosis, the subject—composed of drive + trauma = ego—shows what defense his ego is, that is, himself or herself as always subject to the process of negation in which, paradoxically, the integration of his ego has already been accomplished (*Comment finissent les analyses*, 53–55). A subject's ego is "shown," then—is a kind of *donner-à-voir*—as the inverted form of a fundamental relation to one's own ideal ego. Thus, Kris' patient reveals who he is *at the level where the subject is a defense*. One might even picture a subject as a *che vuoi?* graph rather than a "whole" person. In the patient's choice of friends, for example, his brilliant scholar friend would represent his own unconscious ideal ego *at the surface* of his language. But what does this tell us about the real?

Lacan considered Kris' interpretation of his patient's belief that his own article was a plagiarism as true, a correct interpretation, arguing that the subsequent actions of the patient proved this. The whole of the subject's history unfolded, revealing his lack as the lack of an image of the *real* father—enjoying, powerful. He lacked the *symbolization* of—quite literally, he had no *form* for—the image of a father who could *enjoy* anything. Given that jouissance, be it a jouissance of meaning, being or the body, translates itself via the body, Lacan says that the

> properly speaking penile [nature] of this need for the real, creative and powerful father, had taken the form in this patient's childhood of all sorts of games, such as fishing games—will the father catch a bigger or a smaller fish? etc. Although the immediate reaction of the patient upon producing this material was to remain silent, at the next session he said—"The other day, on leaving, I went into such and such street . . . and I sought out a place where I could find the dish I am particularly fond of, fresh brains" (Seminar I, 60).

Lacan describes the analysand's quest for "fresh brains" as a moment of passing through an impasse, of unknotting a knot in the real. Indeed, Lacan's own solution to Freud's impasse, the impasse of psychoanalysis as set forth in "Analysis Terminable and Interminable," places the beginning of psychoanalysis at the point where Freud dead-ended in the impossibility of termination. Placing the sexual impasse within the impossible of the Oedipus, Lacan located the *ça* or libido of the Freudian *Trieb* before even the earliest constitution of any ego, making of primordial jouissance a "first orientation."

If one places "fresh brains" within the context of the primordiality of the oral drive, the first orientation towards jouissance, then "fresh brains" is not a metaphor. And Lacan knows this, although he does not put it this way. "Fresh brains" is a metonymy, an answer which points to what Jacques-Alain Miller has called a pre-symbolic real (which Lacan categorized more broadly as *lalangue*), although pre-symbolic does not mean a non-symbolization as in the case of the genital plane for the Wolf Man. Ernest Lanzer had foreclosed only one signifier, the phallic signifier for sexual difference, the key signifier. Thus, his language was drenched in the pre-symbolic real from which a piece of flesh—not symbolized—became concretized in a hallucination.

Kris' patient needed a new symbolization of his real father. In what Lacan called Kris' second interpretation, he read the article his patient thought he had plagiarized and told him that he was wrong, that the *ideas* in it were the patient's, that the author had actually stolen them from *him*. In other words, they are stolen *ideas*, not *plagiarisms*. *You* have ideas in *your* head, Kris was saying. His patient was stunned because in his unconscious identifications, he had nothing worthwhile in his head, no *ideas*. When an obsessional says "I'm guilty. I did it," chances are, Lacan said, he did.[35] But, of *what* is he guilty?

This patient's worst fears *were* true. He *was* a plagiarist, but not of ideas. He was a plagiarist of identifications. His dilemma was the following: How can I have creative, new ideas if my father was a wimp, a loser, a nothing? His repetitious "I am" (my "I" is) *that* (*ça*) shows the killing side of the real when rooted in primordially negative identifications whose archaic imprints constitute a subject's ego as a fiction of certainty.

Kris told his patient that his life "behavior" had been shackled by his identification with his father who had been crushed by the grandfather, a highly creative and productive man. What the patient needed to seek in the signifiers that represented his father to him—not *in* his father qua person—was a "grand" father, not a wimp who is a perpetual failure. And Kris' interpretation worked miraculously because, Lacan says, it was true. The analysand was suddenly relieved of the burden of defining his "I am" in terms of a father whom he, in fact, does not have to *be*. He became free to define himself via a hidden, or latent, identification: the "grand" in the Name-of-the-Father. And, immediately, the burden of a repetitious—both negative and deadly—jouissance of the signifier around the Father's Name was lifted.

When a certain impasse in knowledge—by definition indicating the presence of the real, or *unconscious* material—is passed through, the subject in analysis can reformulate himself or herself via new identifications. These add to, and displace, the old ones that constituted the synchrony of the signifiers and the diachrony of "speech," there where the Other and the *ça* are joined. In the "fresh brains" case, the subject underwent a transmutation of diachronic jouissance via *signifying additions* to his synchrony of signifiers.

Lacan went in the opposite direction from the post-Freudian attempt to cure by "enlightenment," creating a new superego while obliterating desire. By referring to the Wolf Man and the "fresh brains" analysand, Lacan intimates as early as Seminar I that the only way to disempower the primordial grip of the death drive—the real of it—is to not give up the little piece of jouissance that remains.[36] But, as the development of the Freudian Field since Lacan's death has demonstrated, negative jouissance can only be dropped piece by piece as words and images are rewoven in the talking cure. The cure bears on energy and the body, then, the ultimate remainder being the subject as object in the fundamental fantasy out of which any subject's *Weltanschaaung* is constructed. As one detaches oneself from the deadly jouissance of signifiers that one cannot utter, but merely repeat dumbly, one becomes capable of realigning one's libido around Eros. But this is no simple matter of reducing the ethics of desire to the demand for jouissance. The constant, defiant presence of the impasses of the real *in* language stand as proof positive that the empirically invisible is *not not there*.

Notes

1. Ellie Ragland-Sullivan, "Lacan, Jacques," *Feminism and Psychoanalysis: A Critical Dictionary*, ed. by Elizabeth Wright (Cambridge, Mass.: Blackwell Publishers, 1992), 203.

2. Lacan answered Freud's question concerning how repression works by linking Freud's idea that the unconscious does not know negation (i.e., does not follow diachronic time), to an understanding of how the *nachträglich* functions within logical time. Trauma, paradoxically, has a repressing action that, nonetheless, returns into language or thought *after the fact.* "Repression and the return of the repressed are the same thing," Lacan says in Seminar I—the return of the past which structures the future (191). See also *"Perspective de la fin de l'analyse de l'Homme aux loups,"* *La Conclusion de la Cure: Variété Clinique de la Sortie d'analyse* (Paris: Eolia/Diffusion Seuil, 1994), 44–47.

3. Adolf Grunbaum, *Validation in the Clinical Theory of Psychoanalysis* (New York: International Universities Press, 1993).

4. Jacques Lacan, Seminar XX, *Encore.*

5. Slavoj Žižek, "The Real and its Vicissitudes," *Newsletter of the Freudian Field,* vol. 3, nos. 1 & 2 (Spring/Fall 1989), 86–89.

6. Jacques Lacan, Seminar VII, chapters 8 and 10.

7. Sigmund Freud, "Three Essays on Sexuality" (1905), SE VII, 123–245.

8. Jacques-Alain Miller, *Réponses du réel,* unpublished course.

9. Jacques-Alain Miller, *Donc,* unpublished course, 1993–1994.

10. Jacques-Alain Miller, *Montré à Premontré,"* *Analytica* 37 (1984), 28–29.

11. Jacques-Alain Miller, *De la nature des semblants,* unpublished course, 1991–1992.

12. Jacques-Alain Miller, *Extimité*, unpublished course, 1985–1986.

13. Jacques-Alain Miller, *Donc*, June 22, 1994.

14. Malcolm Bowie, *Lacan* (Cambridge, Mass.: Harvard University Press, 1991).

15. Jacques-Alain Miller, "A Reading of Some Details in *Television* in dialogue with the audience," *Newsletter of the Freudian Field*, vol. 4, nos. 1 & 2 (Spring/Fall 1990): 24–29.

16. Jacques Lacan, *Les complexes familiaux* (Paris: Seuil, 1984).

17. Jacques Lacan, *Écrits: A Selection*, 315.

18. Jacques Lacan, Seminar IX (1961–1962): *Identification*, unpublished seminar.

19. Jacques-Alain Miller, *Les divins détails*, unpublished course, 1989.

20. *Perspectives de la fin . . .* , 47.

21. Hervé Castanet, *Réel et éthique de la psychanalyse* (Nice: Z'Editions, 1990), 74–75.

22. Jacques-Alain Miller, "Language: Much Ado About What?," *Lacan and the Subject of Language*, ed. by Ellie Ragland-Sullivan and Mark Bracher (New York: Routledge, 1991).

23. Jacques Lacan, "Le séminaire sur *La Lettre Volée*," *Écrits* (Paris: Seuil, 1966).

24. Sigmund Freud, *Beyond the Pleasure Principle* (1921), SE XVIII, 3–66.

25. Sigmund Freud, "Analysis Terminable and Interminable" (1937), SE XXIII, 209–54.

26. Jacques Lacan, Seminar XI, 203–215.

27. Jacques Lacan, Seminar XXII (1974–75): *R.S.I.*

28. Jacques-Alain Miller, "A Reading of Some Details . . . ," *op. cit.,* 29.

29. See the film *Rainman* where Dustin Hoffman plays the role of a schizophrenic. Although he has been portrayed as an *autiste savant*, he is, according to the differential clinic of diagnosis established by Lacan, a schizophrenic. Autistic children are, by definition, not *in* the symbolic, even if they have some access to language, while schizophrenics such as Rainman experience the symbolic as directly attached to the real. They speak and act *as if petrified* in language. See Alexandre Stevens, "Two Destinies for the Subject: Neurotic Identifications and Psychotic Petrification," *Newsletter of the Freudian Field*, vol. 5, nos. 1 & 2 (Spring/Fall 1991): 96–112.

30. *"L'analyse et son reste: Le testament de Freud,"* in *Comment finissent les analyses*, ed. by the Association Mondiale de Psychanalyse (Paris: Seuil, 1994), 47–71.

31. Jacques-Alain Miller, "Marginalia de Milan sur *Analyse finie et infinie*," *La lettre mensuelle de l'E.C.F.*, no. 121, July 1993: 18.

32. Anne Dunand, "The End of the Treatment," *Newsletter of the Freudian Field*, vol. 4, nos. 1 & 2 (Spring/Fall 1990): 129.

33. Jacques Lacan, Seminar IV: *La Relation d'objet*, text established by Jacques-Alain Miller (Paris: Seuil, 1994).

34. *Comment finissent les analyses, op. cit.*, 58.

35. Marie-Hélène Brousse, "Freudian interpretation and the subject's lines of fate: interpretation and structure," *Analysis*, no. 4 (1993), 9.

36. In "To Interpret the Cause," Miller explains Lacan's reformulation of Freud's pleasure principle and reality principles. Representations constitute the Lacanian Other, the field of meaning that Freud tried to pinpoint with the reality principle. What Lacan called jouissance, by which he reinterprets the Freudian pleasure principle, refers to the libido. In making meaning, one is substituted for the other, language for libido or libido for language, leaving an irreducible excess that Lacan called a quota of affect. This quota is object *a*, a *cause* which cannot be translated into signifiers, but which, nonetheless, was constituted for particular meaning from the outside world, albeit, constituted in the pathway of the drives. Jacques-Alain Miller, "To Interpret the Cause: From Freud to Lacan," *Newsletter of the Freudian Field*, vol. 3, nos. 1 & 2 (Spring/Fall 1989).

A DISCUSSION OF LACAN'S "KANT WITH SADE"[1]

∞

Jacques-Alain Miller

Part I

Jacques Lacan's "Kant with Sade" is probably one of the most difficult texts in the *Écrits*, and I think it would be appropriate to consider a number of passages from it at this conference on "Lacan, Discourse, and Politics." I believe that, in a way, "Kant with Sade" is a rewriting of Freud's "The Economic Problem of Masochism." As I said yesterday, using Kant and Sade, Lacan dramatizes the problem enunciated by Freud, that of the sadistic superego.

I want to begin with a simple detail: the title, "Kant with Sade." That's a strange "with." Why "with"? Why use that preposition to connect Kant and Sade? I wonder if there are any books with such a title: someone *with* someone else? What is the meaning of this "with"? What is usually the meaning of "with"? It could imply companionship: someone who accompanies someone else. It's difficult to imagine Sade accompanying Kant. They would make very strange companions indeed.

Consider the numerous examples of couples in literature. Consider, for instance, Don Quixote with Sancho Panza. In Baltasar Gracián's *El Criticón*, you have Critilo with Andrénio, Critilo being the critical mind and Andrénio being the innocent, naive dupe. In English literature we might think of Dr. Johnson with James Boswell. James Boswell was modest enough to entitle his book *The Life of Dr. Johnson*, leaving out his own name. But we nevertheless read it as the life of Dr. Johnson *with* James Boswell. We might also think of amorous couples: Pyramus and Thisbe, Daphnis and Chloé, Héloïse and

Abelard, and perhaps even Moby Dick and Captain Ahab. We could construct all kinds of modalities of companionship, companionships that would be interesting to study side by side. The famous couples in literature might provide us with the meaning of this "with."

Question: Doesn't it also evoke the idea of the double, the imaginary couple?

Miller: The double, well, yes; perhaps when Kant was dreaming he dreamt that he was Sade!

Slavoj Žižek: The example that comes closer, though it involves a rather different logic, is Sherlock Holmes with Watson. Watson is a sort of stupid companion, but really Sherlock Holmes wouldn't be Sherlock Holmes if he weren't seen through the eyes of Watson. He is Sherlock Holmes only as a result of Watson's idiotic view. Here it is quite different—I mean, Sade is not Kant's idiot.

Miller: As a matter of fact, Lacan thinks that Kant was Sade's idiot. Lacan says, in effect, that Kant and Sade were the precursors and consequences of the Declaration of the Rights of Man. There is a certain solidarity between them. From Don Quixote and Sancho Panza up to Sherlock Holmes and Watson, one member of the couple is always apparently noble and the other ignoble. One may be deemed the mind, and the other the body. In some ways, this kind of couple is reflected in "the Freudian couple": the pleasure principle and the reality principle. Clearly, Don Quixote has something of the pleasure principle about him, which contrasts with the supposed commonsense of Sancho Panza.

The Lacanian "with" here is something else at the same time. It is the utilitarian sense of "with," for example, the sense in which one uses Sade to read Kant. As you say in America, "I use Lacan to read so and so." Lacan uses Sade to read Kant and to reveal something hidden in Kant's work. That doesn't nullify what I said earlier: there is something classic about this particular couple. Kant could be viewed as the purest mind that ever lived, and Sade as the basest person ever to live. But what is specific to the Lacanian will and its "with"—the with of the will—is this sense of instrument. As Lacan says, this is specific to Sade's subjective position, because in perversion he is precisely that: an instrument.

That is rather surprising. It is the opposite of what is commonly thought about perversion. It is commonly thought that the pervert uses other people, other peoples' bodies, without due respect for their status as subjects. Lacan's fundamental clinical thesis regarding perversion is the opposite. Lacan asserts that the pervert devotes himself to the Other's jouissance, the Other's sexual enjoyment, trying to restore lost sexual enjoyment to the Other.

I don't particularly like the expression, "using Lacan." I wonder why I don't like it. Perhaps it's because I'm not sure it's a good thing. Perhaps to me Lacan's work is an end in itself. But if that is the case, it isn't any better than using Lacan. In effect, Lacan's work gets used. He produced his work in order for it to be used, but chiefly for analytic purposes. He offered his work up for this kind of use. But the use of his work for strictly academic purposes always met with resistance on his part. He didn't want to be put to such use. Nevertheless, he was clearly fascinated with James Joyce's comment about giving work to academics for at least three centuries to come. Lacan quoted that.

It's always a question: to whom is a discourse really addressed? Lacan said the very same thing about André Gide, observing that some intimate papers Gide apparently wrote only for himself were in fact already prepared for his future psychobiographer. The most intimate of his productions were already preserved for the future. Where then does true intimacy lie? The public is already present at the core. So who did Lacan address? He always said, "I speak for analysts." He said that many times—so many times that you could wonder what was hiding behind that assertion. He knew very clearly that you always speak for the universities as well, because universities preserve, and at the same time deflect, the knowledge of all times. Thus, Lacan apparently spoke for his audience of analysts, his students, but I believe he also wrote for other addressees. A lot of his students, his analysands in training as analysts, believed that Lacan wrote and spoke for them alone. When they discovered that Lacan had readers around the world, and that analysts in South America and in other European countries were also reading Lacan, they felt dispossessed, even though Lacan continued to repeat to them so frequently, "I am speaking and working for you."

Comment from the audience: If Kant, when seen through the eyes of Sade, is not the Kant that we normally take him to be, I wonder if it goes in the other direction as well—perhaps Sade is not who we think he is from Kant's perspective?

Miller: When you see that it works in one direction, you immediately want it to work in the other direction too, that is, to be reciprocal. Lacan devoted a whole paragraph here (which is a lot for him) to the question of reciprocity. Reciprocity would mean that if Sade provides the truth of Kant's work, Kant provides the truth of Sade's. If, for instance, Gérard Miller is my brother, then I'm Gérard Miller's brother: it's a reciprocal relationship. Even there, however, even in the difficult relationship between brothers, there is some asymmetry. For instance, since I am the eldest, he has always been a brother. I have not always been a brother, and that is something which renders the relationship asymmetrical.

Lacan's emphasis throughout "Kant with Sade" is to construct non-reciprocal relationships and to demonstrate that what is fundamental in the logic of the subject is always non-reciprocal relationships. Perhaps I could quickly read the part I alluded to. "Reciprocity: a reversible relationship because it is based on a simple line uniting two subjects who, from their reciprocal positions, hold this relationship to be equivalent." That's a logical definition of the mirror stage when we understand it, not in terms of images, but in terms of subjectivities. You might say that it's a logical definition of intersubjectivity. Reciprocity, which Lacan defined as such, can only be situated with great difficulty as the logical time of any crossing over of the subject in his or her relation to the signifier, and still less as a stage of development.

It is interesting to consider what you said about Kant providing the truth of Sade's work, because there is a crucial text by Kant on the origin of absolute evil: "On Religion and the Limit of Simple Reason." Kant was the first to consider what would happen if a radically evil will existed, if pure will—as pure as the will he had defined, a will submitted to the formal nature of the moral law—were radically evil. Perhaps you can give a better definition, Slavoj.

Žižek: Until Kant, the ethical or good was always associated with some logical consistency or purity, and evil was always associated with the empirical, that which is dependent on contingent, worldly objects, etc. To be evil meant to be attached to some empirical object.

Miller: For instance, to love money, pleasure, etc.

Žižek: But Kant's idea here is that it is possible for somebody to be evil beyond the pleasure principle—to put it in Freudian terms—to be evil out of principle.

Miller: To want evil for evil's sake. Not evil for the sake of money, pleasure, etc., but evil for evil's sake (just as you might want good for its own sake). That would be the position of a saintly devil, or something like that—a devil who would foment evil for evil's sake. That is really the crux of "Kant with Sade," and it's surprising that Lacan doesn't quote Kant's "On Religion and the Limit of Simple Reason."

Question: Weren't there some ancient Christian heretics who embraced the principle of evil for evil's sake?

Miller: It's the problem of the devil. I appreciate your reference. Lacan refers to that in Seminar VII, *The Ethics of Psychoanalysis*. It is there that this couple, Kant with Sade, first appears.

Žižek: There are a lot of literary students here, and for them I think the crucial literary figure to evoke is the romantic Byronesque hero: for example, at the end of Mozart's *Don Giovanni*, when Don Giovanni is confronted with the statue. From the perspective of the pleasure principle, what would Don Giovanni do there? Repent for his sins? He knows perfectly well that if he repents for his sins he can be saved. Thus, from the perspective of the pleasure principle, it would be best for him to repent. But he says, 'No, I will persist in it; I will persist in my evil as a matter of principle,' although he knows he will be forever condemned. It seems to me that when Lacan refers on the first page of "Kant with Sade" to the notion of happiness in evil (*bonheur dans le mal*), the perspective is definitely romantic.

Miller: Exactly. Perhaps, before going any further, I could try to articulate more precisely the link between Kant and Sade, which in itself seems scandalous: Kant, the purest mind, the philosopher of pure duty, going hand-in-hand with the vile Sade who spent years in prison and who is repulsive to all morality. Lacan's thesis is that something is begun by Kant and continued by Sade. At the end of the path running from Kant to Sade and traversing the nineteenth century—above all, the literature of the nineteenth century—you have psychoanalysis. Indeed, in the second paragraph of "Kant with Sade" we find a definition of the historical condition of the possibility—to use Kant's expression—of psychoanalysis itself. Which is rather surprising, because we are used to thinking about Freud's scientific precursors. We know that he was a student of Helmholtz's and that he himself was a kind of positivist. Lacan offers a completely different view, placing Freud on a path that Byron traveled before him, a path trodden not by Helmholtz or laboratory scientists, but by Kant, Sade, a romantic hero, Baudelaire, Barbey d'Aurevilly, etc. Lacan says that someone like Sade, with Kant as a precursor, was necessary for Freud's path to be passable.

Thus, it's not exactly the logical condition of possibility that Lacan is referring to when he says that Freud's work depends on Kant and Sade. It's something much more refined than the logical or epistemological condition of possibility. To be able to do something you need a kind of consent from the milieu, from the spirit of the time—if not from the *Zeitgeist*, at least from the *Geist* of the nation. For instance, to be able to practice Freudian psychoanalysis in a Lacanian fashion, you need some kind of consent from the depths of the people. And if you don't have that, it's difficult—just ask Stuart Schneiderman. It is difficult when the society's values contradict the goal of analysis. That's what I believe Lacan means when he says, "*pour que la voie de Freud devient praticable* (for Freud's path to become passable)." He says that there is something "*qui chemine dans les profondeurs du goût*"—something which makes its way into the depths of taste. During the nineteenth century, something made its way into the depths of taste which enabled Freud to follow his path.

It's very difficult to give a precise meaning to "the depths of taste." Let us keep in mind that Lacan is speaking of taste here in an essay on Kant. You know that the first part of Kant's *Critique of Judgment* is concerned with the judgment of taste, which is neither logical nor demonstrable. The judgment of taste—for example, when you say that something is beautiful—is not demonstrable. There is no criterion of the beautiful. And since that is so, there is no matheme of the beautiful, to use Lacan's term. There is only a "patheme," something you experience—*pathos*, a feeling you have. But at the same time, to say that something is beautiful is not the same as to say it's tasteful. That is, when you say it is beautiful, you require everyone to say it's beautiful: there is a supposed universal pleasure in the beautiful, even though there is no universal rule to prove that it is beautiful. There is no rule or criterion for the beautiful which you could apply to a painting, by taking out a little apparatus and reading from its dial whether or not the object in question is beautiful.

That's the aesthetic problem, which is distinguished from the ethical problem in Kant's work. For ethical questions, you do have a universal criterion. You have a demonstrable rule: if you want to know if something is moral or not, you call Kant; Kant comes along with his little machine; you describe your action; you put it in the machine; and at the end it says "It *is* moral" or "It is *not* moral." Whereas for the beautiful, for questions of taste and aesthetics, there is no such machine. It's interesting to see that Lacan combines aesthetics and ethics: "Kant with Sade" is a text on ethics, but it begins with a reference to something which escapes the universal rule of judgment.

Comment from the audience: I'd like to give a parallel example from a work of literary criticism by John Bailey which is called *The Characters of Love*. Bailey compares descriptions of the annunciation to the Virgin Mary, and he gives two different descriptions of what is naturally pleasing, aesthetically speaking. An artwork that would fail to be aesthetically pleasing might be a modernist painting of the Virgin Mary standing at the kitchen sink, with a packet of soap powder beside her. It would be ineffective, because, after all, she really was the Virgin Mary, and that's all we can say about her. As for an example of something that is aesthetically pleasing, he mentions a painting (I can't remember who it is by) of the Virgin Mary, and says this is obviously aesthetically acceptable to us, tasteful, and beautiful because the Virgin Mary looks as if she had been invited to a cocktail party. Thus, what is presented here as an aesthetic judgment quite clearly has an ethical basis. I wonder how you would rate that in describing the difference between the aesthetic and the ethical.

Žižek: I think the thing to do is to include the third Kantian term, the sublime. I think that the judgment that something is aesthetically beautiful but still objectionable (such as the example of the Virgin Mary in the kitchen) is possible only if you already implicitly define the beautiful in opposition to the sublime. This is only possible in so-called post-Kantian modern art, which was made possible by Kantian philosophy itself, the Kantian aesthetic. Thus, to answer your question, you get involved in the whole problem, first taken up by Walter Benjamin and today by François Lyotard, of the difference between the beautiful and the sublime, because modern art is supposedly work that refuses beauty.

Miller: Now in this context, where Lacan uses the expression "in the depths of taste," all the logical conditions of the possibility of something may be satisfied—that is, something may be perfectly well proven—but it's something else for people to desire to pursue it. By the phrase "the depths of taste," Lacan implies that people also have to like it, that it has to be a cause of desire. How can something become a cause of desire? The logical foundations of psychoanalysis lie therein, I would say. But, for people to get into it, there have to be personal reasons and a change in taste as well.

Question: But is it necessary to like something in order to desire it? Isn't it possible for something to come to the fore that people desire even though they don't like it at all?

Miller: Yes, it's quite possible.

Response: Sometimes people go out and spend four million dollars for a painting they don't really like, but that they desire. They have to have it.

Miller: You know that the schools of antiquity were progressively deserted. They were schools to which students came to hear people speak. They were what Lacan, when he founded his own school,[2] called "a refuge from civilization and its discontents." He viewed his own school on the model of the schools of antiquity: a place of refuge from civilization and its discontents. When we read Plato, it is clear that there was passion around the schools—people wanted to know if the playboys of the time would come to hear Socrates or not. It was trendy. It was big news.

It's amazing to see how, in the course of history, after Christianity appeared, the schools were progressively deserted. That was due to a change in taste. To the philosophers of that time, who were educated in the schools of antiquity, Christianity seemed so crude and base that they could not understand how people could be fascinated with it. In the course of time, they refined Christianity.

There you see that kind of mysterious change in taste which Lacan, when he speaks of changes in discourse much later, calls the emergence of a new kind of transference. We can view all this as a long preparation for Freud's version of transference, which has produced a change of taste in our own century. It's clear that whatever you think of psychoanalysis, it has produced a change of taste in our century.

Allow me to emphasize a sentence in which Lacan describes the schools of antiquity: "There one paved the way for science by rectifying one's ethical position." What he means by ethics is the kind of relationship established between the subject and the other. He certainly isn't saying that science has no ethics. On the contrary, he is saying that ethical factors are part of the condition of the possibility of the emergence of the scientific mind or subject: prior to science there is an ethical stance. When Lacan says, "The status of the unconscious is fundamentally ethical," it may seem that he is saying that about psychoanalysis alone. But he could say the same for science. The status of science is fundamentally ethical. It demands, for example, that the subject refrain from doing something he would like to do, and that he be subservient to the supposed facts, number them, etc. He must believe that the numbers of mathematics are already written in the real, that is, that nature is written in mathematical language, as Galileo wrote.

Question: In science, don't you also have to work with the question of your own desire?

Miller: Yes. In the story of Descartes' life, we see Descartes as a man of desire, and one famous moment in his life is when he has dreams of a masked man. In some sense, it is through an asceticism that he arrives at the scientific position. Even if we can say that science rejects desire, that doesn't mean that it rejects ethics. Rather, in science, the definition of one's ethical position paves the way for science.

Let us take the example Lacan discusses: the Academy, the Lyceum, and the Stoa (the Academy is associated with Plato, the Lyceum with Aristotle, and the Stoa with the Stoics). Ethical reflection in the Platonic circle had to do with mathematics, the preoccupation with numbers, insofar as it was linked with Pythagoreanism. With Aristotle comes the emergence of logic, if we take the scientific part, which is in some ways still valid. And with Stoicism we have the beginning of the scientific analysis of language as well as symbolic logic. These different schools were where people came chiefly to ponder the question of the meaning of life, the question of desire, the question of the supreme good, that is, all the pre-Kantian questions: "What am I to do?" "Which objects are good?" They all came seeking the good object. Is sex a good object? And how much sex is good? Is wealth ever good?

They were all told, in some way, what they had to sacrifice: not too much of this, and not too much of that. But at the same time, all this paved the way for the scientific approach. In fact, you could say that in the Lacanian sequence, ethics precedes science. In between, you have something like aesthetics or taste. That's what is defined here. Kant and Sade constitute a rectification of ethics. Then, at the aesthetic level, you have the literature of the nineteenth century, and then you have Freud.

A very central role is assigned here to literature, and if we consider the seventeenth century, we could speak of the epistemological break in the seventeenth century, as Koyré does. Koyré's view was later accepted by all epistemologists. We accept Koyré's argument because it seems very clear that a new way of tackling physical reality emerged, that of applying mathematics to it. We accept the idea of an epistemological break at that time.

"Kant with Sade" is devoted to what we might call the ethical break. Lacan presents Kant's ethics as an ethical break. With it, a new world emerges in which psychoanalysis becomes possible. What exactly is that break? Lacan defined this formative condition of the possibility of psychoanalysis as the theme (which Slavoj alluded to) of happiness in evil. The subject of happiness in evil seems a bit surprising at the beginning of "Kant with Sade." "Happiness in evil," as Lacan says (*le bonheur dans le mal*), is not a very common expression. Why does he put it in quotation marks? Is it a quote? Let me translate it into Freudian terms: happiness in evil means taking pleasure in pain. This formulation is the literary precursor of the death drive. In order to come up with the concept of the death drive, you have to conceive of the possibility of finding satisfaction in aberration, and even in aberrant acts directed against yourself, that is, finding satisfaction in aggression for the sake of aggression. That is what the death drive and the Freudian superego are all about.

Let us consider the superego. Everyone has been talking about fiction: Freud's work is fiction, as is everyone else's. Well then, let's take Freud's work as fiction: Freud as a writer of fiction presents us with a certain character named Superego. We can consider eighteenth century literature as preparing the way for this Superego character. Just as Don Quixote has forerunners in earlier works, and Rameau in *Les liaisons dangereuses* has Richardson's Lovelace (from *Clarissa or the History of a Young Lady*, 1748–1749) as a forerunner, you might say that Freud's Superego has a forerunner, for instance, in some character from Byron's work.

Think of the seducer. The methodical seducer wants to have women, not so much for sexual enjoyment, as to destroy them—for purposes of mastery. We are familiar with this devilish character, who appears in conjunction with the theme of happiness in evil. This character is modeled on Richardson's Lovelace. So let us take the superego as a kind of character. Its forerunner in the eighteenth century is a kind of devilish character who dupes people and pursues evil for the sake of evil, just as the superego pursues aggression for the sake of the pure satisfaction of aggression.

Let us not forget that all this, for Kant and Sade, is contemporary with the French Revolution. That is precisely when destruction on a large scale was manifested. In some ways, Lacan's text also explains the relationship between the Declaration of the Rights of Man and the Terror; Hegel shows that there is a clear link between them, and Lacan explains that here. That's why the French can't handle their bicentennial: they would like to revere the Declaration of the Rights of Man—which is so famous and good for everyone—and separate it from the Terror; and yet at the same time they would like to repeat what the most logical people (who also happen to be counterrevolutionaries) said at the time: that the Rights of Man were the seeds of the Terror. Edmund Burke was clearly the most intelligent man of the period. When everyone in England was in favor of the French Revolution, Burke already saw that it would end badly. That is not to say that I'm in favor of Burke. But he was, in fact, the most lucid analyst of the French Revolution. He knew that if you break with tradition—if you try to begin anew—you upset everything, and the death drive triumphs.

In some ways, that is Kant's ethics. Before Kant, the question of ethics was, "Is this good enough for me?" "And what would be best for me?" That is the Kleinian question; thus, Melanie Klein is pre-Kantian. She has a formula for the supreme good: it is the good object as such, that is, the breast. In antiquity, ethics required that you delicately choose more of this and less of that: moderation. At that time there wasn't any mass terror. Of course, sometimes everyone in a town got killed. But generally speaking, it's only in the nineteenth and twentieth centuries that mass destruction has occurred (it was announced by Nietzsche), and that we are really in the era of Kant and the death drive—Kant's little black box being used to say what is moral and what is not moral. Kant's black box is equipped with the universal criterion of morality: if you want to know whether an action is moral or not, you just try to imagine it as a rule for *everyone*. It's a logical device, and doesn't take into account any other considerations. It destroyed all previous systems in which, for instance, there was one action that befitted a nobleman and another that befitted a commoner, one morality for women and another for men, and different actions that were appropriate depending on your age. With Kant, there is all of a sudden a universal criterion, which as Lacan says, clears all this away, leaving only the terrible logical machine. The result is that one of the great moral issues of our time in America—the abortion question—makes for a great universal debate. It is in some ways structured in Kantian terms: that is, is it or isn't it valid for everyone?

Žižek: The abortion debate clearly shows the limit of this Kantian formalism, because the point is, how do you define universality: is the fetus a human being or not?

Miller: Yes, you have to know if the fetus is part of humanity or not—that's true.

Perhaps I could say a bit more about what made it possible for the theme of "happiness in evil" to catch on. It might be said to have begun in the middle of the eighteenth century, before Kant and Sade. Lovelace is perhaps the very first manifestation of the devilish seducer. If I remember correctly, Richardson has Lovelace say that the devil is part of his [. . .]. He is a seducer with a system, but he is clearly the kind of character that captures the imagination throughout the second half of the eighteenth century. What is fascinating is that he contradicts the old Socratic idea that nobody is bad voluntarily, that is, that no one is willfully evil, but that being or doing evil is merely the result of a misunderstanding regarding what ought to be done. In the middle of the eighteenth century this changes, and you see the change in literature first. This leads, at the end of the century, to Kant's reflection on pure evil, and it also gives rise to the fascination with the Marquis de Sade. You see the same theme in the materialistic philosophers of the second half of the eighteenth century, for example, in LaMaitrie's "Discourse on Happiness" where, in pre-Sadian terms, he recommends crime. He says, "I recommend crime, but pay attention: I recommend peace of mind in crime." You have Sade, you have Byron, you have the character of Melmouth the Wanderer, and you have Baudelaire: *Flowers of Evil* is a study of whether one can find happiness in evil or in goodness. The problem—it's a common topic at that time—is that happiness in goodness means boredom.

You cannot say that someone who does bad deeds is always unhappy. Quite the contrary! Consider the nineteenth-century French author Barbey d'Aurevilly, who wrote a short play called *Happiness in Crime*. Since many fictional characters present us with jouissance in evil, they may be deemed precursors of the superego, the superego that fundamentally wishes you harm. That's the context in which to read "Kant with Sade": using Sade to read Kant. Kant presents us with the demands of duty through what he calls the fact of pure reason—that is, "the voice of conscience." And the voice of conscience appears to be nobody's voice or the subject's own voice, to recall what Slavoj said—that is, the subject hears his own voice as the voice of conscience. In some sense, duty in Kant's work appears as the subject's own voice, but it is completely impersonal, as everyone is supposed to hear the same voice. It is the impersonal "auto-affection" of the subject. Hence, what, according to Lacan's reading of Kant, Sade helps to reveal, is that this voice is not nobody's. It is the very same voice as *the voice of the drives*. That is, it is *the voice of the sadistic superego*. It is the voice of the devilish character.

Whereas in Kant's work there is no one else, that is, the subject "auto-affects" himself with the voice of duty, Lacan reveals a division: there is someone else who enunciates the duty, and *he who enunciates the duty is not dutiful. He who enunciates the duty is not subject to the duty he enunciates.* He is a vicious character.

Thus, in some sense, Lacan provides a critique of Kant, because Lacan says that while Kant reveals the truth, he nevertheless suppresses a fundamental element thereof. But at the same time, Lacan says something else. He says that, if you read Kant with the help of Sade, you see that Kant himself is subversive, that in some way this new ethic of Kant's, which dismisses the old hodgepodge of the ethics of antiquity, has something subversive about it. Lacan says that if you read it from his point of view, the *Critique of Practical Reason* has a flavor of eroticism, an innocent eroticism. Lacan says that because he reads the *Critique of Practical Reason* as veiling a hidden object. It is like the dance of the seven veils: you read a chapter, and you think you'll find the object, but you never do. Lacan, looking as he is for the hidden object in the *Critique of Practical Reason*, says that for him Kant's text has something erotic about it.

Comment from the audience: What has so far not been mentioned is the passion to tell the truth: the ethics that precedes science is the passion to find out what's true. That was Plato's enormous passion against the rhetoricians.

Miller: Could we say that Sade had a passion for truth?

Response: Yes, I think so, because before Sade, evil had not been mentioned. Everybody had been keeping the real heart, the evil heart, hidden.

Miller: I wonder if Sade had such a passion for truth.

Response: He may have had less than Kant, who was very interested in how we can tell the truth, how we know we've got the truth.

Žižek: But isn't one of the points of Kant's revolution precisely that, whereas for all philosophers before Kant, the knowledge of the supreme good was in a way always intimately linked to a knowledge of the supreme truth, for Kant there is a clear and almost radical disjunction between the two. His whole point is that, as an ethical person, you follow a certain voice from nowhere, but that doesn't imply any knowledge of truth.

Response: His forerunner is Newton. He is very interested in how Newton managed to find out the way things work and how we can know.

Žižek: In Newton's work, things are more complicated; the problem with Newton was that he wasn't Newtonian enough. Seventy-five percent of Newton's writings were religious. He didn't accept the basic fact that the universe is a meaningless mass to be symbolized with mathematical signs alone. Newton wasn't yet prepared to achieve that. He still wanted to stick to the notion that the universe is a kind of symbolic, metaphorical universe that has hidden meanings, etc. But to be radically Newtonian implies accepting that the universe as such is a totally meaningless system that can be expressed only in mathematical formulas. That opens the way for Kant's totally formal ethics.

Miller: Perhaps we should recall to mind Kant's fundamental law: act in such a way that the maxim of your will may always be valid as the principle of universal legislation. As an exercise, let us consider what the following have in common: the fundamental law of Kant's pure practical reason, and a saying Lacan quotes from Jarry's play *Ubu Roi*: "Long live Poland, because without Poland there would be no Poles." Lacan tries to formulate Sade's fundamental law using Kant's method. Stuart Schneiderman referred, in his presentation, to the fundamental rule of analysis; this could be an exercise to try to formulate the fundamental rule of analysis on the model of the Kantian axiom as well. That would thus also be an exercise to try to formulate the fundamental law of analysis using Kant's method. What would be the formula of free association? I propose this one, which I wrote down while I was listening to Stuart's presentation: "Speak in such a way that your speech will not be determined by any rule." That would be the rule made precisely to enable the subject to discover the rule that determines speech, that rule being the fundamental fantasy. In Kant, you have the fundamental law. In analysis, you have the fundamental fantasy. Indeed, the whole of Lacan's analysis of Sade is grounded on Sade's fundamental fantasy.

Let us take this mysterious fundamental fantasy. Kant speaks of the fact of pure reason. Let us speak of the fact of the unconscious as such. There's a similarity there, with the difference that the fundamental fantasy is constructed during the analytic experience itself. Analysis really is a process of simplification—you call it "shrinking." I find it marvelous that analysts are called "shrinks," because analysis involves the shrinking of the libido and the progressive construction of the fundamental fantasy from various fantasies, the construction of the subject's fundamental maxim, to use Kant's term. It is equivalent to the fundamental maxim of one's conduct, that is, the law it obeys. And it constitutes meanings and signification. That is, the fundamental fantasy is essentially a formula that says, "Act in such a way that your will always obeys the formula."

Žižek: I think there's a paradox in the fundamental rule of psychoanalysis. On the one hand, of course, it's impossible to follow the rule of so-called free association. All analysands probably know that they always cheat in a way: you never really follow it. So you cannot abide by it. But, on the other hand, you can't escape it. For example (I'm following Michel Silvestre here), when you are speaking as an analysand to your analyst, you can't free associate for a while and then turn to the analyst and say, "Okay, now I want to speak to you seriously as one person to another." Everything is already subsumed under the rule of free association. That is the paradox.

Miller: The paradox of free association—that is, the question of whether one is following the fundamental rule or not—is more palpable for obsessive neurotics than others. Hysterical patients are different, because they are looking for the truth, the truth marches on, and they have no time to inquire if it's free association or not. But the logic is there, you are right. There is a paradox in the rule itself.

In any case, we can construct the fundamental fantasy like that, just as Lacan constructs the Sadian maxim. The Sadian maxim cannot be found in Sade's own work; it's a formulation offered by Lacan.

We might try in a similar manner to reformulate the fundamental rule of analysis. There are people here who are trained in the analysis of texts and the analysis of propositions, so perhaps we can find a parallel between the fundamental rule of pure practical reason, "Everyone has to act in such a way, etc.," and the sentence, "Long live Poland, because without Poland there would be no Poles." Reflect on the structural identity, the similarity of the two sentences. What is the relationship between Kant's fundamental law and the "long live Poland" sentence?

Part II

The parallel between Kant and Sade established by Lacan is an asymmetrical parallel, as we saw in discussing the "with" in the article's title. The article is organized as follows: there is a parallel between Kant and Sade, and Sade completes Kant's analysis; then come considerations on Sade, which appear to fall in two parts, with two schemas; there is another part of the text, which seems more diffuse and general concerning fantasy, law, desire, and the position of psychoanalysis; and then a final section provides an assessment of Sade's position. We have to keep this map in mind, and see how we can tackle the problem.

I had an afterthought concerning "with" and what I said about reciprocity. Normally, the relationship denoted by "with" is reciprocal. That is, if Smith is with Jones, Jones is with Smith. In the relationship denoted by "with" in the modality of companionship, we can see something else. Sancho Panza is not with Don Quixote in the same way Don Quixote is with Sancho Panza. Aeneas is not with his companions in the same way his companions are with him. That is, they are more with him than he is with them, we might say. They are followers and he is a leader. That is an example of a "with" which is not reciprocal. That's the type of "with" we have here, a non-reciprocal "with." In another sense, we could say that Sade is a follower of Kant's, *Philosophy in the Bedroom* following the *Critique of Practical Reason*.

Let us not forget that we ended the first session with a problem, an exercise, which was to compare two propositions. Let me ask a question: Is it true that if you don't have Poland, you don't have Poles?

Response from the audience: One hundred twenty-five years of Polish history demonstrates just the opposite.

Miller: That's exactly why Lacan uses the example. There may very well be Poles throughout the world but no Poland. The gist of Lacan's remark on this exclamation in Jarry's play is thus that it disconnects the existence of Poland from the existence of particular Poles: it disconnects the set and the members of the set. Polishness is independent of Poland. Poland has ceased to exist for years and yet Poles remain, hoping for the second coming of Poland. Lacan quotes this statement about Poland to contradict it. We are in a dimension where, in spite of the fact that Poland and Poles are linked analytically—that is, linguistically and logically—in reality, to bring together Poles and Poland, you need something else. It's not simply that there is a relationship of membership: a Pole is someone who is a citizen of Poland; Poland is the land of the Poles. That is undeniable. That logical, linguistic relationship cannot be eclipsed. But in spite of the logical, linguistic level, historically speaking, there can very well be Poles but no Poland. You need something further to bring the two together.

Now let's see how this relates to the analysis of Kant's fundamental law according to Lacan. This supposed law of morality doesn't mention any specific act that you have to carry out. It's not the ten commandments: it doesn't say you have to honor your father and mother, abstain from stealing, or tell the truth; it doesn't specify anything you should or should not do. Kant's fundamental law doesn't specify any object which you ought to protect, respect, or touch, or on the contrary, not touch. It doesn't say, "Pray in the direction of Mecca five times a day," "You ought to circumcise your male child," "Go to communion," etc. All of that is eliminated. Kant's fundamental law is a true bulldozer in the field of ethics. That's why Lacan speaks of *déblaiement*–of clearing away–at the beginning of his article. Kant clears away the whole field of ethics with it. He clears away the tradition of ethics in antiquity: a discriminating taste for various kinds of objects.

That, for instance, is what fascinated Michel Foucault about ancient Greece, where ethics was very similar to hygienics. The question in Greek ethics was, "What is good for me?" What is good for you is perhaps a little sex–not too much–and to have it with a choice object, not base objects. It is to eat, certainly, but not too much, and to have a little wine, and a little dancing, and sleep in moderate quantities. That was ethics. It was grounded in a highly discriminating taste for various objects in the world. There was no transcendental object to respect. You had to know the world around you, what was harmful to you, and what favored good health. The completely ethical person was in good health. There was a connection between good health and moderation which completely disappears with Kant.

Kant's ethics is thus a kind of Terror–radical and destructive–because in it the world disappears: one's father, mother, neighbor, the neighbor's cows, the neighbor's sheep, wine, women, men, children; all that disappears. You have a formal law and that's it. A formal law is a law which does not specify an object. All content of the law disappears, and we have but a formal criterion of morality. Before that, ethics required you to get inside the world, learn what was best, and even discover the supreme good, which was hidden somewhere. Kant, however, takes an eraser and annihilates all of that, leaving a void or vacuum. Hence, Kant's ethics make present a void. Lacan speaks of this, using the French word "*réjection*." (In French, "*réjection*" is a bit contrived now.) Rejection is fundamental in Kant's ethics. The question is, "What is left?"

The way Lacan looks at Kant's fundamental law is not dissimilar to the way he looks at Descartes' cogito. In Descartes' work, Lacan sees the same kind of operation: first you have the mind with imagination, memory, perception, mathematics, etc. Descartes erases all that, and the void which is left he calls the "cogito"–that is, the pure fact of thinking, which remains undeniable, something which cannot disappear. In Kant's work, this void is a void of all that is pathological in the subject, "pathological" here meaning pathos, emotion, all the subject's sensory interests, everything that gives pleasure. In Kant's law, the dimension of pain and pleasure disappears. His law doesn't say, "Act in such a way as to obtain pleasure," or "Act so that you can be happy," or "Act in such a way that you prevent pain." Pleasure and pain no longer count. Lacan thus describes Kant's law as implying a "complete rejection of the pathological." What's left? Only the criterion of morality.

Yesterday I emphasized the fact that we do not have a true criterion of beauty. The fact that we do not have a true aesthetic criterion is the subject of Kant's *Critique of Judgment*. But we do, according to Kant, have a true criterion of morality—that is, a logical criterion. That is what Lacan emphasizes when he speaks of the rights of logic. It's a funny expression: "the rights of logic." It sounds as if, in order to enter the country of morality, you have to show your passport. It's like getting searched before you get on a plane. That's the way it is with Kant: you leave behind all your pathological luggage, you go through the door, and then the Kantian door makes a sound—"yes" or "no." The only luggage you are allowed afterward is pain, because to obey this fundamental law is generally painful. Kant says that to truly obey the universal criterion of morality, which forbids you to do anything which everyone couldn't do, means that you can't do an awful lot of pleasurable things.

But in spite of the universal criterion of morality, you remain a pathological being. You still experience pain and pleasure. Even if you do not act so as to obtain pleasure and avoid pain, you nevertheless experience them. Because of the fundamental law of morality, you are, for instance, always obliged to tell the truth—even to a dictator who may use it for evil purposes. The result may be that you'll suffer pain.

Kant's logical criterion is universalizability. That is, when you have an action in mind, you put it in the universalizing black box, and an answer comes out: moral or immoral. For instance, are there circumstances in which I am allowed to lie? What if the dictator asks me to reveal what I saw? Am I morally free to lie? Kant says no, because if lying were morally allowed, no one would ever believe anyone else. But such a conclusion is only possible in some transcendental space, because in fact people lie all the time, and we nonetheless continue to speak to each other. We lie all the time, not because we are liars, but because we do not know the truth.

Comment from the audience: There is another position, the classic position before the House Committee on Un-American Activities, where if one were a communist, one's response was, "I refuse to answer the question on the grounds that it might incriminate me."

Miller: Yes, the Fifth Amendment. That is grounded in the fundamental right to preserve one's own life. It means that, in some way, the highest value is protecting one's own life. That conflicts with the fundamental law, because the fundamental law does not say to act in such a way that you will never harm yourself. On the contrary, by obeying Kant's fundamental law, you harm yourself quite a bit. Thus, the philosophy behind the Fifth Amendment conflicts with Kant's fundamental law. If it allows people to remain silent, it's because they would harm themselves by speaking. Nobody ought to speak. As soon as you speak, you are a goner—good for the gallows. Under the Terror, that is real life.

Comment from the audience: Some subjects, though, will give their life with pleasure.

Miller: That's precisely the dimension we see with Sade: the fundamental law of self-preservation is not valid.

Comment: The right to and the obligation to, though, are not the same.

Žižek: The whole point is that there is a distinction in Kant's work precisely between what is legal and what is moral.

Miller: Let us continue with the Kantian criterion. Lacan shows that the functioning of this criterion is based on an analytic [as opposed to a synthetic] link. That is to say, the most ordinary mind can distinguish without previous instruction which actions can or cannot be universalized. It's very important to Kant that his criterion of morality not be something for academics, for those with the highest level of education. It's a criterion that the simplest person can understand and apply immediately.

Take Kant's famous example of the deposit. Suppose I have formulated a maxim to increase my resources by every sure means. I don't live my life by the fundamental law, but by a principle of my own. Now I want to know if this maxim can also take on the value of a universal law. I take out my little black box and ask if my egoistic maxim, "Increase my resources by all sure means," can be universalized—that is, whether, for example, everyone is authorized to deny that they have received a deposit when no one can prove that such a deposit was made. According to Kant, I would immediately see that such a principle would self-destruct as a law because no one would ever again make a deposit. Lacan analyzes that by saying that you can't have deposits if you do not have a depositary worthy of the name: "No deposits without a depositary." It's analytic. It's grounded at the logical, linguistic level, as is "No Poles without Poland." It's the same structure.

Lacan simplified Kant's argument by saying that what is essential in arguments in which you apply the universal law is that you rely on what is in the concepts themselves. Morality, in such instances, is mere logical consistency. You demand logical consistency, and if it is not forthcoming, your maxim self-destructs like the tape in *Mission Impossible:* first you hear a tape-recorded message which asks you to do something which is apparently impossible, and then it self-destructs. You could imagine the fundamental law itself playing on a tape recorder—and it's so impossible to realize that, in the end, it self-destructs. Kant found it a great comfort that you could put your egoistic maxim into a universal machine and have it self-destruct, proving that it is not moral. In some sense, Kant reduces ethics to logic.

What Lacan introduces here is the idea that we could come up with a more synthetic foundation for moral law, synthetic being the opposite of analytic. Perhaps this analytic circularity is not enough to ground ethics; we need something other than definitions of words. Lacan introduces this idea with the example of Poland, where at a certain level you have the same kind of logical consistency: Poland is the land of Poles, and a Pole is a citizen of Poland. But Poland doesn't always exist, even though Poles do; thus the relationship between them is not only analytic, it must also be synthetic.

We can provide a very simple diagram of the difference between the two sentences. Kant's moral law defines the country of morality and says who may cross the border into that land. As Kant himself says, he is not at all sure that there is anyone in the land of morality. Because although there might be people who act in ways that seem truly moral, they might be acting that way because they enjoy it. And if they enjoy it, you can't be sure they are doing it out of pure respect for the moral law. Thus, what we might call Kant Land is perhaps empty—that is, it is a country with no inhabitants. In the case of the Poles, it's just the opposite. In one case, you have a country without people, and in the other, you have people without a country.

What are Poles without Poland? Poles without Poland deplore the fact that Poland does not exist, and they dream of Poland. When Poland doesn't exist you cannot define a Pole as a citizen of Poland, so you define him as someone who dreams of Poland, who loves Poland. You describe him as motivated by a kind of courtly love for Lady Poland, for instance. Try to say to a Pole when there is no Poland that he is not a Pole, and he won't agree, because for him Poland is the other Pole, as it were, of his desire. I say that because Lacan makes the same point in "Kant with Sade." Lacan says that jouissance is at one pole of a relationship with an other, which is a hole it is excavating in the other. At that level, the dictionary is of no help. You cannot simply analyze the dictionary meaning of the word. You cannot, at that level, know what being a Pole means. For instance, you wouldn't say, "Long live Israel because without Israel there would be no Jews."

I believe that the very simple structure we have here lends itself to a lot of interesting associations, and we could spend a lot of time on this parallel. I intended it to be merely a preliminary exercise, a bit of jogging with Lacan.

Now that we have analyzed Kant, the task is to introduce Sade alongside Kant. We have to take into account Kant's phenomenology, that is, the way he describes this fundamental law. He describes it not only as a logical formula. It is at the same time the voice of conscience. Lacan makes a lot of the word "voice," as Kant uses it. Lacan draws a correlation between the fact that, in Kant's work, at the very moment all objects disappear at the level of the law, the voice remains, and the fact that, in Descartes' work, when all the contents of self-consciousness disappear, something is left as a remainder, which is "*cogito ergo sum.*"

In Kant's work, the remainder is a voice, the voice which appears at the very moment that it makes the object disappear. What remains is the voice of conscience, a voice which has something of the signifier about it, because it's a voice with a formulation, a voice that says something. Slavoj alluded in his paper to the importance of the place of the voice in Lacan's graph of desire—the voice which, in some way, is what remains in the locus of the Other. The voice in Kant's work is senseless, because Kant's universal criterion would make a mess of our world. But it's a voice which says something nonetheless. That is, it doesn't make everything disappear. At some level, it is senseless, but it nevertheless has signification in Kant's work. If we had time, we could redo the long analysis of the voice of conscience, for instance, in Heidegger's *Being and Time*, where there is a beautiful and convincing analysis of the structure of the voice of conscience and of the consciousness of the sense of guilt.

Let us try to write the relationship between the moral subject and this voice. The voice formulates an imperative, and if we write the subject as S, we can represent as follows the fact that the voice commands: V → S. In Kant's work, there is a relationship between the voice that formulates the fundamental law and the subject: the voice commands the subject. But to Kant, the voice is an auto-affection of the subject. It is not someone outside of himself who speaks; it is from the very core of his identity that he hears this voice.

In a way, in Kant's work there is nothing else concerning the voice: it is an auto-affection of the subject. That is the very definition of the fundamental law. While we might say there is a voice which commands the subject, in fact, the voice is only the subject's return arrow: V ↻ S

The voice itself is a form of the subject. Kant doesn't introduce any division between the voice and the subject. The voice is the subject returning on himself.

That is precisely the assumption that Lacan refutes by using Sade. With Kant, the situation can be structured using two terms, V and S; using Sade, Lacan brings in two other terms: *a* and $. There you have the four terms of the two schemas in "Kant with Sade":

$$\text{Kant: V} \rightarrow \text{S}$$
$$\text{Sade: } a \quad \$$$

Thus, Sade really helps to complete the relationship. What I am providing here is a very simplified introduction.

Now let Sade enter; everything's prepared for him! We will not make him go through the electronic metal detector because he can't make it; we will smuggle him in! To smuggle him in, Lacan disguises Sade exactly *à la mode de Kant*: he disguises Sade in Kantian clothing. Sade leaves behind his old clothes and comes dressed as a fake Kant.

In discussing Kant, Lacan presents the very formulation found in Kant's text. In discussing Sade, on the contrary, he himself composes Sade's supposedly Kantian maxim. It does not appear anywhere in Sade's texts, though something similar to it can be found in *Juliette*.

In Seminar VII, Lacan provides a more direct quote from Sade: "Lend me the part of your body that can satisfy me for a moment, and if it pleases you, enjoy that part of my body that can be gratifying to you." In "Kant with Sade," Lacan makes a far more convoluted proposition from that. It is a parody of Kant. Sade, dressed up in Kantian clothing to show his stuff, is asked, "Please formulate your fundamental law." He does the best he can, with his various sexual obsessions, and what he formulates is not so well behaved. It seems universal, but I'm not sure it could pass muster.

Let us enunciate this bizarre maxim:

"I have the right to enjoy [*le droit de jouir*] your body," anyone can say to me, "and I will exercise that right without any limit to the capriciousness of the exactions I may wish to satiate."

That's the best Sade can do in the attempt to be like Kant.

Now, if you had no sense of humor whatsoever you might say, "How dare Lacan associate this filthy Sadian maxim with the exalted Kantian maxim?" There are people who really are shocked by this. You should realize that Lacan does this in jest. Like you, he knows that you can leave your children in Kant's hands and have nothing to worry about. You couldn't leave your children with Sade that way. Lacan isn't saying, "Sade is as good a fellow as Kant is." Everyone can see the difference between them. Rather, it is a kind of parody, and Lacan deems it an instructive parody. What he is saying is, "Well, we could dismiss Sade. Sade himself doesn't mean to be taken so seriously, because he's a humorous man. But perhaps we can take it just a bit more seriously and look at what we can do with it."

Everyone can protest that it is intolerable to associate Sade with Kant. Lacan repeatedly says here that he is praying for a sense of humor. He defends his position here on the basis of the fact that Freud himself wrote an article on humor in 1927, in which he explains the relationship between humor and the superego, noting that humor depends on the superego. Humor is a kind of representative of the superego in the dimension of comedy. I don't have time to comment on that in detail, as I would have to refer to Freud's text on humor. That's the only point in the entire text, I believe, where Lacan uses the word "superego," although the entire text has as its psychoanalytic focal point the concept of the sadistic superego and of pleasure in pain. That's part of the eroticism of reading Lacan. Lacan speaks of the eroticism of reading Kant, because there is a veiled object, which you can never grasp. There is eroticism of the same sort in reading Lacan, because sometimes you believe you have it, when in fact it is already elsewhere. The Other jouissance is also present here.

Now that we have taken some precautions concerning the parallel between Kant and Sade, let us approach things in the American way. Imagine Sade in front of the Committee on Un-American Activities. He is asked, "What is the governing principle of your conduct?" And he replies, "The principle governing my conduct is the following: 'I hold that I have the right to enjoy your body,' anyone can say to me, etc." The Committee on Un-American Activities says, "We can't give this guy a visa. Suppose he wants to use a machine gun against someone? We only allow American citizens to do that!" Thus, they would refuse to let him enter the United States.

But along comes his lawyer, Jacques Lacan, who says, "I'm going to demonstrate that Sade's principle is perfectly valid and that it's as beautiful and moral as Kant's. On what grounds do you object to Sade's principle? You object that Mr. Sade alone endorses it. But as a matter of fact, if we consider only the form of what he's saying, it is undoubtedly a universal principle. He is not saying, 'I consider that I, Sade, have a limitless right to do whatever I want to any part of your body.' He is not a Gilles de Rais—a *grand-seigneur* who maintains that he does something simply because he has the power to do it. My client, on the contrary, has formulated a principle for everyone. He is a very modest man, for he says that anyone and everyone can say to him that they have the right to enjoy him. My client allows everyone to enjoy all of his property and even his body. Thus, Mr. Chairman, you must at least acknowledge that it is a universal principle formulated in all modesty.

"'The consequences,' you will retort, 'are horrible: one can imagine what would happen in Washington if anyone could say to someone else, "I'm going to enjoy you without any restrictions." What would happen to the Strategic Air Command?'

"In fact, however, it's you who are not at the Kantian level, for at the level of a fundamental law, pathological consequences must not be taken into account. We are not saying that the world will be *happier* because we respect the universal law. 'Let the world perish,' as Nero said. Nero, in the same vein as Rais and Sade, said, 'Let the world perish rather than the fundamental law.' So, all those consequences which seem horrible to you are simply pathological reactions which must not be used against my client to forbid him from entering this country."

Comment from the audience: Do you think that Lacan would act as his attorney? I think Lacan would just smuggle him in!

Žižek: A good attorney would do more. He would quote the passage by Kant which goes in the same direction. In the *Metaphysics of Law*, Kant defines marriage as follows: "Lend me a part of your body," etc. Kant says that "marriage is a mutual contract."

Miller: He doesn't say, "any part of your body"—

Žižek: No, not just any part!

Miller: "Marriage is the reciprocal lending of the genital organs." He doesn't go as far as Sade.

Žižek: No, but it's a step in the right direction!

Miller: Yes, it's a step in the right direction. But it's also a step in the opposite direction, because Kant defines marriage by mutual property: mutual property of a part of the body.

"My client, on the contrary, rejects all property rights one person might have to another. Jouissance rights, yes; property rights, no. We can say, for instance, that it's very important for every woman to lend herself to the desire of every other person, and it's very important for men too to offer themselves to everyone who desires them. He justifies that as a human right: no one is anybody else's property. He says, 'Never may an act of possession be exercised on a free being.' It's in the part of his book entitled 'Frenchmen, One More Effort if You Want to be Republicans.'

"It is just as unjust to exclusively possess a woman as it is to possess slaves. All men are born free; all have equal rights. It can never be legitimate to exclusively possess another person. Thus, a woman cannot justify refusing someone who desires her by evoking the love she has for someone else, because this motive is one of exclusion, and no man may be excluded from the possession of a woman when it is clear that she is a possession of all men.

"This is what leads my client to conclude that a man who wants to enjoy a woman is entitled, if the laws are just, to summon the woman to a special place, and there, with the blessing of the matron of this temple of Venus, she has to humbly and submissively satisfy his every whim and fancy. And men would have to do the same for the women who desire them.

"Do not try to imagine such a world. That's not the point of the fundamental law. If you tried to imagine such a world you would judge my client according to possibility: is it possible or not? But I would object: the question of possibility must not be asked in this trial, because what counts here are universals and logic, not possibility."

All of these arguments can be found in "Kant with Sade." There is no reciprocity here, because the moment a man wants a woman, he may call for her and she will have to come. It is not reciprocal, but another time she may grab someone and do the same with him. That is the distinction Lacan draws between reciprocity and *la charge de revanche*. Let us take an example: You are at a restaurant and the woman you are with says, "It's on me." You yourself are not going to pay a second time (so it's not reciprocal), but you might say, "*À charge de revanche*"—that is to say, "When we go out to eat next time, I'll pay." In other words, "my turn next time." The difference between this and reciprocity is important, because on one occasion you may have complete mastery, but on another you may be the slave. This promise of switching sides is very colloquial in French.

Lacan writes, "*Un énoncé, excluant comme tel la réciprocité, la réciprocité annule la charge de revanche*": reciprocity annuls the principle of "my turn next time." He takes the French expression, "*à charge de revanche*," and makes a substantive of it, "*la charge de revanche*," which is perfectly understandable, but incorporates a twist, a bit of "linguistrickery." You see the importance of distinguishing reciprocity, which is an immediate relation—if I am X to you, you are X to me; if I am master to you, you are master to me, which is stupid—from role reversal where first I'm master, and you're slave, but next time, the tables will be turned.

Lacan says, "My client subjects himself to another's law. 'I,' '*Je*,' in French, is subjected to any other: A → *Je*. Thus my client holds that the other has the right. And that's why, in my *Écrits*, I wrote that Sade's regime is a regime of the other's freedom. His discourse of the right to enjoyment situates the other as its enunciating subject. Not as the subject of the enunciated or statement, because in the statement it is: 'anyone can say to me.' The 'me' designates the subject of the statement. But what props up enunciation is the other as free to do whatever he wants with me.

"Hence my client is much more honest than Kant. Kant leads us to believe that the subject is speaking to himself, enunciating a law that terrorizes him. Whereas Sade presents us with a formulation in which the distinction between subject and other is explicit. He reveals the division of the subject, whereas Kant makes us think it is an auto-, non-divisive affectation."

Lacan writes: "The bipolarity by which the moral law is instituted is but the splitting of the subject which occurs in any intervention of the signifier—namely, that of the subject of enunciation from the subject of the statement." "The moral law," says Lacan, "has no other principle. Still, it is necessary that it be pronounced." Lacan finds that in "Long live Poland," because he considers the exclamation to imply the presence of the subject of enunciation. And that conforms, if not to what Jakobson says, then to what Damourette and Pichon say in their treatise on language.[3]

Lacan asserts that the Sadian maxim, pronounced as it is by the other—that is, by anyone—is more honest than appealing to the voice within. Thus, Sade is more honest than Kant, because Sade's principle is not supposedly enunciated by the voice within, but rather is explicitly enunciated by an other. The Sadian maxim unmasks the splitting of the subject that is usually covered over. The Sadian maxim shows us the difference between two positions of the subject: the fundamental subject [of enunciation] and the subject of the statement.

That's why it's so difficult to remember the formulation of the supposedly Sadian maxim: "'I have the right to enjoy you,' anyone may say to me." This involution makes it rather difficult to remember, because the first "I" is not the subject of the statement. It begins with "I," but this "I" is already a quotation. And it is revealed as a quotation only retroactively. You might try to abstractly define "enunciation" and "statement"; I suggest you do the opposite: use Lacan's text to see what meanings are attributable to those two words.

Now we have to reproject the explicit split between the statement and enunciation onto the subject. That is, the subject is split into two parts. We won't designate the subject anymore as S as we did before, but rather as $, because it is split between the Other and the subject.

The Other is not situated in the same place as the subject, but in another sense the whole schema represents the Other's place or space. In one paragraph, Lacan makes the Other other than the subject, and in another paragraph, the Other is the place of both the Other and the subject. That's also true in Schema L where you have the ego (a), the other (a'), and S:

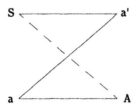

The Other is situated in the lower right-hand corner, but at the same time the entire process occurs in the Other's locus. That is, the Other is situated at one vertex, alongside other terms, but all this is at the same time within the Other.

That's why we see in Lacan's work the problematic of the signifier of the Other (A) in the Other's locus: the Other is a set that contains itself. The very last point Lacan makes in his article on psychosis is that the Name-of-the-Father "is a signifier of the Other, as locus of the law" in the Other—as the locus of language (*Écrits*, p. 221). We have the Other as the name of the set, and the Other as an element in the set:

This is an early view of Lacan's which implies that there is an Other of the Other; that's why he denies it at the fundamental level later, saying, "There is no Other of the Other." Thus, there is a considerable evolution in Lacan's writing, from the idea that there is a fundamental guarantee of the Other to the idea that there is no such guarantee.

Thanks to Sade, who renders the split in the subject explicit, we can complement our S with $. With Sade we see an explicit splitting of the subject. We are also going to complement the V—which, as I said before, designates the voice of conscience, and which Lacan takes as the will [*Volonté*], the pure will in Kant's work—with the symbol of the voice as object *a*. Under Kant's pure will, we are going to give its full value to the voice as object *a*. This abstract will is nothing without the voice which props it up and which is the remainder when all objects have disappeared.

Now we have four terms. Lacan doesn't indicate where they come from in the text: they just crop up all of a sudden. Having motivated the four terms here, we now have the elements with which to construct the schemas:

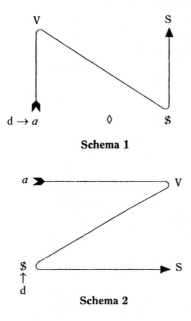

We now find ourselves on the threshold of the questions of fantasy, jouissance, desire, and so on. But we are out of time. Will Sade ever get along with Kant? Will Sade escape the Committee on Un-American Activities? We'll leave those questions open and go to the banquet!

Notes

1. [This lecture was given in two parts in 1989 at Kent State University in the context of a conference on "Lacan, Discourse, and Politics." It was transcribed by Mark Bracher and edited by Bruce Fink.]

2. [See "Founding Act" in *Television: A Challenge to the Psychoanalytic Establishment*, New York: Norton, 1990, p. 104.]

3. [Damourette, Jacques and Edouard Pichon. *Des mots à la pensée : Essai de grammaire de la langue française*, 7 volumes. Paris: Bibliothèque du français moderne, 1932–51.]

PART V

CLINICAL PERSPECTIVES

AN INTRODUCTION
TO LACAN'S CLINICAL PERSPECTIVES

∞

Jacques-Alain Miller

Dr. Françoise Gorog, the head of the clinic here at Sainte-Anne Hospital, asked me to speak today, and I intend to present a number of elements of Lacan's clinical work. I will try to be simple and provide a summary of the main trends in his work.

Lacan worked at Sainte-Anne Hospital, the main psychiatric hospital in Paris. It dates back to the eighteenth century, and quite a lot of the history of psychiatry took place here, especially in the nineteenth and twentieth centuries.

I will stress three main lines of Lacan's work. First, he systematized, radicalized, and in some ways simplified Freud's work in such a way that we can use a very simple grid to diagnose "mental structures," so to speak. This simple grid covers all mental categories: neurosis, psychosis, and perversion. Lacanian clinicians no longer even see that as original, as it is so ingrained in our minds. But the DSM III is there to remind us that this fundamental grid is not so widely recognized. We don't always think about it because it is really what we learn as beginners. I once spoke with an analyst in Chicago who said that ego-psychology is like wallpaper in the United States: it is so much a part of the general background that no one sees it anymore. Similarly, Lacan's grid is our wallpaper: we wouldn't know what to do in the clinic without it.

Mental structure means that there is no such thing as a mental continuum. Such a continuum would allow you to say that someone is a bit psychotic, but sometimes neurotic and perverted as well. You find this kind of perspective in American and English clinical settings where, for instance, the structural differences between psychosis and neurosis are blurred. In such circles, you could offer up a diagnosis including a mixture of perversion and psychosis, the "borderline" category being there to help completely blur the picture. When we read their clinical accounts, we often feel lost. Our little map is not being used in them.

Structure means that there is no such mental continuum. In the clinical exercise in which we engage when we teach, presenting a case and talking about what to do about it, a deliciously pleasurable moment inevitably arises when we have to decide where we are going to situate the subject in question. It is a magnificent moment where clinical mastery supposedly shows itself, a moment that doesn't really exist in circles where this grid is not used. Sometimes we hesitate between hysteria and psychosis, and we consider that we ought to know whether a given subject lines up on one side or the other, though we do not yet know. We can only make a diagnosis after further observation. In two or three cases, Lacan himself, while conducting certain live case presentations, which he did for years, preferred to wait for further indications before offering up a diagnosis.

Structure thus means that there is no continuum. Second, it means that you can encounter the same descriptive elements in different categories. Nevertheless, the presence of particular descriptive elements does not constitute proof of any one specific structure. Descriptive elements tell us nothing if they are not considered in relation to other elements. For instance, you may find hallucination in both hysteria and psychosis, and so hallucination as such is not, in and of itself, proof of structure because you have to consider it as an element of a structure that is codified by other elements. If you find an element like hallucination, you still have to ask very precise questions to distinguish between the different structural categories.

A much debated question is, for example, where homosexuality should be situated, for it may certainly be present in perversion but we know it also plays a role in psychosis—to the extent, in fact, that Freud himself considered paranoia to be a defense against homosexuality. A psychotic subject may be characterized by homosexual object choice; he may, in other words, have a perverse mode of sexual enjoyment. Thus, the existence of homosexuality is not as such sufficient to justify a diagnosis of perversion.

While Lacan systematized Freud's clinical work, he also twisted and radicalized it by indicating one central mechanism for each of the three structures. Things are not so clear-cut in Freud's writings. Lacan had, so to speak, French or Cartesian conceptual requirements: if there are three structures, there should be one central mechanism for each of them. He pinpointed in Freud's work a specific term for each: in neurosis it is *Verdrängung*, usually translated as "repression"; in psychosis it is *Verwerfung*, Lacan's famous "foreclosure"; in perversion it is *Verleugnung*, which is usually translated in English as "disavowal" and in French as *désaveu*. In the end, Lacan preferred the French term *démenti* for *Verleugnung*, which is translated into English as "denial." *Verleugnung* has a long history in Freud's work: it is found, for instance, in his short article entitled "Fetishism" and in the Wolf Man case; it is a constant in Freud's work and Freud attempts to distinguish those three mechanisms in a clear-cut way, but they nevertheless overlap in his writings. People can always say that Lacan injects what he thinks into Freud's work or, on the contrary, that he clarifies the very logic of Freud's thought.

A great deal of Lacan's analytic teaching is devoted to the construction of three distinct modes of negation. Lacan presents them as follows: *Verwerfung* in psychosis is the negation of the signifier of the father, *Verleugnung* in perversion is a specific mode of negation of the signifier of the phallus, and *Verdrängung* in neurosis is a much broader negation of the subject himself. Each one of those mechanisms in itself warrants a full lecture.

Within each of those categories there are, of course, further distinctions. Lacan again and again drew parallels among the three categories. Every time Lacan grappled with a new concept or stressed a new perspective on clinical work, he applied it to neurosis, psychosis, and perversion. In psychoanalysis, every time you achieve a new perspective, you can complexify it according to three registers. Those are obviously not the only registers; we have, for instance, other clinical categories such as man and woman, and male structure and female structure, which clearly cut across the three main clinical categories. If, for example, Lacan says that perversion is a male privilege, things become more complex if we combine the binary structure of male and female and the threefold structure of neurosis, psychosis, and perversion. We could say that perversion is a male privilege, while all true psychotics are would-be females. Lacan forged a now famous phrase regarding psychosis: *"pousse à la femme"*; psychosis is would-be female territory. In neurosis we distinguish between hysteria and obsession, and we usually associate male and female with obsession and hysteria, respectively. Still there is no obligation to postulate that no males are hysterics. At times we focus on neurosis as such, and at other times on the distinction between hysterical neurosis and obsessive neurosis—with the proviso that Freud considered obsessive neurosis to be a dialect of hysteria, hysteria being the central core of neurosis. Occasionally, we focus on a further neurotic entity known as phobia. In Lacan's work you at times find a binary opposition between hysteria and obsession and at other times the threefold distinction between phobia, hysteria, and obsession. In general, our references are Freudian. We refer to Dora when it comes to hysteria, to the Rat Man when it comes to obsession, and to little Hans when it comes to phobia.

In psychosis, the Schreber case is central, but the main distinction Lacan draws is between paranoia, which is a classical psychiatric category, and other forms of psychosis. In those others, one finds the vague term "schizophrenia."

Lacanians have inherited classical German and French psychiatry, augmented by various Freudian notations. Their categories do not go much further than that, practically speaking. In perversion, we essentially use the classical French or German clinical categories, but we distinguish perhaps more clearly than in America and England between perverse phenomena, which we take to be elements that may very well be present in psychosis and neurosis, and "true perverts" who are defined in some sense by not being analyzable or by the very fact that they very seldom enter analysis. Thus, psychoanalysis is not our sole frame of reference.

As I mentioned above, Lacan systematized Freud's clinical perspectives and adopted much of classical French and German psychiatry. He incorporated the latter without much reformulation. Proof of that can be found in the *Écrits*: though Lacan explored the Schreber case at length, he relied upon his psychiatric experience in understanding the dimensions of psychosis. He did so as an analyst, but did not attempt to reformulate subjective positions which lie outside the grasp of analytic operation. As a result, in the 1960s and 1970s his students had to learn about classical French and German psychiatry, which was not exactly accessible in France at that time. We had to republish many works, including those by Kraepelin and Clérambault. Lacan incorporated the classical psychiatric treasures, which have now been replaced in psychiatry by drug treatment which has blurred all clinical distinctions. On the contrary, we have saved all of the earlier detailed clinical observations. Certain psychiatrists have conserved them only as a kind of museum piece. We believe these clinical perspectives are operative. Lacan required us to learn about the history of the concept of paranoia, even though it is pre-Freudian, for Lacan considered it well grounded, albeit in need of some reformulation.

The concept of schizophrenia, on the other hand, is post-Freudian. It was introduced by Bleuler, after having read Freud's work, and attempts to extend to psychosis Freud's theory of neurosis. Like Jung, Bleuler tried to transfer Freud's understanding of neurosis to the realm of psychosis. Freud was always wary of the category of schizophrenia, and in Seminar III on psychosis, Lacan begins by mentioning that.

As we have seen, Lacan systematized Freud's work and incorporated a great deal of classical psychiatry. Let us now move on to a third point. Lacan's clinical work is first grounded on Schema L. I'm not going to explain once again the construction of this very simple cross. At the time of "Function and Field of Speech and Language in Psychoanalysis" and Seminars I and II, Lacan's idea was that the symbolic cures; the cure is symbolic, and the analytic cure is essentially situated on the symbolic axis, impeded only by its encounter with the imaginary axis. The basic idea was that what we call mental illness is essentially due to some kind of defect in the symbolic relationship, some defect in the symbolic axis. Even in Seminar III, when Lacan defines psychosis, he defines it essentially by the imaginary: he in some sense equates psychosis and the imaginary. The imaginary in Lacan's work is psychotic as such, and you see that one can reread the mirror stage as describing paranoia: there is a fundamental conflict with the other because the other is usurping my role; the mirror stage is structured by projection. At times, Lacan emphasizes the subject's native paranoia, the subject being situated at the imaginary level, the symbolic order being what allows one to accede to normality, symbolic normality. But even in the end, Lacan very much enjoyed saying that psychotic subjects are completely normal. Which meant that the symbolic order is what is abnormal and that human nature is fundamentally paranoid.

Seen from the point of view of the symbolic, one could emphasize the subject's native hysteria. That is why Lacan uses the symbol $ for the subject: the subject as such is a hysterical subject. As an aside, I would say the notion of the subject's native paranoia is akin to the Kleinian theory of the psychotic core of all subjects; that is why Kleinians are interested in the mirror stage. Lacan's mirror stage is now part of standard Kleinian training, but Kleinians stop there. One could take the mirror stage as the subject's fundamental stage of development and assert that everyone is psychotic at heart. And one could view analysis as a return to that psychotic core; but when Lacan speaks of the subject's native paranoia, he views analysis as something completely different because to his mind the cure does not involve going back to the imaginary axis but, on the contrary, elevating the symbolic axis.

By using this very simple structural grid, you understand why Lacan stresses that psychosis, if you understand it as the dominance of the imaginary relationship, is not dialectical because the dialectic concerns the symbolic axis. Psychosis has a specific inertia when compared with the dialectical potential of neurosis. Don't think that when we say "dialectical" we are merely talking philosophy; you can truly see what dialectical means in case presentations. In psychosis, we find no true speech, that is, no creative speech which implies a dialectic. That is why foreclosure may be distinguished from repression: foreclosure is a non-dialectical mode of negation. "I don't want it; well perhaps I want it if it is given to me; but if it is given to me, why is it being given to me—perhaps I have to refuse it." There we see dialectical negation: you have to go through various negations to reach something positive and you take into account what the other may think and what you think. In case presentations, you can detect non-dialectical elements where there is no give and take. The very fixity you find in psychosis is a clinical criterion: the non-dialectical fixity of particular elements.

In Seminar III, you still find the prevalence of the imaginary in psychosis. Lacan asks, "What in psychosis stops the symbolic relationship from prevailing?" "What is the defect in the symbolic which explains the dominance of the imaginary relationship?" That is where Lacan introduces the notion of the foreclosure of the Name-of-the-Father, that is, the absence of the fundamental element in the locus of the Other. Let me immediately translate this theme and clarify Lacan's theory of the Name-of-the-Father.

The fundamental element in the Other is the Name-of-the-Father. In order for the subject to be situated in his or her proper place in the symbolic order, the subject must refer to a phallic signification. That is the basis of Lacan's developed theory of psychosis. There is, of course, a predominance of the imaginary relationship, but it is due to a defect in the symbolic relationship, and that defect may be a difficulty with the Name-of-the-Father or a difficulty with phallic meaning. That is the structure of the very complicated schema you have in "On a Question Preliminary to Any Possible Treatment of Psychosis." These two elements, the Name-of-the-Father and the phallus, are taken by Lacan from the simplified Oedipal structure.

At the same time, in Seminar III Lacan says that psychosis involves the reduction of the Other to the other, which is another way of saying the same thing: the collapse of the symbolic into the imaginary. That is the first way Lacan explains how the psychotic subject may feel certain that someone is sending him messages. It doesn't solve the question of the real. What is the real when the symbolic has not been constituted? Lacan answers that question in Seminar I when he says that, in psychosis, the whole of the symbolic order is real: when the symbolic dimension is lacking, the whole symbolic is experienced as something real. The lack which is present in the symbolic order may appear real to the psychotic subject. We will come back to what real signifies in that context. There are various phenomena which the subject tries to describe: a feeling of disunity, of his body, that the end of the world is near. If such phenomena were in the symbolic dimension, they could enter into a dialectic with the Other. In psychosis, however, they appear to the subject to be what is most real in his world.

We use the notion of the real in psychosis as non-dialectical to help distinguish hysterical phenomena from psychotic phenomena. Psychotic hallucinations are taken by the subject to be what are most real in his experience; he speaks of them with complete certainty which is not open to doubt. This is fundamental, and we grasp that by listening. We cannot film hallucinations nor can we observe them, though we may observe that a psychotic formulates his hallucinated messages silently. So what do we focus on? Their enunciation.

When someone says something, there is a statement or proposition on the table. But you can also focus on the position the subject adopts toward what he says. In other words, you can concentrate on his meta-linguistic position. How does he himself view what he is saying? Does he view it as something he knows, believes, or ascertains; as something he is sure of, as something that is open to doubt, as something someone may object to; or is it a thing to him? When it is not open to any dialectical process, it is what we call an elementary phenomenon of psychosis. The subject considers such phenomena undeniable and may even be surprised by them—he himself may consider it strange that the President of the Republic takes the time to speak to him personally in his head, but he cannot deny that experience. Even if some part of his ego agrees that such a thing is unthinkable, he may not be able to deny it: to him it is the most real and certain aspect of his experience. Certainty is a term that fascinated Wittgenstein, for the best of reasons, but this certainty is not simply philosophical in nature. It concerns experience, and in case presentations you can sense at times in what a subject says that it has this quality of unshakable non-dialectical certainty—that it is not provocative certainty, designed to get a rise out of the Other. If an analyst is talking with a subject with hysterical hallucinations, he can make them dissipate or worsen depending on how he reacts. As Other, his belief in them or disbelief can make them wax or wane. If he knows how to present his own disbelief in those phenomena—since in hysteria, the desire of the subject is the Other's desire—the enormous phenomena progressively decrease. That can never happen with a psychotic.

You must also carefully distinguish between visual hallucinations and auditory hallucinations which you don't find with the same precision and credibility in hysteria as in psychosis. In hysteria, hallucinations are not as clear as in psychosis: they are frequently presented as blurred perception, whereas in psychosis they are very clear and well defined. In hysteria, they are presented in the modality of uncertainty, while in psychosis they are presented as what the subject is most certain of.

Foreclosure is a mode of negation which brings out the undeniable. Non-dialectical negation makes things seem undeniable. It is an open question as to what analysis can do, once all these fine things have been distinguished. What can we do with perversion, psychosis, and neurosis?

HYSTERIA AND OBSESSION[1]

∞

Colette Soler

Hysteria, Obsession, and the Freudian Problem

My theme here, hysteria and obsession, concerns differential diagnosis. It is a theme that comes under a more general one, namely, what is neurosis? "Hysteria" and "obsession" are terms that come from clinical psychiatry, which was basically constituted in the nineteenth century. Freud adopted these and certain other psychiatric categories. The framework of my theme here is the fundamental distinction between psychosis, neurosis, and perversion. In psychiatry, neurosis, psychosis, and perversion are defined by the kinds of symptoms associated with each category; thus they are considered to be descriptive categories. Here I will be speaking only about neurosis. The question is: What can psychoanalysis say about neurosis?

The question can be formulated differently, for Freud said that the neuroses are transference psychoneuroses. Thus the question is, what does transference reveal about hysteria and obsession? That is, what does transference bring out that is not brought out in psychiatric observation? Psychoanalysis, which I will define more precisely later, uses the old psychiatric categories, but claims to have found new diagnostic criteria, psychoanalytic criteria. Some of you may think that neurosis, perversion, and psychosis are old-fashioned because they are categories from the nineteenth century. Our claim is that, using these old categories, we have founded new diagnostic criteria. It is not with the help of modern-day psychiatry because contemporary psychiatry has forgotten the nineteenth century diagnoses. Perhaps that is due to pharmacology, but I assume there are other reasons as well. I think it would be useful to begin here with a return to Freud.

For ten years Lacan taught us to return to Freud. It was because he thought at that time that psychoanalysts had forgotten Freud's work and deviated from his orientation. I won't provide a historical study of Freud here. I merely want to stress Freud's main ideas regarding the question: What is neurosis?

Defense Against an Incompatible Idea

I shall mention only a few of Freud's papers where he discusses neurosis. First, I will talk a little about "The Psychoneuroses of Defense" (1894), "Further Remarks on the Psychoneuroses of Defense" (1896), "The Aetiology of Hysteria" (1896), and "Project for a Scientific Psychology" (1895), the latter being Freud's first text on neurosis. Freud himself thought, after writing this first text, that there were things that required correction in it, but he also felt that it contained a number of valid ideas. We also have Freud's important case histories, "Dora" and the "Rat Man," and two articles written in 1924 by Freud: "Neurosis and Psychosis" and "The Loss of Reality in Neurosis and Psychosis." I could quote many sentences from these articles, but I shall quote only one or two.

In the introduction to "Further Remarks on the Psychoneuroses of Defense," Freud repeats his thesis regarding the psychoneuroses of defense: neurotic symptoms arise "through the psychical mechanism of (unconscious) *defence*—that is, in an attempt to repress an incompatible idea which had come into distressing opposition to the patient's ego" (Standard Edition [hereafter SE] III, 162). He also indicates that he considers "defence as the nuclear point in the psychical mechanism of the neuroses" (Ibid). It is a very simple notion: *There is a defense against an incompatible idea.* In other words, something in what we call the subject is pushed aside.

What is that something? Sexuality. The incompatible idea is linked to sexuality. Freud says, "We are to regard the sexual experience of childhood as the cause of hysteria and obsession" ("My views on the Part Played by Sexuality in the Aetiology of Neurosis" [1905]). I merely wanted to remind you of this well-known thesis. Now perhaps we can comment on this thesis.

What is the first notion implied by the theory of the "incompatible idea"? It is the same as Freud's last notion in 1938, the idea of *splitting*. The term "split" is used by Freud in his first article and in his last article, "The Splitting of the Ego." The incompatible idea is pushed aside or split off. When Lacan later introduces the idea of the divided subject ($), it is not a conceptual bomb—it is explicit in Freud's work. What is different is the way Lacan introduces the split in the subject: the way he explains it and the way he justifies it.

The second point I want to stress is perhaps self-evident, namely, the relation Freud establishes right from the beginning between the unconscious and sexuality. The idea that is pushed aside is linked to sexuality. Freud elaborates on this point in great detail and continually changes his perspective in certain ways. Regarding the split, however, there is no change: it is present until the very end of his work.

Frustration of the Child's Sexual Desires

What is Freud's notion of sexuality at the beginning? It is the notion of seduction, traumatic seduction. Freud believed his hysterical patients at the beginning. They were women who said—albeit not so easily, through free association and with the help of interpretation—that they had been seduced by their fathers or by a similar figure. Freud changed his mind on this point later after having recognized that behind the traumatic scene, behind the supposed seduction, was fantasy. This was a very important step because it permitted him to discover infantile sexuality and what he lays out in the *Three Essays on the Theory of Sexuality*. There is a relation between the step he makes and the discovery of infantile sexuality.

Freud, as a psychoanalyst, discovers in his patients' speech certain sexual representations, perverse sexual ideas. That is a fact, the first fact. He then has to attempt to understand that clinical fact. At first he thought that the perverse representations were the result or effect of seduction by an adult. Thus he concluded that a subject's perverse ideas represented the sexuality of the adult who had seduced the subject as a child. He did not conclude that the perverse sexual representations belonged to the subject; rather, he thought they were memories of a traumatic act, an event that was contingent, not necessary, an event that might occur in the case of a given individual or that might not.

It was only when he began to realize that that would imply that virtually everyone had been seduced that the conclusion imposed itself upon him that the child has perverse sexual representations of its own very early in life. That is what allowed him to abandon the traumatic seduction theory and discover infantile sexuality. Thus there was a shift from trauma to fantasy.

An additional change took place. In a later text, "Neurosis and Psychosis" (1924), Freud says that the etiology of all neuroses and psychoses is the frustration of rebellious infantile desires. That frustration always comes from the outside. There is a big change between the first and the last theses.

Let me point out that when Freud speaks about *Versagung*, frustration, he is not referring to the frustration of love. It is not Winnicott's idea. A lot of mileage has been gotten out of the term "frustration" since Freud's time. Winnicott speaks of the "good-enough mother" and grants a major place to the frustration of love. Freud and Lacan never suggest that the frustration of love produces neurosis. Sometimes an early, excessive frustration of love can lead to what Spitz calls "hospitalism," as in the case of children who suffer premature abandonment. I am not saying that the deprivation of love has no effect. It depends on when it occurs. But such deprivation doesn't cause neurosis. According to Freud, frustration does not concern love but sexual desire, that is, jouissance. Or as Freud would say, "sexual pleasure" or "satisfaction."

The Loss of Sexual Satisfaction

The second point I want to stress has to do with Freud's different emphases in his theory at the beginning and at the end. At the beginning, when Freud believed in the theory of trauma, he thought that the true cause of neurosis was the intrusion of sexuality, that is, the encounter with a *surplus or excess of sexuality*. But when he made the transition from seduction to fantasy, Freud discovered infantile sexuality and emphasized the *loss of sexual satisfaction* as the cause of neurosis. At that point he discovered the notion of castration.

First he discovers infantile sexuality and later castration. He puts forward a theory of the sexual causation of neurosis, but sexuality is only a half-cause. The other half is defense. Freud's construction is very simple; it is made up of two terms: (1) sexuality and (2) defense on the part of the ego. Sexuality itself is divided by Freud into two component parts. There is the "incompatible idea" or "representation" of sexuality, which Lacan identifies with the signifier. But there is also affect, the "quantum of affect" or sexual excitation itself. Affect is not an idea: It is something actual in the body. Here you can see the link between sexuality and the unconscious because for Freud the unconscious has to do with sexuality. We see that in Freudian theory a distinction is made between sexuality, which passes into an incompatible idea or representation (*Vorstellungsrepräsentanz*), and the quantum of affect. Here we have an anticipation of Lacan's distinction between the signifier and jouissance. This famous Lacanian distinction is closely related to Freud's earliest and latest notions.

Defense	Incompatible Idea
$\dfrac{\text{Ego}}{\$}$	Sexuality *Vorstellungsrepräsentanz* (Signifier) / Quantum of affect (Jouissance)

The Choice of Neurosis

Now when Freud says "defense" he implies a reaction of the subject to the sexuality that subject encounters. *A reaction implies a choice.* Choice suggests that the subject is responsible. We may think that sexuality is encountered, that is, that it is heterogeneous to the subject; that would explain why the first sexual experiences are always a bit traumatic—not because they involve seduction by another person, but because sexual feeling, in and of itself, is foreign to the subject. That would allow us to say that, at the outset, the subject is not responsible for the sexual sensations he feels.

But even if we believe that sexuality is real and that the subject encounters it as something that originates outside of himself, the defense is his own answer. That defense is what we now call "the position of the subject," his position when confronted with sexuality as real.

"The choice of neurosis" is an expression used by Freud. There are several hesitations in Freud's writings: he wonders if the choice of neurosis depends on the kind of sexual drives involved or if it depends on the defense, that is to say, on the subject's answer. We can ask whether different drives and defenses are involved in the different neuroses. If they are, this could help us understand how symptoms are constructed. Let me remind you of a few of the answers Freud put forward regarding hysteria and obsession. The answers themselves are not important. What is important is to see how Freud investigates neurosis and the sexual drives. Freud links obsession with the anal drive and hysteria with the oral drive. But in his definitive conclusion, it is not possible to identify one kind of neurosis with one kind of drive—it is a matter of frequency. What remains is the way in which he studies the neuroses.

Let us now turn to the drives. Freud introduces another distinction that is actually situated more at the level of how the subject is situated in sexuality. There are texts in which Freud says the obsessive occupies an active position regarding sexuality whereas the hysteric occupies a more passive position. When he speaks of the hysterical nucleus of obsession, his question is located at that level: The hysterical nucleus of obsession is a nucleus of sexual passivity.

As for the position of the subject, Freud stresses the hysteric's fundamental aversion to sexuality or disgust toward sexuality, which is the hysteric's primary answer or reaction of rejection. On the contrary, Freud stresses that too much primal pleasure is at the origin of obsession. That means that the subject is captivated by jouissance. There is a sharp distinction here between two different subject positions.

It is now necessary to add the mechanism of the "return of the repressed," the mechanism by which symptoms are engendered. There is an opposition between the "return in the body" (conversion) in hysteria and the "return in the mind" in the form of thoughts in obsession. There is also an opposition between what Freud called "compromise formation" and the obsessive mechanism of isolation and juxtaposition in the mind. It would be possible here to inquire how the repressed returns in the different categories.

Marco Mause: You stated your intention at the outset to establish a distinctive psychoanalytic clinic based on transference. I have two questions regarding this intention. The first question, which may be premature, but which has been troubling me for a while, is what is the difference, if any, between hysteria and hysterization? The second question concerns jouissance. You talked of the difference between hysteria and obsession, stating that in hysteria we see an aversion to jouissance while in obsession we see a strong attraction to it. We know that Freud said that symptoms contain an element of jouissance. So how do we locate this jouissance in the two clinical categories?

Soler: The first question regarding hysteria and hysterization is premature at this point in this series of lectures. It will be easier and clearer to explain the difference after we talk about desire and fantasy. All I can say now is that hysterization, as the word indicates, implies a change of position on the subject's part. Hysterization designates a change of position in relation to desire, especially the Other's desire, A. I will address this question further when we speak about hysterical and obsessive fantasies. It is simple: An hysterical subject is a subject who has a special link with the Other's desire. You can see it very easily in clinical work. An hysteric is a subject who wonders what the Other desires or if the Other desires, a subject who questions the Other's desire. Hysterization involves making a subject sensitive to the Other's desire.

It is necessary to remember this when you work with an obsessive subject, for *the obsessive subject annuls the Other's desire.* There is a big difference between the two subjects. This is particularly important when it comes to transference. We'll talk about it again later.

Now for your second question. There is an aversion to pleasure in hysteria, while there is too much pleasure in obsession. Your question was how this difference is manifested in the jouissance of the symptom in the two clinical categories. Aversion does not mean that the hysteric cuts off every relationship involving jouissance. There is a defense against jouissance in hysteria, but there is also a failure: The "return of the repressed" indicates the failure of defense. This failure gives rise to symptoms. Logically, therefore, jouissance is present in the symptoms. The hysterical subject defends against this jouissance.

Similarly, in the case of the obsessive, Freud spoke of an overly strong attraction to jouissance. But he also spoke of a defense against that jouissance. It is interesting: You can refuse what you despise but you can also refuse what you like too much.

We could take as an example the butcher's wife in *The Interpretation of Dreams*, but I'll discuss her in detail in a later lecture. Let us take as an example here the obsessive. If he is excessively captivated or attracted by jouissance, it is because of a primary experience in childhood. But attraction does not mean the subject likes it. When you are overly attracted to jouissance, it is threatening to you. When you cannot help doing something, you have a reaction against it. The hysteric, on the contrary, is repulsed by jouissance. In both cases, there is a defense: one is founded on aversion and the other on excessive attraction.

A symptom is always the result of a failure of defense, a defense against the emergence of an excessive attraction to jouissance in the case of the obsessive, and against the repulsion toward jouissance in the case of the hysteric.

Susanna Huler: There is excessive pleasure in relation to what in obsession?

Soler: Freud's thesis is that the obsessive experiences too much sexual pleasure. Let us begin with a subject who has a sexual experience; he can be struck or attracted: he is captivated by it. He could either be attracted or repulsed. Freud evokes here a fundamental position that appears before ideals come into play: a primary reaction that has nothing to do with education or repression. When Freud set out to explain the origin of the defenses he spoke of education—the repression of the drives due to education. Surely, there is a repression of the drives that results from education. But independently of this, Freud states that *there is something primary which defines the subject as a primary reaction of dissatisfaction or satisfaction.*

Eilata: In listening to you, it seems that obsession and hysteria almost collapse into each other: in obsession we have a kind of "too much" which turns into aversion, and in hysteria an aversion and a defense against it. The question is whether this aversion is itself primary or whether aversion results from too much attraction. Perhaps it could be said the other way around with respect to obsession.

The other thing I wanted to say concerns the original constitution of the subject. You said that sexuality, or the primary trauma, is not caused by someone else, such as a parent, but that it is something in the subject himself who experiences his sexuality as heterogeneous. As a result there is a defensive reaction. Is it possible that there is no defense if things go well? Is there a defense that is neurotic, as opposed to a defense that is not neurotic?

Soler: Let me add something regarding the two primary positions of hysteria and obsession. The subject's primary position, a position that has no temporal beginning (it is something we know about, but for which we cannot find an originating event), is a problem. What is it in our experience that gives us a sense of this opposition?

The obsessive generally feels guilty and his guilt may at times be so great that Freud is led to wonder if there is any difference between obsession and melancholia. The hysteric, on the other hand, accuses the Other: It is always the Other's fault. Obviously one can also find accusation in the obsessive and guilt in the hysteric, but the main axes of their discourses are, in the one case, guilt and, in the other, accusation. This is why Freud, in deciphering symptoms, finds shame regarding the first sexual experience in the obsessive, and accusation of the Other for having a sexual, seductive intention in the hysteric. The clinical evidence for this is very strong.

All of this is obviously very complicated, but the fact that the obsessive takes the sexual blame or fault (in French the word "*faute*" has two meanings: sin and lack, fault and deficiency) upon himself, feeling guilty and shameful, is linked to the fact that he is greatly attracted to the sexual experience. The hysteric's accusation is related to the fact that she feels an aversion toward sexuality.

In conclusion, when we speak of a primary experience or position, that is, about something which is not directly visible in the phenomena, we are talking about feelings *deduced from the subject's current position.*

Perhaps I should add something here. A moment ago I indicated that the division in the sexual field is that between the signifier (the representation of an idea or ideational representative) and what Freud called affect, equivalent to what Lacan calls jouissance. But there is a further distinction between jouissance, which belongs to the realm of feelings and sensations, and the object—the object in the sense of that which conditions jouissance. It is logical that when one's feeling about jouissance is aversion, *one is pushed to denounce the object.*

On the question of defense, Lacan's main text is the one dedicated to a paper by Daniel Lagache [not included in the current English edition of *Écrits*]. There is always a defense. What is the difference between a neurotic and a non-neurotic subject? That is a big question. First I will say that there is a big difference between the two and then that there is no difference between the two. Thus there are two answers.

There is a difference at the level of the phenomena: There are people who have obsessions of such severity that life becomes impossible for them, and there are people who manage to live more or less well, that is, with all the difficulties of life, love, and work, but who do not form obsessive or hysterical symptoms. That is a fact. Thus, there is a difference and that is why some people go into analysis and others do not.

Yet, at the same time, there is no difference because you can find something like a symptom in everyone, though its meaning is not exactly the same as in the case of the neurotic. If a symptom is something in which the subject's sexual jouissance is localized, every subject necessarily has a symptom.

What is the something in the symptom in which jouissance is localized? It is always a signifier. But a signifier can be incarnated, that is, it can be an object at the same time. Perhaps you have heard Lacan's strange expression: "For a man, a woman is a symptom." A woman localizes a man's sexual jouissance. In that sense she is a symptom, an object. At the same time she is a signifier in two senses, not only because all women are signifiers but also because traits of perversion are always involved in object choice. The object chosen is a signifier qua woman, and she has certain traits that make her *this* man's Woman. That is the problem of object choice.

What do I mean when I speak of traits of perversion or perverse traits? I do not mean that everyone is a pervert. I mean that we all see our sexual partners as having certain signifying traits, features, or characteristics that allow us to displace and localize perverse jouissance onto them as objects. Perhaps this will become clearer in what follows.

Hysteria and Obsession: Two Forms of the Split Subject

When Lacan returned to Freud, he did not return to the idea of the presence of sexuality in the unconscious. He returned to what Freud had said about unconscious mechanisms, what Freud called "the work of the unconscious." Thus the texts that interested Lacan in his return to Freud were those concerning dreams, witticisms, slips of the tongue—in a word, unconscious formations. Why so? Because Lacan's intent was to make psychoanalysis understandable. His path is a logical one. He starts out from the following consideration: In psychoanalysis we work with speech alone. That is a fact. We obtain effects with speech on something that apparently is not speech: symptoms.

Thus at the outset, it is not the dimension of jouissance in the symptom that is taken up by Lacan, but the dimension by which the symptom is linked to speech. Lacan provided many formulations regarding neurosis, but they have to be situated as a function of the structure he elaborated when he formulated them. For example, you find the following striking formulation in "The Agency of the Letter in the Unconscious" (1957): "Neurosis is a question." That can only be understood if you know what Lacan says about the subject as the subject of speech.

I have to mention something you already know. Lacan distinguished between the ego and the subject, between ego and I. When I say that Freud's notion of the splitting of the ego is the same as Lacan's notion of the divided subject, there is a problem if you don't know that the ego in Freud's work is not merely what earlier theory referred to as the ego. It is not easy to say whether the Freudian *Ich* is the ego or the subject. Lacan's first step was to distinguish between the ego and the subject: The subject is the one who speaks.

But this formulation immediately introduces confusion. Perhaps it is the confusion between psychology and psychoanalysis. Psychologists, particularly clinical psychologists, also work with speech. So we must be precise. It is better to say "the subject of speech" because when you say that you are not saying that the subject is the *agent* of speech. The subject of speech is obviously the subject who speaks, but the point is that he is *determined* by speech. In psychoanalysis, everything you know and do is conditioned by the way you know and do it, that is, by speech.

But at this point, you might think that speech merely expresses another reality. Many people believe that speech is a way of expressing something else–feelings, thoughts, etc.–and there is something of that order in language. Everyday we use language to make ourselves understood. So we are inclined to assume that, first, there is something to express and, second, that we use speech as an instrument to transmit that something. At a certain level of experience, it is not false to say that there is a certain function of speech that is a function of communication and expression. If Lacan had said only that, he would have said nothing new because it is a very old and common idea.

Lacan's thesis is that the subject is not the agent but rather the effect of speech. Psychoanalysis has to do *not* with the entire person but only with the subject, with the person to the extent that the person is transformed by speech. Obviously this thesis requires demonstration. It is not my topic today but we need to keep it in mind.

I shall return to the split, the split in the subject Freud introduced between the patient and sexuality. Lacan introduced this split in another way after having first discussed the structure of speech and later the structure of discourse. We write the subject as follows: $. I could approach the subject in different ways, for example, by studying what speech is. In "Variations on the Standard Treatment" (1955), Lacan constructs what speech is. He introduces the partner of speech who is not the same as the sexual partner: the Other (Å) who is no one. The Other is a partner that can answer. I could also develop the subject as presupposed by the signifying chain. Perhaps today, in order to introduce clinical cases, I will take up the subject as a subject of desire. We have to keep in mind the idea that desire is the effect of the signifying chain. What psychoanalysis calls desire is not need. It is something that implies a lack and a quest for an object that cannot make the lack disappear, but that can make the lack less painful.

Our question now concerns hysterical desire. Let us take the case of the butcher's wife. I don't know if all of you know the case well. It is an example of Freud's (SE IV, 146–51) on which Lacan comments extensively in the "Direction of the Treatment" (1958; see section V, entitled "Desire Must Be Taken Literally"). There Lacan explains his then-held views concerning desire. The example is of interest to us here because it involves a case of hysteria.

The butcher's wife has a dream: "I want to give a dinner but I only have a slice of smoked salmon. I intend to go shopping but I remember that it is Sunday afternoon and all the shops are closed. I think I will order by phone some supplies but the phone does not work. At the end I have to renounce my will to give a dinner party." If you merely treat the manifest content of the dream, it is a dream that presents the failure of desire in the sense of a preconscious desire: the failure of a wish.

What does Freud say about this dream? First, he knows that the patient has a female friend who likes salmon very much but prefers not to eat it. She likes it but is used to depriving herself of it. When you desire something and you deprive yourself of that very thing, what you are doing is continuing to desire. That is, when you refuse the very thing you want, you maintain your desire as unsatisfied. Lacan translates this by saying that salmon is the signifier of the female friend's desire.

Freud also knows that his patient, the butcher's wife, behaves in the same manner with caviar. She claims to have a strong wish for caviar but when her husband proposes to buy her caviar because he loves her, she refuses decidedly. She behaves in the same way as her friend, and we can say that caviar is the signifier of the patient's desire.

In the dream, caviar does not appear—we see only salmon. Lacan deduces that the dream is a metaphor. Metaphor is the substitution of one signifier for another: S_2/S_1. But this is only the beginning. The problem is to understand how this simple demonstration that the dream is a metaphor illustrates why desire must be taken literally. The dream concerns the hysteric's desire. The question is: How is the representation of desire by a signifier to be interpreted? Freud himself interprets the caviar his patient desires as a signifier that designates a relatively inaccessible object of her time and place. A Russian patient, perhaps, would not have dreamed about caviar because for her caviar would have been a common object. For the butcher's wife, however, caviar is an inaccessible object and is thus a signifier of her desire as unsatisfied. But with enormous subtlety, Lacan adds something further here: If caviar signifies unsatisfied desire, the desire for caviar signifies the desire to have an unsatisfied desire. That is, the desire for caviar is a metonymy of a desire as unsatisfied.

Why does Lacan speak about desire for an unsatisfied desire? It is because Freud introduced it, saying that the behavior of the two women friends means that they want to have or they desire an unsatisfied desire. Thus Freud discovered that there is a desire for privation in hysteria—a desire for privation as a condition for desire. This means that desiring may, in and of itself, be pleasant.

Now for the central question. Lacan asks: What does this desire for an unsatisfied desire mean in the unconscious? It is an important question because, up until now, we have been speaking about a conscious desire. The hysterical subject knows that she is toying with the idea of caviar in order to remain unsatisfied in some respect. She says it and she knows it. Now if we want to situate the true desire implied in this little comedy—and this example is a

comic one although sometimes there are hysterics who push the hysterical position to tragedy—we need to see how many terms are involved in this story. We
have the two friends: the patient (the dreamer) and her friend. We also have a
man, the husband. Our question is, what about the subject? What about the
desire of the dreamer? To grasp the subject we have to find the subject's identifications.

We have a first and obvious identification: The metaphor involving salmon
and caviar indicates a substitution between the patient and her friend. The
choice of privation common to both indicates a substitution that reveals an
identification. The butcher's wife behaves like her female friend. We can speak
at this level of an *imaginary* identification: The butcher's wife wants to resemble her friend. But not completely, for she identifies with her friend in only one
way, involving one trait alone: her unsatisfied desire. It is a trait that makes the
friend inimitable. I quote: "If the patient identifies with her friend it is because
she is inimitable."

The friend is impossible to imitate and the patient tries to imitate this inimitable friend, that is, to imitate her very unusual trait. But why does she think
that the friend is inimitable? It is not only because the friend deprives herself
of salmon. There is another reason that involves the husband and the friend.
Freud indicates that the husband has a peculiarity: He likes curvaceous or
slightly plump women. The friend is thin and thus is not his type. But strangely
enough, in spite of that, the patient notices that her husband always speaks well
of her friend. The hysteric pays close attention to the Other's desire. In this
case, we see the special attention she pays to her female friend's desire and,
even more so, to her husband's desire.

Here we see the question that is constitutive of the hysteric's desire. Lacan
formulates it as follows: "Has he [the husband] too not got a desire that is somewhat thwarted when everything in him is satisfied?" Between the patient and
her husband everything is all right. He loves her, desires her, and gets off on
her sexually. What more can he ask for? You see here that the hysterical quest
for a bit of unsatisfied desire concerns not only herself but the other as well,
the partner. Now we understand why the female friend seems inimitable to the
butcher's wife: She doesn't understand how her friend manages to interest her
husband who otherwise seems so satisfied.

Lacan formulates the hysterical question precisely: "How can another
woman be loved? Isn't it enough for the patient to think that her husband
should consider her highly? How can another woman be loved by a man who
cannot be satisfied by her (the friend)?" We know about the satisfaction
between the patient and her husband, yet something remains enigmatic. He
likes and is interested in the friend who is not his kind of woman. We see here
(thanks to the caviar) that the hysterical subject is interested in something that
is not satisfaction. Generally speaking, if you like caviar you eat it when you can.

In other words, you generally try to satisfy your desire. Here we see a subject who does not seek satisfaction of her desire but who instead is interested in the Other, in the Other's lack. This concerns what in French we call the *"manque du sujet,"* the *"manque à être,"* that is, the "want-to-be" of the subject.

We see that the hysteric, as subject [$]—not as the counterpart of the friend, nor as someone who manages or fails to resemble her friend [that is, not as an other (a–a')]—is equivalent to the question about the husband's desire. That is to say, the husband is present as an Other, a barred Other, *Ⱥ*, insofar as he desires. The hysterical subject's question is: How can he desire this other woman? Lacan says that "the subject becomes this question." The woman identifies with the man through this question. On the imaginary axis we have an imaginary identification between the patient and her female friend. But here, between the subject ($) and the person who incarnates the barred Other (*Ⱥ*), there is another identification: hysterical identification with the man.

Schema L

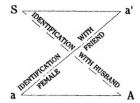

That's not all. If the subject identifies with the man via this question, it still remains to be seen what it is that she wants to *be*. That is a different question. The subject investigates the Other's desire in order to answer the question: What is the subject as a being?

This provides a third identification. Lacan formulates the unconscious desire of the butcher's wife as follows: "To be the phallus, if only a somewhat thin one." That is, to be ("to be" is the expression of desire—the grammatical infinitive is the way desire is formulated) the signifier of the Other's desire: the phallus (Φ). Her unconscious wish is to be the phallus. Now we can say something more precise.

The hysterical subject is structurally linked to the Other. She is alienated from the Other's desire. If the hysterical subject is a question, she finds her being in the Other's lack. Now there is an equivocation in the statement, "The subject is a question," for it can mean different things. But it is similar to the statement "Neurosis is a question."

If neurosis and the subject are questions, it is because we are speaking of the subject of speech, of language, and of what happens to the subject who is determined by speech. He who does not know what he is, is a subject by definition: he asks himself, "What am I?" The subject of language necessarily does not know what he is. Why? Because if he asks, "What am I?," he can only reply with signifiers. He can say I am a professor, a teacher, the butcher's wife, my father's daughter, etc. Every answer thus provided can be written $S_1/\$$, that is, a signifier that represents the subject. But in the same movement the subject's being is lost and changed. I won't develop this point though it is an important one in order to situate neurosis.

There is a twofold lack: a "lack of knowing" and a "lack of being"; a "want-to-know" and a "want-to-be." The neurotic subject seeks an answer to these questions by way of the Other's desire. We can say the same thing differently. In the Other of the signifier, the Other has a locus. There is no signifier of the living being; there is no signifier of sexual difference. That is why there is a question.

Before taking any questions, I want to stress something. I want to stress that the example of the butcher's wife shows three levels:

1. The level of the ego at which we see an imaginary identification (a real identification between the images of the two egos). Here the patient's desire is the other's desire, the friend's.

2. The level of the subject as desire. Here we see an identification between the woman and the man as barred Other ($\cancel{A}$). At this level, her desire is the Other's desire.

3. The level of being, that is, being the phallus (Φ), the phallus as the signifier of the Other's desire.

Here there is a question: What is the phallus? You can find different statements about the phallus in Lacan's work. The phallus is a signifier, according to Lacan, but a signifier of what? In certain texts he says that it is the signifier of desire; in others he says that it is the signifier of jouissance (e.g., "Subversion of the Subject"). How can we settle the contradiction? There are two ways, one complicated and one simple. Here I will discuss the simple one.

The phallus is the signifier of lost jouissance. There are two aspects to that: (1) You can say the phallus is the signifier of desire to the extent that desire implies a lack of jouissance; in that case we write $(-\varphi)$, castration; (2) you can also say that every plus of jouissance is linked with a minus of jouissance, and it depends where you situate the phallus, on the side of the minus or the plus. In the hysteric's case, it is clear that the phallus is a signifier equivalent to $\cancel{A}$, a signifier of what is lacking in the Other: $S(\cancel{A})$. When an object is situated in the hole or lack in the Other, that object takes on the value of the phallus. That is why I wrote the phallus as representing the being of the subject in the Other.

Adrianna: You said that the butcher's wife is the signifier of the Other's desire (her husband). Is that equivalent to saying that she is the object of her husband's desire?

Soler: I didn't say that the butcher's wife was a signifier of the butcher's desire. On the contrary, I wanted to stress that she is an object and feels like one. She is an object of love and of jouissance. Her question is: "Am I also the signifier of what remains as a lack or a want in him?" It is in that respect that she identifies with her friend.

Shlomo Lieber: Why is it that the hysteric can hold onto her desire only through the Other's dissatisfaction (Ⱥ), for desire in general has its origin in dissatisfaction? That is the question of desire for every person. It may be that I did not understand and that the answer has to do with the structure or the history of the hysteric, a structure that has a historical basis you did not talk about. If the hysteric is every person in the sense that she raises the question of the subject, then how is she different from any other person, particularly from the obsessive?

Soler: Let me say something about history and structure. The French word for history is *"histoire"* [which also means "story"]. Lacan wrote *"hystoire"* indicating that in every story there is something of the hysteric. But for Lacan, structure determines history—not every event in it—but the development of a subjective history or story is a manifestation of structure. Following Lacan's orientation, I don't see anything that would allow one to say that structure is the effect of history. That is never the case.

The hysteric shows us that there is a subjective or unconscious strategy to recoup or cure the "want-to-be" and the "want-to-know" using the Other. It's very obvious in love life when someone says, for example, "If he or she abandons me I will cease to exist." It's a simple sentence. But what does it mean if not love, with all of its meanings of jouissance, desire, and affection. Love grants us a modicum of being. That is why it cures the "want-to-be." That is also why Lacan says that to love is to give what you do not have. It is a beautiful formulation. To love is to give your own want, your own lack. And love makes the other's being, the partner's being, your lack or want. In the social relationship of love, being is at stake.

The neurotic strategy is very clear in hysteria, but the obsessive strategy is a bit different. At the beginning of his teaching, Lacan opposed what he called hysterical intersubjectivity to obsessive intrasubjectivity. Surely, the neurotic is someone who manages to dissimulate the link between himself and the Other's desire. You see this immediately in experience. The hysteric, in general, has many relationships as well as many problems with people. What happens when the hysteric has a problem? She talks about it with a lot of people who then talk among themselves. Immediately a collective problem is created. The hysteric maneuvers. Take Dora, for example. It is clear that Dora manipulated her entire little world. The typical obsessive, on the other hand, is a man who stays in his study and thinks about his problem all by himself. The obsessive's immediate tendency is not to go out and talk with people. It is rather to put his head in his hand and think without stopping.

On the descriptive level, the hysteric and the obsessive have very different styles and that indicates something: The link with the Other's desire is not as questioned in obsession. On the contrary, it is avoided. Perhaps we will further develop the topic of the obsessive tomorrow, but there are two points that warrant mentioning now:

1. In obsession, the link with the Other's desire is not absent but dissimulated, covered over.

2. The repressed term comes back in the mind. The obsessive manages to close off his own division through the return of the repressed in the mind.

When S_2 is repressed in hysteria (S_2 is the term that represents what Freud called the repressed), you have a lack in the signifying chain. You receive an "I don't know" or something of that nature from the hysteric in response to the question: "Why do you do that?" Where does S_2 go? Where is the missing term? We know it is somewhere. Obviously we can say in the unconscious. But where is the hysteric's unconscious? In the body, for example, or in the Other. But for the subject, the second term is lacking: She is a question. The question is "Why does he do it and why do I do it too?" This question is always present for the hysteric.

It is not the same in the case of the obsessive because the repressed term in the obsessive comes back in the signifying chain itself. That is why Freud said that there is something strange in obsession where the repressed is generally enunciated by the subject. Sometimes he says it right at the beginning of analysis, but it is repressed all the same. In what sense is it repressed? In the sense that he does not know he has said it. He does not know that it is what determines his behavior. Thus there are certain things the obsessive does not know. He too is a divided subject. For example, he does not know why he had a particular thought or does not realize how important an event was. If you reread the case of the "Rat Man" in Freud's writings, you will see many examples of this that are very precise. Freud himself stressed, for example, that the Rat Man's mother told him that she wanted him to marry a rich woman, and that that was the event that triggered his neurosis. He told Freud that, but it remained unknown to the Rat Man himself.

The return of the repressed in the signifying chain dissimulates the gap in the obsessive, that is, sutures it. That is why the obsessive must undergo hysterization in order to enter analysis. It is also why you find hard-core obsessives who never even think about going into analysis because their symptom is itself a kind of suture. A change has to come about before the obsessive asks to start an analysis.

Liliana Mauas: I can safely say that I have met the butcher's wife, a woman who presents a complete description of her history in a well thought out manner, a history of loneliness. She is as lonely as the obsessive you mentioned. She articulates something but does not know how important it is, even though it seems very important to her. She talks about her relations with very important, successful, rich, and famous men who are satisfied with their women. She falls for these men, not on account of their charm and glory, but at the precise moment in which she discovers in them a defect or deficiency, however minor, that she subsequently aspires to satisfy with her entire self. She dedicates herself to making good the deficiency while wondering how they can accept the compensation she constitutes for them—after which they go on with their lives. My problem concerns the encounter with a presenting statement which seems to be or should have been the product of work. She presents her story as an obsessive might: she seems to enunciate the repressed but not realize its significance.

Soler: An hysteric is capable of describing her behavior, but that is not the return of the repressed; it is merely the capacity that every subject has, in general, to discern the repetition that orients her love life.

With your subject the problem is what she is asking for when she presents herself or describes herself. She's a woman, of course, and she is presenting her symptomatic love life to you as a question. She is clearly an hysteric: She presents herself as a question to the analyst. Perhaps you have the answer. But the problem is how to pass the answer onto the subject, because it is true that you could use the schema of the butcher's wife. You see that this woman is interested in men in terms of what is lacking in them. She explains that she is dedicated to the lack in the Other. That is what we call *"une prise de conscience,"* an insight.

But you must not believe you have the answer because what you see, as well as what she sees, is her intention to place her being in the Other's lack. The question, "What do you want to be?" is a question she has yet to answer. Let me be more precise. When we say the subject wants to be the phallus, that is not the last word. We see that the analytic relationship has something to do with bringing the question back to the Other. The patient presents herself as a question, but what should the analyst's position be in relation to this subjective question? The analyst should not give an immediate answer. You can imagine the effect of saying to her, "You want to be the phallus!"

When the subject presents her demand to the analyst, the analyst responds with a question of his or her own, namely, "What do you want?" That is why I said that "What do you want?" is the answer. It is only when the analyst responds by asking this question that the subject is able to give an answer, the answer that is her fantasy. The question posed by the Other, formulated by Lacan as "*Che vuoi?*" ("What do you want?" in Italian), allows the subject to change the question she was presenting and to ask herself, "What does the Other want from me?"

In the beginning of analysis there is necessarily a reversal in the question. The subject presents her question, an *x*, and the analyst's maneuver consists in making the *x* change sides. That is, the analyst has to raise the question: "What do you want?" It is a condition for making the subject's answer appear, that is, for making the subject's fantasy appear: for fantasy interprets the Other's desire.

Tamar Kafri: I have a question regarding your talk this morning. You spoke of attraction and aversion as primary positions that precede culture and education. Does that mean that they are inborn or constitutional? How are these two positions related to castration? Where do you locate castration in your scheme?

Soler: It's an opportune question. When we speak about something primary there is always the risk of understanding that there is something like nature, a native constitution. In this case it is true that Freud and Lacan differ, for Freud develops the idea that drives are natural. In his thinking, the problem concerning the lives of living beings has to do with the regulation of the drives, that is, with making them sociable or compatible with relationships or social bonds. Thus Freud talks about drives and education. If I translate the term "education" into Lacanian terms as "the Other of discourse," I have to stress that for Lacan the drives do not precede the Other's influence. The drives are effects of the Other. That is why he says simply that it is due to demand, demand that is firstly the Other's demand, that needs become drives.

Our animal needs (as can be seen with a dog or a cat) are transformed by demand. For example, it is very obvious to us that the oral and anal drives are not natural. There is no anal or oral *drive* in the animal kingdom. There is a need to eat and to excrete, but there are no drives. I cannot develop this point now, but the drives come into being by way of the Other's demand. It is very obvious when one observes children that what Freud calls fixation is linked with the mother at the beginning, with her demand that the child eat and become toilet trained. So there is a link between the Other's demand and the drives. Lacan writes the formula of the drive as follows: ($ \lozenge$ D).

The Other's demand obviously implies the envelopment of the Other's desire. Thus there is also a link between the drives and the Other's desire, but the first emphasis is on demand as the cause of the appearance of what we call drives. Thus drives are not natural: They are the effect of the Other. That is the first point.

The second point is that the subject is also the effect of the Other. When I said something was primary you must not forget that the primary subject is secondary to the Other. Conclusion: Something can be primary, that is, present from the beginning, and nevertheless be a product of structure.

Desire and Jouissance in Hysteria and Obsession

Now we will talk about desire and jouissance in hysteria and obsession. Hysteria and obsession are two modes of what Lacan called "separation." I will not explain what separation is exactly. I will merely say that separation concerns being in relation to the Other. We have to start with the subject: when you say "subject" you imply a want, castration. Want is not something simple. There are different wants: the "want-to-be," the "want-to-know," and perhaps the "want-to-come."[2] Thus we begin with a subject who lacks.

This subject addresses the Other in order to ask him for something, to find a complement in the Other. What does he encounter in the Other (*A*)? He encounters signifiers and speech. He finds a plus, a complement, something that compensates for his own lack, the lack produced by the very fact of his being a speaking being. He encounters speech, speech, and more speech. But in the Other he also encounters the "Thing" (in German, *das Ding*). "The Thing" he encounters is an enigma—something unknown in the Other.

For the first time, perhaps, a question arises for him. Children very often wonder "What does she (my mother) want?" The child can say to himself: "She tells me to be quiet, but when my little sister is very bad, my mother is full of admiration toward her." The child starts asking himself, on account of the contradiction in the mother's discourse, "What does she really want?" She says to me, "I adore you my little child," but when it's nine o'clock she says to me, "Go to bed" or "I have other things to do." So what does she really want?

Finally, the child may ask, and sometimes he really does ask: "What would you do if I died?" Generally speaking, the child *encounters* the enigma of the Other's desire in the Other's discourse by way of contradictions and silence in that discourse. You can see why Lacan criticized Winnicott's notion of the "good-enough mother," a mother who is supposedly always present, always sustaining the child with her love. The risk is that the good-enough mother may be too good. What does that mean? She may prevent the encounter with the Other's desire, and that encounter is necessary for the child because it is with the Other's desire that the child tries to answer his own question and situate his own being.

Let us assume that the encounter has occurred and that there is thus lack, not a lack of lack. The subject addresses a demand to the Other, a demand that assumes the form of a question: "What am I for you, the Other?" What can the

Other answer? The Other does not answer. Why not? Not because the Other is bad. The Other does not answer because he can't answer: by definition he does not know what his own desires are. So surely when you ask the Other: "Tell me, what am I for you," the well-intended Other could try to answer. The more he answers the less you know, because when he tries to answer he continues to use his signifying chains, words, words, and more words. And that is why the subject finds proofs beyond words, especially in acts, in the Other's behavior. In other words, the subject becomes an interpreter. The Other can't answer so the subject interprets: he invents the answer to the question "What does the Other want?"

Where do we find the answer the subject constructs? In the fundamental fantasy. The fundamental fantasy is *an invention that determines the subject.* Here we have to be precise. We write that fantasy like this: ($ \lozenge a$). It is a link between a subject and a desired object, an object capable of compensating for the lack in the subject. The object in fantasy has a twofold status: It is the object that is lacking in the subject, and the object that fills the lack in the subject.

Fantasy gives us the answer to the question of desire. But this answer is the subject's answer, the answer defined by the subject and that defines the subject. It is not the Other's answer.

Lacan says that man's desire is the Other's desire. But while man's desire is the Other's desire, man's fantasy is not the Other's fantasy. In "Subversion of the Subject and Dialectic of Desire" (*Écrits*, 321), in the paragraph where Lacan defines the two positions, obsession and hysteria, he speaks about fantasy as desire for the Other or the Other's desire (*le fantasme comme désir de l'Autre* allows for both meanings). How can we understand this expression?

We have to understand it as meaning two things. The first meaning: *Le désir porte sur l'Autre,* desire concerns the Other. The second meaning: *Le sujet désire en tant qu'Autre,* the subject desires qua Other, that is to say, the subject's desire is unconscious. This formulation (fantasy as the Other's desire) does not mean that the subject's fantasy is the same as the fantasy the Other has. This is because the Other has no fantasy. Why is that? Because the Other does not exist!

There is a difficulty in understanding this because the Other is not a living entity. The Other is the set of signifiers: language or speech. What is the difficulty? The difficulty, it seems to me, is that we use examples of human-involved situations to help us understand. I took the example of a child and its mother. Now who would say that the mother does not exist? No one, surely. The mother exists. But what does not exist is the mother as Other. The mother in my example incarnates the Other who does not exist. It's true that the real mother, the living mother, as a subject has a desire, jouissance, and a fantasy. That is to say, she is also a subject, but qua Other she does not exist.

Question: Does that mean she is in the position of an object?

Soler: That's a good question. Sometimes we say "primary object" when speaking about the mother. The mother is an Other (A) because she speaks, and a small other or counterpart, written in Lacanian terms as the image of the counterpart, i(a). She is also an object. What we call "object" in the descriptive sense is not something simple. The object in the descriptive sense can be three things:

1. If you address your demand to this object it becomes A.

2. It may become your reflection in the mirror, someone you look at and want to resemble: i(a). That is a simplification.

3. The object can also be an object of jouissance or desire (object *a*).

$$\text{Mother} \begin{array}{l} \text{A} \\ \text{i(a)} \\ \text{object } a \end{array}$$

Let me stress again that the neurotic constructs his fantasy because he has encountered the Other's desire. He has encountered desire as Other. Here we have to speak about angst. I don't like the word "anxiety." In French we have the word "*angoisse*," which resembles anxiety but differs from angst. Anxiety is not as strong as angst; it refers to a state of waiting, of expectation mixed with worry or preoccupation. It does not convey the sense of crisis found in angst. That is why I cannot use the word "anxiety" for angst.

On the horizon of fantasy you always have the presence of the barred Other (Ⱥ). That is why fantasy is always linked to angst. What is the cause of angst? The first answer given by Lacan is that angst is caused by the Other's desire. Why? Because the Other's desire is an x, and an x, an unknown, always produces anxiety.

Lacan provided a parable to help us understand anxiety: Imagine a giant female praying mantis approaching you while you are wearing a mask without knowing what kind of mask you are wearing.[3] If you happen to be wearing the mask of a male praying mantis without knowing it, you have a reason to feel angst. You see here the limit in which angst appears. Angst is linked to the x but it is not the x itself that arouses anxiety. It is, rather, the object you might be without knowing it.

Two things can be said about desire that are apparently contradictory. You can say and prove clinically that desire as an x (unknown) produces angst. But at the same time you can say that desire is a defense against the certainty of jouissance. So we can say that there are two gradations of angst that can be seen in Lacan's little parable. If you are face to face with this praying mantis and you are wearing a mask without knowing what the mask is, you will feel angst because you don't know what you are. That is the first gradation of angst, linked with the uncertainty concerning the object that you are. But if you know that you are wearing the male mask in front of this female praying mantis, the certainty of the angst is greater and justified. As you can see, the uncertainty of not knowing what object I am is better than the certainty of knowing what object I am.

The obsessive and the hysteric are situated at this precise limit. Both question the Other's desire and this gives rise to angst. But this angst, this position of questioning the Other's desire, permits the neurotic to avoid the certainty of being an object and of knowing what that object is.

You can see the difference here, for example, between the neurotic and the pervert. The pervert does not interrogate the x of the Other's desire. The pervert has certainty: He possesses a certainty of being, a certainty of the object that needs to be placed in the lack. The pervert places a plus of jouissance there and has no question. He has knowledge.

Let us turn now to the difference between obsession and hysteria. You know that Lacan's famous formulation, which, as you will see, is very firmly grounded in clinical experience, states that the hysteric sustains her desire as unsatisfied (as we saw in the case of the butcher's wife) while the obsessive maintains his own desire as impossible. What does that mean? It means that the unconscious strategies concern different terms in the fantasy. In hysteria we see a strategy on the side of the object. The name Lacan gave this strategy is evasion or side-stepping (*dérobade*). The hysteric slips away as object (*elle s'y dérobe comme objet* [*Écrits*, 321]). Usually this requires a complicated strategy. What does it mean to slip away as object? Such evasion produces a clear result: the creation or maintenance of a lack in the partner.

The hysteric is someone who is always absent at the right moment, who always fails the partner. That does not mean that she is physically absent. She may be present physically but not subjectively. When you see someone engaged in a serious affair with a partner, you need not conclude that she is *not* a hysteric; perhaps when she is in bed (and generally the problem is in the sexual relationship) she is physically in bed, but in her mind, in her subjective position, she is dreaming about another partner or dreaming that it is not her who is in bed but another woman or a man. By keeping her desire unsatisfied, *the hysterical subject refuses to be the cause of the Other's jouissance.* When we speak about the maintenance of an unsatisfied desire, we have to see that *it is a strategy with respect to jouissance.*

Now for the obsessive. The obsessive's strategy concerns the subject side of the fantasy. Lacan says that the obsessive sustains desire as impossible. He also says that the obsessive annuls the Other's desire. In "Subversion of the Subject" (*Écrits*, 321), he says: "The obsessive . . . negates the Other's desire, in forming his fantasy by accentuating the impossibility of the subject vanishing."[4]

Now why does Lacan talk about the vanishing of the subject? It's the vanishing of the subject when faced with the object. In the encounter with the object of desire and jouissance, the subject disappears. That is what Lacan calls "fading." The obsessive is a subject who refuses to fade, who refuses to be eclipsed by an object.

Let me provide an example of an obsessive subject. You will be able to see that the obsessive is also capable of manipulating other people. This particular man has a lover and what does he do? He calculates the precise moment at which he will make love to her and sees to it that another woman phones him at exactly that time. He makes love with one woman and talks to the other on the phone very calmly and collectedly at the same time. The essential point is not to stop making love while he is answering the phone.

What is he doing? He is trying to prove to himself that there is no object that is capable of making him vanish. It is a strategy of mastery. It is as if he were trying to demonstrate that he is the master of his own desire. Lacan says that he annuls the Other's desire. It is another way of avoiding the encounter with an object that could be the proper object of desire. He tries to be the master of his desire, but also to always be thinking. One form of the vanishing of the subject in love is the cessation of thinking. In general, during jouissance, one does not think. Perhaps a lot of thinking is necessary for jouissance in the case of the obsessive and a lot of speech in the case of the hysteric. But at the moment of jouissance, the vanishing of the subject is equivalent to the cessation of thinking.

In this example you see a subject who continues to talk and think at the critical moment. The hysterical subject is not present, she is absent. The obsessive is lost in thought, present in his thinking and not at the right place. This illustrates what I was saying yesterday when I said that the obsessive plugs up the lack with signifiers, with thoughts.

A last remark. The obsessive, much like the hysteric, also refuses to be the cause of Other's jouissance, to be used by the Other for the latter's supposed jouissance. In both cases, neurosis emphasizes in desire the dimension of a defense against jouissance.

Tamar Kafri: You spoke of the object of desire. Does desire have an object?

Soler: Yes, desire has an object, an unusual object, and its peculiarity is indicated in the expression Lacan proposed later in his teaching: "the object cause of desire." Maybe I should say something about why he said "object cause." At first, Lacan developed the thesis that there is no object of desire. In what sense is there no object of desire? In the sense that desire is first of all a lack, a want.

That is, we can establish an equivalence between desire and the subject's lack: castration. Thus castration is the cause of desire. That is, lack produces the vector of desire. The first idea emphasized by Lacan is that no object will ever be able to fill the lack brought on by castration. Thus desire is always desire for something else. The hysterical subject makes this very evident: There is no convenient object of desire. That is, all the objects with which we may offer to satisfy her desire will always be unsatisfactory to her. Desire is the infinite recurrence of the want. And the want is what sustains the infiniteness of desire that always runs ahead.

But there is another side or aspect to the experience: The subject always repeats the same thing. That is, desire is not only the metonymy of the want-to-be. Desire is always desire for something else, but desire nevertheless always searches for the same thing. Both are true for the subject. Desire is precisely determined in the fantasy where it is linked with an object particular to each individual subject. Thus, we have two contradictory affirmations. Lacan manages to condense both aspects of desire into a formula, saying there is no object capable of plugging up desire, yet the subject always searches for the same thing. Lacan says that the object as cause is not ahead but behind; something is lost and searched for or followed at the same time. I can draw this structure with a circular vector of desire.

$$d$$
$$a \, (-) \Rightarrow a$$

You see here an object that is both at the origin and yet still sought for, behind and yet ahead. Generally, we write this object (a) as an equivalent substitute for $-\varphi$ (castration). So there is an object cause.

Rivka Amir: Yesterday you said that neurosis and the subject are both questions. That is because we are talking about the subject of speech. You demonstrated the hysterical subject's question in the case of the butcher's wife. And today you said that the obsessive and the hysteric both question the Other's desire, but I couldn't figure out what the obsessive's question is. You spoke of his *strategy* in relation to desire and in relation to his being a subject. What is his question and what is his relation to speech? You also emphasized that when he annuls the desire of the other, it is not the Other (A) but the other as partner.

Soler: It's a big question and I could talk about it for a week or more, but for now I will only make a few remarks.

What is the fundamental question? It is the question of being: What is being? "Neurosis is a question that being poses for the subject" (*Écrits*, 168). What would be the formulation of this general question for both subjects? In

"Subversion of the Subject," Lacan says that the fundamental question for the subject is "What am I as a being"?

This question concerns us as living beings. It is a question that has two sides and two formulations. The first formulation is "What am I as someone who exists?," that is, as someone brought into the world by my parents. The second formulation is, "What am I as a sexual being?" Lacan shows that the two sides of the question are distributed between the obsessive and the hysteric. The hysteric essentially incarnates the sexual question: "What am I as a sexualized being?" The obsessive incarnates the question of existence: "What am I as a living being?" But every subject is engaged in both questions. Lacan illustrated this very convincingly with the case of little Hans who asked himself in relation to his mother both about the why of his existence (to be) and about his penis (to have).

Thus there is in obsession a precise question about being. The only problem in obsession is to make the question appear, because, as I said, the obsessive's strategy is to behave as if it were possible to provide a signifying answer where there is no signifying answer.

Nechama Gesser: You have indicated that the obsessive is usually male and that the hysteric is usually female. Assuming we are not talking about empirical observations, would you please specify what underlies this assumption?

Soler: Statistically speaking, there are more obsessive men and more hysterical women. In general, there is something like a "predisposition" to hysteria among women and to obsession among men. That was stressed by Freud from the beginning to the end of his work. Now what is the logic behind it? If we say that there is a structure we have to postulate that it is not random.

The first question, that of existence, is present in every subject, whether hysterical or obsessive. That is, the question whether I am desired by the Other or whether I was desired as a child by the Other. If the answer is yes, then as what?

Now, the question "What am I as a sexual being?" is also present in both structures but we can understand why the question about what I am as a woman is more frequent. That is, the hysterical question of what I am as a sexual being is more present for women because there is no signifier for woman in the Other. There is nothing in the Other that says what a woman is as a partner of jouissance. Woman remains an enigma for everyone, for women as well as for men. But when you are the enigma, on account of having been born a female, perhaps you can understand the tendency to ask yourself "What am I as a woman?"

For a man the question about Woman concerns the object. But for a woman the question about Woman is a question about her own being. And that is why it is not illogical for the hysteric to investigate the being of a woman by questioning the Other's object, that is, the man's. In other words, it is possible to say what a man is: A man is castrated. In Seminar XX, Lacan says that it is possible to say, using set theory, that all men are subjects of castration using the following formula: $\forall x \Phi x$. That is, for every x the phallic function is true. Every man is a subject of castration. This is precisely what permits him to use his organ.

Castration does not mean impotence: *It means a loss of a part of jouissance that conditions man's sexual desire.* Thus castration is the precondition for sexual potency. I could almost say that castration, what Lacan here calls the "phallic function," allows for identification of the sexual being in man. That is why we can say Man: All men are alike in castration.[5] The only question that remains for man is to know whether he is alive and why.

Women, too, have a relation to castration, but not all of them. There is a problem of translation because in French, when we say *"pas toute/s"* there are two possible meanings: not all of them and not the whole woman ($\overline{\forall x}$: not every x and not all of x). We have to consider both meanings. I will address the solution to the question. We can understand why women are more essentially concerned with the mystery of femininity. The expression *"pas toute/s"* implies a greater diversity in the sense that it is more difficult to say "all are alike" when you are speaking about women than when you are speaking about men. No woman is the same as any other.

Nomi Huller: How do you relate this to what Freud said in 1924 about the Oedipus complex regarding the woman who is afraid of losing love and the man who is afraid of castration.

Soler: Thank you for this opportune reference because it is right on target. As for men, fear of castration goes quite well with the affirmation that every man is castrated. Now, regarding women, you know that Freud, toward the end of his life, was concerned with the question: "What does a woman want?" That *is* the hysterical question. When I say the hysterical question I don't mean that only hysterics can raise it. The hysteric incarnates the question and that is not the same.

What is the relation between the affirmation that there is no signifier of Woman and a woman's fear of losing love? That is exactly the question in the case of the butcher's wife. The answer is simple: Women "cure" the question of their being by finding being in a man's desire. What is a woman? We don't know, but she can almost be a man's object. A woman prefers to almost have the being she can have in the Other's desire, even if she does not like it much, rather than not know what she is or not being. Surely, the fear of losing love is precisely linked with the absence of the signifier. "To be the phallus, if only a somewhat thin one," is the answer of the butcher's wife. Being the phallus is not an ideal but it is *something*, given that a woman cannot be Woman.

Hysteria and Obsession in the Transference

This afternoon I want to say something about hysteria and obsession in relation to transference. At the beginning of an analysis we have to obtain a change in the subject's position, and there is an asymmetry between hysteria and obsession in this regard. When we held the Fourth Meeting of the Freudian Field on hysteria and obsession in Paris, we published a volume of what we called "reports."[6] It was a volume lacking in unity. Every group in the world wrote whatever it wanted.

There was, however, one point on which all the reports agreed: It is hard to get the obsessive to enter psychoanalysis while it is hard to get the hysteric to leave correctly. That was noted by very different clinicians from all over the world, and I was quite struck by it.

We can understand why it is easier to get an hysteric as opposed to an obsessive to demand something from an analyst. The hysteric is linked, prior to psychoanalysis, to the Other's desire. Lacan emphasized that when he said that hysteria is a discourse, meaning that it is a social bond. The hysteric is never alone, and when she encounters in her own life a symptomatic problem, her first tendency is to address another person. Since Freud, since the presence of psychoanalysts in the world, there is an offer, there is a person who offers to listen.

With the obsessive the situation is a bit different because, as I said, the obsessive manages to suture his subjective division. In the strictest sense, the obsessive symptom itself is what Freud called *Zwang*, a compulsive thought of jouissance. Thoughts of jouissance are not thoughts about jouissance; they are thoughts that serve as a *vehicle for jouissance*. The result is that, in the obsessive's thoughts or signifying chain, we have, side by side, thought as a defense and thought as a vehicle of jouissance. The result is the sense of absurdity felt by the obsessive, when, for example, he cannot help thinking about insults, or when he is full of doubt and inhibition that make it impossible for him to arrive at a conclusion due to contradictory terms in his thoughts.

We must reread the case of the "Rat Man" in which we find a simple example constructed by Freud. In any case, *here the symptom does not demand, it satisfies*. That does not mean that it is pleasant. The symptom plugs up subjective division, dissimulating the function of the cause. Something must be changed in order to make a demand appear. It is necessary to tear the obsessive from his own intrasubjectivity before starting psychoanalysis. This is contrary to hysterical conversion that seems to be nonsubjective, not a phenomenon of the subject. Such a symptom pushes one to demand, not necessarily to see an analyst, but a physician, for example.

What makes the obsessive request to start an psychoanalysis? Generally, it is angst: Something happens that threatens the subject enough to push him into crisis. Here we can take the example of the Rat Man. What pushed the Rat

Man into analysis was an encounter. Prior to this encounter, the Rat Man was very happy. We know that he was in the army and that he was preoccupied with demonstrating how a reserve officer was capable of being a better military man than a professional officer. That gave him a great deal of pleasure—Freud says so explicitly. So we have in this case a subject identified with the signifier "officer" as an ideal:

$$\frac{\text{Officer}}{\$}$$

We know that this ideal identification was related, for the Rat Man, to his father who had been an officer, and who was perhaps not a very honest or courageous figure.

Engaged in this endeavor, the Rat Man encounters a man known in the literature as the "cruel captain" who makes him go crazy. Why? Because he discovers in the discourse of the cruel captain a sadistic jouissance revealed in the latter's tale of torture. It is the encounter with the evil jouissance of the cruel captain that leads the Rat Man into analysis. Something encountered in the Other unravels the suture.

It is not always on the side of the Other that something appears that undoes the suture. I could mention a case of a man who came to analysis when he discovered that he couldn't cope with the strange behavior he found himself engaging in. When he had to cross a road, he couldn't help crossing it without seeing the traffic light. He understood, obviously, that it was very dangerous. Here it was a *passage à l'acte*[7] that triggered his entry into analysis. In any case, you always have to look for the triggering element. When you can't find it, you need to be prudent.

For example, when an obsessive comes to see me, complaining only that "This can't go on anymore," I am very prudent. Because many people spend their entire lives complaining of just that. In and of itself, it does not prove that anything has changed in the subject's suture. It is a demand, surely, a demand for help and an understandable one, but it is not the same as hysterization. Hysterization brings out $\cancel{A}$, that is, the fact that the Other is barred. The effect of hysterization is to put transference into action in the sense of the subject-supposed-to-know (*sujet-supposé-savoir*).

There is an equivocation here. In French the word "*savoir*" can be used as a verb (to know) or a noun (knowledge). That is, in French this expression means either: the subject who is supposed to know (verb) or the subject presupposed by knowledge, by unconscious knowledge. In English, subject-supposed-to-know renders only the first meaning. In other words, the problem is not to obtain a demand from an obsessive because he does demand. The problem is to obtain a demand addressed to a subject who is supposed to know. That is, you must obtain a change from a simple demand for help to a demand for analysis—a demand that brings out what the unconscious knows about the subject. It is only when the bar on the Other appears that the function of the subject-sup-posed-to-know can appear.

In the case of the hysteric, a change must also be obtained from the initial position. We don't have to maneuver to obtain a link between the hysteric and the subject-supposed-to-know because it is a given in the very structure of hys-teria. The position of the hysteric in relation to the subject-supposed-to-know is: "Please tell me something about myself. Please give me an interpretation." The subject, divided by her symptom, addresses someone else, a supposed master (an S_1), a master from whom the subject can demand knowledge. "What do I have? What am I?" The hysteric has a demanding position and you have to obtain a change. You have to make the subject perceive that she is the one who has to produce the answer.

The hysterical answer appears in the case of the butcher's wife. She pre-sents Freud with a dream of failure, whereas Freud's thesis is that dreams are wish fulfillments. And she asks: "How do you work that one out professor?" Her transferential position in relation to Freud can be formulated as follows: "Show what you know, and we'll see how much your knowledge is worth!" Thus the hysterical subject, with her questions, situates herself as the master of knowl-edge, that is, as the subject who, at the end, will be able to say if the knowledge produced by the Other is of value or not. Perhaps you remember Dora's state-ment, when Freud, at the end of a session, expressed to her his satisfaction, say-ing something like "It was a good session," meaning that it was good work. Freud was very pleased with himself. And Dora answered: "No big deal." Here you see the divided subject as master.

While the obsessive tries to be the master of desire via his own petrifica-tion, the hysteric makes herself master of the Other's (the partner's) desire and knowledge. In the hysteric, you have to obtain the change that can be written as follows:

$$\frac{\$}{a} \rightarrow \frac{S_1}{S_2} \quad \Rightarrow \quad \frac{a}{S_2} \rightarrow \frac{\$}{S_1}$$

Hysteric's Discourse   Analyst's Discourse

The subject must cross over to the position of the one who works.[8] Only then can the analyst assume the role of the one who commands and sustains the work with his or her desire. It is not so easy to make the hysteric work because she is always trying to make you work.

Thus in both hysteria and obsession you have to obtain a change at the very outset. Once analysis is underway, the maneuver of transference in the two clinical pictures is not the same. Why? Because in the case of an obsessive, you have something a bit strange. It is difficult to make him enter analysis but once he has entered he is very pleased with free association. Why? Because it involves thinking and more thinking. That is, there is an affinity between the obsessive symptom and analytic technique: certain obsessive subjects associate perfectly. As soon as you manage to forge a link between the obsessive and the subject-supposed-to-know, the suture is reconstituted. The patient speaks calmly, but does not want to hear the analyst: The analyst has to be quiet. Perhaps he would like to forget the analyst, he would prefer a mostly dead analyst, at least a very silent one. That would give rise to a very lengthy analysis.

Thus the problem of transference with the obsessive is not only the hysterization at the beginning, but the maintenance of hysterization or the management of the production of the moment of hysterization.

Transference actualizes symptoms. That is true in hysteria as well. Perhaps the analyst cannot help an analysand who makes himself an incarnated mystery. You know, I suppose, that the hysterical subject tries to constitute herself in the transference as what is lacking in the analyst. Thus, for example, the subject will come late and the analyst will wait or else the subject won't come at all and the analyst will wait again. Or when an interpretation is made, the subject will immediately produce a new symptom and the analyst will be left with a new question about what is happening. The hysteric tries to sustain the analyst's desire as unsatisfied. Doing so, the hysteric forces the analyst to produce answers and maneuvers. Stated differently, the hysteric tries to constitute herself as *agalma* for the analyst and that is why the analyst's presence is a bit disturbing to her.

How can I explain what agalma is? You have an example of agalma in the case of the female friend of the butcher's wife. An agalma is an enigmatic something that makes someone interesting. It is linked with desire and it is the name of the object cause of desire when it functions as a mystery.

I have said something about the beginning of transference in general. Now I will talk about the end.

There is a big debate about the end of analysis in the psychoanalytic movement. The question is whether an analysis has a proper end, not merely a point at which analysis stops. Freud simply states that analysis ends when the analysand stops coming to speak with the analyst. That is, the end takes place when the analyst and analysand don't meet any more. Freud also mentions that there is an obstacle to the completion of an analysis: castration. The subject never stops his revindications regarding castration, that revindication being addressed to the analyst.

If you reread the last two pages of Freud's "Analysis Terminable and Interminable," you will see how Freud situates the dead-end: Something is directed at the analyst by the analysand, something like a protest or revindication concerning the lack that always remains in the end.

You know that Lacan maintains that there is no dead-end. What does that mean? It does not mean that castration is cured by analysis. But something does change in relation to castration at the end of analysis. The change is that the analysand may be able to understand through analysis that the subject is equivalent to castration. That is, he will be able to stop asking the Other to resolve his castration.

The general idea is that something can change and that it is what Lacan called the neurotic's passion. The neurotic's passion is to address his complaints to the Other and to suppose that the Other is the agent of castration. Thus something can change: It is a possibility rather than an impossibility.

In fact, if you reread the two last pages of Freud's text, you will see that he does not stress the dead-end so emphatically. In the last paragraph of the text he says that we have to permit the subject to choose his position. This implies that it depends on something having to do with the subject, something that the subject either agrees or does not agree to sacrifice or give up. In the end, the subject can renounce the "effect of being" he seeks to receive from the Other. We saw the "effect of being" when we spoke of the butcher's wife. This is surely more difficult for an hysteric than for an obsessive.

Liliana Mauas: If I understood correctly, yesterday while speaking about defense in relation to the subject, the object was presented as something tenuous, something that opposes rather than changes. We did not speak about change in the object. My question, despite the difference that may be emphasized between defense and repression, is as follows: Freud says that resistance is the clinical expression of repression; Lacan situates resistance on the side of the analyst; how are we to view what we see as defense in analysis?

Soler: First, we must make a very clear distinction between defense and resistance. The reference here is Lacan's "Direction of the Treatment." Defense is something inherent in the subject. As for resistance, there is a big debate around this concept in psychoanalysis concerning who resists and whether there is resistance. It is simpler to say that the principle of resistance in psychoanalysis has to do with the heterogeneity between speech and the real. Anyone encounters resistance when he tries to say that which is most intimate or real in himself. Thus resistance lies between the real and the symbolic. It is not something like an intention on the subject's part. The real resists crossing over into the symbolic. Defense, on the other hand, implies intentionality: the subject's position in relation to the real.

Susy Pietchotka: Does a male hysteric also ask "What does a woman want?" Or does he ask "What am I as a sexual being?"

Soler: Lacan always insisted that hysterics are not necessarily women in the civil sense. In the civil sense, there are hysterical men as well. What is clear is that *an hysteric is not a woman.* Lacan asks whether or not it's possible to make the hysteric become a woman in analysis. What does that mean?

First, we can evoke the hysterical woman's identification with a man. We see it clearly in the case of the butcher's wife where her primary identification is not with a woman but with a man. That is why Lacan uses the expression: *"L'hystérique fait l'homme."* There is a double meaning in this expression: she plays the part of the man and at the same time she fabricates the man ("makes the man"). Lacan always stresses what he called *"le naturel,"* the natural talent with which women *font* the man. I don't really understand the expression "the hysteric is *a* woman."

We can say, first, that the hysteric *fait l'homme* and that that is related to what she wants: to make Woman exist, to sustain what, if it were possible but isn't, Woman would be. Perhaps this point is not unrelated to the end of the hysterical woman's analysis. The French expression, *"se faire à être,"* means to become able to bear or stand something; it also implies that something is given up. It is difficult for the hysteric to become accustomed to being only *a* woman and not Woman, that is to say, to be one woman, only one, meaning that there are others and that she is not unique.

The hysterical man is faced with the hysterical question whether he is a man or a woman. He wants to know on which side of the sexuation formulas he is situated. His question is the same as that of the hysterical woman, as is his doubt about sex and his demand. As an hysteric, he demands from the Other and he tries to find a part of his being in the Other's desire.

Shlomo Lieber: You spoke of desire and of neurosis as a question, that is, of the subject as a question, without saying anything about the analyst's desire. Hopefully the analyst too is a subject, someone who fails or suffers. We know that hysteria gave rise to psychoanalysis or that psychoanalysis developed alongside hysteria. . . . My question concerns the subject who constructs the logic we are learning today. Could you say something about the analyst's desire and how it relates to desire in general, to the soul.

Soler: The analyst's desire is a big question. I didn't talk about it here because my theme was hysteria and obsession. If I had talked about transference, I obviously would have talked about the analyst's desire. Well, it's impossible to speak about everything at once. Let me try to answer your question briefly.

First, something about the analyst as a person. The analyst was necessarily an analysand and perhaps still is. I say this because it's possible to continue one's own analysis while being an analyst. Surely, as a subject, the analyst is at the same level as his patients. That is, he suffers, he is neurotic, cured more or less, not always. Not just anyone can be an analyst. A change, a metamorphosis, says Lacan, is necessary to permit someone to work as an analyst. What this change is is not so easy to explain in a few words. But I will say that, according to Lacan, what operates in treatment is not the desire of the analyst as a subject. That is because the analyst's personal desire is sustained by his own fantasy. But if you are an analyst, you don't analyze with your fantasy. The metamorphosis in question presupposes something like a change at the level of fantasy: "the crossing of fantasy."

More simply, it is something that permits the analyst to put aside his own particularity as a subject. It is necessary for the subject who wants to become an analyst to have acquired some idea, feeling, or knowledge about his own phantasmatic peculiarity. It is necessary for him to be able to take into account the analysand's particularity.

Now for the analyst's desire. The analyst's desire is far more desubjectivized than we think. That is to say, it is a function in a structure. The analysand's partner must lend support to the x of the Other's desire. On the side of the analysand you have demand. You need someone who will take charge of presenting the dimension of desire, but it is not the analyst's personal desire that is at issue in analysis. The point is to analyze the analysand's desire as implied by his demand. Stated otherwise, what gives rise to the need for the analyst's desire is the analysand's demand. The analyst takes charge of the analysand's desire, of the question "*Che vuoi?*"

Thus there are two aspects to the question about the analyst's desire. The first is, in what ways must a subject change in order to become an analyst, to become someone with "the analyst's desire"? The second is, what is the function of the analyst's desire in treatment? These are two different matters.

Nechama Gesser: When you talked about the change that needs to take place in the obsessive and the hysteric when entering analysis, you used the word "maneuver" several times. Could you elaborate on this word and say if there is a difference in the function or role of the analyst at this stage of analysis and in analysis itself?

Soler: I used the word "maneuver" because I am used to using it. Lacan uses the word in the expression "the maneuver of transference." It implies that the analyst has to do something: it is not enough for him to sit in his armchair and remain quiet. The analyst has to say something at the right moment, of course, but he also has to do something regarding time, money, and presence. The maneuvers of transference are all the interventions the analyst makes in words or deeds. Perhaps the word "maneuver" has a bad connotation, but it implies a calculation. I think that the latter meaning needs to be stressed: The analyst has to do and say something, but not in just any old way.

The second part of your question concerns the difference between the beginning and later moments in analysis. At the beginning, the analyst's goal is to produce transference, to make the subject enter into the transference. It's not the same thing perhaps as maneuvering the transference but the two are closely linked. What is definite is that the analyst's desire operates from the beginning until the end.

Rivka Amir: I find it very hard to understand what a desire without a subject— a subjectless desire—could be. The analyst's desire is not his desire as a subject— I think that's what you said. I tried to imagine Freud interpreting the dream of the butcher's wife, and I thought that that dream would be impossible to interpret if he tried to interpret it on the basis of his own desire as a subject. He had to give up his own desire to interpret it. Is that what you mean by the analyst's desire?

Soler: I agree that something has to be given up in order to be an analyst. What was Freud's desire? Reread the last two pages of Seminar XI where Lacan discusses the analyst's desire in relation to Spinoza's and Kant's work. I can't go into it in detail here, but Lacan clearly prefers Spinoza. Spinoza's desire, according to Lacan, is that of a subject who manages to reduce desire to the universality of the signifier. It's only understandable if you read Spinoza. Spinoza's desire is to identify the object or reduce it to the universality of the signifier. Lacan says this position is untenable for us now. Kant, he says, is closer to the truth (see the *Critique of Practical Reason*).

What is Lacan's thesis about Kant? In "Kant with Sade" he says that Kant's desire is that of sacrifice. That is, to desire is to sacrifice what Kant called "the pathological object." In Kant's vocabulary, "pathological" means the object of particular interest, tenderness, and jouissance as well, that is, the object to which one is attached. Thus Kant's moral law consists in sacrificing every particular interest, everything pathological; it requires the subject to do without the pathological object. It is what Lacan calls a "pure desire," that is, a desire without a particular object. Spinoza, on the contrary, wants to identify the universality of the signifier with the particularity of the object.

Now for the analyst. Lacan discusses Spinoza and Kant to hone in on the analyst's desire. He says that the latter is not a pure desire. He uses an expression that is a bit difficult to understand at the outset: the analyst's desire is a desire to obtain absolute difference. What is absolute difference? There is an opposition between the universality of the subject of the moral law ("universality" meaning the same for every subject) and the idea of absolute difference. When you have something absolute, you can be sure the signifier is not involved because nothing is absolute in the register of signifiers: everything is relative to something else. When you see the word "absolute," you can be sure that only one element is involved.

What is the absolute? The object is absolute in that it does not obey the division of signifiers. But there is another absolute when one signifier is subtracted from the chain of signifiers; in that case it functions as something real, not as a signifier. Thus to obtain absolute difference from the patient, the analyst's desire aims to bring out in the analysand not what is universal, but what is particular, singular, and true for him alone. The last aim Lacan mentions in Seminar XI, about which I still wonder myself, is "to obtain absolute difference." Lacan does not say that the analyst desires "to know absolute difference," but rather "to obtain" it or produce it. If you obtain something, perhaps you know about it at the same time, but knowing is not the same as producing. To produce is to bring about a change in the analysand, a change that allows the fundamental element of his particularity to appear.

Notes

1. [This article includes four lectures given on December 3 and 4, 1989, as part of the annual "Seminar of the Freudian Field" held in Israel. It was initially edited and circulated by Yotvat Elberbaum and Susy Pietchotka; it has been extensively revised by Bruce Fink for this publication.]

2. [The French, *manque à jouir*, implies a failure or inability to come.]

3. [The female praying mantis devours the head of her male partner while mating with him.]

4. The English translation is no good. In French the word is *"il nie"* (he negates). That is a big mistake. "To deny" is the verb used in perversion. Obviously there is also negation in perversion but there is a problem with the word "to negate."

5. All people inscribed in castration have something in common at the level of jouissance, not at all levels.

6. [*Hystérie et obsession*, Paris: Navarin, 1986.]

7. [A putting into action or effect of something, an enactment.]

8. [On the left we have the hysteric's discourse, where the subject ($) is the agent who questions or interrogates S_1 (the master or master's discourse), which is expected to produce new knowledge; on the right, the subject is in the position of being interrogated by object a (the analyst as desire) and must produce something herself.]

CLINICAL VIGNETTE:
A CASE OF TRANSSEXUALISM

∞

Françoise Gorog

"I don't want to be a woman; I already am a woman." That is how one patient, who chose the name Jean for himself, explained to me what led him to request surgery so his anatomy would come into line with his feminine being.

Jean considered his anatomy to be somewhat foreign to him: it was that of a being who was not a full-fledged man but rather already akin to a woman. Indeed, according to Jean, his masculine organ was hardly developed. He compared it to his twin brother's, and had, since childhood, always found it small in size. Moreover, he had had to undergo an operation for phimosis which was unsuccessful, and also had three further operations for the same problem.

At age ten, a gynecomastia—the medical term he himself used—appeared; in other words, breasts began developing. This led to a visit with a doctor. The doctor recommended that they wait and see, no doubt feeling that the gynecomastia was not terribly noticeable. Jean's father, however, was the one who most wanted him to be treated with male hormones so these unwelcome ectopic organs could be dealt with.

Jean considered his voice too to be feminine and shrill, never striking the deeper notes that a boy's changing voice normally reaches. His father wanted to help him change his voice by encouraging him to smoke cigars and drink alcoholic beverages.

His hair was left long and curly throughout his childhood. While his brother was the spitting image of his father, Jean closely resembled his mother. Both his mother and grandmother dressed him like a girl, and he spent his time cooking, cleaning, ironing, and knitting with the two of them. He and his mother or grandmother would go to the market hand in hand; he felt boundless love for his mother and was his grandmother's confidant.

The games he played were little girls' games. He told me that, at age seven, he felt left out at school and was laughed at by his schoolmates. They went so far as to call him a "pansy" and a "girly" "front side and back." Cooking and taking care of the ill were the two skills he developed most.

Jean worked in the restaurant business at certain points in his life, and was the personal nurse of an old lady he devotedly watched over; he also took care of third world children while working for the International Association for the Handicapped.

Jean sensed that his femininity was somehow already contained in his mother's desire for a daughter. She had had male twins instead, and he told me that his brother "had kept all the masculinity for himself." She had picked a first name for him that could easily be feminized—José, all one had to do was add a silent "e" to the end to turn it into a girl's name, and his father supposedly switched around the twins' first names. Jean, whose name is in fact Alain-Jean, nevertheless considered his middle name, Jean, to be ambiguous. That is not the case, however, in French, but he adopted the English pronunciation, Jean, in order to turn it into a girl's first name. He managed to get his first name, Alain, struck off all his official identification papers.

Jean studied transsexualism in great detail, and drew up a list of all the advantages and disadvantages of having the operation. Having worked in the health professions, he was aware of the risk involved and of all the possible surgical complications that could arise. He was willing to run those risks, just as he was more than willing to forego the possibility of ever having a child or of ever having an orgasm again.

According to Jean, he was getting along quite well sexually in his present state. He was able to reach orgasm by fondling his breasts, and also had male sexual partners that he fooled by adopting the same method used by eunuchs to fool men who are unexperienced or want to be fooled. He pulled the wool over their eyes so well that, when he was hospitalized, a boyfriend showed up who believed he was coming to a maternity ward to "see his pregnant companion."

Jean had already had a child: a daughter who died of leukemia at age three. He said he felt more like her mother than did his wife, and that he conscientiously looked after her throughout her illness. Jean had already engaged in similarly maternal behavior when a half-sister came into the household due to his mother's remarriage—he tenderly raised that half-sister as if he were her own mother.

Jean liked to emphasize this devoted, conscientious facet of himself, manifest in the maternal devotion he showed his half-sister and later his daughter, as well as his concern for all those who suffer. What he quite willingly de-emphasized were the times when he was engaged in prostitution, times we know about from medical records dating back to prior hospitalizations.

Rather quickly, however, a number of elements began to seem atypical, leading me to suspect that I was dealing with a case of psychosis. According to the most official criteria in the DSM III, psychosis rules out the possibility of authentic transsexualism.

First of all, I noticed a kind of *fluctuation* in his demand to become a woman through surgery. Indeed, in the history I reconstructed, it turned out that, from age fourteen on, Jean had gone to the hospital several times asking to be operated on and had left the hospital considering himself a man and in love with some woman he had met at the hospital.

Second, after having stressed his ability to have sexual relationships with men, Jean emphasized the element of deceit involved in all of those relationships. He claimed to be able to exploit everyone—his sexual partners as well as his co-workers. But this exploiter could also at times be exploited. Indeed, he had had many botch-ups in his relations with women and had been called a jerk and laughed at on several occasions.

His wife supposedly married him only because of his stable income; their marriage allowed her to regain custody over two children she had had earlier and who had been placed in specialized institutions. His last lover, an alcoholic who he claims to have helped out, eventually threw him out of the house and orchestrated his loss of all their joint possessions in Belgium. There was, overall, a persecutory tone in all his relationships with women.

After having run the gamut of traditional roles played by transsexuals in the literature on the subject—he even worked as a call girl at one point—Jean, in talking to me one day about the woman he would like to be, said that, "When I look at myself in the mirror, I say to myself, I sure would like to make it with her." Jean developed his desire to be a woman, but held typically "masculine" jobs—airline pilot and foreman—adding an unusual touch to the clinical picture typical of transsexuals.

The woman he would like to be is, in fact, the woman he says he read about in the *Talmud*: a woman who knows everything—a woman who has no need to learn because she already knows it all. Such a woman can do without men; she is made of the same stuff as Jean's great-grandmother who was strong enough to defend her home against the Nazis during the occupation at the risk of her own life.

The woman Jean would like to be thus hardly fits the model of a "true woman," a woman who is always lacking in some respect. Jean's ideal embodies absolute power, is not decompleted, and is closer to certainty than to belief.

In time, Jean spoke to me more and more of his great-grandmother. The woman was, as it turned out, deaf from age twenty-five on, and it was with the sign language used by deaf mutes that he claims to have communicated with her. Once a certain confidence arose between us, Jean was willing to talk about the secret bonds between his great-grandmother and him.

The woman apparently conducted black masses, participated in Sabbaths, and was devoted to Satan. Jean accompanied her and had supposedly inherited her gifts—not all of them, however, for he refused to give himself over fully to Satan. Jean nevertheless claims that he can, with a single glance, stop a brawl, predict the future, its failures and successes, foresee the gender of children yet to be born, and even foresee death—in particular he claims to have predicted the death of his daughter, and that of his mother and father who he says died in a car accident on the same day his daughter died.

Translated by Bruce Fink

"BLACK JACKET":
A CASE OF TRANSITORY FETISHISM

∞

Claude Léger

Lacan produced the signifier "*lalangue*" to give us a means of approaching a question which almost always arises in the analysand's mind during the analytic process concerning the use of his or her "mother tongue." Through the play of substitution, this reference point becomes the very link of the symptom to the symbolic, that is, the articulation which opens up the space of interpretation. I'll try to briefly show how psychoanalysis arrives at the dialectic which founds structure as well as discourse. "Dialectic is not individual," Lacan says in "Function and Field of Speech and Language in Psychoanalysis" (*Écrits*). The psychoanalyst must commit himself to deducing the consequences: "Let him be well acquainted with the vortex into which his period draws him in the continued enterprise of Babel, and let him be aware of his function as interpreter amid the discord of languages."

The unconscious is structured like a language, but *lalangue*, by contrast, doesn't place the subject in the same sort of subordination to the signifier. Some of these "*lalangues*" even go as far as to soak up (*tamponner*) what other languages make structural use of (*capitonnent*)–*lalangue* is both material and foreign, and inclined to borrowings.

Moreover, language can become more complex due to particular sorts of dichotomies between the vernacular, the oracular, and writing; we see this with the *Kana* and *Kanji* in Japanese. In 1885 in Paris, Freud had hoped to learn French by going to the *Théâtre Français* (today the *Comédie Française*), but his migraines stopped him from understanding what the women were saying.

He was, however, in his element when attending the theater of Salpétrière Hospital, where the great Charcot's performances no doubt dazzled him, but not to the point of totally blinding him to the meaning of the choreography being staged.

Later on, Freud revealed that he dealt with the question of *lalangue* in his practice as an unconscious formation, without requiring analysis to be conducted in the patient's mother tongue, so as not to disrupt the whole signifying process. Even though there are only two references to this point in his work, they are significant enough to warrant our attention. The first is *"Glanz auf der Nase"* episode in his 1927 article, "Fetishism" (which Freud treats in a quasi-Lacanian way, so to speak), where the displacement from one language to another, in this case German to English, which the patient had learned as a child, allows the object as gaze to emerge. Moreover, this entails the question of the link between fetishism and voyeurism, in Lacan's grammar: *"ça me regarde"* ("it is looking at me" and "that's my business") like the nose in the middle of a face. The second refwolf manerence in Freud's work is the role of the Russian language in the analysis of the Wolf Man, the German in which the analysis was conducted being a foreign language for the patient. I shall only note that, from the Russian *babuska* (butterfly) to *grusha* (pear), wasp, *Wespe* in German, is inscribed which, losing its wings, falls out of the German language in which the dream is told, to produce the initials of Serguei Pankejeff (S.P.), also causing the knell of *las cinco de la tarde*, the fatal hour of castration, to toll.

These two examples encourage me to question the effect of having read Freud in the case of an industrious analysand I treated. However, before I come to this, I would like to point out that, to my knowledge, only one author has tried, since Freud, to theorize the problem of bilingualism in analysis. Edith Buxbaum, a student of Richard Sterba's, who emigrated from Vienna to the United States, published an article in the *Psychoanalytic Quarterly* in 1949 on "The Role of a Second Language in the Formation of the Ego and the Superego." Her examples all spring from the specific context of the German emigration which followed the Nazi takeover, though her work also applies to analysands whose experience of a break with their mother tongue did not result from that event. The author stresses a not uncommon phenomenon, the dichotomy which separates the two languages between speech and writing. While James Joyce's solution is to fabricate a universal language in order to cut himself off from English and find in soliloquy the space of the Other, writing usually serves to establish a pact whose secret is akin to that of incest. In language there is a certain tendency to establish a rapport, which prompted even Karl Abraham to refer to the extravagances of Kleinpaul as falling into the trap of a fantasy of "linguistic sexualization." But, as the latter author mentions, there resides in *lalangue* a magic of special relevance to the obsessive who can ensure "in another language" that "things happen, or on the contrary that he will not do them," in other words, he can make speech unreal.

It is precisely this last adjective which Freud uses in 1915 to qualify transference; he uses it at a stage when his conception is no longer solely based on a repetition of what escapes remembering—and hence on the trauma theory—but on an enactment of what Lacan calls "the reality of the unconscious" and which leads him to formulate that if "transference is simply the real in the subject," that is because the real exists and is elsewhere. This implies bringing into play the Other (and the Other's desire), the place the subject in analysis covers over with the object long enough to construct a fantasy. It's the passage from a particular difficulty to a possible articulation that I'm going to speak about, where, instead of a bottle-opener, that of the *"che vuoi?"* graph, the subject uses a coat hanger.

Dennis B. is an Englishman in his thirties. When he came into analysis with me, he had already been living in France for five years and teaching English to adults. In his own words, it was to "break with England" and because he was attracted to French culture that he crossed the Channel. He admitted straightaway that when he has to speak about things sexual he sometimes forgets his mother tongue.

Two symptoms brought him into analysis, and he described them with nosological detail acquired from reading Freud while studying philosophy. The first consisted of a long-standing submission to obsessive rituals which he feared would worsen and invade his public life, having long been held in check by private practices (masturbation). The second took the form of an insistent question: "Why does a fetish influence my sexual relations?" The objects in question were women's classic black velvet jackets which, when worn by his partner, assured his jouissance. He constantly tended to "inferiorize" himself with women, and thus feared that a woman would be disappointed (*déçue*) in him at the fatal hour of coitus. The English accent with which he pronounced the French *déçue* revealed it to be a Freudian slip (*dessous*: underneath, below, underside, etc.). However, what I perceived as a topological inversion (*dessus—dessous*; over—under) returned much later on in a striking and indeed staggering form. This was already clear when I agreed to take Dennis into analysis on the basis of his inability to pay, his "minus value" (as opposed to surplus value), which I attributed to his status as an immigrant worker. Otherwise I would have more easily identified *des sous* (money) in his complaint, which I took to be a load of rubbish.

The young man complained that his symptoms had plunged him into a state of depression for around twelve years, and he found an analogy in a prolonged separation from his mother, at the age of four, when he had to be hospitalized for a serious illness. His exaggerated preference was for women to whose caresses his fetish was attached, and his choice most often fell upon suitably dressed prostitutes, with whom he played a passive role, the very condition of his pleasure, without fear of humiliation.

I should point out that the word *fétiche* has the same double meaning in English as in French: "lucky charm" or something "tacked on" and thus artificial. In accordance with the logic which followed from this, Dennis' reveries were very warlike and drew basically on the glorious history of England, especially the period between prehistory and history: "the dark ages." His conjuratory rituals aimed specifically at postponing the moment of masturbation: he had masturbated from the age of eleven and had not forgotten the slightest detail of the very first occasion. The way in which his transference was structured became clear early on, in a dream at the beginning of his analysis. In this "part" (French *partie* = English "part," but *une partie de golf* = "a round of golf") of the analysis, he set into play one of the mainsprings of the transference: "The scene is a warship, in the officers' wardroom. I am lying on a seat close to a form. A Japanese person enters and says 'This is your lobby. It's not that expected.'" It was only in the next session that he completed these incomplete phrases. The Japanese person added: "It is the way you treat your prisoners," an affirmative sentence which then evoked for him the memory of accounts of intolerable cruelties that the Japanese inflicted on their English prisoners during the Second World War, heard around puberty directly from one such unfortunate prisoner.

As for the first sentence, he gave me a remarkable translation: "lobby" became *vestiaire* (cloakroom) instead of *vestibule*: he then associated from "lob" which reminded him of a book read long ago at college, *The Language of Business*, which the students called "L.O.B." for short. This latter signifier reminded him of another: "lob-lollies," a nickname given to the assistants of military surgeons on ships, formed from "lob," a stroke in tennis, and from "lolly," of which the most current meaning is lollipop. Indeed, one of the functions of these assistants was to throw "lollipops" to the fish whenever limbs were amputated.

This crossroads of signifiers, revolving around castration, became clearer in the course of his analysis and led me to discover that "lolly" also means "cash," and that in this dream it was a case of throwing money out the window. It was also later that I realized to what extent Dennis felt he was the prisoner of a will, a desire to which he remained subject despite having crossed the Channel. We have here the configuration on the basis of which he decided to end his analysis.

The crux was the changing status of the black jacket, and the textual knowledge tied to it through the progression of signifiers up to a point of resistance; in the folds of the material he met the line of a possible cut, to which he responded by deserting.

He viewed black jackets as ritualistic or even sacrificial garments, worn by priestesses—prostitutes—who were also in the habit of wearing tags around their necks with their first names engraved on them like serial numbers. These names are usually false; they are *noms de guerre*. Dennis' father also used a *nom de guerre*: during a stint in a factory as part of his training as an engineer, he had decided to change his name, John, a bit too upper class, to Jack, much better suited to his situation. He had kept this assumed name ever since, and Dennis could thus claim to be Jack's son.

At the time he felt his first masturbatory excitement, Dennis had among his teachers a certain Miss Jackson, a beautiful woman who generally wore a plain waisted jacket called a *jaquette* in French, a word which, moreover, the English language has borrowed from the French and which derives from "Jacques," the typical restive peasant of the *Ancien Régime*.

The scholarly reference is important here. (Dennis had always been a good student; he became an industrious analysand, constantly striving to distinguish what he referred to as the banal part of his analysis—that is, everything that was reduced to rhetorical formulas, products of his reading of Freud and Lacan—from an ineffable part that he situated in a firmament like the stars in a constellation.) High on the copper dome of the planetarium in London, in the construction of which his father had participated, was inscribed the phallic enigma that the analyst, in winching it up, had to allow him to go decipher. His fixation on Jack and J.B., his father's initials, was reversed by the lens of this optical apparatus into B.J., the initials of black jacket, whose velvet serves as a screen to the fantasy, including its "wet" veil. A fan of the most subtle signifying games, Dennis referred to his ejaculations as "quotations." But he needed to take one further step to spread out the whole web which covered the absence, and it was the return of a childhood memory which allowed him to do so. In that memory, he was asking his mother, who had just bathed him, about the origin of children; she explained to him that it was thanks to his "gibby" that daddy sowed his little seed, and she pointed to his penis. This memory also evoked another from an earlier time: "My mother told me that one bought children in shops and that they were very expensive. She added that if the family wasn't rich, it was because of this investment. "My response," said Dennis, "was to be a good child, worthy of such an investment."

Dennis decided to stop his analysis, having articulated this original link and the hold it had had on him. His excuse for leaving was that his apartment had been burglarized—for the second time since the beginning of his analysis—and he needed to find a more secure place to live. He had to take out a loan in order to buy a studio, and the expense made the continuation of his analysis impossible. In transferring the investment, Dennis found a most curious way of instating himself in the place of the Other. In his very last sessions, he discovered that the nickname his father gave his mother, Joy-Bell, also contained the initials J.B.

And there was a legend that the cockneys, with their famous East-End accent, had to be born within earshot of the ringing of the bells of Bow Church, near White Chapel, the area where, at one time, a notorious Jack was at large: Jack the Ripper.

Thus, before ending and dumping me at that point, Dennis shot an arrow from his tensed bow, to avoid a blow that he felt would be fatal to him. At the beginning of the analysis, I had refused to take his phonematic imprecisions (such as *déçu*) at face value, questioning what was beneath his disappointment. He wrote to me telling me of his decision to stop and the last sentence of the letter read: "I hope that you aren't too disappointed (*deçu* without the accent) in me."

From "black jacket" to "gibby," from the jacket (*veste*) to invest, we can see what Lacan calls "the affinity between sexuality and the play of the signifier." This deployment is not, of course, the whole of an analysis: I would even say that, viewed from this angle, Dennis ended where he started. He remained at the preliminary stage, backing away, just as he did in his conjuratory rituals against masturbation, from the showdown with the Other's disappointment. However, these preliminaries weren't totally ineffectual, for Dennis almost succeeded in hanging up the jacket in the cloakroom. This was marked by two events: a first burglary, which he blamed on his favorite prostitute, to whom he had lent a large sum of money. Shortly after this incident, Dennis met an American woman with whom he came to an understanding—he sometimes made her wear the black jacket, but it was no longer like before. She was the first woman with whom he'd had a relationship in two years, that is, since the beginning of his analysis which had begun in the throes of a stormy split. Before becoming the silky envelope of that which brought happiness, the jacket was the content of a less happy encounter—then it took on the form of a veil whose very texture covered the top half of the maternal body like a gigantic pubic fleece, camouflaging intolerable castration.

In unravelling the folds of the signifying chain through regular defecation, Dennis, who came to France to write in exile, ineluctably narrowed the virtual space where an object found its place as soon as the consistency he stubbornly insisted on crumbled away, transmuting into coarse fabric before disappearing from view, letting lack emerge in the form of an empty apartment, like an undressed woman. The jacket was only held up by a button which, with the sliding of his gaze from the vulva to the belly button of a naked young girl, had, since puberty, concealed the question: to what was the sash attached? Hence the extraordinarily precise memory of the first time he masturbated, which took place against the musical backdrop of the song "Buttons & Bows." There were no buttons without bows.

Confronted by this knowledge, Dennis, in accordance with the terms in which he had first posed the problem, "discharged himself." The vanishing point was already no longer crucial by the time it came; Dennis didn't give either me or himself the choice. The end of his analysis was inscribed in the *mal de mer/mère* (sea/mother sickness) of his crossing or transference. *Übertragung*, after all, also means translation. Just as there were two burglaries, of which one was in fact a relief while the other was an unbearable loss, there were two attempts to escape: the first, from the signifiers of his mother tongue, an ocean on which he was tossed around like a buoy; the second led to his being locked up—the officers' square or wardroom (*carré*), found once more on the anxiety-producing blank sheet of paper, emerging from the empty apartment that Dennis filled with the object of his fantasy.

Let me conclude by stressing that to set the Other in place, Dennis needed this displacement (*Verschiebung*) which, like transference, has its Freudian roots in dreams, and which Lacan equates with metonymy and desire. Desire for Dennis was in little bits of wood which warded off misfortune for him: the habit went back to a story he had heard about the poet, Robert Graves, who claimed that he only survived the butchery of the trenches thanks to an amulet, his pencil, which protected him against all the fates, including that of bearing his surname, Graves.

As for the maneuver which concerned the upper line of the algorithm of transference, I fear that Dennis confused it with the entrance under the planetarium's dome, at once turning the copper cauldron upside down, risking losing a bone in order to make for himself a chef's hat, sheltering him from bad weather; from top to bottom, he made a choice with irremediable consequences. Not tolerating being cut in two, specifically in two languages, he closed the lid on the glimpsed mystery for fear that the crucial cut of the tailor's scissors, too skilled in making jackets, might make a cut which would be fatal to him.

In conclusion, we are faced with a fetish object embued with signifying power: the reversal of the father's initials designates the penis which makes the little boy into a phallus for the mother. Just as Dennis struggled against the guilt linked to masturbation by means of conjuratory fetishes, so the black jacket later served, not to cover the lack in the Other—his mother's castration—but like the black veil for little Hans, to fix the boundaries of the gulf against which Dennis barricaded himself.

Here we are right at the border separating neurosis from perversion. Lacan ended his *Écrits* on the question of the division of the subject (in "Science and Truth"): the "no" (*pas*) of "no penis" (*pas de penis*) is a negative, but also a step (*pas*), a passage, like the Straits of Dover (*Pas de Calais*).[1] It is one step forward, two steps back.

Notes

1. [Cf. Sigmund Freud, *The Interpretation of Dreams*, Chapter VII.]

A CASE OF CHILDHOOD PERVERSION

∞

Dominique Miller

I would like to discuss a case history published in the *Complete Works* of Ferenczi, entitled "A Little Chanticleer." It is a case of a boy who is five years old when Ferenczi first meets him. Freud alludes to it in *Totem and Taboo* and compares the case with that of little Hans, though he makes a distinction between them: Hans is characterized by a phobia, while this child, named Arpad, is characterized by a perversion.

Arpad is a perverse, sadistic child who exhibits a fascination with pain and violence. A second feature which suggests true perversion is the exclusiveness of his sadistic behavior. His libido is essentially focused on sadism. His drive is fixed and needs a fixed object in order to be satisfied. Perverse subjects are said to be happy because they are not like neurotics, who are in constant search of an object by which to obtain satisfaction. Perverse subjects are set apart by the fact that they actually possess the object of their desire. The metonymical nature of the object characteristic of neurosis does not appear in perversion.

In this particular case, the objects around which the question of desire revolves are cocks or chickens, hence Arpad's fascination with hen houses. When no hen house is available, Arpad recreates one at home. He himself cackles with great skill. Ferenczi says,

> His mental activity and skills are curiously focused on the feathered species. He cackles and crows "cock-a-doodle-doo" masterfully. At dawn, the sound of a loud "cock-a-doodle-doo" wakes up the whole family. He has a sense of music, but only sings songs about hens, chickens, and other feathered creatures. He

particularly likes a popular song about buying a turkey cock, two chicks, two cockerels, and one pullet. He only draws birds with long beaks, his only toys are chickens and hens, and with them he engages in various games.

His single-minded interest in poultry, Ferenczi says, constitutes his main characteristic.

Let us now consider his sadistic side. Arpad is bewitched by the slitting of chickens' throats. He enjoys going to the market and badgers the cook or his mother until she buys a chicken. (Note that women are always involved.) Once purchased, the cock or chicken must not stay alive: it must be killed. According to Ferenczi, the slitting of the chicken's throat is a feast for Arpad's eyes; he becomes very excited, dances around the carcass for hours, and imitates the slitting of its throat.

I will attempt to reconstruct the history of this perversion in accordance with the Oedipus complex and Freud's theory of the libido. Ferenczi tries to isolate the moment of the onset of this perversion, and in that sense remains faithful to Freud. It is important to proceed as Freud did, distinguishing the moment of onset from the causal moment which preceded it.

Ferenczi isolates these two moments. When Arpad is two and one-half, an event occurs: his encounter with sexuality. When he is three and one-half, a second event takes place which triggers his perversion. Between two and one-half and three and one-half, the child is not yet a pervert; it is only at three and one-half that the trauma experienced a year before is interpreted, triggering the perversion. This pattern is always the same, demonstrating the usefulness of Lacan's formulas: a first signifier, S_1, is introduced, and then a second signifier, S_2, interprets it.

Ferenczi begins his description of the case with the second event, not with the first traumatic event. At three and one-half, Arpad is on vacation in a town in Austria. There he discovers a hen house. From that moment on, he becomes entirely taken with it. Every morning at dawn he rushes to the hen house, gazes at the animals tirelessly, copies their calls and postures, and cries and screams when he is forced to leave. He keeps on cackling, crowing "cock-a-doodle-doo," and answers every question with animal calls. His mother is afraid he will forget how to speak normally.

A year before that, Arpad was on vacation in the same town. One day he went in the hen house and urinated. A chicken approached and bit him on the penis. A servant dressed the wound, and then someone cut the chicken's throat. Arpad told this story to explain his fear of chickens and his pleasure when they are dead. It is of course his own discourse about the event. Did it really happen or is it a fantasy?

Freud came up against the same kind of difficulty concerning trauma. He could not decide whether it had really occurred or simply been fantasized. He finally solved the problem by assuming that reality is fantasmatic in nature. At the moment of trauma, something happens about which the subject cannot say anything. This unspeakability led Freud to suppose the existwolf manence of a traumatic event, and even to invent it, as he actually did with the "Wolf Man." Freud invented a primal scene: the Wolf Man as a child witnessing sexual inter-course between his father and mother *a tergo*. Freud had to invent it; he had to influence the Wolf Man so that he could remember the event.

In Arpad's case, this particular event suggests the possibility of castration. The chicken, by biting him on the penis (which must be distinguished from the phallus), raises the question of the Other's desire—a question which has no place in the symbolic.

Two signifiers, the words "chicken" and "kill" signal this particular event. But they don't fit into the symbolic chain, and are therefore meaningless and frozen. It is difficult to tell whether or not this event really occurred. It simply re-emerges a year later when he rediscovers the hen house. The symptom takes shape to interpret something which is present but unsymbolized. Perversion symbolizes this traumatic real.

The symptom is a mode of symbolization. There is another deciding factor which reveals a perversion: the fact that Arpad can no longer speak when he approaches the hen house. This encounter stirs up something real which was latent until then. $ is a presentation of the subject who can no longer speak and determine himself in the signifying chain. The subject is adrift in the signifying chain. This encounter with the real strikes him dumb and triggers the perversion.

We can compare this development with the course of the drive. First he loses his ability to speak, and then he passes through the Other—but here the Other is reduced to the level of an imaginary double or other. The chicken becomes the other who is both different and similar, similar in that the subject can imitate it, and inflict the castration he himself had experienced a year before. Perversion is a means of inflicting castration upon the other. In sadism, as we see it in the Marquis de Sade's work, the subject rids himself of the bar of subjective division and thrusts it upon the other. The sadist takes a whip and beats the other, especially a woman who must bear the bar in his stead. Lacan shows how the whip marks on the woman's body stand for the bar of the subject ($). The subject thrusts onto the woman his own bar by beating her. Our little "cock man," Arpad, inflicts castration upon the chicken. The chicken cannot stay alive, cannot remain intact. The slitting of its throat is necessary, but not sufficient; the chicken must also be plucked. This chicken object takes the sub-ject's place. We can consider the structure of perversion as an arrangement in which the object, in fantasy, becomes the subject. Then what about the pervert? He becomes the object. Arpad's fascination with the object, the fact that he has no choice but to gaze at a scene in which the chicken bears the bar of his own subjective division, suggests that he has become the object.

In a third stage, Arpad becomes another subject. He recovers language, though in a curious way, since he keeps talking about cocks and hens, and keeps on cackling, imitating cocks and hens. Arpad has become a chicken. Far from the hen house, he invents a game which amounts to a perverse scenario. Through this game he tries to symbolize something of his perversion. The game proceeds as follows: with a bit of paper he makes a hen or a cock; then he puts it up for sale, his sole aim in doing so being to kill it. He imitates the cook or his mother slitting the chicken's throat under the tap. He shows how the cock bleeds, and at the end imitates its dying.

This scene is an accurate reproduction of a real scene. The scenario takes place in the oral register, and the paper used to make the chicken comes from his father's newspaper. Something which belongs to the father's symbolic world mediates the game, and thus the paternal function is not absent from this imaginary scenario. The scenario presents a fantasy, which is situated along the imaginary axis a-a'. Perversion requires an imaginary axis along which the relation between the subject and object can be produced.

In "Kant with Sade" (*October*, 51, 1989), Lacan formulates the structure of this fantasy as $a \rightarrow \$$, object a working the subject. There is a conjunction between this axis and the imaginary axis, a-a'. Ferenczi reveals an important aspect of the imaginary scenario: while Arpad is cutting the chicken's throat, he is acting symbolically, for, as Ferenczi says, this game does not require a knife—any object can be used. The knife is all the more symbolized since Arpad is willing to call any object a knife. It is a representation of the bar on the subject ($\$$).

By imitating the slitting of the chicken's throat, Arpad can once again become a subject, for the chicken is no longer frightening. This scenario restores the child to his position as subject of desire.

Between neurosis and perversion there is a reversal. The neurotic subject is in the place of the object in fantasy, while in perversion it is the object which occupies the place of the subject. Moreover, the neurotic has to construct his fantasy in order to accede to it, while in perversion fantasy is already constructed in reality, and the subject thus already has access to it.

Object choice in neurosis and perversion is based on the phallus. This is illustrated by Arpad's chicken. The chicken is a valid object choice since it can be castrated. Castration is the requirement for phallicization. The chicken can stand for the phallus provided it is marked by a cut. To be divested of its feathers, wings, and tail, it must be alive when purchased. However, the crest on its head must be spared so as to avoid any confusion.

A fetish exemplifies the phallic value of the object. A fetish object derives its attraction from the fact that it can be extracted or removed: a braid can be cut off, a shine can be detached from the nose, underwear can be taken off. All these objects emphasize the object-like function of the phallus, a function that has to be linked with the signifier, that is, with the veil.

The nature of the phallus is clear, and Arpad is quite explicit about it; he says to a little girl, "I am going to cut your head off; then I will put it on your belly and eat it." The phallus is feminine. Immediately afterward he explains that he feels maternal: "I would like to eat some pickled mother; I would cook it and eat it." In the same vein, whenever he sees a chicken that is alive, he asks his mother to buy it and kill it. The chicken can complete his mother provided it is dead. This necessity expresses the child's sadism. The chicken can take the place of the object of his mother's desire, that is, the object desired by the mother that the child wants to get from her. The mother becomes this pickled chicken with which she feeds Arpad—it is a metonymy of the mother herself. Therefore, it can be either the being or having of the mother.

We can formulate Arpad's fantasy with these two major signifiers, "chicken" and "kill," in the same way that Freud formulates the fantasy in his article "A Child is Being Beaten": "A Chicken is Being Killed." The chicken is situated on the narcissistic axis. The word "kill" replaces the word "love." Through this signifying substitution, hate takes the place of love. Arpad's ambivalent feelings towards chickens demonstrates this substitution. He kisses and strokes the chicken once it is dead even though he wanted it to die. He throws his paper chicken into the frying pan, and then immediately rushes to stroke it. This substitution leads to an extension of the sadistic drive to his relations with his fellow beings. Through his perverse fantasy he is able to avoid castration, but at the same time he discovers via the other that he himself is plucked and eaten.

Arpad is a witness to the scene. His denial of his own castration is superimposed on his denial of the maternal other's castration. In his discourse, the intensification of the sadistic drive reveals his denial of castration: "Now I'm going to gouge out the eyes of this dead chicken," he says. What is the point of gouging out the eyes of a dead chicken? It is explained by the fact that Arpad cannot acknowledge castration. The dead chicken, representing the lack in the Other, blinds Arpad. The blind eyes reveal the Other's lack or desire. This gaze which cannot see becomes both the object as gaze in the Other and his own gaze, the object of his fantasy. Being blind, this gaze leads to the superimposing of two lacks: the maternal Other's lack and the lack in the subject who identifies with the other, that is, with the object. This double castration is unbearable and leads the subject to intensify his denial: he blinds the eyes of a dead chicken, and in doing so blinds eyes that are already blind.

The act is thus reiterated: Arpad wants to gouge out blind eyes. We see something similar in the case of Sade: he wanted nothing on his grave, thereby denying death. By refusing to have his name inscribed on his tombstone, Sade refused the symbolization of death.

Arpad's encounter with Ferenczi at the age of five is his first opportunity to situate his perversion in the symbolic register. His perversion is not yet fixed and in fact changes. At their very first meeting, the child surrenders his perversion to the Other. Arpad selects, among the objects in the room, a wood grouse. He brings it to Ferenczi and asks, "Will you give it to me?" Instead, Ferenczi gives him some paper and a pen. From the outset, Ferenczi situates himself as the Other who is lacking, who does not give objects requested, and asks the child to speak. Arpad tells Ferenczi his story, and refers to his father: "My father is the cock." This assertion is neither right nor wrong. It is not right because the chicken represents the mother's object, an oral object, an object of exchange which is similar to the breast. On the other hand, it is not wrong because, in the work accomplished by the child, we can see an attempt to appeal to the Name-of-the-Father. Here the Name-of-the-Father is not sufficient to explain castration, and the deficiency of the paternal function can be overcome by the perverse scenario.

Arpad says something which shows how the Name-of-the-Father operates in his perversion. He says, "I am a little boy, I am a chicken, but when I grow up, I will become a hen, then a cock, and at last a coachman." The paternal function exists for the child, and he is able to establish a lineage which indicates a progression. First he is a chicken, then a hen, then a cock. But the cock is not as strong as the coachman, and the coachman is not the father. The coachman impresses him more than his father. For the father, there is an Other of the Other. The father serves a paternal function in the field of the Other, and thus is missing. The coachman is stronger than he is. Through perversion, the subject tries to achieve the paternal function, to accede to a phallic power which consists in being a coachman. His meeting with Ferenczi confronts him with lack in the Other.

Arpad asks a neighbor, "Why do people die? Why does God knock me down?" To have access to the lack in the Other is also to have access to his own lack or want (want-to-be): to be a barred subject. Arpad adds, "Once I saw an angel who carried children into the sky." Arpad can find in the field of the Other, in the sky that is God's realm, an element which could complete the Other. He can complete the Other provided an angel brings him there. The angel is an interesting figure, because it is a winged child who wants for nothing, but whose sex is uncertain. Angels can help him become the phallus and thereby complete the Other.

His analytic work ends with the image of the mendicant Jew. People come and see his mother to beg. The Jew who begs for something is a new illustration to him of the lack in the Other. The Jew wants for something and begs for it. Arpad asks his mother to complete the Other. He situates himself in the oral register, in the field of desire he shares with his mother. "Give him what you give me, for if you can give it to him you must be able to give it to me." Arpad finally calls himself a mendicant cock. He is still begging for his mother's object, though he is able to accede to the place of the coachman.

Arpad's story ends with a depressive element. Arpad says to his neighbor, "I will marry you, and your sister, and my three cousins, and the cook. No, I will marry my mother instead of the cook." He swings back and forth between two positions: being a mendicant cock and being a strutting cock (the German expression is literally "a cock in the basket"). Hence, the acknowledgment of his masculinity is in question. His desire to marry his mother is nothing unusual—every normal boy wants to marry his mother—but to be a strutting cock is rather striking. Phallicization is ridiculed in that fantasy. We can assume that the cock "in the basket" will be put up for sale.

This end involves, on the one hand, the phallus, and on the other, the object, the object for sale, object *a*.

FROM FREUD TO LACAN:
A QUESTION OF TECHNIQUE

❧

Robert Samuels

To start off, I would like to issue a warning, similar to the one Lacan issues at the beginning of Seminar I. Lacan argues that Freud's work is not a ready-made system or a fixed body of knowledge. Rather it represents "thought in motion" or "work in progress." The same is true of Lacan's work, for in it we find no systematic presentation of his theory of analytic technique. What we do find, however, is the development of a certain inner logic which, Lacan argues, accounts for the totality of the "Freudian experience."

This inner logic is based on the relation between the three categories, the real, the imaginary, and the symbolic, which for Lacan determine the entirety of what he calls the "Freudian Field." My attempt here will be to introduce these categories and briefly outline how they are related to Freud's theory and technique.

In his first published seminar, Lacan argues that all of Freud's theoretical innovations are derived from practical considerations. We can test this hypothesis by first looking at the way Freud himself divided the movement of his technique into three phases: hypnosis, analysis of resistance, and free association.

Through hypnosis, Freud made the initial discoveries of the unconscious and infantile sexuality. He believed at that time that neurosis was due to an early sexual trauma that had been forgotten yet retained in the subject's unconscious. Through hypnosis, Freud was able to undermine the subject's resistances and retrieve the repressed unconscious truth. However, Freud eventually discarded this technique because some people could not be hypnotized and often old symptoms would be replaced by new ones. Furthermore, Freud argued that since hypnosis totally undermined the role of the ego, it made it impossible to analyze the forces that served to repress the unconscious material in the first place.

Once Freud gave up hypnosis, he then encountered the resistances of the conscious ego. To counteract these defenses, he worked on the analysis of resistances. This brought him to develop a psychology of the ego and its defenses and, in particular, of the process of repression.

However, Freud soon found out that the analysis of the resistances also had its limitations, because it forced the analyst to be too directive and the analysand to become too dependent on the analyst. The analysis of resistance was then replaced by free association, where Freud took a much more limited role in controlling the direction of the analysis.

By moving from the analysis of resistance to free association, Freud moved from a technique that was based on working primarily with ego defenses to a technique that was founded on working through at the level of speech.

I would argue that these three levels of analytic technique correspond to the three fundamental dimensions of analytic experience: the real, the imaginary, and the symbolic. I will now show how the real is tied to Freud's initial discovery of the unconscious and infantile sexuality; how the imaginary defines the resistances and defenses of the psychology of the ego; and how the symbolic accounts for the structure of speech and free association.

In addition, I would like to point out how Freud himself divided his theory of the libido into three stages, which are the initial discovery of infantile sexuality, the introduction of the concept of narcissism, and the final theory of the death drive. I will argue that it is in fact the second theory of narcissism that helps to explain the psychology of the ego, and that the theory of the death drive is tied to Freud's consideration of language.

1	*2*	*3*
hypnosis	analysis of resistance	free association
unconscious	ego	speech
infantile sexuality	narcissism	death drive
real	imaginary	symbolic

1. In his *Introductory Lectures on Psychoanalysis*, Freud argues that what is unconscious is also that which is infantile. He goes on to state that the unconscious is the place where repressed aspects of infantile sexuality are maintained and that these initial desires are indestructible. Freud also adds that, at the level of infantile sexuality, there is no recognition of the incest taboo, the difference between the sexes, or the separation between self and other. In fact, as he points out in the *Three Essays on the Theory of Sexuality*, the initial sexual experi-

ences are essentially autoerotic, meaning they do not need another person or object.

For Lacan, the initial separation from the Other defines what he calls the primitive real. The real itself is opposed to the symbolic world of law, languages, and social relations. This means the unconscious subject of infantile sexuality recognizes no law or other form of social mediation. Infantile sexuality is therefore a threat to civilization and must be repressed. It is a pure instinctual impulse without limits.

In Freud's structural theory, we attach this initial stage of purely instinctual existence to the agency of the id. In Lacan's Seminar I, we see how this category of the primitive real is tied to the psychotic phenomenon of hallucination and the defense he calls "foreclosure." This theory of the real is articulated in his discussion of psychosis and his critique of Jung's and Melanie Klein's work.

2. For Lacan and Freud, the first resistance or defense against this primary state of real existence and the id comes into being through the formation of the ego in the structure of narcissism. The ego is tied to the subject's limit and control of his or her own body. By separating him or herself from others and his or her pure natural impulses, the subject gains a sense of self and unity. However, for the subject to gain access to this unity, s/he must see him or herself reflected in an image or in an other. After all, no one ever sees the totality of his or her own body; one can only see it in the other. That is what Freud calls narcissism and what Lacan relates to the imaginary mirror stage.

We know from the myth that Narcissus falls in love with his own image that he sees reflected in the water. Narcissus' image of himself is therefore found outside in an external object, just as one's consciousness is always consciousness of an object. Furthermore, one only finds out about oneself through the feedback one receives from others.

This is very evident in what we call narcissistic personalities. At this level of pathology, there is a constant need for reflection and feedback from the other. The narcissist can only feel good about him or herself if s/he sees his or her own grandiosity and self-image reflected back to him or her. Kohut develops the differences between narcissistic transference and idealizing transference to account for two ways that the subject attempts to find the unity of his or her ego or ego-ideal in the other.

Lacan argues that this form of ego or self psychology is based on an attempt to re-enact the symbiotic and dual relation between the child and the approving and loving mother. He believes it is a fantasy relationship based on the attempt to refind ideal images of past love and acceptance. In narcissistic transference, the patient refinds his or her own sense of self-unity by having his or her own image reflected back to him or her, and in idealizing transference it is because the analyst is seen as an ideal Other that the subject can idealize him or herself.

To see one's own narcissistic image reflected back to oneself or to be in relation with an ideal Other are two ways the ego serves to reinforce itself and attain the pleasure principle. In the analysis of the ego it is precisely this relation of narcissism and the defenses and resistances of the ego that are most essential. In Seminar I, Lacan examines this form of analysis in his critique of Heinz Hartmann's and Anna Freud's work.

3. The third level of analysis concerns the symbolic order of speech and the death drive. Freud himself places the death drive beyond the pleasure principle of the ego. From the beginning of his work, Freud constantly points out different phenomena of language and representation that go beyond the subject's own intentionality, consciousness, and well-being. Slips of the tongue, bungled acts, and jokes are all ways that the subject does or says something that he or she doesn't want to say or do. These unconscious slips represent for Freud the truth of the subject's repressed desire.

Through these unconscious formations, Freud discovered that language can divorce itself from the intentionality of the ego. It is as if the ego were dead or non-existent when confronted with these symbolic acts.

It wasn't until he began to formulate his theories of the death drive, the superego, and masochism that Freud began to describe the way the subject could do or say things that were not conducive to his or her own well-being. Through the analysis of traumatic dreams, negative therapeutic reactions, and childhood games, Freud articulated his theory of the death drive that explained why someone would continuously return to negative experiences. He argued that an experience which could not be controlled or mastered in the past could be mastered through a symbolic form of repetition.

The study of the drives also brought Freud back to his theory of perversion and masochism. While neurotics restrict their sexual life to imaginary fantasy and symptoms, perverts are said to act out their desires through their drives. However, these drives usually take on a repetitive and self-destructive mode.

I believe that a lot of the cases we now call borderline personality disorders are actually what Freud calls perversions. The combination of acting out, lack of impulse control, unstable relations, splitting of object and self representations, and low frustration tolerance also applies to sado-masochistic pathologies. This level of pathology is not centered on the narcissism of the ego, but rather on the drives and the superego. For it is the agency of the superego that Freud uses to explain the fundamental masochism of the subject. The superego represents the internalization of social laws and traditions that go against the ego's own narcissism and pleasure principle.

Freud argues that the superego gets its energy from the id, yet it is formed through the resolution of the Oedipus complex, which occurs after the formation of the ego. The logical structure of the second topography moves from the id to the ego and on to the superego, yet the superego itself depends on the initial position of the id.

This complicated structure derives its logic from Freud's theory of symptom formation. The first stage is based on the initial fixation of the subject at the level of infantile sexuality, the second stage is based on the repression of that fixation by the ego defenses, and the third stage is based on the return of the repressed, meaning a return to the first stage but now at the level of a symbolic substitute. The movement is then from the real id of infantile sexuality, to its repression by the imaginary ego, to its return at the level of the symbolic superego.

The very process of analysis serves to reverse this structure. Through symbolic free association, one attempts to go beyond the defenses and resistances of the ego in order to attain unconscious desires and thoughts:

unconscious id   resistance of the ego   symbolic speech

Lacan argues that this same structure has determined the history of psychoanalysis. The initial discovery of the unconscious and infantile sexuality has been repressed by ego psychology, and Lacan returns to the repressed Freud through his theory of the importance of language in analysis.

ON PERVERSION[1]

∞

Jacques-Alain Miller

One more effort! You are tired, and I am too. So let us say, like Sade—*one more effort!*

Sade said it in a title: "Frenchmen, one more effort if you want to be Republicans." Apparently this one last effort which Sade considered necessary did not materialize in France. A few years later, France gave itself to Napoleon Bonaparte who put Sade in jail. Since it was not a success, I shall not say—"Americans, one more effort if you want to be Lacanians"—God forbid! I was told last night that when Lacan triumphs in America it will be an Americanized Lacan, pre-packaged for supermarkets. So I'll just say, "Americans, one more effort before going home."

As a matter of fact, going back home could be the question. Is sexual enjoyment located at home or not? That is perhaps the negative of our theme here: "Gender and Perversion." But certainly I will not say, "Americans, one more effort if you want to be gays."

Framework

In spite of the fact that perversion sometimes lends itself to proselytism, the pervert presenting himself as able to reveal the truth of enjoyment to the non-pervert, a pervert may suffer because he has knowledge of sexual enjoyment that he cannot communicate. Thus the pervert lives in human society, sometimes in a tiny, secret society of initiates. I do not come to praise perversion, but I do not come to bury it either. I come to provide the main coordinates of my view of perversion. I could call this talk, though it would be a bit ambiguous, "A Key to Perversion." Let's say that if I manage to condense what I want to say into one hour, including questions and answers, this talk will be entitled "Fundamentals of Perversion: An Outline According to Classical Psychoanalysis."

Just a word concerning classical psychoanalysis.

It is not ego-psychology. Ego-psychology is a deviation of psychoanalysis. It deviates from the mainstream of Freud's theoretical construction regarding the unconscious along two lines. Ego-psychology lops off Freud's first topography, thus eliminating the very concept of the unconscious and its foundation in the structure of language and the function of speech. Second, ego-psychology unduly singles out Freud's second topography, and changes and inverses its meaning. While Freud, with his second topography, explores the dimension beyond the pleasure principle, ego-psychology establishes the ego as the truest agency, the autonomy of which analytic treatment is supposed to restore.

Classical psychoanalysis is not object relations theory, which is also a deviation stemming from Karl Abraham and Melanie Klein, a dialectical negation of the first deviation.

Nor is classical psychoanalysis the blend of ego-psychology and object relations theory attempted by contemporary American psychoanalysts, that takes into account the semantic relationship to others while retaining the structural framework of ego-psychology.

Classical psychoanalysis is Freud's entire theory, including the inner logic of its changing and sometimes contradictory expression made explicit by Lacan. That is to say, it is the whole of Freud's work as opposed to a partialization thereof, and it is also Freud logicized such that Freud's self-contradictions are not used against him. What I am calling classical psychoanalysis is, I believe, the basis of our common endeavor, and that is why a lot of the talks here have tried to show how Lacan extends Freud: how he reorders Freud's teaching and provides a consistent sequel to it. Lacan explores the clinical practice which stems from it.

This is what I believe our framework is.

The Perverse Analysand

In speaking about perversion, I cannot help thinking about my patients—my clinically perverse patients.

They are mainly male homosexuals who come to analysis day after day, year after year, and they say, "We are among the most honest, the most truth-seeking, the most self-searching patients." I hope I don't sound too moralistic. But I'm prepared to sound even more moralistic if it is necessary to dispel the cloak of infamy from a call to hidden desire, to perversion. Lacan did it wittily when he spoke in French of *père-version*, a word which is untranslatable, made up of *père*, father, and *version*. It implies *a turning to the father, a call to the father*, which perhaps is also a very profound reminder that perversion is, in no sense, a subversion.

This perversion, this turning to the father, is nowhere more patent or explicit than in the case of female homosexuals who constantly attest to an intense love for the father, legitimating the use of the Freudian term "fixation"—the paternal fixation of the female homosexual. A fixation on a memory of the disappointment met with by this love for the father, a disappointment encountered with the father as love object, followed by a turning away from the love object, triggers an identification with it according to Freud and Lacan's classic deduction.

Male and female homosexuals do come to analysis; they may be analysands. As for sadism, masochism, and voyeurism, I have not seen analysands, strictly speaking, whose pathology gives clear evidence of the primacy of such ways of obtaining sexual gratification. Sometimes they come, but they don't stay. I am currently supervising a case of a true exhibitionist who is actually in treatment, who is actually doing analysis, much to my amazement.

A psychoanalyst who takes on homosexuals as analysands certainly has some self-searching of his own to do. I say "self-searching" to emphasize that clinical perversion throws the analyst's most intimate judgment into question, throwing into question the point up to which he himself has moved on the path of sexual enjoyment. Certainly he has to screen out his prejudices, his married life with children, the supreme good according to psychoanalysis. This is not an abstract question—it is something you have to ask yourself in this situation. Is the analyst unduly hostile to a homosexual choice he himself has perhaps rejected, or is he perhaps unduly friendly? Is it enough to suspend any will to normalize? Is it possible for an analysis to reach the proper end of its road without removing the fear of womanhood? What is one to do with female homosexuality, so paradoxical from the analytic perspective, so paradoxical that Lacan once proposed to call heterosexuals all those who love women.

Perversion requires the analyst to suppress all countertransference in favor of the analyst's desire, that desire which operates through the suspension of all beliefs and knowledge, through the introduction of a question mark in the place of the signified. It does so to split the master signifier in its nonsensical nakedness from the constant crystallization of enjoyed meaning, which Lacan called object *a*. You mustn't take at face value the subject's announcement that he is a homosexual. One man may believe he is a homosexual because he slept with a boy once when he was fourteen, and another may believe he is not a homosexual even though he sleeps with two or three different boys a week.

It is a question of meaning. You are in analysis as soon as you no longer know what words mean. You are in analysis as soon as lexical meaning is progressively undone by new meaning surging forth from actual speech, new meaning constructed in analysis step by step or rather mistake by mistake. As a rule, you cannot escape the necessity of asking the person who comes to see you for analysis, "What do you expect from analysis?" I call that the "hook question": "What made you go for the hook on the analyst's line?" The analyst has to promise something in response to the patient's expectations. You have to weigh the patient's hope against what you do or do not promise.

When someone defines himself as a homosexual, he defines his subjective position with respect to his object choice. It seems to him that the most important characteristic of his subjective position is his *Objektwahl* [Freud's term for object choice], that is, he characterizes himself by the sex of the person or persons from whom he expects sexual gratification. A subject who defines himself as a homosexual may expect a change in his object choice, or he may expect analysis to cure his symptoms, for example, discontent, anxiety, and depression which he feels are due to his object choice.

The question that must be raised is: "Is it conceivable for an analyst to promise a change of object choice?" The analyst generally doesn't promise anything, but especially cannot promise a new object choice.

Desire and Enjoyment

As Lacan says, homosexuals exist, but you can't cure them. That is one of the differences between the neurotic and the perverse subject position (the clinical pervert).

Simplistically put, the neurotic is fundamentally uncertain about sexual gratification, and doesn't know where to find it. What he does know is that there is a deficit somewhere concerning sexual gratification. Thus the neurotic initiates a labyrinthine search for the lost object and that is what we call desire; the Latin origin of "desire," *desiderio*, means a "longing for" that implies an absence. The pervert has found the object, that is his problem; he is certain about his ways of obtaining sexual gratification, but that is not why he comes to analysis. Perhaps he feels it is not what it ought to be; he has found sexual gratification but it is not the right kind. Either you don't find it, or if you do, it is not the right kind.

Few perverts ask to undergo analysis. We might conclude that perverts are unanalyzable, but the fact is they simply don't come asking to undergo analysis. They don't come to seek out the lost object; thus, it is just plain common sense to believe that, in some way, they have found it and can expect nothing from analysis. The effect known since Lacan as the "subject supposed to know" doesn't arise with a true pervert, demonstrating that the subject supposed to know always arises in the place of sexual enjoyment. You need a certain void or deficit in the place of sexual enjoyment for the subject supposed to know to arise. I usually present this by saying that, "The pervert has the answer, which stems from the real of his subjective constitution." He has an immutable, constant share that is always ready to use—it is *at hand,* an *at hand* enjoyment.

Desire is something else altogether; it is a *longing for.* Desire supposes a toleration of absence, of *not having,* and desire in this sense is essentially a question, perhaps a question about desire itself. To simplify the question, let us juxtapose desire as a question and the constancy of jouissance as an answer, an answer which is already there. The perverse analysand is a paradoxical analysand. As a true analysand, he must have a question. Therefore, in some sense, perversion disappears on the couch—either perversion disappears on the couch, or the patient disappears from the couch.

If we say "perverse analysand," we must also say that he expresses certainty regarding the ways and means of his sexual enjoyment. Perhaps he is suffering from that certainty and at the same time raising the question of his desire, as if at another level he were not satisfied with his satisfaction. This fact forces us to distinguish jouissance and desire: on the one hand, we have jouissance characterized by its inertia—and Freud himself speaks of the inertia of libido during the years and years of true analysis—and on the other hand, desire as a question, metonymic desire, that is to say free desire, hidden, fulgurating or inhibited desire that is fundamentally perplexed. That is the paradox of the perverse analysand: he is someone who has a sure answer but is nevertheless perplexed.

The Concept of Libido

You can see that I don't approach perversion from the perspective of criminality, but rather from that of morality. I consider the pervert as a full blown subject. I do not consider perversion and the mechanism of perversion as intra-subjective; in other words, perversion is not a raw instinctual drive reigning free, as some have interpreted Freud's *Three Essays on the Theory of Sexuality* to imply.

In classical psychoanalysis, perversion is not a raw instinctual drive; it is cooked, so to speak, not raw. It is a highly complex structure which is as sophisticated and full of intricacies as a neurosis. The pervert remains a subject throughout what we may call his oscillation. I would proscribe all debasement of perversion. But the difficulty lies in the fact that, in large part, perversion is not a native psychoanalytic concept. Perversion is a clinical concept I hope to define which encompasses all kinds of atypical, aberrant, or abnormal sexual behavior. The diagnosis of perversion may be based on the objective data of deviant sexuality. Perversion might be thought to cover all troubles in sexual relationships, all troubles in one's relationship to the other sex, but as a matter of fact we do not call all such troubles perverse.

For instance we don't call inhibitions in sexual relationships perverse. When we speak of perversion, believing we know what we mean, we always imply an active sexual behavior that deviates from the normal ends and means of human sexuality. Perversion involves the notion of action. A classical thesis in psychoanalysis holds that neurotics may have perverse fantasies, but should not for all that be diagnosed as perverts. What we require is a dimension of action, that is to say, a broader notion of sex. Fantasy is not enough for a diagnosis of perversion. But as I have already very simply presented the concept of perversion, you can see that it throws into question the very notion of normal human sexuality. The norm is fundamentally biological: reproduction. Freud goes so far as to suggest that foreplay is perverse.

From the point of view of analysis it's a question, for instance, why men are attracted to women at the same time that they perhaps despise women or always reproach them with something. We know that men reproach women with not being men. That's why at the end of *Some Like It Hot*, Tony Curtis says to Jack Lemmon, "Nobody's perfect."

Freud considers that, from the point of view of psychoanalysis, object choice is problematic. We are not preoccupied with some sort of supposedly natural, biological, preordained object choice. Freud broadens our understanding of the term "homosexuality." There is no such thing in the Freudian Field as a sexual instinct which is a natural impulse toward the opposite sex, an impulse that would know its pre-ordained aim.

That's what Lacan writes as $, the subject with a bar, where the subject does not refer to the individual or to any biological aim, and the bar nullifies all outside determinations, introducing a cut, gap, or discontinuity in any chain of determination. That is why it is only concerning $, a subject strictly speaking, that we may think of object choice. Object choice is unthinkable if it is not related to an undetermined subject.

At the same time it is not an undetermined choice; the indeterminate subject is not an autonomous ego, and thus Freud and Lacan speak of a constricted choice, a choice dependent on conditions. Indeed, perversion throws the very concept of sexuality into question. If the biological concept of sex implies a complementarity of the two sexes according to the thesis of sexuated libido, perversion attests to the fact that human subjects can seek sexual gratification outside of the normal biological coupling of the sexes. We are not here to praise perversion, but we are not here to bury it either. In other words, we have to create a concept of a form of sexual gratification which may or may not be realized through normal coupling; and which may be realized with an individual of the opposite sex, but without normal coupling, or with an individual of the same sex, or with an individual of another species, or with an inanimate thing.

That is what Freud created with the concept of libido: a concept of sexual gratification which may be realized in various ways, not infinitely various ways, but in many different ways. Psychoanalysis has created a very broad list of libidinized activities. To fuck is to satisfy libido, but to eat, shit, see, speak, think, write, and even walk may satisfy libido as well. Freud brings about an extraordinary extension of the concept of libido and of sexual gratification which we might have thought reserved to the sexual. Libido plays an important role in the distinction of the stages of development.

Libido is a quantity which cannot be calculated, but whose introduction enables us to equate a wide variety of activities and behavior—eating, shitting, thinking, and writing too, since sublimation also attests to libido. In Freud's terms, sublimation means satisfaction without repression that does not derive from sexual contact with members of the opposite sex.

There is a question in psychoanalysis as to the connection between sublimation and perversion, and not a few true perverts have enormously contributed to human sublimation—no other clinical structure involves as many literary references as perversion. The point is not to either confuse or distinguish sublimation from perversion conceptually, but to see that they stem from the same question: satisfaction from activities other than fucking. We have to assume there are other satisfactions in life, otherwise we wouldn't be spending two days in this dark basement talking about perversion!

Satisfaction as Object

This implies a new concept of the object, a concept of the object which is distinct from that implied in the expression "object choice." We know what we mean by "object choice": the object of the choice—a man with a mustache, a tall or very strong man; or a curvaceous woman, etc. The whole imaginary may come into play here. But we need another concept of the object, if we take seriously what I said before. We need an object for the satisfaction involved in writing, thinking, walking, etc.

Let's call it a "libido object"; it's a libido object for a libidinal subject. We may think it is material, for instance, in fetishism where the object chosen is usually a woman, whether beautiful or not. But fetishism means that beauty is nothing but a prop for the libido object, so much so that the libido object perhaps takes the place of the object chosen: first, the woman with high heels, then just the high heels. In the example of fetishism, which is so instrumental in distinguishing what Lacan calls "the cause of desire," we see the fetish as a condition for sexual enjoyment of the chosen object. But at the same time it is erroneous to limit this libido object to the fetish as material. For instance, in his article entitled "Fetishism," Freud doesn't discuss a material object. On the contrary, the example he proposes first is an effect of mistaken translation: *Glanz auf der Nase* (a shining on the nose or glance at the nose)—an error of translation between German and English. Thus, the libido object is not necessarily material. Here the woman seems to be nothing but a necessary prop for this shining on the nose. Furthermore, women's noses usually do not shine because they powder them.

Let's just say we have to distinguish between the chosen object and the libido object. But second, we need a new concept of instinct, that is, of the impulse toward the libido object. That's what Freud calls drive, "*Trieb.*" What is the libido object? It isn't material. The Freudian drive, which is a satisfaction-seeking *Trieb*, doesn't seek any object in particular. It seeks satisfaction. The object that corresponds to the drive is *satisfaction as object*. That is what I would like to propose today, as a definition of Lacan's object *a:* object *a* is satisfaction as an object. Just as we distinguish between instinct and drive, we have to distinguish between the chosen object and the libido object, the latter being *satisfaction* qua *object.*

The sexual *Trieb* thus does not go toward the opposite sex. There are multiple impulses, multiple drives, and psychoanalysis points to the problem of the integration of multiple drives. We have to recognize that the concept of perversion, the original concept of perversion, has been perverted. According to Freud, children are naturally polymorphously perverse. Thus for Freud, perversion is natural, that is, primary. Perversion is more primal than the norm, that norm being secondary or even cultural for Freud—though not for Lacan. In psychoanalysis, there is a problematic of normalization, of normative integration of multiple drives.

But this makes no sense if we do not admit that the drive is by its very nature perverse, and that perversion is the norm of the drive. Thus, what is problematic is the existence of a sexual drive toward the opposite sex. Lacan's thesis here is that there is no drive toward the opposite sex; there is only a drive toward the libido object, toward partial satisfaction qua object. To take a person, a whole person as an object, is not the role of the drive; it leads us to introduce love. Freud says the drives are our myths, and love was a myth long before Freud. If you take drives seriously and even if you take drives at the level of the real, you have to take love at that level too. To go from drives to desire, to introduce the absence necessary for desire, you need the mediation of love.

If drives are Freud's myth, what Lacan tries to do with object *a* is explain the inner logic of the Freudian myth of the drive, just as he tries to explain the inner logic of the Freudian myth of the Oedipus complex. It is clear in Lacan's work that, as there is no sexual *rapport*—no fixed sexual formula, as he puts it— perversion takes the place of what doesn't exist as a fixed sexual formula. Perversion means innovation, invention of ways of relating to the opposite sex; perversion is a way of relating to the opposite sex. Woman remains present at the very core of male homosexuality. The problem is that innovation is not all that innovative; Lacan was waiting for a new perversion to appear.

What kind of object is connected to the drive? It is not a whole person. It is partial, and there is constancy: the constancy of object *a*. I can't dwell on that here. . . .

Generalized Perversion and the N-operator

That is enough to justify what I would call "generalized perversion." If we say the drives are essentially perverse, we have a level of generalized perversion, of primary and generalized perversion, perversion for everyone. This level calls for a normalizer, and so we may define restricted perversion, that is to say perversion as a distinct clinical structure, as a result of the failure of normalization; or we may note, for instance, that in some sense normalization is always partial. This problematic of generalized perversion and the introduction of a normalizer can be found explicitly in Freud's work: for instance, when he speaks of the necessary synthesis of the partial drives under the supremacy of the genital organs.

In Lacan's work, this translates very precisely as the relationship between object *a* and the phallus. What Freud calls the synthesis of the partial drives under the primacy of the genital organs finds a very simple, logical translation in Lacan's work in the tension or opposition between object *a* and the phallus.

Lacan shows that the primacy of the genitals is a negative primacy, that is, that object *a* is connected to minus phi (−φ), which translates the Freudian supremacy of the genitals, but takes into account castration. Lacan introduces the whole problematic of the connection between satisfaction and the signifier, and various definitions of the phallus as the symbol of the place of satisfaction or as the signifier of jouissance, which attempt to explain what Freud calls the synthesis of the partial drives under the primacy of the genitals. In Lacan's work, that synthesis translates as the connection between jouissance and the primacy of the phallus as signifier. Lacan tries to elaborate it logically. Freud recognizes the perverse components of supposedly normal sexuality, and views them as remainders of primal perversion. If you take them as remainders of primal perversion, you have to define the aim of treatment as that of completing normalization, of absorbing the residue. Lacan defines the aim of treatment differently: it is not to complete normalization or absorb non-normalized residues, but to give permission for perversion, permission for object *a*.

Don't take that at face value! Let me explain it first.

The normalizer—I could call it the n-operator—in psychoanalysis is classically presented as the Oedipus complex. At one point, Lacan tried to provide a linguistic formula for the Oedipus complex which he called the paternal metaphor. You can distinguish two things: you can say that before the activity of the n-operator, you have the pure drive, and that perversion is connected to the drive that has *not* undergone normalization. Or you can say that perversion is connected to the drive that *has* undergone normalization. I would say the latter is the classical psychoanalytic perspective on perversion, as opposed to any biological approach to perversion, but to many it is a cryptic approach.

The classical psychoanalytic approach is that the n-operator always functions in perversion—that is, perversion is fundamentally approached from the Oedipus complex. Lacan was interested in W.H. Gillespie's work because Gillespie concluded from Freud's work that the Oedipus complex and the castration complex are essential in perversion. In Lacan's view, however, the pre-Oedipal drive is not pre-linguistic or raw; the drive is a highly elaborate concept compared to "natural needs." The drive is not primitive and "pre-Oedipal drives" are not pre-linguistic. What Lacan called the Other is already there in the drive. Thus the drive is cooked. Not only is it not raw, but all of Lacan's demonstrations regarding the drive show that the drive is, indeed, very sophisticated.

To Deduce the Drive

Lacan tried to deduce the drive in the sequence *demand, desire, demand for love, and drive.* That's the simplified sequence: first there is what you ask for (demand), then desire in the sense of "Do I want what I am asking for?", then the demand for love which is to ask for the Other, and finally *the drive which is not to ask anyone any longer.* Conceptually speaking, first you have the distinction between the signifier (S) and the signified (s) from "The Agency of the Letter." But that is equivalent to the distinction between demand (D) and desire (d), which is equivalent to the distinction between the enunciated (e) and enunciation (E), which is equivalent to the distinction between the signifier (S) and the subject as the signifier with a bar ($).

$$\frac{S}{s} \Rightarrow \frac{d}{D} \Rightarrow \frac{E}{e} \Rightarrow \frac{\$}{S}$$

Thus the drive as Lacan writes it is characterized by the fact that the element underneath is at the same level as the element on top. That is, he writes the drive like that: S with a bar, lozenge, and D for demand ($\$ \lozenge D$). It's a demand which is no longer interpretable because you have interpretation when you have two distinct levels. You know you are dealing with a drive in analysis when there is nothing more to interpret. And that's why, classically speaking, it is always from the point of the drive that interpretation is given, that is—it is the instrument of interpretation. Analysts speak of drives when interpretation is no longer conceivable.

Thus you see the contrasting relation between the drive and desire in Lacan. In the case of desire, asking is essential; poor blind desire has to ask its way about. That's why Lacan says the most essential object *a* in neurosis is demand itself.

This makes no sense if you believe object *a* is something substantial and material. Demand is the essential object of desire in neurosis. But the drive is characterized by the fact that, in human behavior, there is sometimes speech in which you are not asking your way. The drive does not ask its way. That's why it might be said that perversion is when you do not ask for permission—with the exception of masochism, and that is the paradox of masochism. In masochism the other's consent is essential. Perhaps we will have time later to get to the question of demand in masochism.

With the drive you can always ask, who is driving? Is there a pilot in this drive? In some sense, the drive seems to go adrift (*à la dérive*). But in fact it is desire that drifts, whereas the drive knows its way. Drives may seem to err, drives may seem to be prone to aberrations and abnormalities. But as a matter of fact, drives know their way toward satisfaction as an object. Lacan simplified this when he depicted the drive as a circuit around the object, the latter being *the result or product of a circuit*. The drive is language, and it is essentially a program. It is something that is previously written. In "Drives and Their Vicissitudes," Freud approaches drives from the point of view of grammar and grammatical inversion. However, this leads Freud to sustain a symmetrical relationship between sadism and masochism, and between exhibitionism and voyeurism, a symmetry which is criticized by Lacan.

You can understand from the matheme ($ \lozenge D) why Freud speaks of the silence of the drives. He couldn't speak of the silence of the drives if it was not essential to pinpoint the position of the drive with respect to speech. There is no function of speech in the drive because the drive is beyond demand, but the structure of language is nevertheless implied therein, which is why Freud's perspective is grammatical. We can connect satisfaction and castration. What is castration in Freud's work? It is a sacrifice of satisfaction. It is the sacrifice of the satisfaction at hand, that is, masturbation, as a precondition for openness to the opposite sex.

Lacan situates castration as the fundamental effect of language on satisfaction. We have accounts of this in Freud, for example, in his myth of the libidinal body whose satisfaction is progressively evacuated until libido is restricted to very few zones. When we speak of perversion as restricted—that is, as a specific clinical structure—first we present it as a particular way of negating castration, of rejecting the necessary sacrifice of satisfaction. What Lacan is saying isn't very different when he qualifies the perverse operation as bringing jouissance back to the Other, restoring object *a*—which represents the sacrifice of satisfaction—to the Other; we can represent the Other as the body from which satisfaction was evacuated.

When we write *A̸*, A is castrated, and in this sense perversion may be spoken of as fear of castration, fear of the Other's castration essentially. That's why female homosexuality is especially paradoxical, because in female homosexuality, the absence of the organ functions as a condition of love. That is why Lacan hesitated to qualify female homosexuality as perverse. Female homosexuality is constituted in the register of love, rather than in that of perverse satisfaction.

Perversion and the Other

We don't have much time left, so I will not be able to distinguish the three clinical structures—neurosis, psychosis, and perversion—according to the three fundamental mechanisms found in Freud's work, which were logicized by Lacan: repression (*Verdrängung*) for neurosis, foreclosure (*Verwerfung*) for psychosis, and *Verleugnung* for perversion which is sometimes translated as denial, though there are many problems with that.

To condense Lacan's approach to perversion, I would say there are two fundamental ways in which he qualifies the elements necessary to supplement the Other: first in the register of desire, and second in the register of jouissance. The first involves being the phallus which the Other is lacking (that is the topic of identification with the imaginary object of desire as phallus), the second the level of jouissance (that is the formula for perversion); the first involves being the phallus, the second involves being object *a*.

This leads me to introduce another fundamental thesis which is not found in Lacan's work, but is apropos: *there is no negation of the Other in perversion*. It is false to believe that in perversion the Other doesn't exist; on the contrary, the pervert needs the Other to exist. The pervert needs the Other much more than an obsessive neurotic; for example, an obsessive neurotic needs nobody, and it is very difficult for him to open up. The obsessive neurotic spends a lot of time talking to himself; he is characterized by intra-subjectivity, not intersubjectivity.

The Other is necessary in perversion. Think of the exhibitionist. For the exhibitionist, the public, or audience, is essential. To exhibit one's genitals to the mirror is of no interest, except to the obsessive neurotic who, like the Rat Man, may open the door to show his genitals to the dead father. But to the exhibitionist, it is opening the door to nobody, because for him the dead father doesn't materialize like it does for Hamlet.

The exhibitionist needs the Other. It is of interest to him to show his genitals to women to try and produce shame in the Other, shame for not being the same. The exhibitionist tries to make Woman exist; indeed we might say that Woman doesn't exist *except* for the exhibitionist. Voyeurism involves trying to see a woman as devoted to the jouissance of her own body and making her realize that, even when alone, she is being watched by another. The Lacanian structure of exhibitionism and voyeurism is as follows: exhibitionism involves the attempt to make the gaze appear in the Other. The exhibitionist shows his organ, but the erection is on the side of the female gaze; the true erection is generally on that side. The voyeur brings in the gaze himself to obturate the hole in the Other, to make the Other whole.

Here too there is a tension between perversion and sublimation which we must try to understand. Does sublimation require the object not to exist so that you can create something? In perversion, on the contrary, you need to make the Other exist to be the instrument of its jouissance. That is why sublimation is often the salvation for perversion.

Lack of Time

I won't have time to develop the function of Woman as Other—Woman is central to perversion because Woman is man's Other, because Woman is Other as such, or Otherness. That is why what is normal is always only "norm-male," so to speak.

I won't have time to talk about normal male perversion either, which I have been working on in Paris.

Let us conclude on this point: if the true pervert makes himself be object *a*, we can very simply deduce from Lacan's formula why it is incompatible with analysis. The analyst, in the analytic operation, makes himself be object *a*. Is that to say that the analyst is a pervert? Certainly not.

I'll stop there now and take questions. I hope to follow up in two months at Kent State.

Answers to Questions

"Kant with Sade"

The worst pervert is he who speaks in the name of morality. The true perverts, the ones you never see in analysis, are the judge, the priest, and the professor—all those in a position of authority who control the jouissance of others. The worst perversion is righteousness. That is what Freud teaches us. Moral conscience is fed by exactly the same energy that would have gone into drive satisfaction but has been renounced. The criminal pervert is not the opposite of the righteous judge: the righteous judge is the worst criminal.

He who pretends to incarnate the moral law is the true sadist. You may believe, for instance, that "Kant with Sade" is really a far-fetched idea of Lacan's, but it was not Lacan who invented the notion of the sadistic superego. One of the secrets of "Kant with Sade" is that it speaks of *Freud with Melanie Klein*, of the post-Oedipal superego and of Klein's pre-Oedipal superego. Freud himself knew very well that the secret of moral conscience is its sadistic element. He alludes to Kant in "The Economic Problem of Masochism." On page 167 of Volume XIX of the Standard Edition, he says: "Kant's Categorical Imperative is thus the direct heir of the Oedipus complex."

It is a reference to Kant's principle of higher morality, and Freud says that the Oedipus complex proves to be the source of our individual ethical sense and of our desexualized morality. But he notes that, in true moral masochism, morality is re-sexualized. He alludes there to the fact that the cultural suppression of the instincts stops a large part of the subject's destructive impulses from being exercised against others; instead they are exercised against the subject himself. Thus Freud here refers to the sadistic superego that increases its sadism against the ego. It translates in Lacan as "Kant with Sade."

"Female Perversion"

You have to look for female perversion where it is invisible. Female narcissism may be taken as a perversion, as an extension of the concept. It is because Woman is Otherness as such or the Other that she spends so much time in front of the mirror—just to recognize herself, or perhaps to recognize herself as Other. Even if it is a myth, it is very important. You may find female perversion in narcissism, at the core of one's own image, or as Freud proposed, in the child—the child used as an object of satisfaction.

In the latter case, we have the mother and the imaginary object, the phallus. The mother here is responsible for the perversion of the male child, but at the same time uses the child as an instrument of jouissance. According to the preceding formula, you could call that perversion. Was the first perverse couple mother and child? Lacan, in the fifties, suggests that it is in the connection between the mother's own body and the child that you may find a concealed expression of female perversion.

Insofar as female homosexuality eliminates the male organ, there is some difficulty placing it in the register of perversion proper. Lacan noted that it doesn't have the social importance of male homosexuality. According to Freud, male homosexuality is a fundamental social bond: it is a principle of the social bond. Female homosexuality doesn't have that function; it may be of great *cultural* importance, but is not of fundamental *social* importance.

You ask me, "If it is not a perversion, what would you call it?" It could rather be called "female homosexuality," or perhaps "heterosexuality," which Lacan defines as "love for women." You have to consider female homosexuality in hysteria, which can disappear like magic when a woman enters analysis. As long as she can love the analyst as inaccessible, the longing for love which is realized in female homosexuality may immediately shift into the transference and you may witness a magical cure. Others take a very long time.

Note

1. [This lecture was given in New York City on April 2, 1989, and was the closing talk of the Paris–New York Psychoanalytic Workshop entitled "Gender and Perversion," organized by Stuart Schneiderman. It was transcribed by Josephina Ayerza and edited by Bruce Fink. Jacques-Alain Miller was kind enough to reread and correct the text for the present publication.]

PART VI

OTHER TEXTS

"A CIVILIZATION OF HATRED": THE OTHER IN THE IMAGINARY

∞

Maire Jaanus

What do we call a subject? Quite precisely, what, in the development of objectification, is outside of the object.
—Lacan, Seminar I

"Is Psychoanalysis a Humanism?"

How other is the other in the imaginary? Is the otherness of the other in the
imaginary order more marked than the otherness of the other in the symbolic
or the real? The problem of otherness preoccupied Lacan all his life[1] as his ever
more intricate and paradoxical schemata of the outwardness of inwardness, and
the reverse, show. My focus here is on the otherness of the imaginary, predom-
inantly in Seminar I, in which there is as yet no schema R, nor even schema L,
although the latter is clearly adumbrated.[2]

The central other in the imaginary–the fellow human being, the semblable,
the recognizable self-likeness–*appears* to be a separate enough entity, but
turns out, in fact, to be an alter ego, libidinally chained to the narcissistic image
of the ego.[3] Without the radical otherness of the symbolic, therefore, a pure
imaginary would, at core, be wholly narcissistic, and thus the least other. The
imaginary other "isn't an other at all, since it is essentially coupled with the ego,
in a relation which is always reflexive, interchangeable–the *ego* is always an
alter ego."[4]

Lacan opposes the libidinized structure of the imaginary, source of all erotic-aggressive relations, to the nonlibidinal order of the symbolic. ("Libido and ego are on the same side. Narcissism is libidinal.")[5] Identificatory and sexual fusions, rather than simply synthesis as traditional psychology believed,[6] are the imaginary's aim.[7] The imaginary ego is constantly affirming or negating its identificatory oneness with the other or its difference from them. "I am you" or "I am not you" is what the imaginary tirelessly reiterates. But when the ego affirms itself, it negates the other, and when it affirms the other, it negates itself:

> Every imaginary relation comes about via a kind of you or me between the subject and the object. That is to say—If it's you, I'm not. If it's me, it's you who isn't.[8]

This bondage and subjection to the other is at once this order's strength and weakness. On the one hand, living predominately in the imaginary, libidinally invested in everyone and everything, means never to see the other or the world symbolically and scientifically. On the other hand, never developing an imaginary, and thereby the crucial link with the other, or losing it, as for example in the case of Schreber, means to have no human subjectivity and no capacity for inter-human relations. For Schreber, other men seem merely "cursorily improvised or fabricated men" ("flüchtig, hingemachte Männer") that have suddenly been "miracled up," while he himself is "the only real man left alive."[9] Having eliminated all others in the imaginary, Schreber must attempt to reconstruct them by coupling with God. To turn himself into a woman as he must, he "draws" around himself the outline of a woman as he stands before a mirror. And, "it has become so much a habit with me to draw female buttocks on to my body," he says, "that I do it almost involuntarily every time I stoop."[10] The effort to actualize his sexual transformation and to establish a relationship with God needs the imaginary.

The relativity of the ego[11] makes life in the imaginary a struggle of identifications and de-identifications, fusions and defusions, idealizations and devaluations, loves and hatreds. Only in alliance with the symbolic does this imaginary strife cease in a sublimation or an absolute identifications with mass groups, nations, ideologies, God, or the entire cosmos as such. As Dostoevsky has his Grand Inquisitor say, the drive for unity is an inalienable drive in humankind.

> [T]he craving for universal unity is the third and last anguish of men. Mankind as a whole has always strived to organize a universal state. There have been many great nations with great histories, but the more highly they were developed the more unhappy they were, for they felt more acutely than other people the craving for world-wide union.[12]

The imaginary wants the totality, the oneness, the completeness, the dialectical synthesis in which its own unrelieved, dialectical dividedness, ambivalence, and aggressiveness would cease as it once ceased in the unitary mirror image.

The imaginary is the "human" order or the order of "hominisation" (141), connected to a human body and its narcissism.

> The language embodied in a *human* language is made up of, and there's no doubt about this, choice images which all have a specific relation with the living existence of the human being, with quite a narrow sector of its biological reality, with the image of the fellow being. (my italics)[13]

This "human language" of the imaginary recognizes or misrecognizes everything as "human." If there is an otherness of nature, of God, of symbols, or words, this fundamentally anthropoid and sexualized order has the least capacity for sensing it. The questions then that the imaginary raises are: Is there anything wrong with our making the very universe and God into a metaphorical likeness of our ego? And, more radically, "Is psychoanalysis a humanism?"[14]

If humanism continues to be defined as it has been since the Renaissance, the answer to the last question is negative. What "humanizes" the human animal is neither his reason or his heart, his fellow human or God, but the law of speech (87). "If one has to define the moment at which man becomes human, we can say that it is the moment when, however little it be, he enters into the symbolic relation" (155). The analytically defined "human" is not the traditional dual knot of living flesh and eternal spirit, but a subject constituted by the force and structure of speech and language. And language as such has nothing human about it. Signifiers are dead. "Humans" incorporate this deadness. Lacan attempts to comprehend the full significance of these facts, so contrary to traditional humanism. It is because of this paradox—the fact that something radically Other than the human constitutes the human—that Lacan can say that Freud's "discovery is that man isn't entirely in man. Freud isn't a humanist."[15]

"Hominisation" is a partial and incomplete account of human formation, because the human being is the *tripartite* being of the orders of the real, the imaginary, and the symbolic. "The core of our being does not coincide with the ego,"[16] nor with any single one of the orders, and most significantly, life and death are not distributed within these orders in the way Western culture has traditionally believed.

Phenomenological experience furnishes the symbolic with a necessary ballast that it lacks and makes it "a human language in the most down to earth and most ordinary sense of the word human, in the English sense of 'human,'" but the symbolic order which founds the speaking subject is nonetheless "absolutely irreducible to what is commonly called human experience."[17] In order for a human person, capable of empathy with his fellow others, to come into being, it is important for the languages of the symbolic and imaginary to overlap and to be imbedded in each other, but these two languages are not identical.

The imaginary is fastened to the bodily: "In man, the relation to one's own body characterizes, in the final analysis, the restricted, but really irreducible, field of the imaginary."[18] The imaginary field is centered and born in the body, and developed via the image of the body and the bodily ego. This field of lived, human experience nourishes but also obscures the symbolic.[19]

Language, by contrast, has a relational and abstract structure that seems by traditional definitions nonhuman, albeit not necessarily inhuman. However, the more radically the imaginary is symbolized, and the human element thereby reduced, the more the purely formal and numerical aspects of the symbolic can come to be foregrounded. Human relations can then become mere calculations for a maximization of production and money, in which everyone is assigned a statistical, numerical, or economic value. In such an act of symbolization, love, hate, and ignorance of the human other, the great passions of the imaginary (271), can come to be ignored. Thus, whereas the pure imaginary may produce crimes of passion, the symbolic is capable of massive crimes of inhumanity.

Otherlessness

The case of Robert, the main case presented in Seminar I, is a harrowing example of a failed humanization. Robert is a child on the border between the human and the nonhuman. Initially, he is without either the imaginary or the symbolic function (100). He does not *recognize* or *know* his fellow being or himself. The ego's function, which is to develop and to give form to narcissism, is not operative in him (115). It is possible that he has never even *seen* his fellow other or himself in a human image. Thus, Robert is a case as close to otherlessness as we have.

A state of otherlessness is, of course, a myth. It is the postulation of the state of a non-subject to which nothing is alien. In this pre-imaginary condition, the container and the contained are one. There is no separation of the mother (container) and the fetus (contained) or of the fetal body (the container) and what it contains (food, urine, etc.). In this otherlessness, the subject has not yet produced itself. It has not yet emerged from objecthood. For Lacan in Seminar I, the objectification of the object produces the subject. The subject is "what is outside of the object" (194).

At the very beginning, then, is an object that, after a long development, becomes a subject. The object splits and produces the first pre-otherness from within itself as its own product. The first pre-other, the indispensable particle necessary for the birth of the pre-subject, is a remaindered piece of an initial, seemingly "unified" non-subject.[20] Pre-otherness is "objectal" or an otherness of objects. Originally, therefore, the subject *is* an otherness or it is in any case not a subject. It is not its own beginning.[21] Only with the aid of the otherness of images and words can the object begin to be a subject.

The child Robert is in the midst of the inaugural struggle of objectification. He is as it were the object objectifying itself in order to begin to become a subject. He is trying to shed his objecthood, to shift from otherlessness to the acceptance of pre-otherness. But the genesis of this first otherness terrifies him. Any kind of partitioning of his body terrifies him. He is afraid to eat or to sleep, to pee or to pooh. He is afraid of his own instinctual life and organic processes. The biological crises he has suffered, such as hunger to the point of acute wasting (91), have marked him with an extreme organic fear and fragility. Even the most ordinary somatic movements are a threat to his existence and biological integrity (99). Inborn visceral and bodily changes and exchanges strike him as fearful upheavals and fill him with wild anguish. Because of neglect and abuse, nature itself has, as it were, been de-natured in him and disturbed at its foundations.

Robert is "acutely confused as to his own self, the contents of his body, objects, children, and the adults who surround[ed] him" (94). His identification with objects is only beginning; the few objects that are part of his daily life are the symbols of the contents of his body. "The sand is the symbol of feces, the water that of urine, the milk that of what enters his body" (95). But even these few objects are not clearly differentiated for him and he does not distinguish his own physical persistence from theirs. They *are* he. And for this reason, they obsess him and are able to cause him panic:

> A bit of sand fell on the ground, unleashing unbelievable panic in him. He had to gather up every last bit of sand, as if it was a piece of himself, and he howled—Wolf, Wolf! (95).

Robert is as yet the victim of the objects with which he identifies as his traumatized fear of bodily partitioning (an example of what Lacan calls later "the fall of the object *a*") reveals. What is outside of himself, he perceives as being his very innermost self. The founding and necessary act of the expulsion of a piece of his own body to the outside strikes him as a terrifying dispersal of his being. He is not yet the master of the dialectics of inside and outside nor of that of part and whole. And thus, he is without any assurance that the scattered sand on the ground that he fears himself to be can once again become a unified whole object.[22]

Defecation is for Robert a type of auto-destruction because he is unsure that after such an expulsion he will once again be replenished, filled up, and returned to himself. He is not certain that his bodily unity is guaranteed beyond its excretions and discharges or that the loss will be balanced by food. How can one afford to defecate, if one may never be fed again? How can one tolerate self-division, without a warranty that self-division is self-multiplication, increase, and growth?

Robert can also not bear to be undressed. "His clothes were for him his container, and when he was stripped of them, it was certain death" (96). Instead of a body image to certify his unity, he has only his clothes, these items of which he can hence not bear to be deprived. His inability to separate the container and the contained makes him fearful of destroying one together with the other.

Robert has no assurance that he exists. And therefore, he may at any moment *not* exist. His fear is archaic and elemental, focused on sheer survival as such. The one semi-symbolic word, "wolf," that he has to sustain him is merely an image-word. Insofar as he recognizes himself or any other at all, it is in a ferocious image. He is the wolf (95). Otherness insofar as it exists has a wolfish rather than a human form. His full metamorphosis from animal to human via the mirror and the other has not yet occurred.

"Wolf," linked to the primitive traumas that he has suffered, indicates what meaning, if any, human others have for him and how he symbolizes his world. The word lays him open to a specific relation to his surroundings and reveals that he lives in the terror of need and of hunger, of what to eat and of who will be eaten. He is an object of cannibalistic absorption in a dialectic of eat or be eaten. Seemingly he experiences himself primarily as the other's object of consumption, the object that perishes, that is doomed to vanish. Tragically, precisely because he is potentially human, Robert is not blessed with the indifference to destructive devouring that we assume is part of the mental structure of the animal world.

On the level of need (but *only* on this level, as Lacan says) is there *not* an inadequation between the object and desire. Here alone the object fulfills imagined want so that there is the possibility of a closure. In the state of need, therefore, the cannibalistic core of imaginary identification: "I am you" and "you are me," can become literally and horrifyingly true. In atrocious famines, "when there is nothing left to eat, you eat your child . . . you are all his and by the same token, he is all yours" (210). Purportedly, in certain Australian tribes, "pregnant women are capable . . . of inducing abortions so as to feed on the object of the pregnancy" (211). Mutual consumption is the real object relations underground of the imaginary's identificatory and fusionary drive. An object of need that satisfies an imperious hunger is obviously not an other, autonomous *subject*. If an other is destroyed, as in cannibalism, and I am merely its food or it is merely mine, it is not even an other autonomous object. Destruction as such does not indicate a true recognition of otherness nor therefore the presence of the symbolic.[23]

Robert lacks access to the fully emancipated symbol, to a word freed of the burden of images. His one, main word is overshadowed by its image, a feral and highly anxiety-provoking one. The image keeps his primitive, nonhuman "world" before him and signals his proximity to it. Symbolically, "wolf" ties him to a restricted reality that operates as yet on a "mythical, folkloric, religious, primitive plane." It is part of a "complete filiation, which connects up with secret societies, with everything that implies in the way of initiation, either in the adoption of a totem, or in the identification with a character" (101). A wider repertoire of images and of object-and-ego-identifications would make possible a more differentiated, more objectified, mobile, and wider reality. A world of words would make the control of meanings possible. The more abstract word, opaque to reality, would give the child a separate, other, logical, and scientific world. But Robert has no access to such a humanized or verbalized "reality." His imaginary, like his symbolic, is elemental, almost non-existent. It contains no humans, no recognizable self-likenesses. He is a child in the pre-imaginary real. And even if Robert did develop the imaginary other, this fellow being might always be linked in his unconscious to the image of the wolf, the pitiless other, the animal.

Robert is the prime example in Seminar I of what the real might be for someone compared to reality.[24] The establishment of what I will call reality, or what is a different, humanized, symbolized level of the real, requires images and words. Reality is "a work of transcendence introduced by the symbol into the primitive reality" (87). Without much reality, Robert is abandoned to the real, in his case to a catastrophic war with his own organism and its contents that he seems to be losing and that may terminate in psychosis (106). This real is limited and claustrophobic, as Robert's intense anxiety and obsessions demonstrate. In it, there is no possibility for play or freedom because these require the availability of substitutes that are only given together with the imaginary and the symbolic.[25] Without an imaginary to shape his hallucinatory perceptions into realistic forms (*Gestalten*) in an external world (*Umwelt*), he remains a child who "lives only in the real" (103).

Robert is without all that imaginary development would give him. He is ego-less, and therefore without a feeling for himself (*Selbstgefühl*), for objects, or for others. He is unable to "corpo-reify" his world,[26] to make it a world of things, contoured in the image of his body. Thus, his surroundings are shapeless, unordered, and obscure. He lacks the feeling of at-homeness in the world that a symbolized body would give him.

> the corporeal image ... makes up the unity of the subject, and we see it projecting itself in a thousand different ways, up to and including what we can call the imaginary source of symbolism, which is what links symbolism to feeling, to the *Selbstgefühl*, which the human being, the *Mensch*, has of his own body. (125)

The realization of body symbolism, the basis of all imaginary symbolism, and of the first, natural symbols, such as that of the sun and moon, etc., fails in Robert. These first symbols, born in the imaginary, give human language "its weight, its resources, and its emotional vibration."[27] The archaic coordination between the body image and the world is also the bedrock of the sense of intimacy with the universe. An unsymbolized body leaves Robert in an unsymbolized and unfamiliar world. His world is not a "mirrored" one; it never feels as if it were *his* world. Without a body image, bodily motor activity and self-control can also not be mastered. Robert's motor movements remain disorderly, uncoordinated, and without an aim. Without a body-ego, he can only make gestures once and if they fail, he cannot correct them (92, 106).

It is because Robert has almost no reality (of objects, words, or fellow others) that he has "sunk under the real" (100). The most crucial missing element is the power to *call* on another human being; Robert can only call "wolf." The ability to call would station him in a dependency relation with the human other. The call reaches beyond dichotomy or bipartition because although it represents the *possibility* of refusal, it does not *imply* refusal. On the contrary, it alone consolidates the imaginary interhuman link and establishes communication. (87). Robert's main word is not the call to an other; it is, in fact, not much more than a random sound fragment that he has absorbed and that represents him because he repeats it. Potentially porous to language, as all human animals are, this word that has entered him *is* him, but it is at the same time everything that can be named. It is a sound with a signified at once so total and nonspecific that it is almost meaningless. "Wolf" is "identified with only what is most devastating, most fascinating in the primitive experiences of the subject" (102). It exemplifies the fundamental relation of man to language in its most reduced and most frightening form. This word *is* speech in its nodal state (104).

"Wolf" is an "unanchored" word in that it is not moored as yet in "discourse" or in that part of language, governed by logic and grammar, which helps create "reality." "Reality," as Lacan says, "is what makes it so that when I am here, you, my dear lady, cannot be in the same place" (267). Reality and discourse are logical. They obey the law of contradiction, for one, which, in its ontological form, decrees that two things cannot be in the same place at the same time. It is the presence of such logic that would help alleviate part of the severe confusion Robert suffers.

Since "wolf" is not anchored either to any kind of imaginary symbolization of his own body or of the world of objects, except in a most general way, the word can also not provide him with any kind of self-exaltation or narcissistic ego support. Rather, the word is for him a terrifying experience of an imaginary break-in of a "ferocious figure" (102). Or, equally frightening, it is the experience of the break-in of a brute symbolic commandment into the wordlessness of the biological.

This cry is the summation of something catastrophic that cannot be spoken and that may only vaguely be seen. And this catastrophic symbolic totality or generality seizes the child in a blind and tyrannical way. It defines his situation as a human as such. It is law "entirely reduced to something, which cannot even be expressed, like *You must*, which is speech deprived of all its meaning" (102). In its most rudimentary form, then, law is a sound commanding our attention, possessing us without our knowing why or how or what it signifies. Law is the signifier as a senseless, causeless imperative that has the power to make the human its object. It operates in a blind and elemental way as fate does.[28] In the midst of the senselessness and confusion that Robert is in, this mere root of language is nonetheless for him "the summary of a law" and his potential link to other human subjects (103). It is the very thing he needs to begin, to take his place and to construct himself (104). Robert is only negatively and destructively linked to the community of humankind as his primitive symbol "wolf" indicates, but he *is* linked.

The use of the word "wolf" disappears after an extraordinary self-baptism in which the child names himself and blesses himself with milk and water. It is a ritual scene that seems to mark the child's release from the real into what might become reality.

> Robert, completely naked and facing me, collected up the water in his cupped hands, raised it to the level of his shoulders and let it run the length of his body . . . he said to me softly—Robert, Robert.
>
> Then he took his glass of milk and drank it. Then he . . . [made] the milk run over his chest, his stomach and along his penis with an intense feeling of pleasure. Then he turned towards me, showed me this penis, taking it in his hand, with an air of complete rapture. Then he drank some milk, thus putting some both inside and outside him, in such a way that the content was both contained and container at once. (98)

In this rapturous and moving scene, the child discovers and affirms his bodily reality as a reality of felt pleasure. There is pleasure seemingly in the sensation of touch between his skin and the liquids of milk and water. And there is as if a memory of the pre-birth state as a state of goodness that is also affirmed. The baptism in any case is a *Bejahung* of a first union of flesh and water. The fundamental goodness of these primary relationships of pleasure are then sealed with an affirmation as well of a relationship of pleasure between the flesh and a name. It is the moment of the embodiment of speech. In reality, there is pleasure; in the real there is pure anxiety. This child who only knew anxiety begins to know rapture.

The name, Robert, is free of any appalling images like "wolf." The nomination is instead filled to overflowing with volumes of self-love. The narcissistic pleasure indicates that this signifier has reference in this instance to the *touched* and *felt* as well as to the *seen* reality of the human body. It is as if preeminently a pre-mirror human body-object, and yet it is also the mirror body, because seen by the analyst. However, this body is no longer possessed by any other, and not by the "wolf;" it is an object possessed solely by the self. The child has exorcised the figure of the wolf, the ferocious figure by which it was beset. The analyst is there only as a mirror, in which the child is seen and *recognized,* but not consumed. Robert uses the milk and water as if to outline his new body for himself and the analyst. He feels gratitude and happiness to be with a body that he need no longer fear.

With his auto-baptism, Robert's body becomes the valued site of his sensations of pleasure. Lacan puns on the German *W(ort),* condensing word (*Wort)* and place (*Ort),* to indicate that language is connected to an original site or place (233). And with Robert we see that this place or space is the libidinal body. And although this body is not the real as such, it is at least an indicator in reality of the place (*Ort)* of the ultimate real, libidinal substance. The voicing of "Robert, Robert" conjoins this substance to a name, *W(ort),* and both to the wor(l)d of the human other. The phallus is as if proffered as the culminating mark of this sense of plenitude that enables the child to bridge the abyss between the corporeal and linguistic. Robert's baptism demonstrates with exquisite exactitude that "what speaks in man goes far beyond speech and penetrates even his dreams, his being and his very organism" (260).

Another main sign of Robert's emergence from the real is that he begins to dream. As long as he lives in the real, he does not dream, but as he begins to glimpse reality he dreams. The unconscious that dreams is therefore the effect of a reality which arises together with the other orders. "This child who neither slept nor dreamt, began to dream . . . and to *call* his mother in his dreams" (105, my italics). The dreaming signals the development of his unconscious to which his primitive reality and earliest pre-otherness with its ferocity can be relegated. And the call, albeit made only in his dreams, signals that "the ferocious figure" has been banished by the image of a *human* mother. When there is as yet no being (the triad of the imaginary, symbolic and real), there is no unconscious, and only a separation of the two brings on the need to sleep, which rejoins one state to the other. Sleep and pleasure heal the schism of the unconscious, the alienation induced by the symbolic system. But sleep and pleasure are gifts of the good enough m(other), in this instance, the analyst.

The pure function of language is to assure us that we are (157). It is the assurance that Robert lacked. Images also help provide such a guarantee. Yet words and images entify us only virtually (140). "Reality" is constructed as merely a contrary part of the imaginary and symbolic; it is no more real than these other orders are. Without words and images, it doesn't exist, but even with them, reality is not enough. It remains virtual.

The incompleteness and inadequacy of virtual reality drives the subject to his fellow being in the hope that their seeming substantiality may confirm its own. The subject needs the imaginary other to acquire *more* reality or to escape together with them from this merely virtual and simulated one. The subject needs them also to be recognized, to change its identifications, to experience its sexuality, to dissolve its ignorance, and to release its passions. The imaginary other has many uses but above all this is the other who can be loved or hated.

Imaginary Love

The imaginary is the order of passions and feelings. The three great passions Lacan speaks of in Seminar I are love, hate, and ignorance. The necessary passion in analysis is ignorance because it strives for knowledge, but the transference makes more present and clamorous the passions of love and hatred.

Love is at the junction of the imaginary and the symbolic, while hate is at the junction of the imaginary and the real (271). In love, the ego is willing to lose, even to sacrifice itself for the other, whereas in hate it wants to destroy the other. At the height of passion, as Freud said,

> the ego becomes more and more unassuming and modest, and the object more and more sublime and precious, until at last it gets possession of the entire self-love of the ego, whose sacrifice thus follows as a natural consequence. The object has, so to speak, consumed the ego. Traits of humility, of the limitation of narcissism, and of self-injury occur in every case of being in love.[29]

Love can be a form of suicide, but hatred is murder. Hate is rooted in the real of destruction. It does not have the same intimate relation to sexual pleasure and to the sexual function that love has. In hate, unpleasure is decisive.

> The ego hates, abhors and pursues with intent to destroy all objects which are a source of unpleasurable feeling for it, without taking into account whether they mean a frustration of sexual satisfaction or of the satisfaction of self-preservative needs.[30]

Hate's true prototype is the struggle of the ego for self-preservation.

Both love and hate circle about the scrap of the real that the body represents, but hatred attempts to master the body fatally. Love, by contrast, in addressing the sexual and reproductive body, demands pleasure and immortality. The reproductive body is the individual's access to "the quasi-immortal germ-plasma" and to the imperative of species continuity.[31] The "little death" of sex grants the human being that sense of immortality that it is uniquely in the power of pleasure to confer.

Thus, fusionary love offers the promise of a future and even of immortality. Sex is full of the illusions of pleasure, power, and eternity. Sex is mastery; death is to be mastered. The dead body is a totally mastered body. Hatred has to do with a mastery symbolized ultimately in the dead body. It requires the certitude and finality that only death can provide. Thus, while on the surface imaginary love and hatred appear to be antithetical, they have potentially entirely different destinies. Hatred's destiny has fundamentally to do with mortality and love's with immortality.

Because hate borders on the real, it is more dangerous than love and harder to sublimate. Robert's life of subjection to the real tends to bear this out. He must perforce constantly destroy others, objects, and himself. He tries to mutilate his own body, by cutting off his penis with a pair of plastic scissors (99) and he attempts to throttle the other children (92). Because hate leans towards the real (the body, life itself, objects), hate is older than love.[32] And, for the same reason, hatred tends towards illness, and love, with its greater proximity to sublimation, towards health. Neurosis or illness, as Freud observed, often starts with an expectation of disaster, usually that of death.[33] Given then that the fundamental thought that produces illness is death, hate is the passion that "points the way to" death by pointing to its representative, the instinct of destruction.[34] As Lacan indicates, no such psychological linkage of hatred and death exists in the animal world, which is governed by a regularized and coordinated consumption rather than by a law of radical destruction.

> In fact, everything tells against this thesis [Darwin's] of the survival of the fittest species. It is a myth which goes against the facts. Everything goes to prove that there are points of invariability and of equilibria proper to each species, and that species live in a sort of coordinated way, even amongst eaters and eaten. It never gets to the point of radical destruction, which would quite simply lead to the annihilation of the eating species, who would no longer have anything to eat. (177)

There is death in the animal kingdom, but no imaginary or symbolic *desire* for death.

Because hate slopes towards the real, it is also less satisfied with images than love is. It wants a real and destructive contact with its objects.[35] "Eros desires contact," as Freud said, "because it strives to make the ego and the loved object one, to abolish all spatial barriers between them. But destructiveness, too, which (before the invention of long-range weapons) could only take effect at close quarters, must presuppose physical contact, a coming to grips."[36] Thus, although "touching and physical contact are the immediate aim of the aggressive as well as the loving object-cathexes,"[37] hate "touches" in a way that is cruel or deadly as the amatory contact does not.

Lacan makes a distinction between two forms of love, symbolic love and imaginary love, which echo the classical division of earthly and heavenly love.

The more imaginary love is, the more narcissistic and passionate is its relationship to the other; the more symbolic, the more is the being of the other recognized as another, separate being, ultimately as one who can never provide the clue to the self because a symbolic other is no longer an alter ego or confused with the ideal ego. The analyst's love is the most symbolic. It can only be satisfied by the revelation of the other's originality. The analysand's radical uniqueness would therefore be the analyst's very guarantee of the correctness of the analysis.

Symbolic love does not predominately seek physical or emotional contact with its object. It is not a mere relationship of satisfaction but "an active gift" directed at the being (the tripartite reality) of the other. Without the symbolic speech of love, "all there is is *Verliebtheit*, imaginary fascination, but there is no love" (276-7). Imaginary love, which Lacan also calls passionate or narcissistic love, is a passive desire to be loved (rather than an active loving) and it is "essentially an attempt to capture the other in oneself, in oneself as an object" (276). Narcissism is the very precondition of this love. The other is loved because he is me, or was me, or will be me. The other in imaginary love is, fundamentally, the correlate for one's own being, a support for the narcissistic self. Narcissistic love wants the other to be attentive to, even enslaved to, every aspect and particle of its being.

> The person who aspires to be loved is not at all satisfied, as is well known, with being loved for his attributes. . . . One wants to be loved for everything—not only for one's ego, . . . but for the colour of one's hair, for one's idiosyncracies, for one's weaknesses, for everything. (276)

If the narcissistic lover is seemingly *as* attentive in turn to everything having to do with the beloved, it is because this other is functioning as their counterpart or ideal ego. Thus, the beloved must never step out of the ideal form that has been assigned to him or her. As the self's substitute and correspondent, the beloved must look, speak, and move, as the *ego* requires it to do. In *A Lover's Discourse*, Roland Barthes perfectly captures the moment of the capsizing and despoliation of the image of the beloved when it inadvertently become unequal to this requirement.

> I perceive suddenly a speck of corruption. This speck is a tiny one: a gesture, a word, an object, a garment, something unexpected which appears (which dawns) from a region I had never even suspected, and suddenly attaches the beloved object to a *commonplace* world. Could the other be vulgar, whose elegance and originality I had so religiously hymned? Here is a gesture by which is revealed a being of another race. I am *flabbergasted*: I hear a counter-rhythm: something like a syncope in the lovely phrase of the loved being, the noise of a rip in the smooth envelope of the Image.

(Like the Jesuit Kirchner's hen, released from hypnosis by a light tap, I am temporarily de-fascinated, not without pain).[38]

When the other ceases to be the ideal self, the hypnotic bond between the self and other snaps. As long as the other performs with and for the self, exhibiting and mirroring forth the self's cultivation, urbanity, and elegance, there is fascination and *Verliebtheit*. When, however, signs appear in the other of what the self does *not* want to accommodate within itself, there is a refusal of the other, a dissociation, divorce. The imaginary illusion of similarity and unity is broken. The consecrated image of oneness begins iconoclastically to rip apart. The unholy rip casts doubt on the other as well as the self. Was one blind or deceived? How is it that the beloved other has suddenly so little in common with one's own inclinations and culture? The severance from the love image endangers one's reasons for self-exaltation and the certitude in one's judgment. The experience of de-fascination (Swann's with Odette) signals the loss of an entire repertoire of fond, spell-binding images. Suddenly the world is empty, missing the most fascinating image of all, the narcissistic image of the self. Images as such fascinate, but nothing is more enthralling than the narcissistically invested image of the other who as if steps out of the mirror to play one's own ego.

The imaginary other and the self are tied primarily by means of the image, not the word. The image is the go-between, the broker, and the necessary lure that releases sexual behavior (122). Lacan points to the extraordinary important of the image in animals.

> The male or female animal subject is captivated, as it were, by a *Gestalt*. The subject literally identifies itself with the releasing stimulus. The male is caught up in the zigzag dance on the basis of the relation that is set up between himself and the image which governs the releasing cycle of his sexual behavior. The female is caught up in the same way in this mutual dance. (137)

The other, in the case of the animal, has to do little more than fit the self's programmed body image, but in the human imaginary, it is primarily the self's ideal ego and ego-ideal that need support. Nonetheless, the sudden appearance of the world of two, of the couple, in the natural world as much as in the human, mediated merely by an image, seems inexplicable, somewhat like a miracle, or like a sudden "lapse or flaw (*faille*) in the logic of the universe," as Marguerite Duras put it.[39] Imaginary love entails several flaws. For one, passionate love or imaginary love seems to lead to an abduction or even an annihilation of the symbolic (142). This poses a problem in the analytic love transference. The analysand falls silent. And it is well known that lovers have no care for logic, money, time, or other such symbolic realities. In fact, lovers tend to babble more so than to speak and want only to hear endless variations of the single sentence: I love you.

Roland Barthes speaks of "the fatigue of language itself" in the face of amorous feelings and the indescribable perfection of the loved object. Lovers stutter; their speeches are fragmentary and faltering, non-linear and asysemic. Their language can sound infantile or pusillanimous. The intractability of overpowering feelings inclines them to substitute "a blank word, an empty vocable," like "adorable," for a more just description of the beloved person.[40] Lived love is felt to be beyond words or beneath words but not *in* words. The amorous is something to which language is not adequate. The inadequation that appears tends always to make the language fail, and fail dramatically, but not the feeling. Thus, in the context of the world, the lover's discourse appears as an insignificant sub-language, as kitsch, a babble without much authority, marginal, private, and often seemingly childish.

> . . . the lover's discourse is today of *an extreme solitude*. This discourse is spoken perhaps by thousands of subjects (who knows?), but warranted by no one; it is completely forsaken by the surrounding languages: ignored, disparaged, or derided by them, severed not only from authority, but also from the mechanism of authority (science , techniques, arts). Once a discourse is thus driven by its own momentum into the backwater of the "unreal," exiled from all gregarity, it has no recourse but to become the site, however exiguous, of an *affirmation*.[41]

Puig's *The Kiss of the Spider Woman* is a text that intentionally recreates the sub-language of love. In a highly fractured dialogue, Molina reiterates the classic identificatory confusions, affirmations, and exhilaration's of love after his night of union with Valentin:

> — For a second, it seemed like I wasn't here . . . not here or anywhere out there either.
> — . . .
> — It seemed as if I wasn't here at all . . . like it was you all alone.
> — . . .
> — Or like it wasn't me anymore. As if now, somehow . . . I . . . were you.[42]

Molina has lost himself in the other. His ego, mobilized by passion, becomes an object seemingly capable of fusing or fading, daringly volatile and plastic. He is egoless, placeless, approaching languagelessness, or one might say, to continue Lacan's pun on *Wort* (word) and *Ort* (place), *w(ort)los* (word- and placeless). He no longer has a place or much to say except in and for the other. His affirmation of identity with Valentin expresses itself in fantasies and images of complete fusionary union: "As if now, somehow . . . I . . . were you." Molina in effect says: I am Valentin, or as Emily Bronte, most famously, had Catherine say it: I am Heathcliff. I am the other. This ancient Vedic utterance—"I am you"—is a bond, narcissistic and empathic, loving and hating, unholy and sacred at once.[43] It is the declaration of union at the heart of imaginary love.

To be the other is not to be me. "It's that when you're here, like I already told you, I'm not me in a way and that's a relief," Molina says. (235) To be "not me" is to be free of me. Self-loss can be a relief or an escape or a self-betrayal.

Baudelaire, for one, felt that any kind of human development that entailed a going out of oneself and a loss of one's autonomy was a type of prostitution. To yield one's *ego* to the other is no different or worse than abdicating or selling one's *body* to the other for their use, even if one does it because one adores the other.

> What is love?
> The need to emerge from oneself.
> Man is an animal which adores.
> To adore is to sacrifice and prostitute yourself.
> Thus all love is prostitution.[44]

Baudelaire's stance is seemingly the opposite of that of the Molina's, the Tristan's, and the Werther's, resistant to fusion, although the extreme of his resistance is also the very sign of his own bondedness and his need to work to maintain a distance between himself and the other. Valuing his autonomy, Baudelaire mistakenly placed it in imaginary narcissism, and believed that he should maintain his own ego by the embracement of solitude and the refusal of love.

> Ineradicable desire for prostitution in the heart of man, whence is born his horror of solitude. He wants to be *two*. The man of genius wants to be *one*, and therefore solitary. Glory is to remain *one* and to prostitute oneself in an individual manner.
>
> It is this horror of solitude, this need to lose his *ego* in exterior flesh, which man calls grandly, *the need for love*.[45]

In fact, Baudelaire maintained his ego not by his narcissism but by his symbolic activity and the labor of his poetic writing.

Molina, by contrast, wants to live only under the signifier, "love," and is willing to espouse all that this entails—illusion, loss of his ego, two-ness, self-prostitution. Love is for him the sole escape from solitude and from the confines of his psychic prison as well as from the literal one he is in. It is the ultimate psychic morphine, the only way out of pain and danger.

> — And afterwards, until I sleep, even though you're back on your little cot, I'm still not me. It's a strange thing. . . . And it's like when I'm alone in my

bed I'm no longer you either, I'm someone else, who's neither a man nor a
woman but someone who feels . . .
— out of danger.
— Yes, that's exactly it. How did you know?
— Because it's what I feel.
— Why is it that we feel like that?
— I don't know. . . . (235-6)

In love, one "feels out of danger." Why? Because there is no ego that can be
endangered. Ego loss means also loss of *fear* for the ego. The ego entity that
can be threatened is absent or safely stored in the other. One is fused with the
other and hence stronger. One becomes two. Momentarily one *is* two. In two,
there is more strength and safety than in one. Feelings replace the consciousness that language gives and put in question distinctions that language maintains. As someone who feels, Molina is neither man nor woman, and finally, neither I nor you. The symbolic pronouns that produce distinctions fall away into
sensations and feelings. All distinctions are erased altogether as feeling replaces
language, and thoughtlessness allows the mind rest.

> I feel peaceful. . . . No I'm more than peaceful. . . . I'm really happy. . . . And
> the good thing about feeling really happy, you know, Valentin? . . . It's that you
> think it's forever, that one's never ever going to feel unhappy again. . . . And
> my head feels so empty—no, that sounds stupid: my head's like filled with warm
> mist. (235)

Fulfillment brings with it the illusion of timelessness, even of immortality:
"You think it's forever." And as timeless and immortal, how can one be touched
by pain and danger? Cinematic illusion and intimacy emancipate Molina and
Valentin momentarily from the confines of their prison and the danger that it
inescapably allocates. The power of psychic pleasure gives a short-lived egress
from authoritarian oppression and power, and in the case of the Valentin, fleeting release from the pain of physical torture. This is no doubt why power in its
various forms—parental, church, state—has always tried to maintain control over
various forms of pleasures. Fusionary love, on the contrary, leaves almost literally no space for the exercise of even Molina's and Valentin's own mutual
manipulations and verbal power games. Their erotic union questions at once
their rigid positions and the very language of politics and power.

Discourse and grammar set up differences and maintain them. The symbolic code models subjects in relational and oppositional ways because that is
what the code itself at core is. "This is what I am not. One concludes from that
what I am" (293). The ego at a minimum defines itself by negation. I am not you.
Initially, in their cell, Molina and Valentin spent an enormous amount of time
claiming *not* to be the other. Valentin sees himself as represented by the signi-

fier, "the revolutionary." This is the symbolic ego-ideal that governs and directs him. It is his "guide beyond the imaginary" (141), but as a rather one-sided ideal of the political as the impersonal, it has alienated him from his personal experiences and from love. Somewhat ossified and petrified under his various labels, such as, the Marxist, the enemy, the struggle for justice, not getting attached, etc., it takes considerable effort on Molina's part to reintroduce him to his imaginary-bodily existence and his need for care and love. Finally, debilitated from food poisoning and fearful of death, Valentin utters once again the "call" to a human other. He wants suddenly to dictate a letter:

> Dear . . . Marta: It must be strange for you . . . to get this letter. I feel . . . lonely, I need you so, I want to *talk* with you, I want to be close, I want you to . . . give me . . . some *word* of comfort . . . let me *talk* to you anyway . . . because I'm afraid . . . afraid that something is about to break inside of me . . . if I don't open up to you a little. *If only we could actually talk together, you'd understand what I mean.* (176–7; my italics)

It is a moving, broken oscillation of imaginary and symbolic love. Valentin wants Marta's physical presence and her *words* of love. It is not even definable which he needs and desires more, or which would give him more assurance of being and reality. "'If someone speaks, it gets lighter,'" Freud reported a child saying who was afraid of the dark and longing for its mother.[46] Speech brings light; it makes the absent present; it guarantees that another is there, for what would be the logic or *raison d'être* of speech if no one were there with whom to communicate. If there is an illusion in the speech, it may be that one *can* be understood, but the belief that someone is there to hear is foundational to speaking as such.

Molina's signifiers are entirely in the imaginary and sexual domain. His ideal ego is feminine. His ego-ideal is the female heroine who lives entirely for the real male. "We're normal women; we sleep with men" (203). Molina represents the imaginary that can never completely coincide with or be imbedded in the symbolic.[47] He stands for the nonpolitical, personal, and fictional, which Valentin's kind of ethics needs to become more human. Without the impersonal, there is no law or justice; and without the personal, there is no humanity or love.

For Molina, the imaginary union with Valentin, reinforced in the real, is too powerful an experience to outlive. Their separation therefore produces a fatal desire. "But it's not just some notion that's gotten into my head or something; I'm telling you the only thing I want is to die" (235). Love itself is for Molina the traumapoint, the very point or thing that can no longer be spoken (191). He cannot renounce his identity in a cinematic imaginary, centered on fusionary love, and its realization. Thus, when Molina can no longer be together with Valentin, or be his object, or have him as an object, he must try to maintain their union by some form of incorporation. Assuming Valentin's revolutionary identity (with the aid of a favorite cinematic heroine as the mediator of their differences) and identifying with his political cause are the quickest ways to attain the fatal end and to enact as well an affirmation of love. For what could be a greater affirmation of the other than to be willing to exchange one's identity for theirs, to recreate them, and to act out their life? It is a final yes to the other but also to the self, at once a self-sacrifice and a self-confirmation, just as Valentin suspects (279). An imaginary other who is not relative to the innermost self is never so absolutely affirmed.

What makes anyone else desirable is that they become confused somehow with the images of our ideal ego or ego-ideal that we carry within ourselves. "It's one's own ego that one loves in love, one's own ego made real on the imaginary plane" (142). Love at first sight usually signals that the image of the ideal ego has been triggered rather than that of the more symbolic ego-ideal. This is the case with Goethe's Werther, says Lacan, when he first sees Lotte (142).

> Recall Werther meeting Charlotte just when she is holding a child in her arms–that hits the bull's eye of the narcissistic image of the novel's young hero. If, on the contrary, on the same slope, the other manifests himself as frustrating the subject of his ideal and of his own image, it engenders the maximal destructive tension. A mere nothing turns the imaginary relation to the other either this way or that, giving us the key to the question which Freud raises apropos of the transformation that takes place, in *Verliebtheit*, between love and hate. (282)

The ideal ego produces mad love, idealization of the other, and the enactment of aggressive rivalries; frustrated, it produces hatred. The ego-ideal, more symbolic, makes of the other the one who gives the law to me, who is my master or husband, whom I will obey. The idealization, characteristic of the ideal ego, and the sublimation, to which the ego-ideal can lead, usually operate together, which is why Werther wants to receive the gun with which he will shoot himself (in a sense, the final word and commandment regarding the phallus) from Lotte's hand, and why Molina passes on Valentin's message to his political comrades. "The ego-ideal governs the interplay of relations on which all relations with others depend" (141). Valentin becomes for Molina the only other, besides his mother, for whom he has felt a sublimated, symbolic love (261). And this is why Molina cannot use Valentin as an object of exchange value as the prison system gives him the opportunity to do. He needs rather to keep him as his primary, first object of love and as his ego-ideal.

Love is one of the methods by which we strive to attain happiness, but, as Freud said, the technique of living that makes love central is dangerous.[48] The imaginary which is the domain of the birth of the ego can also be its grave. If I am the other, then I am not. If the other *is* me, then my existence becomes superfluous. Absolute "love is a form of suicide" (149). It can be an abduction of one's own ideal ego and of one's narcissism. And if the ego's love for itself, ever dependent on another, fails or if the ego resides fulfilled in the other, the ego can die.

A Civilization of Hatred

[O]ur civilization is itself sufficiently one of hatred. Isn't the path for the race to destruction really rather well marked out for us? Hatred is clothed in our everyday discourse in many guises, it meets with such extraordinary easy rationalizations. Perhaps it is this state of the diffuse flocculations of hatred which saturate the destruction of being in us. As if the objectification of the human being in our civilization corresponded exactly to what, within the structure of the *ego*, is the pole of hatred. (277)

Up to now, the repertoire of hate images produced by Western culture has not been as rich as its quite extraordinary repertoire of love images. Despite eminent examples, such as those in The Book of Revelation, in Swift, and Flaubert, hatred has remained a relatively unexploited and unworked imaginary field. One reason for this comparative poverty of cultural images of hatred is that the West has always wanted to appear to be a culture of love and peace. Hate corresponds to no one's narcissism or ego-ideal. It does not have the same sexual charge that love has and it is not as entertaining. But above all it is possible that our constant real, historical objectification of hatred in war and myriad other forms of destruction may in fact have made imagining hatred and destruction superfluous.

All this seems, however, to be changing. The amatory phase of the imaginary seems to be ending, while an era of imaginary hatred is predicted as on the rise. Samuel P. Huntington looks ahead to "the clash of civilizations."[49] Barthes mourns the demise of "love-as-treasure" in an ahistorical, synchronic era of photographic presentness, instants, and nowness that no longer values or has time for anything that needs ripening or that has to do with memory.[50] Lacan calls our civilization itself one of hatred. "The objectification of the human being in our civilization corresponds exactly to what, within the structure of the ego, is the pole of hatred" (277).

If classical Greece developed the tradition of the passion of ignorance, and the Christian tradition that of love, is it then the destiny of our civilization to develop the passion of hatred? And does it, indeed, not sometimes seem as if we have come to believe in hate, and rage, and anger as we once believed in love?

We encourage their expression and articulation in ways we never did before; we talk of anger's function, its uses, its positives, and even its genius.[51] We hold workshops and conferences to teach aggression to those who lack it (mainly women) and we think that we can harness its energy somewhat as we hope to do nuclear power for positive ends.

The taboos that characterized anger, hatred, and outright aggression as evil, or immoral, or unmannerly seem to have been lifted considerably; hating is no longer as sinful religiously, nor as rebukable ethically or morally. Standards of civility and sociality have been revised so as to make it on occasion even acceptable. In business and politics, it is an asset, or positively, a requirement. To not be aggressive enough or to lack aggression are more serious character deficits than a lack of intelligence. Aggressivity is important in the marketing of everything, especially his majesty, the ego. In art, it has begun to occupy a central place, even as the portrayal of the passion of love grows ever more abject and even shameful.

Today still, a text of hatred is able to shock. Nonetheless, we are fascinated; images of rage are compelling. In the active infliction and production of pain, there is pleasure and potency. As Freud said, the "sensations of pain, like other unpleasurable sensations, trench upon sexual excitation and produce a pleasurable condition."[52] What we enjoy, of course, is the exciting charge, not the pain.

Kincaid's *A Small Place* is a text that unabashedly symbolizes imaginary hatred. Swiftly and bluntly, it lays bare hate's vicissitudes. Its first brilliant structural stroke is the creation of a polarity between "you," the tourist, and "we," the Antiguans, that quickly becomes an antagonism: it is "you," the stranger, the alien, the invader versus us, the natives. We work, while you play; you come and go, while we stay. You are rich, white, and on holiday; we are poor, black, and above all, pleasureless. It is the difference in the degree of pleasure that rankles most of all. The jouissance, as always, is elsewhere; it is with the other.

In this way, the initial opposition becomes an abysmal estrangement, an accusation, a demand, an imperative, a cause for war or murder. The narrator's voice imputes, charges, denounces, arraigns, and then indicts. The Antiguan list of envies and grievances is long. The opening of the fundamental lack in the self leaves a hole that fills up with hostility and enmity. The deprived ego tries to assuage itself by imagining the tourist as deluded and deceived, swimming in a seemingly emerald, but sewage-filled sea, so that the you have/we have not divide might turn into a you do not have either/ you only think you do. But this flawed and inadequate rationalization is quickly replaced by the more solid and logical accusation that we do not have *because* you took what we had. You robbed us. The tourist is displaced by the colonizers, who came and stayed permanently, and who grew rich on the back of Antiguan labor. Present reality gives way to a past history in which the imaginary passions have more room to expand and grow clamorous.

As the structural breach between the "you" and "we" widens, all neutrality disappears. The volume and momentum of the aggressivity rises. A ferocious and malignant bitterness breaks out that turns the enemy into a full-blown monster. The anger at the other demonizes him. There are accusations that require a trial. You exploited, oppressed, and dominated us. You are racist. You turned us into slaves. And anything is better than being a slave: "Even if I really came from people who were living like monkeys in trees, it was better to be that than what happened to me, what I became after I met you."[53] The other modified us against our will, according to their own.

The change in the self, the anger and the rage themselves, are the fault and the product of the other. What is wrong with the self is due to the other. I *am* you; I am the other, once again, albeit constructed by the very hatred that you caused, rather than by love. I hate you because you hate me. Paranoid or not, the passion of hate is as firm a bond as love. If I am your product or your effect, then you are responsible for me or at least co-responsible. But if the self is the other's responsibility or result or consequence that also means that I am not responsible. I am not an origin and not a cause.

Articulating hatreds that have hitherto never been named is exciting and dramatic. The straight narration of hatred is new, is news as such. It is a new gospel, confrontational and aggressive, bringing tidings of destruction. The expression of hatred becomes a challenge to discover and create ever new images of anger. Narration seems to increase rather than to reduce anger's mass. It is like a harvest of hatreds in which one begins to hope that the accumulated volume and flocculation will itself finally fall on and suffocate the opponent.

Naturally, the other is voiceless. Only the diminished, injured, and offended ego has a voice with which to damage, to diminish, and to make ugly in turn. "A tourist is an ugly human being" (14). The de-aesthetization of the other is followed by their de-intellectualization and de-moralization. The narcissism of the hated one and their ego-ideal must be devalued and destroyed, but only after suffering and torture. The hated one must not be instantly annihilated so that the drive can encircle its object ever again. As Lacan says,

> . . . the imaginary dimension is framed by the symbolic relation, and that is why hate is not satisfied with the disappearance of the adversary. If love aspires to the unfolding of the being of the other, hate wishes the opposite, namely its debasement, its deranging, its deviation, its delirium, its detailed denial, its subversion. That is what makes hate a career with no limit, just as love is. (277)

Fundamentally the other must be dehumanized, turned into something other than human, and not merely the animal or the devil, but into an object, a thing.

"An ugly thing, that is what you are when you become a tourist, an ugly, empty thing, a stupid thing, a piece of rubbish" (17). Hate wants the subjection and mastery of its object. It holds on to it to make it present ever again for one more berating and defacement before the symbolic superego rises up to condemn it.

If the other could be led to self-hatred, self-condemnation, or even self-annihilation, then the accuser might not have to dirty his hands with murder. If the other's narcissistic power and ego-ideal could be sufficiently disturbed, then the "slightly funny feelings you have from time to time about exploitation, oppression, and domination" (10) might develop into full-fledged unease, guilt, and preferably, fear and panic. Hatred wants the hated one to know they are hated, to sense it, feel, see, and hear it. The other must be saturated with this passion. All light but that of hatred must be blocked off from the hated one. They must be mesmerized with the power of hate and then made to fear the edge of destruction, the desire for the other's death glistening at the core of the hatred.

When imaginary envy and hatred have exhausted themselves in the dehumanization and reduction of the other to the worthless thing, to rubbish—rage, still unsatisfied, comes to demand their death. The relentless superego takes over from the voice of the damaged and angered ego. The ego is envious and aggressive, but the superego is impersonal and destructive. The two are not the same voices and do not issue from the same place, *W(ort)*. The narcissistically incensed ego wants the diminution of the other, but the enraged and destructive superego demands their terrorization and death. The superego, a consequence of a schism in the symbolic system (196), comes with the backing of the imperious law. For the superego, the other has in fact as if ceased to be present. This lofty ego listens only to its own impersonal and imperial voice speaking pitilessly of the torture and death of the other.

The tourist-turned-colonist and slave-owner, has now become "the criminal." "When I blow things up and make life generally unlivable for the criminal . . . the criminal is shocked, surprised" (32). The criminal on trial is self-evidently guilty, but goes on pretending to be oblivious to his or her crimes. A criminal must be punished, but what punishment is adequate to the loss and dispossession that have been suffered?

> [N]othing can erase my rage—not an apology, not a large sum of money, not the death of the criminal—for this wrong can never be made right, and only the impossible can make me still: can a way be found to make what happened not have happened? (32)

The book is an invitation to a trial that necessarily becomes a mis-trial. "Can a way be found to make what happened not have happened?" Obviously, neither society nor its courts of justice can undo what has been done. There is no punishment proportionate to the crime. The law, the symbolic, cannot adequately atone for what the heart and flesh have endured. There is a wild dissymmetry between the enormity of the suffering and the most horrendous punishment that the law could mete out. The law is not commensurate to passion, nor fitted to desire, and it cannot redress time. The law is impotent in relation to time past. The law and the individual in historical time do not, in fact, coincide at all. There is no law for rage, just as there is none for extreme love. Imaginary passions fundamentally exceed symbolic reality. The anguished question of the narrator cannot be addressed to society or to the law at all. Finally, it can only be addressed to psychoanalysis. What do you do with the suffering from a wrong that has already occurred and that cannot be made right? Should one accept such suffering or revenge it, attempt to mourn it or forget it, *do* nothing, but write about it, symbolize it?

Symbolization avoids hate's dangerous inclination to the real and its penchant to the violent act. The narrator imagines this most ready path of rage, the one that leads to terrorism and destruction: "Do you ever wonder why some people blow things up? I can imagine that if my life had taken a certain turn . . . there I would be, both of us in ashes" (26). Violence, the murder of the murderers, is not the answer because everyone, most murderers included, are libidinally bound to someone who will in turn seek revenge for their loss. Both end up in ashes.

Symbolization or the expression of anger is itself, in part, a refusal of suffering (although it is a form of suffering itself) and this is to an extent orthopedic and good, but not in itself a healing. The expression of anger helps to reveal the profound deterioration of the entire system of the imaginary other and the ego that occurs with hatred, but it also churns up language to an almost "implicit violence, a reduction of the other to a correlative function of the subject's ego," and it degrades communication (51). Repetition and reiteration reinforce the perturbation of imaginary language and of imaginary relations that develop in hatred. To the extent that such expressions of violence are becoming prevalent today on a worldwide scale, Kincaid's work presents itself as a dynamic, minimalist example of a global rage.

The symbolization of hatred has also necessarily to do with the third great passion, ignorance, and the dialectic of knowledge or benightedness of which it is a part. In fact, Lacan says the three great passions can never be entirely separated (271). And indeed, at the end, the narrator, still searching for an abatement of her anger and a stilling of her inner perturbation, examines once again the master-slave antithesis, attempting to extract from it some new insight or knowledge of the human. She considers the possibility of rebinding the dialectic, after a reduction of both its protagonists.

> Of course, the whole thing is, once you cease to be a master, once you throw off your master's yoke, you are no longer human rubbish, you are just a

human being, and all the things that adds up to. So, too, with the slaves. Once they are no longer slaves, once they are free, the are no longer noble and exalted; they are just human beings. (81)

The "exalted" slave is "just a human being," and the "human rubbish" that calls itself master is as well (81). By the mutual reduction of both to "just human beings," the extreme polarization of the master-slave dialectic is muted. If humanity cannot be united in exalted dreams of universal love and justice, then it must learn to do with lesser dreams of equality and unity in mediocrity, inadequacy, and incompetence. If humanity cannot collectively be elevated and improved, then it must be more accurately assessed as permanently and incurably deficient.

The problem with the universal idea of "humanity," however, is that it eradicates both the psychic particularity and the socio-political one of the individual. The other becomes less and less other. A universal being or abstract humanity is robbed as well of his political and personal force and reality. An illusory lack of alterity reigns. With the universal concept of *Humanität* as such, which is the central synthetic and symbolic concept of the imaginary, little can be done, just as with a world of "just human beings" nothing much can be hoped for or accomplished. The mind may be soothed by its bit of insight and knowledge, however hopeless and pessimistic the mastery, but the other two great passions of the imaginary are neither addressed nor resolved. The narrator's last vision is of dreary mortals who lack the luster of immortality that imaginary love would give them.

Lacan speculates, no doubt correctly, that the objectification and diffusion of hatred in our civilization must on some level appease us. Operating somewhat like a cold war deterrent, the objectification serves to saturate the common and unacknowledged drive of destruction. We can all see that a path for the total annihilation of humanity as such has clearly been laid out. The issue is only whether we will take the path or not or the extent to which we want to realize death. We know little about death; if we knew the real, we would know death, but since we do not, we can know nothing about death unless we die. We know as little about our desire for death except that our hatreds point the way to it. That is why, death is the absolute, that is, the unrecognized and unknown master (287).

Today, we no longer even need nuclear weapons or wars to carry on our games with death. We have learned to package and sell death. One small, inconspicuous gram of Botulin will kill one million people, *one* easily transportable gram of Tetanus toxin will kill *four* million people.[54] Death is everywhere. It is a commodity. Commodified, it can readily be sold and bought anywhere. The question is, who are the buyers and sellers?

Have centuries of the elaboration of love, made the passion of love more clear to us? Will centuries more of the elaboration of hate, teach us more about this passion? Or will we remain forever entrapped in a demand for fascinating images, no matter whether these are of pleasure or pain, of life or death? And will this demand for a spellbinding imaginary world forever halt, stop, cloud, ground up, and interrupt our perceptions, and possibly, our rearrangement of the orders of the symbolic and the real?

The Elephant

> For human beings, a word or concept is nothing other than the word in its materiality. It is the thing itself. It is not just a shadow, breath, or virtual illusion of the thing, it is the thing itself.
>
> Think for a moment in the real. It is owing to the fact that the word "elephant" exists in their language, and hence that the elephant enters into their deliberations, that men have been able to make decisions regarding elephants, before even touching them, which are more far-reaching for these pachyderms than anything else that has happened to them throughout their history—the crossing of a river or the natural decimation of a forest. With nothing more than the word "elephant" and the way in which men use it, propitious or unpropitious things, auspicious or inauspicious things, in any event catastrophic things have happened to elephants long before anyone raised a bow or a gun to them.
>
> Besides, it is clear, all I need do is talk about it, there is no need for them to be here, for them really to be here, thanks to the word "elephant," and to be more real than contingent individual elephants. (178)

The elephant on the cover of Seminar I is simply a photographic image. There is no real elephant nor is there the word for one, and yet the image readily conjures up both the word and the real thing, leaving us more than satisfied with having just the image. For the human being, the image or the word "is the thing itself. It is not just a shadow . . . or virtual illusion of the thing" (178). By virtue of the ligatory power of the three orders, things that are in fact constituted in a disparate, complex, tripartite structural grid, spring forth before us as complete and whole—seen, named, and real.

The elephant on the cover is there precisely by *not* being there (243). The word's negativity leaves us free to fill the sound with whatever we imagine or desire. The word is merely the audible matter, the phoneme, that we instantly jam with differing significations. It is a signifier in search of a signified or of an image or both. It is senseless sound in need of a human voice to give it sense.

In the beginning, sound and sense or the signifier and the signified are separated and apart. A human voice is necessary for us to join them together. Meaning is provided to each of us first by an other human being. But that is something we have long forgotten. The child hears meanings and these become his or her own. The words of the first others are not in quotations marks.[55] We don't remember who the words belonged to and therefore we do not know later whose voices are speaking in us. Analysis is, in part, the attribution of names and identities to seemingly anonymous voices resounding in the subject. It is a learning to hear who, at any given moment, is in fact speaking in the subject.

The blankness, emptiness, or negativity of signifiers is mysterious and powerful. Lacan's description of how these empty signifiers (the container) seek signifieds (the contained) was applied by Barthes to myths to explain the constant modifications of their contents (245). It is because sound is in a sense "virginal" that it can be inseminated with all kinds of heterogeneous, historical meanings and that it can give birth to new myths. Every new myth, like Barthes' deconstruction of the face of Greta Garbo, is a mosaic, a complex cultural constellation of ancient significations, currently deinvested from the point of view of desire, that are reconstructed into new, libidinized configurations of significance.

Inherently, language does not seem made to designate things as such at all, as it is at bottom simply a system of opposite phonemes, "one sound as opposed to another sound, within a set of oppositions" (248). The semblance of reality in words, or what Lacan calls "the lure of things" in words, is secondary. It is the purely incidental, fortuitous, and enigmatic consequence of negativity, on which theory and philosophy rely for the verification of their truths (248).[56] However, the fact that the seeming realness of truth is merely a lure, given within the structure of language, does not obviate either the labor of speaking or the need for an ethics of language.

The invention of language as such initiated the forgetting of the real a million years ago or more. Instead of living in the real, we began to create reality. The real elephant was displaced by "the reality" of the elephant, ever dependent on words and images. The elephant in reality, never free of imaginary or symbolic colorations, modifications, and inhabitancy, is an "hominisation," that has deleted the real elephant. But the symbolic is also the basis of the freedom which enables us to alter and modify our realities, as the very existence of our evolutionary, and often revolutionary, history shows.

Our language-enforced separation from nature is also a danger in that it aggravates the forgetting of the real and the indifference to reality that shows up in our willful hominisation and destruction of the environment. We cannot stop tampering with the environment, or for that matter, with our bodies. We replace nature with civilization and cities, the human voice with machine discourse, and our native bodies with virtual body parts. We seem to be in the process of displacing ourselves wholesale into an altogether virtual reality.

The destruction of nature entails the destruction of all that is non-linguistic and closer to the real than we ourselves have been for more than one million years. We know how to preserve the symbolic and the imaginary, but only nature knows how to preserve the real. At stake then, in the issue of the environment, is the real itself and the memory of the real. Only in nature is there a memory of the real.

The question is, to what extent do we need the real or, at the least, the non-linguistic, as figured forth by nature for one? Can the orders ever be balanced if the material pertaining to one of them is diminished? If we cannot afford to lose a phoneme, can we afford to lose a butterfly?

Science and technology are major and magnificent consequences of our historical labor in the symbolic. With seemingly small, insignificant symbolic inventions, we have managed to disturb, decompose, and dissolve our reality again and again, producing revolutionary changes (274–5). The upheaval of life by the symbol, whether we call it "conquest, rape of nature, transformation of nature, hominisation of the planet" (265) is a reality. Symbolic languages, however, are indifferent in themselves to the negative and positive effects and consequences of their operations.

Today's technology, for example, enables us to simulate the reality of the elephant in a way that seemingly begins to make even the reality of elephants almost superfluous. In fact, all that we are used to calling reality begins in this era of miniaturization, hyper-reality, and the satellisation of the real, "to appear only as some vast useless body, which has been both abandoned and condemned."[57] The simulated elephant is ever further away from what was once the real and also further away from the human voice that might transmit the animal's meaning to a child in a human communication. The elephant is subjected to technological reality and distanced from the symbolic-imaginary voice and the human reality and law that are its work.

> The symbolic system of the sciences tends towards the *well made language,*
> which one might consider to be its own language, a language deprived of all
> reference to a voice. (265)

The inevitable movement of the symbolic towards self-realization as a pure science and as technology may be at the expense of the human, the being embedded in his or her images and in a reality. The symbolic system's inherent non-humanness and negativity entail a complete forgetting of and indifference to the imaginary dimension, on the one hand, and on the other, an oblivion to the real. Its tendency is seemingly toward a ruthless destruction of nature and the planet, a sacrifice of the real and all reality, in favor of its own hyper-reality, ever more removed from the real. Science, for all the blessings and benefits it confers, seems also to be a collusion with this inanimate hyper-reality, full of merely simulated animation. The law and rule of a science without the human voice might just not be bearable or enough for all the animate things that wish to live and breathe in a reality in contact with the real.

Notes

1. In "The Other Is Missing" of January 15, 1980, Lacan wrote, "If it should happen that I go away, tell yourselves that it is in order–to be Other at last." *Television: A Challenge to the Psychoanalytic Establishment,* ed. Joan Copjec, trans. Denis Hollier, Rosalind Krauss, Annette Michelson, & Jeffrey Mehlman (New York: W. W. Norton & Company, 1990), 135.

2. For schema R, see Jacques Lacan, "On a question preliminary to any possible treatment of psychosis," *Écrits: A Selection,* 197. For schema L, see Jacques Lacan, Seminar II, 109, 243.

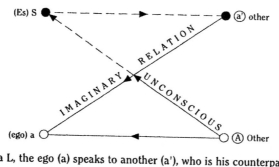

In schema L, the ego (a) speaks to another (a'), who is his counterpart (*Gegenbild*) about itself (S), unaware that the radical otherness of language has split it into something speaking both from the unconscious (Es) and consciousness (S) (or from $ as Lacan will later write it). This ego is oblivious as well to the fact that it itself (S) is symbolic and speaking at all entirely thanks to the symbol (A) that makes it human. Analysis, therefore, is the opening up of the subject to this awareness by shifting it from the dialectic of S, a, and a', to the dialectic of S, Es, and A. The first triangle constitutes the imaginary and produces "communication," the second triangle is symbolic and leads to "revelation."

3. "The image of the ego–simply because it is an image, the ego is ideal-ego–sums up the entire imaginary relation in man" (Seminar I, 282).

4. Lacan, Seminar II, 321.

5. Ibid., 326.

6. Lacan, Seminar I, 52-3, 166.

7. "The function of the imaginary . . . is present everywhere, and, in particular, whenever identification is at issue." Ibid., 281.

8. Lacan, Seminar II, 169.

9. Sigmund Freud, SE XII: 68. Lacan says, "The Other being truly excluded, what concerns the subject is actually said by the little other, by shadows of others, or, as Schreber will express himself to designate all human beings he encounters, by *fabricated* or *improvised* men. The small other effectively presents an unreal character, tending towards the unreal" (Seminar III, 53).

10. Freud, SE XII:32–3.

11. "Analytic theory defines the ego as always being relative." Seminar III, 22.

12. Fyodor Dostoevsky, *The Brothers Karamazov*, trans. Constance Garnett (New York: W.W. Norton & Co., 1976), 238.

13. Lacan, Seminar II, 319.

14. Ibid., 68.

15. Ibid., 72.

16. Ibid., 44.

17. Ibid., 319–20.

18. Lacan, Seminar III, 11.

19. "We are embodied beings, and we always think by means of some imaginary go-between, which halts, stops, clouds up the symbolic mediation. The later is perpetually ground up, interrupted" (Seminar II, 319).

20. This is the remaindered piece that Lacan calls later the "object a." The splitting that creates the archaic object a may in some as yet unknown and very distant way be connected to the dynmaism of cell division that lies programmed in the biology of the DNA molecules.These founding divisions in the organism would then be the underpinning of the experiences of change and exchange, such as the filling and emptying of its container, that the symbiotic fetus has later. The more developed fetus also begins to perceive alternations of sound and silence and of darkness and light. These latter experiences of fetal *pre-otherness* and of adaptations to self-division and differentiation are, however, put at risk after birth when sustenance and comfort come to depend on a reliable human other to consistently supply need.

21. Later, Lacan postulates the lamella or life as such as the beginning. Life is what the human animal lost in the course of its evolution to humanness. However, the more subjectivized the object becomes, the more its beginnings become an ever more distanced and lost zeropoint or *Nullpunkt* to which we have no access. Thus, we can never know this time of objecthood. The subject's time begins with the simultaneity of the three orders, with sound, sight, and pleasure/pain perceptions even in the womb. See Lacan's Seminar XI, and various essays, including my own on "The *Démontage* of the Drive," in *Reading Seminar XI: Lacan's Four Fundamental Concepts of Psychoanalysis*, eds. Richard Feldstein, Bruce Fink, and Maire Jaanus (New York: State University of New York Press, 1995) for a further development of these ideas.

22. The very genesis of an inside and an outside that precedes the genesis of the external and the internal (the division of psychic and material reality) is impaired in him. Robert cannot master the commencement of subjectivation. There is a miscarriage of the emergence and formation of the first layers that might cover the hole into which the primordial object "falls" as soon as its objectification (or what we could also call its subjectification) starts.

23. "What I am teaching you to place as the axis of the symbolic relation . . . is recognition" (Seminar I, 216).

24. To elaborate fully, the different ways Lacan uses the terms real and reality (as well as "primitive reality," "primitive real," "the human real," "the real world," etc.) in Seminar I could be a paper in itself. It may appear that he is not entirely consistent as, for example, when he says the real is "that which resists symbolization absolutely" (66), but then also that the real is that which *is* constituted by the imaginary and the symbolic (74), however, from the context of the seminar, it is possible to say that in the latter case he means another dimension of the *order* of the real, that is, the level constituted together with the symbolic and imaginary (since his whole point is the fact that the orders arise together), which yields what he calls being and revelation.

For the purposes of this paper, "reality" refers to a symbolized-humanized *psychic reality* and to the *external reality* that normally accompanies the former within a condition where both realities are, more or less, shared and held in common with other humans. The real, or what Lacan also calls "the primitive, nonsymbolized real," (58) refers to the something that is normally outside of the subjective domain altogether (and therefore in the domain of objects), and also to the something which is fundamentally unknown to subjects, but that can, under unusual circumstances, such as a psychotic break, appear in the subject as an immediate external reality, that is nonetheless unreal and not shared by other subjects, and therefore, a radically individual, purely psychic, and normally, unconscious reality that has mysteriously acquired the status of both external and psychic reality and that is for the subject more real than either of these forms of reality.

25. "Normally it is through the possibilities of play in the imaginary transposition that the progressive valorization of objects comes about, on the plane that we commonly designate as affective, through a diversification, a fanning-out of all the imaginary equations which allow the human being to be the only animal to have at his disposition an almost infinite number of objects—objects marked with the value of a *Gestalt* in this *Umwelt*, objects isolated as to their forms" (Seminar I, 83).

26. Jacques Lacan, "Geneva lecture on the symptom," *Analysis*, no. 1, 1989: 9.

27. Seminar II, 306.

28. The law becomes comprehensible to the subject only with the development of the superego, which is born consequent to a schism produced within the symbolic system (196). The superego's dialectic of you must or you must not is both a recognition and misrecognition of the law. In the neurotic, it is invariably the misrecognition that is dom-

inant, making their morality almost always "a senseless, destructive, purely oppressive, almost always anti-legal morality" (102). In Robert, of course, neither a superego or this dialectic are operative.

29. Sigmund Freud, SE XVIII: 113.

30. Sigmund Freud, SE XIV: 138.

31. Ibid., 125. See also Seminar I, 120–1. The literal death that occurs with the act of reproductive copulation in some less complex forms of life is simultaneous with the assurance of species continuity.

32. Ibid., 139.

33. Sigmund Freud, SE XIII: 87.

34. Sigmund Freud, SE XIX: 42.

35. In melancholia, that object is the ego itself, which the superego, having become a "gathering place for the death instincts," seeks to destroy. Ibid., 54.

36. Sigmund Freud, SE XX: 122.

37. Ibid., 122.

38. Roland Barthes, *A Lover's Discourse: Fragments,* trans. Richard Howard (New York: Farrar, Strauss and Giroux, 1978), 25–6.

39. Marguerite Duras, *La maladie de la mort* (Paris: Les Editions de Minuit, 1982), 52.

40. Barthes, *A Lover's Discourse,* 19–20.

41. Ibid., 1.

42. Manuel Puig, *Kiss of the Spider Woman* (New York: Random House, 1980), 219. Future references in the text are to this edition.

43. See also Karl F. Morrison, *"I Am You," The Hermeneutics of Empathy in Western Literature, Theology, and Art* (Princeton: Princeton University Press, 1988), 10, 189, *et passim* for a phenomenological approach to identification.

44. Charles Baudelaire, *The Intimate Journals of Charles Baudelaire,* trans. Christopher Isherwood (Boston: Beacon Press, 1957), 40.

45. Ibid., 47–8.

46. Sigmund Freud, SE XVI: 407.

47. There are obviously further problems posed by the character Molina and his psychic structure, such as his limited access to the symbolic, his perversions, his gender confusions, and his homosexuality, that would need another paper to develop, which would have to draw on other works of Lacan.

48. Sigmund Freud, SE XXIII: 81-2.

49. Samuel P. Huntington, *The Clash of Civilizations? The Debate* (New York: Council on Foreign Relations, Inc., 1993).

50. Roland Barthes, *Camera Lucida: Reflections on Photography*, trans, Richard Howard (New York: Hill and Wang, 1981), 94.

51. "I think anger can be kind of genius if it's acted on." Barbara Charlesworth Gelpi, Albert Gelpi eds., *Adrienne Rich's Poetry* (New York: W. W. Norton and Co. Inc., 1975), 111.

52. Freud, SE XIV: 128.

53. Jamaica Kincaid, *A Small Place* (New York: Penguin, 1988), 37. Future references in the text are to this edition.

54. *"Tod und Terror aus dem Labor,"* *Der Spiegel* (no. 34/22.8.94), 23.

55. A comment made by my friend, Halina Morell.

56. Lacan refers to St. Augustine as someone who fell into the trap of this lure because negativity had not yet been developed in his time (Seminar I, 252, 259).

57. Jean Baudrillard, *The Ecstasy of Communication* (New York: Semiotext(e), 1987), 18.

LOGICAL TIME AND THE PRECIPITATION
OF SUBJECTIVITY

∞

Bruce Fink

> "Reflection" is an activity of the ego which demands time, and it
> becomes important when the affective level involves large quan-
> tities. Hence it is that where there is affect there is hastiness and
> a choice of methods similar to that made in the primary process.
> —Freud, *The Origins of Psychoanalysis*

In my talks here on subjectivity, I have proposed that the Lacanian subject
be viewed as the breach between or connecting up of two signifiers. Today I shall
illustrate this hypothesis on the basis of Lacan's 1946 article, "Logical Time and
the Assertion of Anticipated Certainty."[1] While this text may seem at first rather
dated in terms of Lacan's later developments of the 1950s and 1960s concerning
the symbolic order and subjectivity, one nevertheless finds therein a great many
later notions in embryonic form or at least implicitly at work. It should also be
kept in mind that it was somewhat rewritten for its 1966 publication.

I do not assume that the reader is to any degree familiar with Lacan's argument in the article (as the translation has yet to be widely distributed), and it
will be necessary to lay out the three-prisoner problem in some detail in order
to show precisely where and how "a precipitation of subjectivity" can be seen
to take place therein. I will confine myself at first to an explanation of Lacan's
claims, engaging in a judgement thereof only when I first come to the "time for
comprehending." While the "truth-value" of Lacan's argument will be examined
here in some detail, this is not my overriding concern. My primary goal here is
to lay out the argument's manifest and latent premises.

The three-prisoner problem takes its place in the series of logical paradoxes that have arisen throughout the history of Western thought and which have spurred on the advancement of thought. Lacan himself was able to "resolve" what has been known since the time of ancient Greek philosophy as the liar's paradox—the paradox which consists in someone's saying to you "I'm lying," where the very veracity of the assertion is thrown into question by the content of the assertion itself: if the person is lying, then how can you be sure he or she is telling you the truth in saying that he or she is lying?—with his twentieth-century distinction between the enunciating subject (the speaking subject) and the subject of the statement (the word "I" in the statement "I'm lying" which functions as a place-holder for the subject). But still more significant than the fact of having resolved this long-standing paradox is the theoretical advance that was required to come to terms with it.

While the liar's paradox played off of two different functions of the "I," the brain-teaser that Lacan takes up here introduces a time element, an element that has always been rigorously excluded from classical works on logic. Lacan is able to approach such a logical problem (and there are other such problems and paradoxes in the literature involving time) in a new and different way because of his understanding of Freud's notion of *Nachträglichkeit*. It is that same notion which allows him, in the 1950s, to proffer up a first explanation of how meaning is created, and to shed new light on the nature of trauma and symptom formation.

Lacan, exploring the temporal logic at work in unconscious processes, is quite well known for having experimented with the function of time in the analytic setting, as well as in his theoretical writings. His development of the concept of discrete, determinate *moments* in analytic treatment, and of the practices of punctuation and scansion of the analytic session, is based upon considerable reflection on the logic of time in unconscious activity, the creation of meaning, and the precipitation of subjectivity. The theoretical underpinnings of these practices were explored to some extent in my earlier talks on the subject; here I will take up his temporal logic as developed in this 1946 paper. While I take issue with Lacan's argument at certain points, what seem to me most essential are the main outlines of his approach and the implicit premises at work in his interpretation.

1 Structure of the Article

1.1 The Problem

The three-prisoner problem was first explained to Lacan at a cocktail or dinner party. It goes something like this:

Three prisoners in a jail are summoned by the warden. He tells them that he has the authority to release one of them, and that to decide which of the three it shall be, he has concocted a little game for them to play. The winner will go free. He has three white tags (or discs, as he calls them) and two black ones. He is going to pin a disc on the back of each prisoner, but while the other two prisoners will be able to see it, the prisoner to whom it is pinned will not know whether it is black or white. Each prisoner must try to logically reckon—and not simply guess—whether his disc is black or white *without* verbally communicating with the others. As soon as he thinks he has figured it out, he is to run for the door where he should be prepared to answer as to his color and explain how he worked it out.

Having explained the rules, the warden proceeds to pin a white disc on the back of each of the three prisoners, the black discs being left aside. How can the prisoners solve the problem?

1.2 The Perfect Solution

Lacan provides what he describes as the "perfect solution":

> After having contemplated one another for *a certain time*, the three subjects take *a few steps* together and pass side by side through the doorway. Each of them then separately furnishes a similar response which can be expressed thus:
>
> "I am a white, and here is how I know it: as my companions were whites, I thought that, had I been a black, each of them would have been able to infer the following: 'If I too am a black, the other would have necessarily realized straight away that he was a white and would have left immediately; therefore I am not a black.' And both would have left together, convinced that they were whites. As they did nothing of the kind, I must be a white like them. At that, I made for the door to make my conclusion known."
>
> All three thus exited simultaneously, armed with the same reasons for concluding (p. 5).

Lacan then goes on to refer to this perfect solution as a "remarkable sophism, in the classical sense of the term—that is, a significant example for the resolution of the forms of a logical function at the historical moment in which the problem raised by these forms presents itself to philosophical examination" (p. 6).

1.3 The Sophism

The first thing which should be noted is that the sophism, as Lacan calls it here, is not a sophism in the strictest sense of the term. A sophism is "a specious but fallacious argument,"[2] an argument which sounds good and perhaps even seems convincing at first, but which, upon closer examination, turns out to be invalid. The reasoning in question here is that which leads the three subjects, A, B and C, to "take *a few steps* together," enabling all of them to "pass side by side through the doorway." Lacan is not concerned here with putting his solution to the test in an experimental setting (though he claims to have gleaned something nonetheless from his trials "with various groups of appropriately chosen, qualified intellectuals"); he is only interested "in the logical value of the solution presented." His perfect solution is a logical, not an empirical, hypothesis. (The discussion which follows of Lacan's moves in this article becomes quite technical at certain points, and certain readers may wish to pass directly to section 4 below.)

1.4 The Objection

The section entitled "Discussion of the Sophism" which follows Lacan's description of the perfect solution presents an objection to the reasoning based on the conditionality of each subject's conclusion on the others' actions; the same kind of objection arises at three different points in the reasoning:

1. As B's conviction is based upon C's behavior (in the situation of A being a black), "B's confidence must logically dissipate when C stops hesitating; reciprocally for C with respect to B; and both remain indecisive. Nothing, therefore, necessitates their reaction in the case of A being a black. As a result of this, A cannot deduce that he is a white."

2. Even if A has every right to conclude that he's a white, he must revert to indecision when he sees that the others get up with him.

3. Even if A has every right to conclude *once again* that he's a white, he must *once again* revert to a state of indecisiveness when he sees the others moving towards the door in step with him.

Lacan dispels the objection as it arises at each of these three points in showing that it only takes into account the *action* of the participants and not their crucially important *inaction*, that is, their suspended motion: in case one "the fact that neither of them left first," in case two the fact that "they would have to *start up again before him*" and don't, and in case three the fact that if A "were black, B and C *absolutely should not have stopped*," and yet they did. The objection is based on a "spatialized conception"–that is, the movement of the subjects–neglecting the temporal dimension. The pauses (*les temps d'arrêt*) here act as incontrovertible pieces of evidence:

a single hesitation in effect suffices for [B and C] to demonstrate to each other that certainly neither of them is a black. The fact that B and C have halted again means that A can only be a white. Which is to say that this time the three subjects are fixed [or established] in a certainty permitting of no further doubt or objection.

How these hesitations can work in precisely this way will be spelled out further on.

It is in this way that Lacan can claim that "the sophism thus maintains all the constraining rigor of a logical process, on the condition that one integrates therein the value of the two suspensive scansions." But if the perfect solution is considered so water-tight by Lacan, why does he refer to it as a sophism?

Is it because in examining the role of the two suspended motions in the logical process, one finds that their role comes "only after the conclusion of the logical process, since the act they suspend [that of heading for the door] evinces this very conclusion"? Is it, in others words, because the suspended motions— while absolutely indispensable to the conclusion—only come after the fact? How can the conclusion ever be reached if one, the suspended motions are necessary steps in the deduction of the conclusion and two, can only come *after* the conclusion has already been reached? Hasn't the cart somehow gotten in front of the horse?

Yes, but that is precisely the point:

Far from being experiential data external to the logical process, the *suspended motions* are . . . necessary to it. . . . [They] represent nothing, in effect, but levels of degradation in which necessity engenders an increasing order of temporal instances which are registered within the logical process so as to be integrated into its conclusion.

Skirting for the time being all the complexities raised by this latter sentence, note here simply that, according to Lacan, "These temporal instances, constitutive of the process of the sophism, permit us to recognize therein *a true logical movement*" (emphasis mine).

1.5 Spatial vs. Temporal: The Completion of Classical Logic

One of Lacan's interests in this article is to use his perfect solution to show up the deficiencies of classical logic. For the perfect solution, by the end of the article, remains a sophism only in the eyes of classical logic—any sophistic value, any trace of fallaciousness that it might have seemed to possess at the beginning being dispelled by the end for those who lend credence to Lacan's argument. It is not the perfect solution which is found lacking, but rather the very philosophical apparatus brought to bear upon it in judging its veracity:

It is precisely because our sophism will not tolerate a spatialized conception that it presents itself as an aporia for the forms of classical logic, whose "eternal" prestige reflects an infirmity which is nonetheless recognized as their own, that is, these forms never give us anything which cannot already *be seen at a single stroke* [*d'un seul coup*].

Classical logic never gives us anything new, anything beyond what we put into arguments in the form of premises. Its conclusions can be seen immediately—in a single blow, or in one fell swoop, to formulate Lacan's "*vu d'un seul coup*" more literally, sidestepping any allusion to time; it is from the very sterility or infirmity of classical logic's forms that their "eternal" prestige derives. Like Lacan's contradictor in the footnote appended to the above passage (footnote 1), classical logic doesn't wait around for developments, preferring to take it all in with a single glance.

Maintaining this visual/spatial versus temporal opposition, Lacan writes, "*Du premier aspect*"—at first sight, on the face of it, or taken at face value—"the givens of the problem break down" as a logical possibility of three combinations, one immediately ruled out by what everyone sees (that of two blacks and one white), the choice between the remaining two being made on the basis of "a signal" constituted by the experiential given of the suspended motions. The *signal* here is something of a definite spatial component, the displacement of a person (or persons), a movement across a room. It is something available to sight that functions as a transparent sign, similar to the moves executed by bees in what has come to be known as the "wagging dance," forms which indicate the direction and distance to new-found nectar. Lacan, in discussing these forms in "Function and Field of Speech and Language in Psychoanalysis" (*Écrits*, pp. 84–85), refers to them as constituting "a code, or a system of signalling," which is to be "distinguished from language precisely by the fixed correlation of its signs to the reality that they signify." In this at-first-sight breakdown of the givens of the problem, the experiential given of the fit-and-start movements would be read as signals to which but one meaning would correspond; and such signals could only represent what can be seen or localized. But

In complete opposition to this, the coming into play as signifiers of the phenomena here contested (the suspended motions) makes the temporal, not spatial, structure of the logical process prevail. What the *suspended motions* disclose is not what the subjects see, but rather what they have found out positively about *what they do not see*: the appearance of the black discs. That which constitutes these suspended motions as signifying is not their direction, but rather their interruption [*temps d'arrêt*: pause, stopping time].

The signifier gives voice here to what is unheard—silence, inaction, pause; it reveals, brings to light, what is unseen.

2 Temporal Instances

Time forces its way into the perfect solution at three points, functioning in different ways at each of them. The first two points are discussed immediately hereafter, while the third is discussed in section 4 below.

2.1 The Instant of the Glance

While we can suppose it to be taken for granted by the subjects (from the very set-up of the situation, there being two black discs and three white ones) that if any one of them sees two blacks, he immediately knows that he is a white, "the instant of the glance [is nevertheless] necessary for this to occur." For while the formula two blacks::one white may be considered already present "in" the prisoners, it represents "a still indeterminate matrix": *each prisoner must still look and see* if there are in fact two blacks before him. "An instance of time excavates the interval" in which the conditional element—the protasis "if opposite two blacks"—may potentially be transformed into the consequence—the apodosis "one is a white."

In the three-prisoner problem, however, since all three prisoners bear white discs, the protasis is not transformed into the apodosis. The instant of the glance is not sufficient to indicate to the individual the color he bears.

Paradoxically, thus, *the instant of the glance is, in a sense, but a would-be temporal instance.* Nothing is transformed; nothing is deduced; no instance of time excavates an interval, as *there can be no interval without two end-points, and here the end-point/conclusion is inoperative*; no "noetic subject" comes into being—the "noetic" being the first of the three types of subjects to which Lacan explicitly refers in this article (1. the impersonal or noetic subject, 2. the undefined reciprocal subject, and 3. the *personal* form of the subject of knowledge; I will return to these three types further on). The transformation of the protasis into a "*one* knows that . . . ," had it taken place, would have led to a "subjectivization, however impersonal" implied by the use of the third person singular here ("one"). The protasis, "To be opposite two blacks," already constituted a *positioning* of sorts, but the abstract generality of the knowledge in question would have pushed subjectification of this place or position no further than the third person singular (had it occurred), for the conclusion would have been just as valid for A as for B or C. It is a sort of God's eye view.[3]

The glance is nevertheless necessary in the three-prisoner problem, where three white discs are used, for the participants to formulate a hypothesis (see figure below). The noetic subject being short-circuited or bypassed, an abstractly logical, non-positional consideration gives way to a *positional* or *perspectivist* form of reasoning that takes the form of: "if *I* [A] am black, then the others (B and C) must reason as follows: 'seeing as I do one black and one white, etc.'"

$$T_0 \qquad \text{Hypothesis}$$

TIMELINE $\underline{\underline{\qquad}}$ $O \; \text{-} \; \text{-} \; \text{-} \; \rightarrow O$

Instant
of the
Glance

2.2 The Time for Comprehending

The time for comprehending is far more complicated than it may seem at first sight, and before laying it out, I will jump right to *my* conclusions (with which Lacan would not necessarily agree): it *is entirely based on error*, that is, on mistaken reasoning. It is essential to the solution of the three-prisoner problem that the time for comprehending be objectified, in other words, made into something solid, substantial: a signifier. And though it be solidified and transformed into a signifier, this comes about for all the wrong reasons.

This stage of the perfect solution is absolutely crucial, and cannot but remind us of the error involved in the mirror stage: the infant's identification of the mirror image with him or her "self," despite the discrepancies involved in totalization and the right-left reversal occurring in normal mirror-imaging. *Something is irrevocably and irreversibly changed through the error in reasoning needed to bring the time for comprehending to a close, and this error will determine the individual's entire fate thereafter.*[4] *Indeed, the error is responsible for the advent of the subject here, for the all-important precipitation of subjectivity.*[5] And to extend these conclusions still further, I might propose the hypothesis that *certainty is always acquired at such a cost: no error, no certainty.*

Having gotten rather far ahead of myself, let me now backtrack and unpack the time for comprehending step by step.

According to Lacan, the time for comprehending begins with the formulation of an hypothesis: as there are two whites, there cannot be *two* blacks, *but perhaps there is one*—and that could only be me. So suppose I'm black.

Why does the prisoner now consider the possibility that he is a black? Why doesn't he first contemplate the consequences of his being a white like the other two he sees before him? Lacan seems to take it for granted that the prisoners would systematically eliminate the possibility of their being blacks before guessing what is, in effect, the correct solution. I would suggest that, aside from the other reasons one could give—for example, that the reasoning process would be longer were a prisoner to suppose that he were a white like the others,[6] which ultimately is not very convincing—the prisoner's immediate formulation of an hypothesis that he is black reflects Lacan's early notion of underlying paranoia at the root of personality: *the other two are alike, I must be different.* Rather than stubbornly and perhaps arrogantly insisting upon some sort of racial equality or superiority, he immediately casts himself in the opposition, as the underdog, so to speak. This supposition of underdog or minority status is the motor force behind the whole reasoning process. The hypothesis in question is this very supposition.[7]

On the basis of this hypothesis, A reasons as follows: "Were I a black, the two whites I see would waste no time realizing they are whites": for *B and C would each see one black and one white*, and the fact that neither B nor C bolts for the door immediately can but convince both of them that they are whites. B watches C, and C watches B, each ascertaining what Lacan calls a "time of meditation" in the other.

Mere figments of A's imagination, B and C are not considered to be in exactly the same situation as A, nor at the same point in their reasoning. For A, the two blacks::one white combination has already been ruled out, once and for all; not only for himself, but as he sees two whites before him, for all three parties to the game. Yet in going on to postulate that B and C see something different from him at the outset of the game (one black and one white), and that they each then entertain the hypothesis that they are black (thus two blacks and one white), he mentally projects them back to T_0, the instant of the glance. The slightest elapsing of time after the glance, that is, B and C's slightest hesitation after supposedly seeing that A is black, should be enough to convince both B and C that they are whites: if B too was black, C should not have hesitated; and if C too was black, B should not have hesitated.

B and C, in A's imaginary scenario, both now realize they are white. Each of them, having concluded about his own color on the basis of the reflective hesitation detected in the other, constitutes that hesitation as a moment of evidence; he objectifies it as something concrete, solid, and incontrovertible: a bona fide hesitation. The elapsing of time has been concretized in the form of the word or signifier "hesitation," or "pause." (In the diagrams I will label this hesitation H_1, anticipating thereby the other hesitation yet to come, H_2.)

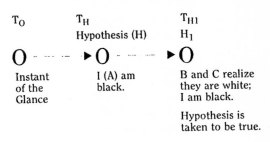

T_0	T_H	T_{H1}
	Hypothesis (H)	H_1

O - - - - ►O - - - - ►O

| Instant of the Glance | I (A) am black. | B and C realize they are white; I am black. |

Hypothesis is taken to be true.

The meaning of this time has become clear, not only for B and C–who, as we recall, are here but marionettes in A's cogitations–but also for A: "this time is, for each of the two whites, *the time for comprehending* in the situation of seeing a black and a white."

2.2.1 Error One: The Equation of Times

According to Lacan, A believes that, chronometrically speaking, the time it took B and C (who supposedly see one black and one white) to realize that they are white is equal to the time it took A himself to think through their reasoning process. Now why on earth would A believe such a thing?

Logically speaking, A has, according to Lacan, had to formulate the following two steps: 1. seeing two whites I suppose I am a black [this corresponds on the timeline to T_H, the time at which this erroneous hypothesis is made]; and 2. B and C each see one black and one white, and as they hesitate, they know they are whites [T_{H1} on the timeline, the time at which A's hypothesis "would be true"]. According to A's supposition, however, that he himself is black, B and C had no need to formulate step 1 and could proceed directly to step 2. Thus, while two distinct "times" have elapsed by the time A concludes he is black, only one has elapsed by the time B and C realize they are whites (assuming, in accordance with A's hypothesis, that A is black). Step 1, the sight of two whites, has been bypassed or excluded for them as a possibility by A's supposition that he himself is black, and seems to be totally forgotten, if not somehow repressed (or even foreclosed) by A when he equates T_{H1} (his position on the timeline after two distinct "times" have elapsed) and T_H (B and C's more logical position on the timeline). The fact is that *something is always lopped off or scotomized when two things are identified*, and it is psychoanalysis itself which teaches us that. While identification of two separate and distinct things (or times) is permitted by the signifier, and by the signifier alone, a remainder or leftover is inevitably engendered.

Lacan proposes that it seems to A that the times are equal because *the whole situation is nothing but his own hypothesis*. But, as we have now seen, were A to be really thinking clearly, there would be no reason for it to "seem" to him that the times are equal. Star Trek's Mr. Spock, for example, would certainly never conflate T_H and T_{H1}! We see here an example of a vacillation on Lacan's part between strictly logical reasons for the prisoner's thought processes, and psychological or experiential or even probabilistic reasons. I would sustain that Lacan slips in an additional premise here.

Could there be any other reason for A's equation than because, in his *imaginary-register-dominated state* (in some sense a paranoid-like state), B and C– as creatures of his own making–obey his every whim and fancy, and A, getting caught up in the *reciprocally specular relationship* he postulates between B and C–Lacan refers to them here as "undefined reciprocal subjects"–mistakes the identicalness of *their* thought processes (and thus of the time they take) for an identity between theirs and his own? I will call this *the imaginary error*, involving as it does the imaginary register. Having initially assumed himself to be different from the others (*viz.* black), he goes on to suppose them to be all too like himself and at the very same stage. The only opposition in play here is same/different.

2.2.2 Undoing the Equation Accepting Lacan's additional premise for the time being, we see that at T_{H1}, A believes that his hypothesis is true, to wit, that he is black. And as each of the prisoners is in precisely the same predicament as A, at this stage in the game all three whites mistakenly believe they are black.

In Lacan's account, temporal tension has not yet accumulated (thanks no doubt to this forgetting, repressing, or foreclosing on A's part); A believes himself to be on a par with B and C: they can now jump up and declare themselves white, while he jumps up and declares himself black. A is in no hurry just yet; when B and C get to their feet, he will too.

But there's a catch: B and C do not budge. A is thus led to think: "Oh no! I am *not* black, *and B and C thus haven't had to make the same supposition I had to make: they've got the jump on me*—if I don't run for the door now, it'll be too late."

In fact, the catch is not even, if we follow Lacan closely, that B and C do not budge—for after all, how much time does a hesitation take?—but rather that A (due to the observed inaction of B and C sitting across from him after he, A, has finished the first two steps of his reasoning process) finally stops equating his thought processes and times with those of B and C, realizing that if he himself is black, the other two have *not* had to go through the same first step as him (*viz.* "seeing two whites, I suppose I am a black"). He is suddenly overcome with the sense that he is lagging behind them. No further elapsing of time need be observed after the first hesitation: A must needs only think, "Oh no! they *haven't* had to make the same supposition. . . ."[8]

Before taking up Lacan's explanation of this aspect of the logical process, I will explore two approaches which present themselves: roads not followed by Lacan. I will then try to explain why Lacan leaves these two approaches aside, preferring another to them.

3 Two Alternative Approaches

There seem, in effect, to be two ways of glossing this particular step, one which involves time, the other which leaves time aside:

> • Atemporally speaking, A's next thought after deciding that the two whites he sees should now spring for the door is that, "Well, if I am black, then

they haven't had to make the first assumption I made, and are thus a step ahead of me."

• Temporally speaking, A, having decided that he is black, is led to throw that conclusion into question *because B and C haven't budged.* Here he first observes an elapsing of time, an indefinite time of inactivity, which then *jars* him back to the question at hand, forcing him to infer something from it. In the second approach, thought is taken to unfold in time.

3.1 An Atemporal Gloss

Let us examine, first of all, what might be construed on the basis of an "atemporal approach," where lightning-fast thought has no need to be jarred into action by further inactivity on the part of B and C.

The first ("imaginary") error is only nullified or corrected by a second thought which effectively bars the equation ($T_H \neq T_{H1}$), but introduces a problem of its own.

1. If I were black, they would have only had to formulate step two of the reasoning.

2. They would thus have the jump on me, and should have run to declare themselves white.

3. What have they been waiting around for?

4. *I* must be white.

The conclusion here seems to result from an ordinary *reductio ad absurdum* argument: there are only two possibilities, black and white; if, supposing the former, experience fails to bear out what that supposition logically implies, then the latter must be true (assuming the prisoners are all capable of thinking the problem through, and keeping track of hypotheses and implications, at the same speed). But the waiting around postulated in line three above seems somewhat problematic, which is not surprising as it is where time explicitly enters the argument.

At the first stage of the reasoning process, A, as we have seen, *erroneously* equates the time it takes him to think through the situation (whereby he is black and the others white) with the time it takes them to realize they are whites. This allows him to "objectify" the first hesitation, that is, to make it into something solid or substantial. What A, in the second stage, considers to constitute a *second* hesitation is built upon that first "hesitation," and is thus dependent on the first error. It is only from the vantage point of H_1 (illicitly reached, as it were) that A can now realize that the time between T_0 and T_H is not equal to that between T_0 and T_{H1}. *A, in this sense, works backward from*

H₁ to see that B and C did not have to bother to formulate the same hypothesis as he; basing himself on H_1, he concludes that they have already hesitated *more* than he at first thought: they have not hesitated once but twice. H_1 is thus not their first, but rather their second pause: H itself is now retroactively read by A as corresponding to a pause on their part, and H_1 as corresponding to a further pause. Whereas he thought they were all in step (which they were as they are all white, but he was nonetheless mistaken as he assumed there were two whites and one black), he now imagines that while he was plodding along the following timeline,

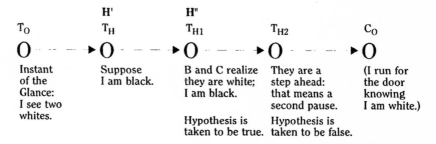

	H'	H"		
T_O	T_H	T_{H1}	T_{H2}	C_O
Instant of the Glance: I see two whites.	Suppose I am black.	B and C realize they are white; I am black. Hypothesis is taken to be true.	They are a step ahead: that means a second pause. Hypothesis is taken to be false.	(I run for the door knowing I am white.)

they were skipping along this shorter one:

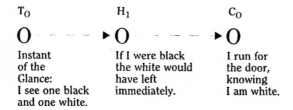

T_O	H_1	C_O
Instant of the Glance: I see one black and one white.	If I were black the white would have left immediately.	I run for the door, knowing I am white.

He cannot objectify a *second* hesitation if he has not already made the first error:[9] he has to first equate the times in order to be able to "disequate" them. Does this second phase in the reasoning effectively *rectify* the error contained in the first? Or does it, rather, *compound* it? A vicious circle or specious sort of reasoning seems to emerge that is of the following order:

> If H_1 (that is, B and C have hesitated once) and I am black,
> then H' and H" (that is, they have hesitated twice) and I am white.

Renaming the hesitations as I have done (see figure above with H' and H") points to the fact that H_1 is *annulled* in a sense by the development of the reasoning: H_1 was not what it seemed to be, but rather something else. Restating the specious progression here, we might say "If H_1 then not H_1." Or again, "If I am black then I am white!"[10]

Now if H_1 is annulled in the course of the reasoning, then the very foundation of the argument is undermined in the course of the argument. Can the subsequent conclusions be of any value?

Let us restate this problem more clearly, using the letters a, b and c to show which hesitation applies to which of the prisoners in the reasoning:

1.	Suppose I am black.	Black
2.	I observe hesitation on the part of B and C.	x
3.	$TH_{1a} = TH_{b\&c}$ (taken to be true).	$Tx = Ty$ (T for Time)
4.	Thus $H_{1b\&c}$.	$\therefore$ p
5.	But then $TH_{1a} \neq TH_{b\&c}$ (we are not in the same boat).	$\therefore Tx \neq Ty$
6.	Then $H'_{b\&c}$ and $H''_{b\&c}$ ($\sim H_{1b\&c}$).	$\therefore$ q and r, that is, ~p
7.	I must be white.	$\therefore$ ~Black

Structurally speaking, it looks as if we have a simple reductio ad absurdum that proves to us that our hypothesis at the outset was false. But let us take a closer look; p is absolutely necessary here to deduce q and r. But deriving, as it does, from two false premises (1 and 3), p is false. Or is it? In logic, one is generally sceptical of conclusions drawn from false premises, for example,

given that a=4, b=5, c=6

1.	a=b	false
2.	b=c	false
3.	a=c	false.

Line 3, like the two false premises from which it is derived, is, as was to be expected, false. But this need not be so. Consider the following example:

given that a=4, b=5, c=4

1.	a=b	false
2.	b=c	false
3.	a=c	true.

Though the premises be false, the conclusion need not be. *The conclusion in the three-prisoner problem*, in accordance with what I've been referring to here as an "atemporal" approach, *though unjustifiably arrived at on the basis of the unfounded deduction p, is nevertheless true.*

We knew at the outset that the premise was false: H_1 was "deduced" only because A erroneously equated T_H with T_{H1}. The subsequent argument showed it to be false, but given its false premise, why lend credence to the subsequent argument? Because it happens to be true. While the reasoning is specious, that is, sophistic, it not only provides the right answer (in this very particular case we are lucky enough to know the right answer), but it is also perhaps impossible to arrive at the right answer in any other way.

This is more than tangentially related to Lacan's frequent references to the Stoic notion that there are arguments whose conclusions are true though their premises be false. *Erroneous premises may in fact at times be necessary for the right conclusion to be drawn.*

Having "arrived at" a conclusion in this specious but unavoidable way, providing a modicum of subjective certainty, *logical certainty can be attained afterward*: through the two suspended motions that come after the conclusion. But how would a "purely logical subject" have reacted?

Mr. Spock (my somewhat facetious example of a purely logical "subject") would, following this atemporal gloss, consider for a moment the possibility that he were black, humanly (all too humanly) fall into the trap of equating T_H and T_{H1}, realize that the others (Vulcans too in this case) would thus be a step ahead, and had therefore hesitated twice. But then suddenly being struck by the specious nature of this reasoning, it would dawn on him that H_1 is not a solid basis, and wonder how H_1 could ever be truly determined. Nothing could bring the time for comprehending to a close for him. Forced at last to realize that the elapsing time must have *some* meaning, he might be led to draw the conclusion that is inevitable though unprovable (at this stage), cognizant of the fact that proof, and thus logical (not merely subjective) certainty, can *only* come afterwards. He rises then to his feet, fully expecting the others to do the same—but then what?

Before mentioning a second possible approach not adopted by Lacan, I would like to suggest a similarity between the nature of the argument presented above and what Lacan says about the specificity of the use of language (and thus of the signifier) by human beings in Seminar IX, *Identification*. There Lacan discusses an animal capable of effacing its own tracks in order to stump hunters on its trail—a prodigious feat in the animal kingdom where the signifier is virtually, if not altogether, unknown. Another kind of animal is supposed to be able to make false tracks to lead hunters and predators in the wrong direction. But according to Lacan, no animal makes real tracks with the intention of fooling the hunter/predator into taking them for false ones.

Such, however, is the storyteller in Freud's *Jokes and Their Relation to the Unconscious*, often mentioned by Lacan, who, in telling a friend of his that he is going to Krakow, elicits the following sort of response: 'Why are you telling me you are going to Krakow, when, though leading me to believe you are thus *not* going to Krakow, you in fact are?!' While it rarely elicits a laugh from readers nowadays, Lacan seems to detect in this story *an essential feature of language: its ability to lie while telling the truth.* The storyteller's intention is to deceive his listener, relying on the latter's undoubtedly time-proven scepticism, hoping the latter will not believe what he says when (for once perhaps) he is telling the truth.

Lacan would seem to be suggesting that this kind of kidding around is not possible without the signifier. What might be called a sort of "breakdown of communication" by some, is in fact an inevitable possibility arising out of our use of language: the insinuation of a gap between word and thing. While tracks are generally *signs* of an animal having passed that way, in the case of the animal mentioned by Lacan that makes false tracks to lead predators astray, they come to mean something else altogether: a hunter, aware of the exceptional intelligence of the particular prey he is tracking, would assume that the tracks he spots are false—why wouldn't the animal have covered them up otherwise? *If they were left behind, they must be false.* At the level of the animal kingdom, a hunter, knowing his particular prey as he does, can be sure of that: there is no independent suspension between what he observes and its meaning. Tracks left by such and such an animal are *always* false: they always mean precisely the same thing *to someone*—the hunter.

Leaving the animal kingdom behind, the manhunter is faced with a far more difficult problem. The same tracks can mean different things at different times: they may have been left accidentally, on purpose, with a deliberate intention to trick, etc. They indicate that a subject, creating space between sign and meaning (thereby making that sign into something else: a signifier), has passed that way.

A realm of intersubjectivity opens up here, where the prey may be tempted to second-guess the hunter's reactions, much as the marble-winning wizard in Edgar Allan Poe's "The Purloined Letter" does in assessing the degree of sophistication of his opponents in their game of odds or evens. "Will he imagine that I've left tracks in order to fool him into thinking they are false when in fact they are real? In that case I should perhaps only leave fake ones!" We see here a sort of multiplication of levels of discourse:

- First order: tracks are signs that an animal went that way.

- Second order: tracks are signs used to deceive—the animal did not go that way.

- Third order: tracks are intended to deceive but indicate, nevertheless, the true direction.

• Fourth order: tracks are not a sure sign of anything; they may indicate either the right or the wrong direction to take.

This proliferation of orders, and the last order in particular, is permitted by our use of the signifier. But what can be seen in both "The Purloined Letter" example and the three-prisoner problem, as well as in the hunter/hunted paradigm, is that, though use of the signifier can get bogged down in specular relations (a-a': the attempt to second guess the other/s by identifying with him/them, that is, by trying to think like him/them), it contains within itself the seeds of another dimension—a relation to the Other.[11]

3.2 A Temporal Gloss

One might try another approach: temporally speaking, A, having decided that he is black and that the others must now know they are whites, is led to throw that conclusion into question because B and C *still* don't budge. He observes an elapsing of time after arriving at that initial conclusion, an indefinite time of inactivity, which then jars him back into a thinking mode. Thought unfolds in time. The elapsing thereof forces him to rethink the situation, and his thoughts come in a certain chronological order and at a certain speed.

A notices that B and C still haven't budged. 'Have I made a mistake?', he asks himself. 'Let's see . . . Oh no! If I am black, then B and C haven't had to make the same hypothesis as me. Hence they're a step ahead of me. Why then have they been waiting? I must be white!'

A calculates as in the atemporal approach above: two hesitations for the price of one; his own single hesitation has in fact been equivalent to two of theirs. Those two hesitations can only mean one thing: his initial hypothesis was false.

The conclusion here is just as specious as in the above example; one might have thought that the "additional" hesitation (or elapsing time) observed by A would somehow make his conclusion better founded. But what could possibly ground a *second* hesitation when the first one is ill-gotten? A beginning and an end are necessary to define a period of time: if the period's beginning is ill-founded, signification can never be closed or completed—that time can never be constituted as such.

4 Subject to Castration: *Lacan's* Moment of Concluding

The approach Lacan adopts makes the two aforementioned lines of inquiry beside the point in certain respects. A, B, and C are, regardless of what he sustains, anything but "purely logical subjects." In Lacan's scheme of things, the sudden realization of the mistake (A's realization that B and C haven't had to make the same hypothesis as him and are thus a step ahead) throws A into a sort of panic. A senses that his previous conclusion (that he was a black) was wrong, but—not being terribly cool- or level-headed at this stage of the game—believes that to hesitate now (to take the time to think things through, for example) would spell his doom. Thus, the moment of anxiety: logical thought is cast aside, if not altogether rendered impossible, by the urgency of concluding. In a fluster, A feels that if he does not act right now, he will no longer be able to tell which way is up; he senses he will get entangled in his own reasoning and that to hesitate now would be fatal.

Lacan himself goes on to show that one (but only one) of the three prisoners *could* fail to jump to the conclusion that he is white at this particular stage in the game, and *nevertheless* correct himself later, thanks to the two suspended motions yet to come. Which is to say the jig would *not* be up were A to hesitate at this point: he would not necessarily be irrevocably thrown into error. How are we then to account for this presentiment of imminent confusion and the precipitated act Lacan attributes to the prisoners?

Lacan's explanation has little if anything to do with "purely logical subjects," as we are inclined to understand that expression: *it concerns, rather, speaking beings subject to castration anxiety.* Lacan's prisoners immediately plunge into error again: in his schema, they make yet another false supposition.

4.1 Error Two: The Dangers of Temporal Tension

While it may have been licit for A to think he was a step behind B and C while he still suspected he was black (ultimately he is not a step behind them, but according to his hypothesis he is), Lacan sustains that *once A has realized that he has made a mistake, the temporal tension he feels lingers on*: he continues to sense that the others have the jump on him.

This is a crucial moment. *A is utterly mistaken!* B and C, being in precisely the same situation as he is (the warden having pinned nothing but white discs on the prisoners), have had to make *precisely* the same presuppositions and hypotheses as he has. Were he to take the time to draw out the implications of what he has just concluded, he would realize that there is a serious discrepancy between his imaginary scenario and what is going on there behind closed doors. If he too is white, then they're all in the same boat, and have been since the word 'go!' But according to Lacan (and he is anything but loquacious on this point), A's first thought after 'Oh no! I'm not black' is *not* 'so we're all white,' but rather 'I'm a step behind!', indicative of a kind of subjective panic.

This is what brings on A's shift into action. A cannot confuse the further elapsing of time with the first elapsing of time (constituted as the time for comprehending when A concluded that he was black), having already constituted or concretized ("objectified" is Lacan's term) it as a hesitation. And A doesn't stick around to tease out nice inferences; the second hesitation (H_2)—that is, B and C's hesitation after A has decided he is black—is virtually swept aside, and is only retroactively constituted by A's jumping to conclusions. A hurdles H_2, in a sense, springing toward the door, "armed" with his conclusion (C_0). The elapsing of time that A considers a *second* hesitation, decisive in determining his true color, precipitates out as a true hesitation only as A rises to his feet and bounds for the door. This can be written as:

$$\frac{C_0}{H_2}$$

H_2 is thus the meaning of C_0, A's conclusion. We would be justified in speaking either of a simultaneous production of C_0 and H_2, or of H_2's retroactive constitution by the action C_0 brings on, schematizing the two possibilities as follows:

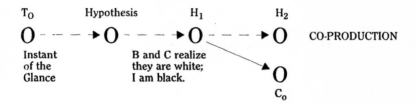

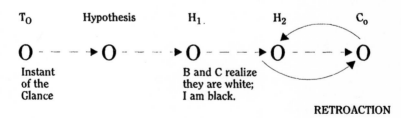

While H_1 corresponds to the time for comprehending, and is objectified by A as he erroneously equates the time it took him to think through his hypothesis with the time it took B and C to realize they must be whites because A is black (or, failing that, is objectified for A when B and C get to their feet and head for the door), H_2 corresponds to the moment of concluding, and is not, according to Lacan, objectified until the second suspended motion (I_2 for "Interruption 2") takes place.

4.2 Urgency of the Logical Movement

Lacan claims it is not due to "some dramatic contingency, the seriousness of the stakes, or the competitiveness of the game that time presses; it is due to the urgency of the logical movement. . . ." What is this "urgency of the logical movement"? Lacan sustains that if A allows himself to be beaten to this conclusion by the other prisoners, he will *no longer be able to tell* that he is not a black; if he does not conclude immediately upon thinking that he is a beat behind them, the time for comprehending loses all meaning. This is not really so. What happens is that by not concluding, H_2 is not precipitated or forged retroactively, and the moment at which B and C spring for the door can then be read as the end-point of H_1 (the time for comprehending); and at H_1, A believes he is black. *It is only by jumping the gun on the basis of specious reasoning that H_2, a crucial moment of evidence, can be brought into being.*[12]

Yet A does not *know* that: he is not aware that if he does not seize the occasion, he will *perhaps* never be able to. And even if he did know it, that would only leave him still more perplexed. Nothing makes the occasion "objectively" seizable: if he were already convinced he were white, he'd obviously seize it, but if he is still pondering the possibility of his being black, why would he seize it now simply because he could never again seize it?

Suppose you're late for an appointment on a busy street you don't know terribly well. You don't know whether the buildings on the side of the street you are on are odd or even, but you see long lines of cars coming in both directions, and you realize that if you do not cross the street now, you will not be able to do so for quite some time. Do you cross?

Here, your chances are fifty-fifty. You have no reason to believe that the house numbers on the other side of the street are more likely to be odd than even. In the three-prisoner problem, on the other hand, once A has erroneously equated T_H and T_{H1}, objectified the time for comprehending and concluded he is black, anything that controverts what he thinks should then take place (that is, that the two whites should jump to their feet) is liable to reverse his conclusion. Given the competition with B and C, he is not likely to take the time to think through every step of the process before concluding.

The street-crossing example above, however, does point to a true temptation. It applies less to some individuals than others: hysterics, for example, are, to make a gross generalization, less inclined to be anxious about being late for appointments than obsessive neurotics. Let us suppose the example involves something a bit different: catching a train or a plane to go on a much-needed vacation. (You have reservations on this one, and all the others are booked solid for the next few days.) You would, no doubt, be tempted—perhaps seriously tempted—to cross that street. And the closer the cars came, and thus the shorter the time remaining during which you could more or less safely cross, the more imperious and urgent that temptation would become.

4.3 Temporal Tension and Castration

Lacan emphasizes what he calls here "the ontological form of anxiety/angst": *"so that there may not be"* (a lagging behind engendering error), and its grammatically equivalent form, *"for fear that"* (the lagging behind might engender error). My point is that the prisoners are in no sense *aware* that their lagging behind in concluding could bring on error (just think of how many errors in reasoning they've already committed); what they are aware of is that their lagging behind in concluding may lead to their not being freed. They are quite clearly in competition with each other to be freed, and as Lacan says, when he relates the subjectification that takes place here to that which takes place in the mirror stage, "the '*I*' in question here defines itself through a subjectification of *competition* with the other, in the function of logical time"; not only, in other words, is there a specular moment in which the other (with a lower case "o") comes into play as such—the moment at which B and C contemplate one another as undefined reciprocal subjects—but *competition is what leads to a surpassing of specularity and to the assumption of a "genuinely" subjective* ("personal" in Lacan's language of the 1940s) *position*, that is, a position as subject in relation to the Other as language.

Competition here is the equivalent of the being-late-for-the-only-train-or-plane feature in the street-crossing example: it generates the *temporal tension* necessary to create a spark which will fly counter to the imaginary axis, instating a symbolic relation. A's initial errors result from his being bogged down in imaginarily considering himself to be like or unlike B and C, his rivals. The complexity of the reasoning involved in the game, the hesitating and the overriding desire to beat the others to the door ironically lead A to conclude that he is white (*like* the others), but this time not because he first makes an hypothesis that he is different from them or that their times are equivalent, but rather because he assumes (in the sense of taking upon himself) the signifying element itself: "white." Indeed, he does not even seem cognizant, in Lacan's account, of the fact that the others too are white. He resolves to conclude about *himself* on the basis of the evidence hitherto observed (though imaginarily motivated, the assumption of the symbolic order—if not of every single signifier—being dependent, no doubt, on a certain level of imaginary relations); this resolve is related to what Lacan referred to as "full speech" in the early 1950s, and clearly turns on the inauguration of a relationship between *the subject as determined by language* and language itself (the signifier "white" in this case). The spark here flies across the imaginary axis (as represented in Schema L), establishing the symbolic one.

Schema L (adapted)

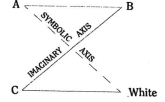

That spark is the subject. The flying of the spark is the process of subjectification. A relation is established between $S(\cancel{A})$ and some term, whether it be "white," "black," "male," or "female," the subject coming to be in that breach between them.

Let us suppose that A allows the others to precede him in concluding and thus to spur on or precipitate H_2 for themselves. A then remains stuck at H_1. Referring to H_1 and H_2 as S_1 and S_2, as I think it is fair to do, A (the prisoner as barred subject, $) is determined by S_1.

$$\frac{S_1}{\$}$$

He is weighed down by it, frozen or immobilized in a sense. Should he instead jump to his conclusion, and thus precipitate H_2 (S_2), he then takes on a new guise; no longer the static, decanted precipitate or subject of meaning ($), he comes to be *the subject in the breach* between S_1 and S_2, and his being is pegged to the a that arises under S_2:

$$S_1 \xrightarrow{\$} S_2$$
$$\overline{ a }$$

It is only by rushing towards S_2 that A (who is of course any one of the three prisoners) can acquire this other status.[13]

Temporal tension is here thus in some sense a leftover, carry-over, or spill-over from the prisoners' imaginary-level rivalry, and forces symbolization (to wit, subjectification) to take place. The subject as meaning settles out in the process: he is alienated by language, determined by the signifier "white," hence castrated. *But his castration antedates the game: had he not already succumbed to the blow of castration, he would never have precipitated the conclusion that he was white, as he does in Lacan's account.* Imagine for a moment the reaction of a psychotic to the three-prisoner predicament: he might prefer to base his conclusion on the fact that one of the other prisoners looked at him askance, or he might simply break down altogether at H_2, when the others jump to their feet, or even at I_2 (see section 7 below). Black or white for him might recall his father's skin color. $S(\cancel{A})$, called upon in every instance of symbolic identification, might be embarrassingly exposed as absent in his case.

But in theory, in any case, the "first" castration came about in the very same way: a path forged between $S(\cancel{A})$—that which has been primally repressed—and "another" signifier. Castration is no doubt always brought into play in the generation of temporal tension.

4.4 The Freudian Subject and the Lacanian Subject

According to my classification here, the emblematically *Freudian* subject is the castrated subject of meaning ($ beneath the bar): a sedimentation of meanings all involving symbolic castration, that is, alienation by and through the signifier. Freud's "*Wo Es war, soll Ich werden*" obviously suggests a *beyond* of this castrated subject of meaning, my claim being here that it is primarily Lacan who brings out, develops, and explores the implications and ramifications of that *Ich* as spark.

Lacan's innovations in psychoanalytic technique seem to me to point to a constant concern with generating temporal tension so as to shake the subject out of his or her impotent slumber, pushing it to the point where a simple letting in of the clutch suffices to start the motor. The technique of punctuation and the variable-length session which derives therefrom are designed in part to generate so much tension around particular terms—often terms which, at a particular point in an analytic process, function as master signifiers—that something gets jump-started: the subject as spark flies between a master signifier and another signifier, breaking S_1 out of its burdensome isolation, and thereby allowing for its dialectization in the analytic process.

5 Certainty and Truth

Leaving aside, for the time being, such considerations, let us now turn to Lacan's claim that the two suspended movements—which I shall refer to here as I_1 and I_2, "I" for interruption—must be integrated into the logical process, that being, in Lacan's mind, one of the thorniest objections to the reasoning presented in the perfect solution. According to Lacan, when any one of the prisoners seizes upon the conclusion that he is a white, he seizes it as something of which he is sure:

> What makes this act so remarkable in the subjective assertion demonstrated
> by the sophism is that it anticipates its own certainty owing to the temporal

tension with which it is subjectively charged; that, based on this very anticipation, its certainty is verified in a logical precipitation determined by the discharge of this tension—so that in the end the conclusion is no longer grounded on anything but completely objectified temporal instances. . . .

Stated more simply, *subjective* certainty already exists at the moment of concluding (C_0), but its status as objective truth has in no sense yet been ascertained. Certainty, interestingly enough, has been attained without an assessment of truth-value having been carried out beforehand. That assessment or demonstration only comes about after the action (*viz.* heading for the door) manifesting that the prisoner has already concluded.

   Certainty and truth are clearly not birds of a feather. Subjective certitude arises here first, the most highly desubjectified sort of verification (as non-subjective as possible) only taking place afterwards. Certainty crystallizes at C_0, verification only being completed after the second interruption, I_2.

T_0	Hypothesis	H_1	H_2	C_0	I_1	I_2

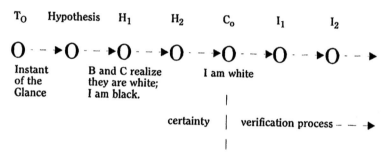

Instant of the Glance	B and C realize they are white; I am black.	I am white

certainty | verification process – – ➤

According to Lacan, I_1 and I_2 are crucial to the working out of the problem: the three prisoners do not seem to him able to make for the door together without doubting their subjective certainty. The very fact that A sees the other two get up at the same time as him throws him into a state of perplexity, putting a stop to his doorward motion.

   Why is this so? Can't we imagine A simply saying to himself, 'Oh that's right, we're all whites and we all must have reasoned in the same way,' and continuing blithely for the door? Why would the three prisoners stop at all once they've started for the door?

   It must be kept in mind here that Lacan is seeking a logically supported conclusion, and does not seem satisfied with the subjective assertion and certainty already acquired by the prisoners. The prison warden demands that their conclusions be based on logical grounds alone, and while subjectivity has been precipitated here, the appropriate sacrifice on logic's altar has not yet been made.

The two hesitations discerned by each prisoner sufficed to allow him to make his subjective assertion, but not to logically confirm, *beyond the shadow of a doubt*, his conclusion.

One of the problems with Lacan's solution here is that it seems to want to stand in for both a *phenomenologically predictive* model and a process whereby a logical proof is completed. In any case, Lacan's disclaimer—his 'test it if you like, but don't expect to get the same results' caveat—shows that it is not the predictive aspect that interests him here.[14] Still, one senses a sort of tug-of-war between what it seems likely that the prisoners *would* do, and what they *have* to do if logical criteria are to be satisfied.

The fact here is that they need two bits of objective evidence, corresponding to the two subjectively determined hesitations, H_1 and H_2. As we recall, T_H was equated by A with the time it took him to think through what he erroneously thought B and C were thinking. And H_2 was literally hurdled over in A's race to the truth.[15]

In any case, though I_1 becomes associated with H_2 and I_2 with H_1 (I will explain how and why in a moment), they do not have the same status as signifiers and no spark or precipitation of subjectivity is generated between them. A, B, and C seem to proceed calmly from I_1 to I_2 to the door with nary a jolt. Nothing is jump-started or precipitated out here.

Temporal tension culminates as the prisoners bound for the door at C_o—subjectivity is there at its climax; from then on, tension is released and the subject slips away as a formal proof unfolds. Truth, as Lacan uses the term here, is only ascertained at the very end, that is, after the two suspended motions. Certainty precedes it. "Truth" here, as in classical logic, is the result of a deduction from premises and propositions: 1. two blacks::one white, 2. I_1, and 3. I_2. It gives us nothing that could not be laid out in the form of an utterly banal argument, the conclusion of which Lacan states in the following thoroughly desubjectified form: "One must know that one is a white when the others have hesitated twice in leaving."

What is, however, unusual about truth here is that, in order to arrive at it, at least two of the three prisoners must *presume* it. Now that is a rather original claim concerning the nature of truth: if it is not presumed, it will never be confirmed. *Truth only comes to be verified through its presumption. Truth depends upon a tendency which aims at the truth.*

Le petit Robert 1: "*Présomption. n.f., 1 • Opinion fondée seulement sur des apparences.*" Opinion based on appearances alone. "*Conjecture, supposition.*"

Isn't this everyday fare for police officers in search of confessions? They confront their suspects with full-blown conjectures for which they have very little evidence, but which experience leads them to construct; their tendency to thus aim at the truth is often what allows them to flush out the truth, to elicit confessions through inadvertent words like "No, it was on the counter to the right" (the knife) pronounced by a suspect caught off guard by the overwhelming veracity of the account.

The difference here is that the tendency aiming at the truth is a trait of the same subject whose truth is on the line. And whereas one might be inclined to associate truth in the three-prisoner problem with the *real* color of the prisoners' discs, this is belied by the example with which Lacan closes the article: that of the precipitation of sexual identity. It seems unlikely that, even at this early stage in his work, Lacan associated "sexuation" (gender identity, we might say in English) with biologically sexual characteristics. One can thus "erroneously" identify oneself as male when one has biologically female genitalia.[16]

Truth must thus be distinguished from biological reality here, just as identification must be understood apart from considerations of true and false. *Identification is neither correct nor incorrect*: identification (which always has a symbolic component) always takes place on the basis of false premises, always involves error, and leads to better or worse results from a social-adaptation point of view. That a boy may identify with a particular trait of his father's has nothing to do with correctness or incorrectness. It just is.

6 Action and Castration

Another interesting feature of Lacan's view of truth here is its association with action, falsehood (or error) being associated with inertia. The action associated with truth is not, however, just any old action, but action manifesting subjectification (a kind of "full act," akin to "full speech"), inevitably resulting in a loss; inertia, on the other hand, smacks of castration, and stems from a refusal to give up anything, in this case to sacrifice one's hesitation and stop wavering—a telltale mark of castration. Hesitation here indicates an inability or unwillingness to precipitate something, to presume something or make a conjecture for which one may suffer adverse consequences. The hesitating prisoner is afraid of putting himself on the line, of going out on a limb and taking chances. This is an example of typically obsessive behavior: a refusal to decide anything until one is absolutely sure (and can one ever be absolutely sure?). The obsessive here wallows in his castration: his refusal to give up anything, to take a chance and risk failure is determinant; he will not allow himself to go beyond a state of impotent hesitation. (It is only when the other two have gotten up, convinced that they are whites, that he will deign to rise to his feet, finally convinced he must be black.)

In Lacan's Seminar XV, *The Analytic Act*, acts are shown to be intimately related to object *a*. While castration is not said to be altogether annihilated in the traversing or crossing of the fundamental fantasy, it seems clear that in order to engage in some sort of genuine act, something must be let go of: something must be sacrificed. The subject must assume the position or function of object–the lost object, like castration, being more or less momentarily swept aside here.

I will not take up the many fine points of Lacan's discussion concerning action, but it does seem clear that in the act, castration is in a sense suppressed, incorporated, and surpassed: *aufgehoben*. In this sense, the Lacanian subject is a going beyond or exceeding of what I've been calling the Freudian subject: the subject as determined by castration.

7 Suspended Motions

Let us now examine the suspended motions I_1 and I_2 in greater detail. Suppose for the time being that all three prisoners have jumped to the conclusion that they are white. According to Lacan, they continue to manifest uncertainty about their conclusion. After setting off for the door, they begin to doubt whether or not they have really grasped the moment of concluding. Lacan does not explain why, but it seems likely that they doubt anew in his model because none of them had been expecting that all three of them would rise simultaneously (and because doubt is an essential element of subjectivity). Lacan claims that it is the second hesitation, H_2, which is momentarily thrown into question here (not the first), and that, while it has already been *subjectively experienced* by the prisoners, it is not yet objectified, but merely *subjectively reappropriated*: 'If I am white, then we are all white.' And the prisoners resume their race toward the door.

But "[e]ach of the subjects, having reappropriated the subjective certainty of the *moment of concluding*, can once again throw it into question"–"can" logically or phenomenologically? Why on earth would any of the prisoners now lapse back into doubt? The question that seems to linger in the prisoners' minds (nowhere elaborated in the article) is: 'Have they really hesitated twice, or just once?' The first suspended motion, I_1, now counts for them as one full-fledged hesitation, already objectified in any case by the erroneous equation of T_H with T_{H1}. But each prisoner *could* now *theoretically* say to himself, 'perhaps I am black, and the two whites I see have only just now fully realized they are whites.' (It seems a bit far-fetched, but whereas, when they were busy jumping to conclusions, at least two out of three of our prisoners were anything but obsessive, here they revert to their fully obsessive "natural" state: if any remaining doubt exists, it must be exploited to the utmost. Every subsisting doubt must be reduced to nought before the prisoner is prepared to really bound for the door– such are Lacan's "purely logical subjects.")

Each of the prisoners stops short a second time, thinking that he is perhaps black. But the second interrupted motion, I_2, short as it may be, suffices to convince them beyond the shadow of a doubt that they are whites like the others. For had A been black, B and C should not have stopped a second time: one single suspended motion suffices for B and C to realize they are whites if A is a black.

I_1 is said by Lacan to refer back to H_2, which is thereby subjectively reconfirmed. I_2, on the other hand, now uses I_1 *as though it were* H_1,[17] and confirms the second hesitation H_2: "The subjective time of the *moment of concluding* is at last objectified here." I_1 and I_2—objectively observable interruptions (observable by outside observers)—have thus successfully supplanted H_1 and H_2. The prison warden now knows what the prisoners have concluded even before hearing them out. Whereas H_1 and H_2 came into play as *signifiers*, revealing to the prisoners something about what they could not see (something involving their own subjectivity), I_1 and I_2 are *signs* available to all spectators. The sign has something inherently objective about it, representing as it does *something* to *someone*—here the two signs tell the prison warden that all three prisoners are convinced they are whites. The signifier, on the contrary, seems to have something inherently subjective about it, representing as it does the subject to another signifier, the subject coming to be in the "interval" (temporal not spatial) between H_1 and H_2.

Thus, Lacan's implicit contention here is that the initial elapsing of time before the prisoners stride toward the door is of no *objective* value whatsoever. Nothing can be deduced therefrom. Contrariwise, the warden can conclude that one single suspended motion (I_1) means one black and two whites, and that two suspended motions $(I_1$ and $I_2)$ mean three whites.

For the one prisoner who has, let us suppose, arrived at C_0 (the moment of concluding) convinced he is a black, the demonstration (starting after C_0, thus once the prisoners are all in motion already, though their motion remains unexplained here) takes the form of a sort of empirical induction:

I see two whites: therefore no one can leave immediately.

Everyone stops: I must be black and the others white.

Everyone stops again: they shouldn't have stopped if I were black, therefore I am white.

8 The Limits of Structure

In this latter situation, the assertion is "desubjectified to the utmost," and can be expressed in the following form: "One must know that one is a white when the others have hesitated twice in leaving." This situation comes very close to representing the workings of structure alone. The prisoner who does not jump to conclusions, simply going through the motions and fulfilling the requirements of a formal proof, demonstrates for us the full extent of the playing out in isolation of structural constraints. He fits the description of the noetic subject mentioned above, a type of subject expressed only in the third person singular: "one knows that . . ." Such a subject can as easily be table, washbasin, ego, or whatever. The expression "desubjectified to the utmost" means that the assertion is not *altogether* desubjectified; something remains that Lacan was willing to relate to subjectivity at that time, but it is not to be equated with the full-fledged subject of Freud's "*soll Ich werden*," reflected in a sense in Lacan's "I hastened to conclude that I was a white. . . ." Whereas the noetic subject is but the bare bones, the structural, positional precondition of the human *parlêtre* or speaking being, *the subject who presumes* takes that infinitely small and at the same time infinitely large step between structure and subjectivity.

We see here how Lacan pursues ever further structure's ground or turf, extending virtually indefinitely the frontiers of structure's dominion. We also see, however, how he shows where structure leaves off, and subjectivity comes in.

Notes

1. *Écrits* 1966; English translation by Marc Silver and Bruce Fink in *Newsletter of the Freudian Field*, 2, 1988.

2. *Oxford English Dictionary*.

3. According to Lacan, the noetic subject "can be as easily god, table or washbasin," reminding us here of the talking podium in "The Freudian Thing" (*Écrits*) which, as a stand-in there for the ego of Anglo-American ego psychology, suggests that the ego as postulated by the latter theoretical perspective has no more elevated a status than that of the noetic subject.

4. Had Lacan presented the time for comprehending as I'm doing here, one might have been able to claim that Lacan persists in qualifying the perfect solution as sophistic precisely because of this error crucial to the solution of the problem.

5. This precipitation of subjectivity takes the form here of jumping to conclusions, or jumping the gun.

6. Suppose I too am white: if B and C imagine themselves to be whites, without ever considering the possibility, even for but a moment, that they are blacks, no one will ever be sure of anything (at least I can't imagine how they could be; we might all just eventually get up and head for the door; well let's try another tack). If anything is to happen, B and C must thus imagine themselves to be blacks. B then says to himself: "A and C each see one white and one black; as neither A nor C immediately ran for the door,

they must both soon realize they are whites and head for the door together. As they have not budged, I must in fact be white." The reasoning process is thus a bit longer, but nothing seems to logically exclude its being adopted by any one of the prisoners: for how could he know in advance that the others would get the jump on him if he assumed he were white instead of black, without having first thought through the whole problem?

7. My claim that the prisoners first suppose they are white *not* for some logical motive, but rather because of a psychological premise, by no means undermines Lacan's argument; it suggests instead that there is an unstated premise at work therein—and I will mention others as we go along—which must be flushed out and examined. This is true of a great many "purely logical" arguments, and the premises here revolve in large part around a particular conception of speaking beings.

8. Alain Badiou, in his critique of Lacan's argumentation in his *Théorie du sujet* (Paris: Éditions du Seuil, 1982), pp. 264–274, fails to include the equating and subsequent "disequating" of times in his own three-step reschematization of the prisoners' reasoning (involving steps he designates as R1, R2, and R3, where $R1 \subset R2 \subset R3$); while his approach is perhaps more logical, strictly speaking, than Lacan's, I would sustain that it eliminates all temporal tension and thus leaves no room for subjectification in the Lacanian sense. I quite agree with his view that "There must thus be something *that Lacan does not mention*" (p. 269), that is, a supplemental premise, but I hardly believe that one could qualify it by saying that "My awareness of haste derives from the fact that the other is perhaps a cretin"! (p. 270). In turning the three-prisoner problem to his own purposes, whereby the game leads to a "free subject" and exemplifies Badiou's *own* notion of subjectification, Badiou not so much criticizes what Lacan proposes (though quite legitimately pointing out that his prisoners do not behave like purely logical subjects) as makes a different problem of it. His account is thus interesting in its own right, but fails to take seriously Lacan's latent premises.

9. Not until later in the game, in any case, for he could in fact objectify it on the basis of the suspended motions which, for B and C, come after their conclusion that they are whites.

10. One might object that H_1 and "I am black" are real "if" statements, that is, hypotheses. But H_1 is now a bona fide premise, not a hypothesis. The argument can thus be restated as:

Suppose I am black.

H_1

Then they are a step ahead: $\sim H_1$

H' and H"

Therefore I am white.

11. The error involved in equating the times in the three-prisoner problem also seems related to the three step creation/genesis of the signifier, as Lacan hypotheses it in Seminar IX, *Identification*: 1. a trace (physical or mnemic), 2. the erasure or forgetting

of the trace, and 3. a circle drawn around the space where the trace had been. Associating the trace here with the instant of the glance, I might suggest we see the lopping off or forgetting of this first time (as A mistakenly equates T_H and T_{H1}) as necessary for something to be symbolized. Something inherent to the construction/generation of the signifier itself is embodied in the game.

12. Should he fail to jump the gun, the time for comprehending is thereby prolonged, spilling over into the moment of concluding. That would not be a fatal error for one of the three prisoners—he being able to correct himself thanks to the two interruptions—though if two of them made the same "mistake," no such correction would be possible.

13. What could we say is produced in the process by way of a lost object, cause of desire? The word "black," a kind of remainder of the signifying material mobilized in the situation, that will henceforth be part and parcel of each prisoner's fantasy?

14. Still I cannot help but find his insistence on the distinction between the subjective certainty of the assertion and the objective or maximally desubjectified final conclusion somewhat exaggerated from a later Lacanian point of view.

15. Why he was so hot-blooded prior to C_0 and becomes so cool-headed afterward is a mystery we must no doubt set aside here.

16. See Lacan's formulas of sexuation in Seminar XX, *Encore,* for example, discussed in my article "'There's No Such Thing As a Sexual Relationship': Existence and the Formulas of Sexuation," *Newsletter of the Freudian Field,* 5, 1991, and in chapter 8 of my *The Lacanian Subject: Between Language and Jouissance* (Princeton: Princeton University Press, 1995).

17. Which has already been "objectified," as we recall. Is I_1 supposed to be "more objective" than H_1?—it seems to be so, in any case, to an outside observer, and at least it is not ill-founded like H_1.

THE ETHICS OF HYSTERIA
AND OF PSYCHOANALYSIS

∞

Vicente Palomera

With Lacan, we can read Freud's texts using the principles they put forward. In his teaching, Lacan constantly returned to these texts to take Freud at his word. As you know, the "return to Freud" was the effect of Lacan's transference onto Freud, and constituted a rereading of the Freudian discovery which was not without consequences, as it renewed a theory and a practice that was beginning to flag.

It is well known that Freud inaugurated an entirely new mode of human relations by listening to hysterics. The birth of psychoanalysis depended on this encounter with hysteria, but we should actually ask ourselves—as Lacan himself did—where have the hysterics of yesterday gone? Those marvellous women, the Anna O's and Emmy von N's, whose lives belong to a lost world. Lacan related the birth of psychoanalysis to Victorian times, since Victoria was she who knew how to impose her ideals in an era which bears her name. Lacan said in his seminar, "This kind of havoc was necessary to produce what I call an awakening." Do hysterics now wreak havoc in the social field?

How, on the other hand, do psychoanalysts of the International Psychoanalytical Association (IPA) face the question of the existence or non-existence of hysteria? The word has disappeared as such from certain psychiatric manuals. In one of the last International Congresses of Psychoanalysis, there was a panel dedicated to hysteria in which psychoanalysts of different persuasions discussed hysteria. Many of them held that hysteria is only a defensive technique to maintain at a distance and under control anxieties which are defined as "primitive," "psychotic," and "asexual." To define hysteria as a defense is not new, and was already thought of by the Kleinians and, for instance, Fairbairn. I'd like to show you how these definitions were bound to lead to confusion, as we can see today. Generally speaking, psychoanalysts have shied away from the challenge of hysteria.

The Hysteric's Discourse

First of all, the hysteric is a particular subject, one who puts her division in the place of power. In the second place, there is an ethics of hysteria, an ethics which is not in the service of the "goods" industry. Psychoanalysis is not an ethics of goods either. The ethics of hysteria is an ethics of *deprivation*, which doesn't mean an ethics of generosity (of giving), but on the contrary, an ethics of dispossession (giving up). It is true that this position, at the very heart of hysteria—the pure hysterical position—is not often fully arrived at, but the hysteric very often affirms her dispossession with ferocity, occasionally achieving sacrifice.

This dispossession is presented to us as a complaint. The most fundamental complaint of hysterics is that of their *lack of identity*, a lack that Lacan wrote with a symbol, $, which means that the subject is separated from her being, and thus from identity, which is why she identifies easily with others. By "unconscious," Freud meant a level where something thinks, where you find articulated thoughts (*Gedanken*). Yet at the unconscious level, you cannot say: "I am"; in fact, you are dispossessed of being. Thus, the unconscious is a level where there is no "self-consciousness," where the subject doesn't find a way of naming herself, because she lacks the fundamental referent, the "I am." By means of $, Lacan transformed Descartes' *cogito ergo sum*, a statement which indicated a level at which the subject would be able to think "therefore I am," that is, a level at which, according to Descartes, you would be able to obtain the certainty of being.

What the hysterical subject intensifies and overtly manifests is this lack of certainty, the lack of an identifying signifier. Hysteria shows up through a void of identification ($) which the subject transforms into a question presented to anyone who occupies the position of master of knowledge (S_1): $ $\rightarrow$ S_1.

Hysteria is a discourse, and like every discourse it implies two partners. In the hysteric's discourse, Lacan isolates one of the partners as the divided subject ($) and the other as the master signifier, or the master who embodies it (S_1). So you have, first, occupying the position of agent, the subject addressing a demand to the Other, the master, that is, commanding the master. The agent's position is a position of power. In analytic discourse, that position is occupied by object a; the object commands the subject to fulfill a certain task, $a \rightarrow$ $.

The first time Lacan wrote his four discourses (see *"Radiophonie"*) he defined hysteria as the divided subject, that is to say as the unconscious in action: "The unconscious in action challenging the master to produce knowledge." What is important here is the identification of hysteria with the divided subject. But, on the other hand, Lacan says clearly enough that the hysteric is also a mastering subject: she occupies the position of agent.

Though you may easily illustrate this with any case of hysteria, I'd rather choose one which is well known to you. Everyone here knows the popular conception of Florence Nightingale, the self-sacrificing woman, the maiden who threw aside the pleasures of a life of ease to help the afflicted, the "Lady of the Lamp," as she was nicknamed, consecrating with her goodness the soldier's deathbed. I have taken Lytton Strachey's picture of Florence Nightingale because one recognizes therein the portrait of a hysteric (*Eminent Victorians*, Penguin Modern Classics, 1980). He describes a hysteric, insofar as Florence's position with men consisted in putting them to work, right up until her death. She wanted to satisfy her vocation to be a nurse. This was her *want* (in both senses of the word), a want that not only remained fixed immovably in her heart, but grew in intensity day by day. To become a nurse implied dispossession. She had brushed aside with disdain and loathing the attractions of her aristocratic milieu. Her lovers had been nothing to her, and she refused to get married. In her thirty-first year, she noted in her diary: "I see nothing desirable but death." Florence made her choice and refused a certain happiness for a visionary good she might never achieve.

The Crimean War broke out, and she was thirty-four when she arrived at Scutari; the organization of the hospitals was horrific, the conditions were indescribable: shortages of everything, confusion, diseases, dysentery, misery, filth, that is, the very image of jouissance. Florence came into that inferno, transforming it into a militarily organized hospital. A passionate idolatry spread among the men, and Strachey summarizes it with these words: "The soldiers kissed her shadow as it passed." A soldier said: "Before she came there was cussin' and swearin', but after that it was as holy as a church." She succeeded in eliminating that jouissance, not without a certain heroism.

Back in England, the Lady of the Lamp fell seriously ill. She suffered from fainting spells and terrible attacks, a mysterious illness that plagued her until her death at the age of ninety-one. "Wherever she went . . . she was haunted by a ghost," says Strachey, "It was the specter of Scutari." I find this a nice way of saying that, in the end, "Scutari" became the signifier that represented Florence ($S_1/\$$). Nevertheless, Strachey wrote that "a demon possessed her," giving her a signifier, precisely when she had rejected every signifier and showing thereby that she was not subjected to or fixated upon any master signifier, but possessed by something mortifying.

The hysteric puts the master to work to produce knowledge, says Lacan. Florence shows this very well. Let's take, for instance, her relationship with Sidney Herbert—who later became War Minister, and who tried to be a man in accordance with Florence's wishes—and then with Arthur Clough, her secretary, and Dr. Sutherland. None of them were men, only fake copies in Florence's eyes. Strachey summarizes it very well: "She worked like a slave in a mine. She began to believe, as she had begun to believe at Scutari, that none of her fellow workers had their hearts in the business; if they had, why did they not work as she did? She could only see slackness and stupidity around her. Dr. Sutherland of course was grotesquely muddle-headed, and Arthur Clough incurably lazy. Even Sidney Herbert . . . oh yes! he had simplicity and candor and quickness of perception, no doubt, but he was an eclectic; and what could one hope for from a man. . . ."

As the years passed, Florence sought consolation in the writings of the mystics, and also in corresponding with Mr. Jowett, who acted as her spiritual adviser. But how could he succeed where the others had failed? Jowett was entirely devoted to her, but Florence felt that she gave more sympathy than she received. "Her tongue, one day, could not refrain from shouting out at him: 'He comes to me, and he talks to me,' she said, 'as if I were someone else.'" With a sentence like this we immediately realize the nature of the hysteric's discourse: the subject ($) in the position of agent, addressing a demand to the master (S_1) to produce knowledge (S_2) which is impotent to speak the subject's truth (a).

$$\frac{\$}{a} \longrightarrow \frac{S_1}{\text{impotence} \quad S_2}$$

The hysteric presents herself precisely as lacking knowledge: "Cure me!" she cries, "try to know what I have!" As a result, like Jowett, the analyst cannot do so. He is impotent in his knowledge of what will cure her. In this sense, hysteria is a challenge.

We don't know much more about Florence. She died leaving nothing but a veil, the very veil she used to wear when she strolled in the park twice a month. What did she hide behind that veil? Strachey sees the visible nothingness she had converted into omnipotence her whole life long: "The thin, angular woman, with her haughty eye and her acrid mouth, had vanished; and in her place was the rounded, bulky form of a fat old lady, smiling all day long. Then something else became visible. The brain which had been steeled at Scutari was indeed, literally growing soft. Senility descended. Towards the end, consciousness itself grew lost in a roseate haze, and melted into nothingness."

Why had she sacrificed all her life? It is an enigma. What we do know is that she didn't give up her sacrifice and that she eluded herself as a question.

Now, thanks to Strachey and going back to Lacan's teaching on hysterical discourse, we are able to reread not only Florence Nightingale's portrait, but also hysterical discourse as such: the hysterical subject is an agent; secondly, she is a subject who eludes herself as object (Florence died without giving away her secret); and thirdly, she is a subject who sacrifices herself.

The Particularity of Hysteria in Lacan's Work

Let us turn now to Lacan's teaching on hysteria.

The first two features I have just given you may seem contradictory: there you see the hysteric defined as subject ($), in the position of agent or power, but I have also said that the hysteric is defined as object. I shall try to show you that there is no contradiction at all.

We can organize Lacan's teaching on hysteria into four periods:

1. 1936 to 1949: The Period of the Mirror Stage

With the mirror stage Lacan formalizes many clinical facts, with a great economy of concepts, after having isolated the imaginary relationship. In the English edition of the *Écrits* (pp. 4–5), you find hysteria defined by means of the fragmented body: "This fragmented body usually manifests itself in dreams when the movement of analysis encounters a certain level of aggressive disintegration in the individual. It then appears in the form of disjointed limbs, or of those organs represented in exoscopy, growing wings and taking up arms for intestinal persecutions. . . . But this form is even tangibly revealed at the organic level, in the lines of 'fragilization' that define the anatomy of fantasy, as exhibited in the schizoid and spasmodic symptoms of hysteria." The fragmentation in hysteria, referred to in the mirror stage, is an early reference to the absence of identification with Woman.

2. 1957: The Hysteric's Question

In "*La psychanalyse et son enseignement*" (*Écrits* 1966), Lacan defines hysteria as an imaginary reversal. We already have a matheme, Schema L. This schema signifies that the condition of the subject is dependent on what unfolds in the Other (A). What unfolds there is articulated like a discourse. This schema indicates an opposition between the imaginary and the symbolic:

 Schema L

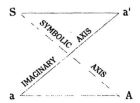

In this schema, a-a' is the relation to the partner, the body image, and the partner's body, as it is developed in the mirror stage.

With the dotted axis, Lacan writes the symbolic relationship, from the subject to the Other, the Other as the locus of language which precedes the advent of the subject in the world. This axis implies a subject, a subject who is presented with the question of his existence, "What am I there?" A question that is posed by the subject to the Other, since it depends on what unfolds in the Other. Lacan says neurosis is a question which finds its strictures in this Other, and it is in the Other too that are posited "the terms without which the subject, whether hysteric or obsessive, cannot accede to the notion of his/her facticity, with respect to his/her sex in the case of the one, and with respect to his/her existence in the case of the Other" (p. 451).

The key to understanding this paragraph is the word "facticity" with its reference to "thingness," a word which designates that in the Other, the locus of all signifiers, signifiers are lacking, that is, the signifiers with which to articulate one's sex and one's existence are lacking. Later in his teaching, Lacan uses the word "real" instead of "facticity."

Hysteria accentuates the facticity of sex. This translates the lack of an identifying signifier for femininity. So when the question is "What is a woman?," this describes the neurosis we call hysteria. It is from this question—"What is a woman?" and unconsciously, "am I a man or a woman?," and at the moment when there is an answer to that question—that the hysterical subject gives a privileged place to another woman, or to *the* other woman, the Woman who would know what it means to be a woman. Nevertheless, there can be other answers; for instance, I am thinking of an analysand whose particularity is that she collects men, and that is her way of trying to learn how to be a woman who would be worthy of the name.

Lacan wrote that the hysterical position is an imaginary inversion, a certain kind of response to her question. Every structure has its question and provides an answer. Thus, the hysteric's answer to her question about sex, to her impossibility to say what a woman is, creates a scene in which she identifies with the opposite sex. It implies an imaginary reversal: instead of identifying with her own sex, she identifies with men.

All this is due to a deficiency at the level of identification, as Freud teaches us, a lack of narcissistic identification. It is like having an anatomy she cannot inhabit. Let us take Dora, for instance: she cannot situate herself where her anatomy summons her to do so; she is fascinated by Frau K, though she identifies with Herr K. You can see this imaginary reversal in another text as well: "Intervention on Transference" (*Écrits* 1966), presented in 1951. It is a perfect example of a critical re-reading of Freud's texts, where Lacan re-reads the question of Dora's symptoms using the mirror stage. There is, first, Dora's identification with her father, favored by the latter's sexual impotence. This identification showed through all the conversion symptoms presented by Dora, a large number of which were removed by this discovery. Second, Lacan wondered why Freud failed to see that Dora's aphonia, which occurred during Herr K's absences, was an expression of her oral erotic drive when Dora was left face to face with Frau K, there having been no need for Freud to mention her awareness that her father had been the object of oral sex.

As you may know, Lacan interpreted Dora's aphonia as an effect of her identification with her father, since "everyone knows that cunnilingus is the artifice most commonly adopted by 'men of means' whose powers begin to abandon them." Had Dora gained access to the recognition of her femininity, she wouldn't have had to remain open to that functional fragmentation (here Lacan referred explicitly to the mirror stage) which constitutes a conversion symptom. Third, in the same direction, Lacan interpreted Dora's pregnancy fantasy and transitory neuralgia as resulting from her identification with Herr K, that is to say, as a function of her virile identification after the rupture which followed the declaration at the lakeside, the catastrophe on the heels of which Dora fell ill. In short, Lacan interpreted all her symptoms as the effect of virile identification. Her symptoms depended on imaginary alienation as seen in the mirror stage.

All this allowed Lacan, in Seminar II, dedicated to the ego and its functions, to make a very precise variation, one which anticipated the discourse of the master: "How can a woman take the place of the master?" Lacan re-read a clinical case taken from a Kleinian, Fairbairn. It involved a woman who suffered from what they used to call "depressive phases." It's a very nice case of narcissistic alienation known as "the woman with the tiny vagina." After all, in this case, you find something real—a tiny vagina—which puts this woman in the position of having to deal with *Penisneid* in a very peculiar way. This example was taken up by Lacan only to criticize the notion of "partial object" commonly used at that time—because her symptom seemed to be the aggression and then the twisting of her own aggression—according to the classic Kleinian sequence "aggression-guilt-depression." Lacan threw overboard all such references to partial drives by saying that all her difficulties and dealings with men were related to the fact that man was her own image, and that that was what she constantly encountered. Aside from that, it is a very important case because we are able to see the distinction between the function of the phallus as a signifier, the penis, and the imaginary genital: in the case of this woman this is marked by a feature of anatomical reality.

3. 1960: Hysterical Sacrifice

In "Subversion of the Subject and the Dialectic of Desire in the Freudian Unconscious" (*Écrits*) there is an important shift in Lacan's teaching. We find a subtle transformation of his previous formulations therein which is the consequence of his having introduced object *a* and the matheme of fantasy: ($ ◊ *a*).

First, you have the subject, divided as an effect of the signifying chain ($); it is no longer biological prematuration that is at stake, following the mirror stage, but a subject who has lost a part of himself, who has been wounded by language. As a result, the subject is not a whole but rather a half. Lacan's idea is that the subject who speaks is a subject who has lost a part. And fantasy depends on that. In the matheme, we see the subject ($) and object *a* placed in opposition.

How does Lacan define hysteria in that article? He defines it in the following way: "Indeed, the neurotic, whether hysteric, obsessive, or, more radically, phobic, is he who identifies the lack in the Other with his demand (D). As a result, the Other's demand assumes the function of an object in his fantasy, that is to say, his fantasy ($ ◊ *a*) is reduced to the drive ($ ◊ D). . . . In the case of the hysteric, desire is maintained only through the lack of satisfaction that is introduced . . . when she slips away as object" (p. 321).

Here Lacan defines the hysteric by putting her in the place of the object, where she operates by slipping away. Lacan also indicates that when she slips away she gets something, she maintains desire, she maintains lack through a refusal of satisfaction. As a result you have dissatisfaction. To keep desire unsatisfied is thus the hysteric's motto. It means two things: to make the Other desire and also to keep desiring oneself. That is very close to the phenomenology of the seduction phantasy discovered by Freud, because it is the Other—the father—who is situated as the agent of desire, and the subject fantasizes herself as being in the place of the object the Other lacks.

On the other hand, to slip away as object implies the presence of the Other she slips away from. In fact, she first and foremost needs the presence of the partner, and sometimes she complains about this *alienation*, saying that she is not autonomous. At the same time, besides this alienation there is also her triumph over the Other, which gives us an idea of what a mastering subject is. Let us recall Fairbairn's case cited by Lacan. The hysteric is a subject who tries to be the master of desire, as the Lady of the Lamp shows us, to make desire burst into flames, in the sense of the Freudian equation "phallus (the signifier of desire) = fire." Sometimes, the hysteric—think of Rider Haggard's book *She*— doesn't know how much longer this position will sustain her (at the end of *She*, the guide, instead of finding immortality for herself and the others, perishes in the mysterious subterranean fire). Thus, the hysterical position is to elude herself as object (to refuse jouissance and to cause desire).

The hysterical subject doesn't want to offer up her division to the Other's jouissance. That is shown in the intrigue (Lacan spoke of "hysterical intrigue"). Here also her sacrifice, that is to say, her intrigue, implies a renunciation of a share of jouissance: she refuses a part of jouissance to the Other and, at the same time, deprives herself of jouissance. She finds satisfaction in her sacrifice. In this regard, Lacan made a very precise remark, in reference to the dream of the beautiful butcher's wife: "She didn't know what Dora knew." What does that mean? Both were hysterics, but Dora was nearer to knowing that what she wanted was deprivation: She wanted to leave Frau K. to men. In "*La psychanalyse et son enseignement*," Lacan pointed out: "The hysteric offers the woman in whom she adores her own mystery to the man whose role she assumes without being able to enjoy it." What the butcher's wife didn't know was that she would find satisfaction by leaving her husband to the other woman.

What the hysterical subject intensifies and manifests is this raising of deprivation to an absolute level, which can eventually manifest itself by the rejection of every master signifier. She is a subject who says no to identifying with the unary signifier (S_1).

4. 1973: The Being of Lack

In 1973, Lacan wrote an introduction to the German edition of the *Écrits*. There he went back to the dream of the butcher's wife and took it as the paradigm of hysteria: "I'm not lavish with examples, but when I proffer them, I elevate them to the status of paradigms." "There is no common denominator of hysteria, and what identification plays on in hysterics is structure, not meaning, as is shown by the fact that it bears on desire, that is, on lack taken as an object, not on the cause of lack" (*Scilicet*, 5, p. 15). That is to say, the hysterical subject demands being, but not just any being; she demands the being of lack. What characterizes hysteria is that the hysteric identifies with a lack of desire, not with its cause. In saying this, Lacan went back to his formulation in "The Direction of the Treatment" (*Écrits*): The desire of the butcher's wife—the question by which she identifies with a man—is to be the phallus (in this text Lacan defines the phallus as the signifier of lack, that is, the signifier of desire). To be the phallus does not provide surplus jouissance; it means being the signifier which indicates the ever present lack in the Other (the slice of smoked salmon in the dream takes on the role of the lack in the Other). In short, what is at stake in hysteria is to be the lack or nothing of desire (the nothing here is an object). The hysteric puts this void in the place of the object, she shows up through this void, transforming it into an eternal question. Hysterical dissatisfaction is correlated with her way of sustaining herself in being as nothing.

Sometimes the hysterical subject takes this position to the point of self-sacrifice. We saw this, for instance, in the case of Florence Nightingale. She sacrificed everything to be a nurse, brushed aside the charms and attractions of her aristocratic environment, refused marriage, and fled from her own country. She was ferocious with men and her heroism went beyond all human considerations. Although her ideals proved her discontent with any master signifier, she called for a new desire, allowing her to struggle against what Lacan called "*la dégradation communautaire de l'entreprise sociale,*" the blind alleys of the Other.

HEGEL WITH LACAN,
OR THE SUBJECT AND ITS CAUSE

∞

Slavoj Žižek

Lacan: From Hermeneutics to the Cause

Lacan's opening gesture consists of an unconditional espousal of hermeneutics. In the first two seminars, he opposes determinism in the name of (psychoanalysis as) a hermeneutic approach: "All analytic experience is an experience of signification" (Seminar II, 325). Here originates the great Lacanian motif of the *futur antérieur* of symbolization: a fact counts not as *factum brutum*, but only as it is always-already historicized. (What is at stake in the anal stage, for example, is not excretion as such but how the child makes sense of it: as a submission to the Other's—that is, parent's—demand, as a triumph of his control, etc.) This Lacan can be easily translated into the later problematic of antipsychiatry or existential psychoanalysis: Freudian clinical designations (hysteria, obsessive neurosis, perversion, etc.) are not "objective" classifications stigmatizing the patient; instead, they aim at subjective attitudes, "existential projects," which have grown out of the subject's concrete intersubjective situation and for which the subject, in his freedom, is ultimately responsible.[1]

However, already in the mid-1950s, this hermeneutic attitude is undermined by a worm of doubt. If nothing else, the fact remains that Freud unambiguously resisted reducing psychoanalysis to hermeneutics: his interpretation of dreams took shape through his break with the traditional inquiry into the meaning of dreams. Freud's resistance, his persistent quest for a cause (in trauma), cannot be dismissed as a naturalist/determinist prejudice. Likewise,

Lacan's similar shift away from hermeneutics involves no regression into natu-ralism, but rather renders visible the "extimate," inherent decentering of the field of signification, that is, the cause at work in the midst of this very field. This shift occurs in two steps. First, Lacan embraces structuralism: the decen-tered cause of signification is identified as the signifying structure. What is at stake in this first shift from hermeneutics to structuralism is thus precisely the question of the cause. As we move *from signification to its cause*, signification is conceived of as the *effect*-of-sense: it is the imaginary experience-of-meaning whose inherent constituent is the misrecognition of its determining *cause*, the formal mechanism of the signifying structure itself.

This shift from signification to the signifying cause (correlative to the notion of signification as an effect) does not reduce signification to a product of positive determinism, that is, this is not a step from hermeneutics to natural science. What forestalls this reduction is the gap that separates the symbolic from the real. Thus, Lacan's next step involves precisely the insight into *how this gap between the real and the symbolic affects the symbolic order itself*: it functions as the *inherent* limitation of this order. The symbolic order is "barred" and the signifying chain is inherently inconsistent, "not-all," struc-tured around a hole. This inherent non-symbolizable reef maintains the gap between the symbolic and the real, that is, it prevents the symbolic from "falling into" the real—and, again, what is ultimately at stake in this decentering of the real with regard to the symbolic is the cause: the real is the absent cause of the symbolic. The Freudian and Lacanian name for this cause is, of course, *trauma*. In this sense, Lacan's theoretical enterprise already lies "beyond hermeneutics and structuralism" (the subtitle of Dreyfuss and Rabinow's book on Foucault).

The relationship between the cause and the law—the law of causality, of symbolic determination—is therefore an antagonistic one: "Cause is to be distin-guished from that which is determinate in a chain, in other words *law*. . . . [T]here is cause only in something that doesn't work" (Seminar XI, 22). The cause qua real intervenes where symbolic determination stumbles, misfires, that is, where a signifier falls out. For that reason, the cause qua real can never effec-tuate its causal power in a direct way, as such, but must always operate inter-mediately, in the guise of disturbances within the symbolic order. Suffice it to recall slips of the tongue when the *automaton* of the signifying chain is, for a brief moment, derailed by the intervention of some traumatic memory.

However, the fact that the real operates and is accessible only through the symbolic does not authorize us to conceive of it as a factor immanent to the symbolic: the real is precisely that which resists and eludes the grasp of the sym-bolic and, consequently, is only detectable within the symbolic in the guise of its disturbances. In short, the real is the absent cause which perturbs the cau-sality of the symbolic law. On that account, the structure of overdetermination is irreducible: the cause exercises its influence only as redoubled, through a certain discrepancy or time lag, that is, if the "original" trauma of the real is to become effective, it must hook onto or find an echo in some present deadlock. Recall Freud's crucial statement on how "a normal train of thought"—expressing a present deadlock—"is only submitted to the abnormal psychical treatment of the sort we have been describing"—to the dream work—"if an unconscious wish, derived from infancy and in a state of repression"—that is, a desire concomitant to the "original" trauma—"has been transferred on to it."[2] Overdetermination means that this statement must also be read in the opposite direction: "An unconscious wish, derived from infancy and in a state of repression, can only exert its influence if it is transferred onto a normal train of thought."[3]

Consequently a certain radical ambiguity pertains to the cause: the cause is real, the presupposed reef which resists symbolization and disturbs the course of its *automaton*, yet the cause is simultaneously the retroactive product of its own effects. In the case of the Wolf Man, Freud's most famous patient, the cause, of course, was the traumatic scene of the parental *coitus a tergo*—this scene was the non-symbolizable kernel around which all later successive symbolizations whirled. This cause, however, not only exerted its efficiency after a certain time lag; it literally *became* trauma, that is, cause, through delay: when the Wolf Man, at age two, witnessed the coitus a tergo, nothing traumatic marked this scene; the scene acquired traumatic features only in retrospect, with the later development of the child's infantile sexual theories, when it became impossible to integrate the scene within the newly emerged horizon of narrativization/historization/symbolization. Herein lies the trauma's vicious circle: the trauma is the cause which perturbs the smooth engine of symbolization, throws it off balance, and gives rise to an indelible inconsistency in the symbolic field; but for all that, the trauma has no existence of its own prior to symbolization; it remains an anamorphic entity that gains consistency only in retrospect, viewed from within the symbolic horizon—it acquires its consistency from the structural necessity of the inconsistency of the symbolic field. As soon as we obliterate this retrospective character of the trauma and "substantialize" it into a positive entity, one that can be isolated as a cause preceding its symbolic effects, we regress to common linear determinism.

This paradox of trauma qua cause that does not preexist its effects but is itself retroactively "posited" by them involves a kind of temporal loop: *it is through its "repetition," through its echoes within the signifying structure, that the cause retroactively becomes what it always-already was.* In other words, a direct approach necessarily fails: if we try to grasp the trauma directly, irrespectively of its later effects, we are left with a meaningless factum brutum—in the case of the Wolf Man, with the fact of the parental coitus a tergo which is not a cause at all since it involves no direct psychic efficiency. It is only through its echoes within the symbolic structure that the factum brutum of the parental coitus a tergo retroactively acquires its traumatic character and becomes the traumatic cause. This is what Lacan has in mind when he speaks of the signifier's *synchrony* as opposed to simple atemporal simultaneity: synchrony designates such a paradoxical synchronization or coincidence of present and past, that is, such a temporal loop where, by progressing forward, we return to where we always-already were. Herein resides the sense of Lacan's obsession with topological models of "curved" space in the sixties and seventies (the Möbius strip, Klein bottle, inner eight, etc.): what all such models have in common is that they cannot be grasped "in a single glance"–they all involve a kind of logical temporality, that is, we must first let ourselves be caught in a trap, become the victims of an optical illusion, in order to reach the turning point at which, all of a sudden, the entire perspective shifts and we discover that we already are "on the other side," on another surface. In the case of the Möbius strip, for example, "synchrony" occurs when, after passing around the whole circle, we find ourselves at the same point, yet on the opposite surface. It is impossible to miss the Hegelian overtones of this paradox: doesn't this repetition of the same, this return to the same, which brings about the change of the surface, offer a perfect illustration of Hegel's thesis on identity as absolute contradiction? Moreover, doesn't Hegel himself assert that, through the dialectical process, the thing *becomes what it is*?

Such a "curved" surface/structure is the structure of the subject: what we call "subject" can only emerge within the structure of overdetermination, that is, in this vicious circle where the cause itself is posited/presupposed by its effects. The subject is strictly correlative to this real qua cause: $-a$. In order to grasp the constitutive paradox of the subject, we must therefore move beyond the standard opposition of "subjective" and "objective," of the order of "appearances" (of what is "only for the subject") and the "In-itself." Likewise, we must reject the concomitant notion of the subject as the agency that "subjectivizes," molds, and makes sense of the inert/senseless In-itself. Object a as cause is an In-itself that resists subjectivization/symbolization, yet far from being "independent of the subject," it is *stricto sensu* the subject's shadow among the objects, a kind of stand-in for the subject, a pure semblance lacking any consistency of its own. In other words, if the subject is to emerge, he must set himself against a paradoxical object that is real and cannot be subjectivized. Such an object remains an "absolute non-subject" whose very presence involves *aphanisis*, the erasure of the subject; yet this presence is as such the subject himself in his oppositional determination, the negative of the subject, a piece of flesh that the subject had to lose if he is to emerge as the void of the distance towards every objectivity. This uncanny object is the subject itself in the mode of objectivity, an object which is the subject's absolute otherness precisely insofar as it is closer to the subject than anything that the subject can set against itself in the domain of objectivity.[4] This is what the Kojevean, quasi-Hegelian, negative ontology of the subject qua negativity, nothing, a hole in the positivity of the real, etc., fails to see: this void of subjectivity is strictly correlative to the emergence, in the real itself, of a stain which "is" the subject. (In the domain of philosophy, perhaps the only concept that corresponds to this uncanny object is Kant's transcendental object: noumenal "In-itself," an absolute presupposition, yet simultaneously pure positedness, that is, the only object thoroughly posited by the subject and not—as is the case with ordinary phenomenal objects—some transcendentally molded stuff in whose guise the In-itself affects the passive subject.)[5]

We can see, now, how Lacanian theory surmounts the antagonism of explanation and comprehension, of signification and determinism: the traumatic real is stricto sensu the cause of the subject—not the initial impetus in the linear chain of causes that brings about the subject, but, on the contrary, the missing link in the chain, that is, the cause as remainder, as "the object that cannot be swallowed, as it were, which remains stuck in the gullet of the signifier" (Seminar XI, 270). As such, it is correlative to the subject qua break in the chain of signifying causality, qua hole in the signifying network: "The subject sees himself caused as a lack by *a*" (*Ibid*).

Between Substance and Subject

Lacan's "Hegelianism" is usually limited to the first, "hermeneutic" phase, dominated by the motifs of intersubjective recognition of desire, etc. (For example, the entire discussion of the status of the signifier "elephant" in Seminar I is explicitly couched in Hegelian terms.) Is, however, the reference to Hegel really crucial only in this first phase and, consequently, devalued with the emergence of the "non-existence of the Other," the real as the hard kernel that resists symbolization, and other late Lacanian motifs? Let us approach this problem via Hegel's proposition on substance as subject. In the classic Frankfurt School and Habermasian notion of psychoanalysis, the motif of "substance as subject" involves the traditional notion of disalienation: "repression" designates the subject's self-alienation, and by accomplishing the gesture of disalienation, the subject recognizes in the alienated substance, in this false appearance of a foreign power, the reified result of his own activity. In short, substance becomes subject when the subject appropriates the alienated substantial content.

As "Hegelian" as it may appear, this conception was never really Hegel's own, and it is precisely Lacan's notion of the subject which enables us to bypass this traditional "Hegelianism"; or, to put it in the language of the triad of positing/external/determining reflection: the Frankfurt School's Hegelianism surmounts external reflection by returning to positing reflection, to the notion of the subject who posits the entire substantial content, whereas Hegel directly opposes such a resolution. How?

Let us tackle the problem at the precise point of the passage of substance
into subject; this point lies at the end of the "logic of essence" where, with the
shift of absolute necessity into freedom, objective logic passes into subjective
logic. In the terms of the last (third) part of Hegel's logic of essence ("Actuality"), the problem of "substance as subject" is set out in the following terms:
how can we formulate a contingency that does not collapse into necessity?[6]
That is to say, the abstract, immediate setting of necessity against contingency
leads to their abstract identity, that is, to the impossibility of their conceptual
differentiation:

- The first attempt to differentiate contingency and necessity, "formal actuality, possibility and necessity," defines categories in a purely formal/logical
  way, without any determination-of-content (contingent is an actual entity
  whose opposite is also possible; necessary is an actual entity whose opposite
  is inherently impossible; possible is an entity which is inherently non-contra-
  dictory); the dialectical analysis of these notions leads to the empty tautol-
  ogy according to which whatever exists exists necessarily since, by the mere
  fact of its existence, its opposite is no longer possible. In this way, thought
  becomes reduced to a formal assertion of the necessity of the most trivial
  empirical reality.

- In the second attempt, "real actuality, possibility and necessity," all distinctions again collapse into necessity. Here, one endeavors to articulate the
  relationship between possibility and actuality in a more concrete, content-
  related way: as the relationship between a determinate state of things and
  the conditions of its possibility, that is, those circumstances that must have
  been present when this particular state of things was realized. At this level,
  possibility does not designate a simple formal non-contradiction; it is real; it
  equals the totality of real conditions. However, a closer analysis again
  reveals the inherent contradiction of the category of real possibility: as soon
  as the possibility in question is truly real, that is, as soon as all conditions of
  a thing are present, we are no longer dealing with possibility but with necessity; a thing necessarily occurs. If, on the contrary, all conditions are not
  present, the possibility in question is simply not yet real.

- The third attempt, absolute necessity, corresponds to the standard notion of
  the dialectical synthesis of necessity and contingency, that is, of a necessity
  that asserts itself through the interplay of contingencies. This necessity encompasses its otherness—it "remains with itself in its otherness"; it contains contingency as its ideal, sublated moment—therein lies its "absolute" character.
  In other words, far from being a process in which "everything is governed by
  absolute necessity" without even the slightest element of contingency, absolute necessity is a process whose very necessity realizes itself not in opposition
  to contingency but in the form of contingency. I could provide endless examples of this necessity qua totality of the process that dominates the multitude

of its contingent moments. Suffice it to mention the classic Marxist example: The necessity of the shift from the French revolution to Bonapartism, which was realized in the contingent person of Napoleon.

A better example of absolute necessity than this unfortunate Marxist reference is Marx's case of the capitalist system as a totality: the capitalist system is an "absolute necessity" insofar as it reproduces itself, its notional structure, through a set of external, contingent circumstances. These contingent circumstances exhibit the structure of real necessity, broadly corresponding to what we usually conceive of as mechanical necessity, that is, a necessity in which the causal chain is linear, running from the circumstances or conditions of a thing to the thing itself as the necessary effect of those same circumstances or conditions. What eludes us when we observe phenomena from the point of view of real necessity is the living totality that reproduces itself through the interplay of contingent linear necessities. For each individual act that pertains to the capitalist system, a set of external causes can be found which thoroughly explains the act's occurrence (why gold was found at a certain place, why some capitalist introduced the first weaving machine, etc. ad infinitum). Yet this "bad infinity" of moments whose occurrence can be explained by the categories of real necessity is in its entirety contingent, since it does not provide an answer to the crucial question: how does the capitalist system qua living totality reproduce itself through this network of indifferent, external circumstances—indifferent in the precise sense that their connection with the capitalist system is contingent and not comprised in the very notion of capitalism? The absolute necessity qua living totality that reproduces itself through the interplay of indifferent circumstances contains the moment of *teleology*, but not in the usual sense of the term. In order to explain any particular phenomenon, we need not have recourse to its alleged external aims; every phenomenon, taken alone, can be explained via real necessity. The true enigma, however, is how the totality makes use of the previously given contingent circumstances for its reproduction. Marx speaks here the language of Hegelian absolute necessity: he points out that capitalism is indifferent regarding its empirical genesis (was it founded on theft? etc.)—once the system achieves its balance and starts to reproduce itself, it posits its presupposed external conditions as its inherent moments.

This, however, is not Hegel's last word. The dialectical synthesis of necessity and contingency cannot be reduced to the preservation/sublation of contingency as a subordinated, partial moment of global necessity—the acme of the dialectic of necessity and contingency arrives in the assertion of the contingent character of necessity as such. How are we to conceive of this assertion? Its elementary matrix is provided by *narrativization*, that mode in which the contingency of past events becomes transposed into a homogeneous symbolic structure. If, for example, we are Marxists, the entire past is perceived as one long narrative whose constant theme is class struggle and whose plot strives towards that classless society which resolves social antagonisms; if we are liberals, the past tells the story of the gradual emancipation of the individual from the constraints of collectivity and Fate, etc. And it is *here* that freedom and the subject intervene: freedom is, strictly speaking, the contingency of necessity, that is, it is contained in the initial "if . . . ," in the (contingent) choice of the modality by means of which we symbolize the contingent real or impose some narrative necessity onto it. "Substance as subject" means that the very necessity that sublates contingency, by positing it as its ideal moment, is itself contingent.[7]

Let us explain this passage in a more immanent way. Absolute necessity as *causa sui* is an inherently contradictory notion; its contradiction is explicated, posited as such, when the notion of substance (synonymous with Spinozean absolute necessity) splits into active substance (cause) and passive substance (effect). This opposition is then surmounted by the category of *reciprocity*, wherein the cause which determines its effect is itself determined by the effect—thereby, we pass from substance to subject:

> This infinite reflection-into-self [reciprocity], namely, that being is in and for itself only insofar as it is posited, is the *consummation of substance*. But this consummation is no longer *substance* itself but something higher, the *concept, the subject*.[8]

This category of reciprocity is, however, more intricate than it may seem: to comprehend it adequately (that is, to avoid the usual platitudes about the moments of a living totality that reciprocally condition each other), we must return to the relationship between $ and *a*. The *a* is an object which is In-itself only insofar as it is posited; as the subject's cause, it is entirely posited by the subject. In other words, "reciprocity" designates that same vicious circle of the real cause and its signifying effects out of which the subject emerges, that is, that circle in which the symbolic network of effects retroactively posits its traumatic cause. Thus, we arrive at the most concise definition of the subject: the subject is an effect that entirely posits its own cause. Hegel says the same thing when he concludes that absolute necessity

> is a relation because it is a distinguishing whose moments are themselves its whole totality, and therefore absolutely subsist, but in such a manner that there is only one subsistence and the difference is only the *Schein* of the expository process, and this [*Schein*] is the absolute itself.[9]

The vertiginous reversal is brought about by the last clause of the last sentence. That is to say, had the sentence ended *without* "and this is the absolute itself," we would be left with the traditional definition of substance as absolute: each of its moments (attributes) is in itself the whole totality of the substance; it "subsists absolutely," so that there is only one subsistence and difference concerns only appearance. (In Spinoza, for example, every attribute expresses the substance in its entirety, that is, the totality of its determinations. The chair and the notion of the chair are not two different entities, but one and the same entity expressed in two attributes, that is, in two modalities of the "absolutely same subsistence.") However—and here we encounter the Hegelian passage from substance to subject—the "absolute" is not this self-identical "absolute subsistence" that remains the same in all attributes, as a kind of kernel of the real. If we accept such a notion of the absolute, the moment of difference (the differentiation of the absolute's content into a multitude of particular determinations) concerns only the "expository process," *Darstellungsweise*—the way we as finite subjects, from our position of external reflection, conceive of the absolute—not the absolute-in-itself. "Substance as subject," on the contrary, means precisely that the "expository process"—the way we, from our position of external reflection, conceive of the absolute—is *the inherent determination of the absolute itself.*

The Syllogism of Christianity

We can see, now, how the reversal of absolute necessity into freedom, of substance into subject, involves a purely formal conversion: at the level of substance, the absolute is a subsistence which remains the same through all its moments; at the level of subject, the absolute is this very *Schein* of the differentiation of moments, each of them containing in itself the totality of substance. The tension between external and positing reflection, between "substance" and "subject," appears in its purest form apropos of the paradox of *social cause*, which is the product of the subject's belief in itself. What does it mean to declare, "I believe in . . . (Communism, freedom, nation)"? It attests to my belief that I am not alone; others exist who also believe in the same cause. As to its inherent semantic structure, the proposition, "I believe in . . ." is therefore reflexive, that is, self-referential; its explicit form (the form of an immediate relationship of the subject to the cause) should not deceive us: to believe in a social cause ultimately means *to believe in belief (of the others) itself.* Here is a characteristic passage from Hegel's *Phenomenology*:

> [T]he absolute being of faith is essentially not the abstract being, the Beyond of believing consciousness. Rather it is the *Geist* of the community, the unity of the abstract being and self-consciousness. That this *Geist* is the *Geist* of the community depends essentially on the doing of the community. For this *Geist* exists only through the productive action of consciousness—or rather, it is not without having been brought forth by consciousness. For although such doing

is essential, it is nevertheless not the sole essential ground of that being, but merely one moment. At the same time, the being [of faith] exists in and for itself.[10]

This is how we are to read Hegel's proposition that "being is in and for itself only insofar as it is posited": not as a subjectivist platitude according to which every being is already subjectively posited, but as the paradox of an object which is *posited* precisely as *existing in and for itself*. (The key to this paradox turns on how the gesture of subjectivization/positing, in its most fundamental dimension, consists of a *purely formal gesture of conceiving as the result of our positing something which occurs inevitably, notwithstanding our activity*.)[11] The social cause, the object of Faith, is produced by the community's labor in its very capacity as the presupposed Ground that exists in and for itself. Hegel asserts the same paradox with regard to the relationship between knowledge and truth: the subject not only passively mirrors truth, he "posits" it by means of his cognitive activity, yet he posits it as "the true existing in and for itself." "The concept to be sure produces the truth—for such is subjective freedom—but at the same time it recognizes this truth not as something produced, but as the true existing in and for itself."[12]

In this precise sense, the "death of God" designates for Hegel the death of the transcendent Beyond that exists in itself: the outcome of this death is God qua Holy Spirit, that is, the product of the labor of the community of believers. The relationship of cause and effect is here dialectically reflected. On the one hand, the cause is unambiguously the product of the subject's activity; it is "alive" only insofar as it is continually resuscitated by the passion of the believers. On the other hand, these same believers experience the cause as the Absolute, as what sets their lives in motion—in short, as the cause of their activity; by the same token, they experience themselves as mere transient accidents of their cause. Subjects therefore posit the cause, yet they posit it not as something subordinated to them but as their absolute cause. What we encounter here is again the paradoxical temporal loop of the subject: the cause is posited, but it is posited as what it "always-already was."

How, precisely, are we to grasp this dialectical unity of God qua substantial Ground of transient individuals and of these same individuals qua subjects whose activity animates God? The "positing reflection," which conceives of religious content as something produced by the subjects, and the "external reflection," which conceives of subjects as passing moments of the religious Substance/God, are each in themselves the whole totality: the *entire* religious content is posited by the subjects, and the subjects are *entirely* moments of the religious Substance which exists In-itself. For that reason, the "dialectical synthesis" of the two moments, that is, the "determining reflection," does not amount to a compromise that concedes to each of the two extremes its partial justification ("religious content is *in part* produced by men and *in part* exists in itself"). Instead, it involves the absolute mediation of both sides in the person of Christ who is simultaneously the representative of God among human subjects and the subject who passes into God. In Christianity, the only identity of man and God is the identity in Christ—in clear contrast to the pre-Christian attitude, which conceives of such an identity as the asymptotic point of man's infinite approach to God by means of his spiritual purification. In the language of Hegelian speculation, this intermediary role of Christ means that Christianity has the structure of a syllogism: the Christian triad of Doctrine, Faith, and Ritual is structured according to the triad of qualitative syllogism, syllogism of reflection, and syllogism of necessity.[13] The paradigmatic matrix of the first syllogism is S-P-U: the ascension from the singular to the universal, with the particular as the middle term that disappears in the conclusion (Socrates is a man; man is mortal; therefore, Socrates is mortal). The nature of the second syllogism is inductive, that is, its matrix is P-S-U: the singular is the middle term which enables us to connect the particular and the universal (this swan is white; that swan is white, etc.; therefore, swan as such is white). Finally, the third syllogism is S-U-P, that is, its middle term is the universal which mediates between the singular and the particular—for example, in the case of the disjunctive syllogism, "Rational beings are either men or angels; Socrates who is a rational being is a man; therefore, he is not an angel."[14]

How is this syllogistic trinity linked to Christianity? The answer is provided by the Christian triad of Doctrine, Faith, and Ritual:

- The content of Christian *Doctrine* is Christ's ascension through his death, which means that the role of the middle term is played by death qua negativity which is the way of all flesh. Death denotes here the moment of judgment in the judicial sense—the sentencing of Christ to death—as well as in the logical sense—the distinguishing of subject and predicate, of the perishable individual and the perennial Universal. At this level, the syllogism is therefore the following: "Christ, this individual, is exposed to death, to the judgment that awaits all particular living beings; but he rises from the dead and ascends into Heaven, that is, is united with the imperishable Universal." In this sense, one could say that the death of Christ in the Doctrine is "objective"—its subject-matter—and not yet existentially experienced. On this account, we remain within the abstract opposition of perishable finitude and transcendent Infinity: death is still experienced as the force of negativity that affects a particular, finite, being; it is not yet experienced as the simultaneous death of the abstract Beyond itself.

- The content of Christian *Faith* is salvation, accomplished by Christ when he took upon himself the sins of humanity and expired on the cross as a common mortal—salvation thus involves the identity of man and God. This identity, which was in the Doctrine a mere object of knowledge, occurs in Faith as an existential experience. What does this mean with regard to the structure of the syllogism? How do I, a finite mortal, concretely experience my *identity* with God? I experience it in my own radical despair, which—paradoxically—involves a *loss* of faith: when, apparently forsaken by God, I am driven to despair, thrown into absolute solitude, I can identify with Christ on the cross ("Father, why hast Thou foresaken me?"). In the identity of man and God, my personal experience of being abandoned by God thus overlaps with the despair of Christ himself at being abandoned by the divine Father, and it is in this sense that we are dealing with the syllogism of analogy/induction: the imposed analogy is drawn between my own miserable position and the position of Christ on the cross. The identity of man and God in Faith is thus not "immediate"; it consists of the very *identity of the two splittings.* The difference between this experience of Faith and Doctrine is thus twofold: the death of Christ is here not merely "objective" but also "subjective," involving my intimate experience of despair; on that account, I find myself absolutely alone, I "contract" into the night of the pure I in which all reality disintegrates. What expires on the cross is thus not only the terrestrial representative of God (as it still seemed in the first syllogism of the Doctrine), but God himself, namely the God of Beyond, God as the transcendent Substance, as the divine Reason which guarantees that our lives have Meaning.

· The content of the *Ritual*, finally, is the Holy Spirit as the positive unity of man and God: the God who expired on the Cross is resurrected in the guise of the Spirit of the religious community. He is no longer the Father who, safe in His Beyond, regulates our fate, but the work of us all, members of the community, since he is present in the ritual performed by us. The structure of the syllogism is here S-U-P: the Universal, the Holy Spirit, mediates between us as particular humans, and Christ as the singular individual—in the ritual of the Christian community, the resurrected Christ is again here, alive among us believers.

Why Hegel Isn't a Humanist Atheist

The crucial feature not to be missed here is the abyss that continues to separate Hegel from humanist atheism according to which God is a product of the collective imagination of the people. That is to say, at first glance, it may appear that Hegel interprets the philosophical content of Christianity as positing just such a "death of God": Doesn't the death of God on the Cross and his later resurrection in the spirit of the religious community amount to the fact that God passes away, ceases to exist as the transcendent Beyond which dominates the lives of men (and this, precisely, is what the word "God" means in the common religious use), in order to be restored to life in the guise of the spirit of community, that is to say, as the result/product of the communal activity of men?

Why does Hegel's work resist such a reading? This resistance by no means attests to Hegel's inconsequence, due to his placating attitude towards traditional theology or even to his political conformism; rather it results from Hegel's having thought out all the consequences of the "death of God," that is, the consequences of reducing all objective content to the pure I. Conceived in this way, the "death of God" can no longer appear as a liberating experience, as the retreat of the Beyond which sets man free, opening up to him the domain of terrestrial activity as the field in which he is to affirm his creative subjectivity; the "death of God" involves instead the loss of consistent "terrestrial" reality itself. Far from heralding the triumph of man's autonomous creative capacity, the "death of God" is more akin to what the great texts of mysticism usually designate as the "night of the world": the dissolution of (symbolically constituted) reality. In Lacanian terms, we are dealing with the suspension of the Other, which guarantees the subject's access to reality: in the experience of the death of God, we stumble upon the fact that "the Other doesn't exist [*l'Autre n'existe pas*]."[15] In the Holy Spirit, the Other is then posited as a symbolic, de-substantialized fiction, that is, as an entity that does not exist as an In-itself, but only insofar as it is animated by the "work of each and all," that is to say, in the guise of a spiritual substance. Why, then, is this spiritual substance not comprehended as the product of the collective subject? Why is the place of the Holy Spirit irreducibly Other with regard to the subject? The answer is provided by invoking the Lacanian concept of the Other.

What is the Other? Let us recall the scene from Act II of Mozart's *Cosi fan tutte* in which don Alfonso and Despina bring together the two couples: they overcome the couples' reticence by literally conversing in the couples' place (Alfonso addresses the ladies on behalf of the two "Albanians"—"*Se voi non parlate, per voi parlero . . .*," and Despina delivers the ladies' affirmative answer— "*Per voi la risposta a loro daro . . .*"). The comical, caricatural nature of this dialogue should not for a moment deceive us: things are for real, and "everything is decided" in this externalized form. It is precisely through representatives that the two new amorous couples are constituted, and all that follows (the explicit acknowledgment of love) is just a matter of execution. For this reason, once the couples join hands, Despina and Alfonso can quickly withdraw to let things take their own course; their mediatory job is done. . . .[16]

In the totally different domain of crime novels, Ruth Rendell exercises the extraordinary power to make some material network function as a metaphor of the Other. In *King Solomon's Carpet*, for example, this metaphor is the railway network of the London subway. Each of the novel's principal protagonists is caught in a closed psychotic universe, lacking any proper communication with fellow creatures and interpreting contingent accidents as meaningful "answers from the real," that is, as confirmations of his or her paranoiac forebodings. For all that, it seems as if their encounters are controlled by an invisible hand, as if they were all part of some hidden scheme materialized in the network of under-ground tunnels and trains, this nocturnal, subterranean Other Place (the meta-phor of the unconscious) which redoubles the "daily world" of the chaotic streets of London.[17]

Here we confront the decentering of the Other with regard to the subject, on account of which the subject—as soon as he returns from the "night of the world," from the absolute negativity of I=I, into the "daily" world of *logos*—is caught in a network whose effects a priori elude his grasp. This is why self-con-sciousness is strictly correlative to the unconscious in the Freudian sense of the term, which is akin to the Kantian infinite judgment: when I assert about a thought that "it *is* unconscious," this is quite different from asserting that such a thought "*is not* conscious." In the latter case, that is, when I negate the pred-icate "conscious," the (logical) subject is simply located in the domain of the non-psychical (of biology, etc.—in short, in the vast domain of all that goes on in our body beyond the reach of our consciousness). However, when I affirm a non-predicate and assert that the thought is unconscious, I thereby open up a third, uncanny domain that subverts the very distinction between psychical/conscious and somatic, a domain that has no place in the ontological/phenom-enological distinction between psychical and somatic and whose status is for that reason, as Lacan puts it in Seminar XI, "pre-ontological."

Notes

1. For a detailed account of Lacan's initial indebtedness to hermeneutics, as well as of his subsequent move to the non-sensical cause, see Jacques-Alain Miller's unpub-lished seminar *Cause et consentement,* 1986–87.

2. Sigmund Freud, *The Interpretation of Dreams* (Harmondsworth: Penguin, 1977), 757.

3. In this sense, the status of freedom in Kant is also real: freedom is the causality of the moral Law as the paradoxical object ("voice of duty") which suspends the phenom-enal causal chain.

4. The paradox of object *a* is that, although imaginary, it occupies the place of the real, that is, it is a non-specularizable object, an object that has no specular image, and which as such precludes any relationship of empathy, of sympathetic recognition. In the course of psychoanalysis, the analysand has to reach the point at which he experiences his impossible identity with this absolute otherness—"Thou art that!"

5. The true import of the Kantian revolution is condensed in the notion of "tran-scendental schematism" which is more paradoxical than it may seem: it means the exact opposite of what it seems to mean. It does *not* mean that, since pure notions are alien to temporal, finite, sense experience, a mediator has to intervene between the intellectual framework of a priori notions and the objects of sense intuition. It means, on the con-

trary, that *time* (since schematism concerns precisely the relationship to time: it relates notions to time qua form of pure intuition) is the *insurmountable horizon of the legitimate use of pure notions themselves*: these notions can be applied only to the objects of temporal, finite, sense experience. Herein lies Kant's break with traditional metaphysics: the Finite is not simply a deficient mode of the Infinite which persists in itself outside time; *it simultaneously involves its own version of the noumenal Infinite.* It is for that reason that the Kantian duality of noumena and phenomena does not coincide with the traditional metaphysical dualism of essence-substance and appearance: with regard to this dualism, Kant introduces a supplementary splitting, the splitting between the noumenal In-itself and—not the phenomenal, but—*the way this In-itself appears within the phenomenal field.* From our perspective, that is, from the perspective of finite mortals whose experience is limited to temporal sense objects, the noumenal sphere appears in the guise of freedom, of the kingdom of ethical ends, etc. If, however, we were to have direct access to the noumenal sphere, bypassing the phenomenal level, the noumenal sphere would lose these very characteristics of freedom, etc.—the subject would be able to discern his inclusion in the noumenal causal mechanism. This *splitting of the noumenal itself* into the In-itself and the way this In-itself appears to us finite subjects, means that "substance became subject."

6. It is easy to discern, in this paradox, Hegel's typical approach: the problem is not how to prove, via dialectical sophistry, the ultimate identity of the opposites, necessity and contingency (as the common notion of "Hegelianism" leads us to expect), but, on the contrary, *how to tell one from the other on a strict conceptual level;* Hegel's solution, of course, is that the only way to differentiate them is to define the necessity of contingency itself.

7. Hegel is here far more subversive than his critics—Schelling, for example—who reproach him for "sublating" contingency in the all-comprehensive necessity of the Notion. Schelling limits the import of notional deduction to the a priori ideal structure of the possibility of a thing—the actualization of this possibility depends on the contingency of the real ground of being, the "irrational" Will. According to Schelling, Hegel's error resides in his endeavor to deduce the contingent fact of existence from the notion: the pure notion of a thing can only deliver *what* the thing is, never the fact *that* it is. However, it is Schelling himself who thereby excludes contingency from the domain of notion: this domain is exclusively that of necessity, that is, what remains unthinkable for Schelling is *a contingency that pertains to the notion itself.*

The relationship between Schelling and Hegel can also be conceived of as the relationship between the two aspects of the Lacanian real: pure contingency of the "irrational," pre-logical chaos, *and* a meaningless logical construct. Hegel's logic ("God prior to the creation of the universe") endeavors to accomplish what Lacan later had in mind with "mathemes": it does not provide any kind of "horizon of meaning," it simply renders the empty, meaningless frame later filled out by some symbolic content (the subject-matter of the Philosophy of Spirit). In this respect, Hegel's logic is the very opposite of Schelling's philosophy in which the real is the domain of the divine drives (Schelling uses this very term: *das Reale, Trieb*). Prior to uttering the Word (*logos*), God is caught up in the unbearable antagonism of expansion and contraction: He utters the Word in order to escape the madness in Himself, that is, the light of the Word "represses" the real of the drives in eternal past. (Cf. Part 2 of Slavoj Žižek, *Le plus sublime des hystériques* [Paris: Point hors ligne, 1989].) It is easy to conceive of Schelling as the forerunner of the late Lacan and to establish a link between Schelling's critique of idealism (reproaching it for not taking into account the real in God) and Lacan's insistence on the real as that which resists symbolization, symbolic integration-mediation; however, such a hasty reduction of the real to the abyss of "irrational" drives misses Lacan's crucial point: the real is at the same time a "matheme," a purely logical formation to which nothing corresponds in "reality."

8. *Hegel's Science of Logic* (Atlantic Highlands: Humanities Press International, 1989), 580.

9. *Ibid.*, 554.

10. G. W. F. Hegel, *Phenomenology of Spirit* (Oxford: Oxford University Press, 1977), 391.

11. For a more detailed examination of this paradox, see chapter 6 of Slavoj Žižek, *The Sublime Object of Ideology* (London: Verso, 1989). The opposite also holds: the fact that something appears to us as a raw, meaningless, unjustified state of things is also a result of our "positing." Suffice it to recall here the early bourgeois opposition to feudal repression. One of the standard motifs of the early bourgeois melodrama (Richardson's *Clarissa*, etc.) is the desperate struggle of the bourgeois girl against the intrigues of the feudal debauchee who poses a threat to her virtue. What is crucial here is the symbolic mutation by way of which the subject experiences as an unbearable pressure upon his free individuality what was previously simply the social surrounding in which he was embedded. It is not enough to say that the individual "becomes aware of" (feudal) repression: what gets lost in this formulation is the performative dimension, that is, the fact that, through the act of "awareness," the subject *posits* social conditions as something that exerts an unbearable pressure upon his free individuality, thereby *constituting* himself as a "free individual."

12. G. W. F. Hegel, *Lectures on the Philosophy of Religion*, Vol. III (Berkeley: University of California Press, 1985), 345.

13. As to this syllogistic structure of Christianity, see John W. Burbidge, "The Syllogisms of Revealed Religion," in *Hegel on Logic and Religion* (Albany: State University of New York Press, 1992).

14. Hegel's logic of syllogism is therefore based on the structure of the "vanishing mediator": what vanishes in the conclusion of the syllogism is the third element which, by way of its mediatory role, enables the final unification (copulation) of subject and predicate. (Hegel differentiates the three basic types of syllogism precisely with regard to the nature of this "vanishing mediator": particular, singular, or universal.) One is tempted to account for Lacan's "impossibility of sexual relationships" in terms of this syllogistic structure: contrary to immediate appearances, the sexual relationship does not possess the structure of judgment, of the copulation between the two subjects involved, but

rather the structure of syllogism. That is to say, the sexual relationship is doomed to fail since, in it, a man does not relate directly to a woman—his relating to a woman is always mediated by a third term, object *a*: John desires *a*, his object-cause of desire; John presupposes that Mary possesses, has in herself, *a*; John desires Mary. The problem is, however, that this *a* is irreducibly decentered with regard to the subject to whom it is attributed: between the *a*, that is, the fantasy in the guise of which the subject structures his relationship toward *a*, and the concrete woman, the real kernel of her being beyond fantasy, the abyss remains uncrossable. *Vulgari eloquentia*: a man thinks he is fucking a woman, but what he is actually fucking is the fantasy attached to this woman.

15. The recent ecological crisis offers perhaps the most stringent experience of $ qua empty, substanceless subjectivity. In it, the very ground of our daily life is threatened, the circuit of the real which "always returns to its place" is perturbed: all of a sudden, the most basic pattern and support of our being—water and air, the rhythm of the times of the year, etc., this natural ground of our social activity—appears *contingent* and unreliable. The vision, proper to the Enlightenment, of man's complete domination over nature and its exploitation thus arrives at its truth in an inverted form: we cannot fully *dominate* nature; what we can do is *derail* its course. It is only here that "substance becomes subject": the subject is bereft of the most fundamental "substantial" support in nature as that which always finds its balance and follows its path notwithstanding the perturbations of social life. The usual reaction to the ecological crisis—the desperate endeavors to find the way back to the "natural balance"—is therefore simply a mode of eluding the true dimension of this crisis: the only way to confront the full extent of it is to assume fully the experience of radical contingency that it involves.

16. At a deeper level, one would have to focus on the enigmatic relationship of Despina and Alfonso: by pretending to play the mediatory role between the other two couples, don't they actually declare love *to each other*? In short, does not the "truth" of *Cosi fan tutte* reside in the fact that its truly amorous couple, hindered in the acknowledgment of love, is Despina and Alfonso? Do they not stage the farce with the other two intermingled couples to resolve the tension of their own relationship? This is the insight on which Peter Sellars' great staging of the opera is based.

17. A further example of this "subterranean" character of the Other is provided by Milos Forman's American films. Although most of them take place in America, one cannot avoid the impression that, in a sense, his American films remain Czech: their implicit "spiritual substance" and elusive "mood" is Czech. The problem we confront here is how it was possible for the specific universe of late Czech Socialism to contain a universal dimension which enabled it to function as the matrix for the (quite convincing) portrayal of modern American life. Among numerous similar examples, suffice it to mention the TV movie on Stalin with Robert Duvall: it soon becomes clear that its hidden reference is mafia-sagas *à la Godfather*. What we are actually watching is a movie about the power struggle in a Mafia family, with Lenin as the aged and mortally ill don, Stalin and Trotsky as the two *consiglieri* fighting for his legacy, etc.

PART VII

TRANSLATION FROM LACAN'S *ÉCRITS*

ON FREUD'S "*TRIEB*"
AND THE PSYCHOANALYST'S DESIRE[1]

∞

Jacques Lacan

The drive, as it is constructed by Freud on the basis of the experience of the unconscious, prohibits psychologizing thought from resorting to "instinct" by which it masks its ignorance through the supposition of morals in nature.

It can never be often enough repeated, given the obstinacy of psychologists who, on the whole and per se, are in the service of technocratic exploitation, that the drive–the Freudian drive–has nothing to do with instinct (none of Freud's expressions allows for confusion).

Libido is not sexual instinct. Its reduction, when taken to an extreme, to male desire, indicated by Freud, should suffice to avert us to that fact.

Libido, in Freud's work, is an energy that can be subjected to a kind of quantification which is as easy to introduce in theory as it is useless, since only certain *quanta* of constancy are recognized therein.

Its sexual coloring, so categorically maintained by Freud as its most central feature, is the color of emptiness:[2] suspended in the light of a gap.

That gap is the gap desire encounters at the limits imposed upon it by the principle ironically referred to as the "pleasure principle," the latter being related to a reality which, indeed, is but the field of praxis here.

It is from precisely that field that Freudianism hews a desire, the crux [*principe*] of which is essentially found in impossibilities.

Such are the outlines moralists could have discerned therein were our times not so prodigiously tormented by idyllic exigencies.

That is what is meant by Freud's constant reference to *Wunschgedanken* (wishful thinking)[3] and the omnipotence of thought: it is not megalomania which he denounces thereby, but rather the reconciliation of opposites.

This might mean that Venus is proscribed from our world, implying theological decline.

But Freud reveals to us that it is thanks to the Name-of-the-Father that man does not remain bound [*attaché*] to the sexual service of his mother, that aggression against the Father is at the very heart [*principe*] of the Law, and that the Law is in the service of the desire that Law institutes through the prohibition of incest.

For the unconscious demonstrates that desire is coupled with[4] prohibition, and that the Oedipal crisis is determinant in sexual maturation itself.

Psychologists immediately turned this discovery into its opposite in order to draw from it the moral of the importance of maternal gratification—a form of psychotherapy which infantilizes adults, without recognizing children any better.

All too often, the psychoanalyst toes the same line. What is eluded thereby?

If the fear of castration is at the crux [*principe*] of sexual normalization, let us not forget that, as that fear no doubt bears upon the transgression it prohibits in the Oedipus complex, it nonetheless brings about obedience thereto,[5] by stopping its slippage in a homosexual direction [*l'arrêtant sur sa pente homosexuelle*].

Thus it is, rather, the assumption[6] of castration that creates the lack on the basis of which desire is instituted. Desire is desire for desire, the Other's desire, as I have said, in other words, subjected to the Law.

(It is the fact that a woman must go through the same dialectic, whereas nothing seems to oblige her to do so—she must lose what she does not have—which tips us off, allowing us to articulate that it is the phallus in its absence[7] which constitutes the amount of the symbolic debt: a debit account[8] when one has it, a disputed credit[9] when one does not.)

Castration is the altogether new mainspring Freud introduced into desire, giving desire's lack the meaning that remained enigmatic in Socrates' dialectic, though it was preserved in the recounting of the *Symposium*.

The ἄγαλμα in the ἐρῶν proves to be the motor force [*principe*] through which desire changes the nature of the lover. In his quest, Alcibiades spills the beans regarding love's deception and its baseness (to love is to want to be loved) to which he was willing to consent.

I was not allowed, in the context of the debate, to go so far as to demonstrate that the concept of the drive represents the drive as a montage.

The drives are our myths, said Freud. This must not be understood as a reference to the unreal. For it is the real that the drives mythify, as myths usually do: here it is the real which creates [*fait*] desire by reproducing therein the relationship of the subject to the lost object.

There is no lack of objects involving profits and losses to occupy its place.[10] But only a limited number of them can play the role best symbolized by the lizard's self-mutilation, its tail being jettisoned in distress. Misadventure of desire at the hedges of jouissance, watched out for by an evil god.

This drama is not as accidental as it is believed to be. It is essential: for desire comes from the Other, and jouissance is on the side of the Thing.

Freud's second topography concerns the pluralizing quartering of the subject that results therefrom—yet another opportunity not to see what should strike us, namely that identifications are determined by desire without satisfying the drive.

This occurs because the drive divides the subject and desire, the latter sustaining itself only in the relation it misrecognizes between that division and an object which causes it. Such is the structure of fantasy.

What can the analyst's desire thus be? What can the treatment to which the analyst devotes himself be?

Will he fall into the kind of preaching that discredits the preacher whose noble feelings have replaced faith, and adopt, like him, an unwarranted "direction"?

One cannot but note here that, apart from the libertine who was the great writer of comedies of the century of genius,[11] no one, not even during the Enlightenment, has challenged the physician's privilege, albeit no less religious than others.

Can the analyst take cover behind this ancient investiture when, secularized, it is moving toward a form of socialization which can avoid neither eugenics nor the political segregation of the anomaly?

Will the psychoanalyst take up the torch, not of an eschatology, but of the rights of a primary aim [*fin première*[12]]?

What then is the aim [*fin*] of analysis beyond therapeutics? It is impossible not to distinguish the two when the point is to create an analyst.

For, as I have said, without going into the mainspring of transference, it is ultimately[13] the analyst's desire which operates in psychoanalysis.

The style of a philosophical conference inclines everyone, so it seems, to highlight his own impermeability.

I am no more unable to do so than anyone else, but in the field of psychoanalytic training, the process of displacement makes teaching cacophonous.

Let's say that, in teaching, I relate technique to the primary aim [*fin première*].

I regretted in concluding that, on the whole, Enrico Castelli's profound question was left aside.

Nihilism here (and the reproach of nihilism) relieved me of the responsibility of confronting the demonic, or anxiety, whichever one prefers.

Translated by Bruce Fink[14]

Notes

1. This is a summary of the comments I made at a remarkable colloquium organized in Rome by Professor Enrico Castelli, the second in a series on ethical problems posed by the effects of science—which Enrico Castelli admirably knows how to raise in questioning aporias.

This colloquium, entitled "Technique and Casuistry," was held at the University of Rome from January 7 to 12, 1964.

I avoided spelling out too quickly, in a way which would not have been controllable, what I have since articulated concerning the drive in my lectures at the *École Normale Supérieure*, which began several days later.

This text was given to the *Atti* of the colloquium to serve as a summary of my paper and my remarks.

2. [*couleur-de-vide* could also mean devoid of color.]

3. [Text in parentheses in English in the original.]

4. [*accroché à*: attached to, hooked onto.]

5. [To the Oedipus complex, it would seem, that is, to an interest in the parent of the opposite sex, or possibly to transgression itself.]

6. [*assomption*: taking or assuming responsibility, taking upon oneself.]

7. [*par défaut*, the expression Lacan uses here to qualify the phallus, has a number of meanings: *juger quelqu'un par défaut*, for example, means to judge someone in his or her absence, or "by default," that person having failed to show up at the hearing or trial. A *défaut* is a fault, inadequacy, defect, flaw, failing, deficiency, imperfection, shortcoming, failure, etc.]

8. [*compte débiteur* means an account that is in the red, overdrawn, or showing a deficit/debit. Further financial definitions include "account receivable" (from the perspective of a person who owes someone else something) and "blank credit."]

9. [*créance* means credit, claim, or debt; it can take on the meaning of "account receivable" from the perspective of a person who claims that someone else owes him or her something.]

10. [Cf. *Écrits*, p. 251.]

11. [Lacan seems to be referring to Molière (1622–1673).]

12. [Eschatology concerns the *fins dernières*, the last or final matters: death, the Last Judgement, heaven, and hell. By counterpoint here, *fin*, which generally means end or goal, also takes on the meaning of matter or concern.]

13. [I would normally translate the expression Lacan uses here, *"au dernier terme,"* by "in the final analysis"; the context, however, makes this infelicitous.]

14. [I wish to express my thanks here to Russell Grigg who made a number of very useful comments on this translation.]

COMMENTARY ON LACAN'S TEXT[1]

∞

Jacques-Alain Miller

Lacan's text, "On Freud's '*Trieb*' and the Psychoanalyst's Desire," is designed to emphasize the disjunction between the drive and desire. It is hard to see that at first because Lacan speaks of Freud's drive and of the psychoanalyst's desire, but the text is nevertheless devoted to the disjunction between the drive and desire. It emphasizes the fact that they must not be confused as Lacan himself had confused them in "The Signification of the Phallus" (*Écrits*).

It is in the present text that we find a sentence I have commented on before: "Desire comes from the Other, and jouissance is on the side of the Thing."[2] What Lacan is stressing here is the disjunction between the signifying order—its locus which is the Other—and jouissance, which is taken up here via Freud's concept, *das Ding* (the Thing), which Lacan had reworked in Seminar VII, *The Ethics of Psychoanalysis*.

The present text runs counter to "The Signification of the Phallus," since the latter is based on the confusion between the drive and desire. Lacan immediately announces that in Freud's work the drive is distinct from any sort of sexual instinct, first of all because it is a quantifiable energy, and second because its sexuality is the "color of emptiness" (*couleur de vide*). What is pointed out by this image is that, in effect, the Freudian drive is not naturally inscribed in the relationship between the sexes. The drive's relationship to its satisfaction obviously does not involve the Other sex[3] as such.

That is why Lacan says the drive is "suspended in the light of a gap." What he is trying to get at with this image is the relation between the drive and the gap which is written -φ. "Desire encounters [this gap] at the limits imposed upon it by the [pleasure] principle," says Lacan. That means that desire is inscribed within the limits of the pleasure principle, in other words, that desire remains the captive of the pleasure principle—this is already indicated by the opposition I have pointed out between pleasure and jouissance. Desire remains captive and what lies beyond it is the value of jouissance (*la valeur de la jouissance*).[4] That is what Lacan emphasizes when he says that "the crux [of desire] is essentially found in impossibilities." What does that mean?

Lacan accentuates the "not" that is present in desire as such, which may go so far as to inspire fantasies of transgression. It is in that sense that he can say that in Freud's own work desire is instituted by prohibition—that is how Lacan takes up the Oedipus complex.

In fact, prohibition, the well-known incest prohibition, translates above all as the prohibition against satisfying desire for the mother (*désir de la mère*),[5] and Lacan had already mentioned in Seminar VII that that is but a metaphor for the prohibition expressed in signifiers (*l'interdit signifiant*) of jouissance. The incest prohibition means: Thou shalt not have access to that which is your supreme jouissance. What reverberates in this story is the prohibition expressed in signifiers which bears on jouissance itself. What Lacan emphasizes here is that, in this respect, desire is always tied to the prohibition of jouissance, and that is why desire's major signifier is -φ. Desire is always instituted by a lack, and hence desire is on the same side as the law.[6]

The more one talks about the fantasy of transgressing the law, the more one is led to say that it is precisely the prohibited object that is the object of desire, and the more one accentuates the fact that desire is submissive[7] to the law. That is the gigantic point that is formulated in this tiny text: desire is submissive to the law. It is in that sense that desire comes from the Other.

Of course, that is not how Lacan presented desire prior to that time. He presented it, on the contrary, as always in violation, always rebellious and diabolical.

But here, in the disjunction between desire and jouissance, desire is the submissive party. Even in the fantasy of transgression, desire never goes beyond a certain point. What lies beyond it is jouissance and the drive of which that jouissance is the satisfaction. In this new conceptual division, jouissance is not tied to prohibition.

The drive couldn't care less about prohibition; it knows nothing of prohibition and certainly doesn't dream of transgressing it. The drive follows its own bent and always obtains satisfaction. Desire weighs itself down with considerations like, "They want me to do it, so I won't" or "I'm not supposed to go that way, so that's the way I want to go, but perhaps at the last second I won't be able to do it anyway."

In other words, the function of desire presents itself both in submission and vacillation, and as closely linked to castration, to castration of jouissance, and that is why the major symbol of desire is -φ.

What is it that gives body to jouissance? How is jouissance incarnated in this dialectic? Lacan's answer is that jouissance is incarnated here in the same way as in the case of the lizard that mutilates itself [jettisoning its own tail when in distress]: in other words, it is embodied in the lost object. And all those objects "involving profits and losses," as he says, are place holders for -φ. In other words, here we can provide the major formula: $a/-φ$. The formula here means that desire is linked to -φ, while jouissance is linked to object a:

$$\frac{a}{-φ} \quad \begin{array}{l} ◊ \quad \text{jouissance} \\ ◊ \quad \text{desire} \end{array}$$

What takes the form of prohibition in the myth is basically loss. Prohibition is the myth of loss. That is what Lacan so prettily calls the "misadventure of desire at the hedges of jouissance." Whenever desire attempts to proceed towards jouissance, like the lizard's tail, it falls off (*ça tombe*). It must be admitted that that is a rather nice representation for -φ, and that it is also a representation for object a, that is, for the lost objects that fill up that emptiness. It is also here that the reading Lacan provides of Freud's second topography takes on its true value when he says, "identifications are determined by desire without satisfying the drive." Desire and the drive are two distinct orders that must not be confounded.

There is a lesson to be learned here concerning the end of analysis, namely that any problematic of desire always leads to identification, suggesting that desire satisfies itself with identification. *Identification is the mode by which desire is satisfied.* Even the hysteric's unsatisfied desire—what is it satisfied by if not by an identification with the other's dissatisfaction? Thus, in a certain sense, desire is essentially satisfied through identification. That is why Lacan says early in his work that desire is desire for recognition. That means that desire is always a desire to be told, "You are this or that." With the notion of recognition, Lacan showed that desire is satisfied via an identification. What Freud termed the drive is something altogether different; it must be distinguished from the sliding functions of desire, because the drive couldn't care less about the desire for recognition. No identification can satisfy the drive.

That must be kept in mind when speaking of the "pass."[8] For, on the one hand, the pass as a procedure promises a form of recognition. It promises the subject identification via a signifier, "AE" [*Analyste de l'École*, Analyst of the School], whereas the drive is indifferent to identification. What needs to be determined is whether the institution of another relationship between the subject and identification can translate into another relationship between the subject and the drive.

Let me return to the formula: $a/-\varphi$. First of all, $-\varphi$ designates a lack in the signifying order, that is, a lack in the Other. It designates a lack of jouissance. That is what we call castration and what Lacan qualifies as an enigma—the enigma that the subject most often resolves to avoid. Secondly, lost objects come to occupy the place [of that lack].[9] That is what Lacan proposes as a link between the signifying order and jouissance. It involves, on the one hand, a lack or -1 in the signifying order that is designated by $-\varphi$, that is, castration, and, on the other hand, the function of the lost object.

Later, Lacan gives a precise meaning to castration. He provides an answer to the enigma by speaking of the sexual non-relationship. He provides the following meaning to that which is lacking in the signifying order: what is lacking above all are signifiers capable of ciphering the relationship between the sexes; the signifier of the phallus comes to take the place of [or stands in for] those lacking signifiers, the phallus then appearing as a cover for the sexual non-relationship—not as the final answer to the enigma but as the false answer to it.

There is no reason to conceive of the two registers with which I began, satisfaction and signification, as body and spirit. On the contrary, the signifier penetrates the body. When we speak of the mortifying effect of the signifier, we note that Freud himself highlighted the fact that the human body is progressively mortified, to such an extent that jouissance is required to take refuge in the well-known erogenous zones. This mortification is so complete that Lacan makes the body the locus of the primordial Other, that is, the locus in which the signifier with its mortifying effect is first inscribed.

In this construction, two terms come to the fore. What happens in Lacan's construction is that the function of the symbolic phallus is erased and desire is devalued. During a whole period of his theoretical elaboration, Lacan tries to prop up the life functions on desire. But once he distinguishes the drive from desire, a devaluation of desire occurs, as he emphasizes above all the "not" on which desire is based. What then becomes essential, on the contrary, is the drive as an activity related to the lost object which produces jouissance, and secondly fantasy.

Fantasy and drive move to the center of his theory, especially to the theory of the pass, as two modes of the subject's relation to the lost object.

What else is fantasy in Freud's own work? It is a meaning related to satisfaction. The production of meaning and the production of satisfaction are best conjoined in fantasy.

In that sense, fantasy becomes an essential term while desire is devalued. What is essential to desire is its impasse. Its crux, says Lacan, is found in impossibilities, and we can say that its action essentially reaches a dead-end (*est dans l'impasse*). That is more or less what Lacan says in his "Proposition de 1967":[10]

"Our impasse [is] that of the subject of the unconscious." One might say: our impasse is that of the subject of desire. The crux of the drive is not found in impossibilities. The barred subject is not in the drive. While the subject and desire are divided, the subject and the drive are not. The drive never comes to an impasse.[11]

That is what Lacan comments on in an amusing way when he says that the subject is happy. The want-to-be is on the side of desire, and that is basically what is written by –φ. But on the side of the drive, there is no want-to-be. What Freud calls the drive is an activity which always comes off. It leads to sure success, whereas desire leads to a sure unconscious formation, namely, a bungled action or slip: "I missed my turn," "I forgot my keys," etc. That is desire. The drive, on the contrary, always has its keys in hand.

In that sense, to remove [*lever*][12] fantasy—fantasy as misrecognition of the drive (and that is more or less how Lacan describes it here), as that by which desire sustains itself in order to misrecognize the direction pointed out to it by the drive (if desire followed the drive it would never lose its keys, but fantasy covers over the drive, and thus desire errs)—what impact does the removal of fantasy have on the drive? What impact does it have on the relationship between the subject of the unconscious and the drive? Can the subject align himself with the drive and with its surefootedness? The problematic of removing fantasy, of traversing the screen it represents, aims at a laying bare of jouissance. It is, as Duchamp says, "The Bride Stripped Bare by Her Bachelors, Even."[13]

The bride is jouissance. Can one marry her?

One sometimes observes at the drawn-out end of an analysis, at the end of an analysis which never seems to come to a conclusion, an intensification of the meaning of the subject's failure, an "I can't do it" which seems to be an inhibition at its peak. It is the exasperation of the want-to-be, of the failure-to-be (*manque-à-être*) what I want, of the failure-to-be what I want to be. It signals the last tie between identification and desire.

The bride is stripped bare by her bachelors, even. Who wants her to be laid bare? Who wants to lay bare jouissance? Who wants to discover it underneath the [fundamental] fantasy?

There are two bachelors: the analysand and the analyst. Lacan completes his "On Freud's '*Trieb*'" with "and the Psychoanalyst's Desire" by saying that the one who wants to lay bare jouissance is the analyst bachelor: his desire is to lay bare the subject's jouissance, whereas the subject's desire is sustained only by the misrecognition of the drive known as fantasy.

Transcribed by Jacques Peraldi
Edited by Catherine Bonningue
Translated by Bruce Fink

Notes

1. [This commentary is a short extract from a two-hour class given by Jacques-Alain Miller on May 18, 1994, in the context of his year-long course entitled *Donc*, given under the auspices of the Department of Psychoanalysis at the University of Paris VIII–Saint-Denis.]

2. [or "and jouissance is related to the Thing."]

3. [The more familiar *l'autre sexe* (with a lower case "a") would normally be translated as "the opposite sex"; *l'Autre sexe* could thus also be translated as "the Opposite sex."]

4. [The French here might also be understood as "jouissance as a value."]

5. [The French here can also mean "the mother's desire."]

6. [The notion of one thing being on "the same side as" or "the opposite side from" another is very common in Lacan's work and is not always easy to translate effectively. When it refers to a diagram, the sides are often graphic and visible. Here one might say that "desire is aligned with the law."]

7. [*soumis* can also be translated as "subjugated" or "subjected."]

8. [On the pass, see in English Anne Dunand's "The End of Analysis" in *Reading Seminar XI: Lacan's Four Fundamental Concepts of Psychoanalysis*, edited by Richard Feldstein, Bruce Fink, and Maire Jaanus (Albany: State University of New York Press, 1995).]

9. [The lost objects take the place or fill up the space or gap in the Other: they stand in for the missing jouissance.]

10. [In *Scilicet* 1 (1968): 14–30.]

11. [*Il n'y a pas d'impasse de la pulsion* could also be translated "There's no such thing as an impasse for the drive" or "The drive knows no impasse."]

12. [*Lever* can also mean to alleviate or dissipate.]

13. [The title of a major, yet unfinished, artistic work by Marcel Duchamp, entitled *"La Mariée mise à nu par ses célibataires, même"* (1915–1923), also known in English as "The Large Glass."]

INDEX